VILLAGE CHINA UNDER
SOCIALISM AND REFORM

鄉村中國

李懷印 著

Village China Under Socialism and Reform

A Micro-History, 1948–2008

HUAIYIN LI

STANFORD UNIVERSITY PRESS

STANFORD, CALIFORNIA

Stanford University Press
Stanford, California

Printed in the United States of America on acid-free, archival-quality paper

Library of Congress Cataloging-in-Publication Data

Li, Huaiyin.

   Village China under socialism and reform : a micro-history, 1948–2008 /
Huaiyin Li.

      p.   cm.

   Includes bibliographical references and index.

   ISBN 978-0-8047-5974-8 (cloth : alk. paper)

   ISBN 978-0-8047-7657-1 (pbk. : alk. paper)

   1. Peasantry—China—Jiangsu Sheng—History.   2. Agriculture
and state—China—Jiangsu Sheng—History.   3. Collectivization of
agriculture—China—Jiangsu Sheng—History.   4. Jiangsu Sheng (China)—
Rural conditions.   5. Jiangsu Sheng (China)—Politics and government.
I. Title.

HD1537.C5L37   2009

951'.13605—dc22   2008032387

Typeset by Westchester Book Composition in 10/12.5 Palatino.

Contents

Illustrations

Five pages of photographs follow page 258

Notes on Weights, Measures, and Currency

1 catty = 500 grams or 1.1 pound

1 dou = 14 catties

1 dan = 10 dou or 140 catties

1 li = 500 meters or 0.31 mile

1 mu = $\frac{1}{15}$ hectare or $\frac{1}{6}$ acre

1 yuan = US$0.41 from 1953 to 1972

US$0.41–0.67 from 1973 to 1980

US$0.67–0.36 from 1981 to 1984

US$0.35–0.17 from 1985 to 1993

US$0.12 from 1994 to 2005

US$0.12–0.15 from 2006 to 2008

Administrative Changes in Qin Village

1955   Two primary agricultural production cooperatives were created in Qin village.

1956   The Qindian Advanced Agricultural Production Cooperative was created, which included two production teams in Qin village and another two teams in the neighboring Ji village.

1958   The Qindian Advanced Agricultural Production Cooperative was renamed the Qindian Company of the Baozhuang Brigade of Shiyan People's Commune.

1959   The Qindian Company was renamed the Suqin Brigade of Qindong People's Commune. The company had five production teams, including one in Qin village (the No. 5 team).

1960   The five teams of the Suqin Brigade were split into eight production teams, including six in Su village, one in Ji village, and one in Qin village (the No. 8 team).

1966   The Suqin Brigade was renamed the Zhigang Brigade. The No. 8 production team of the Suqin Brigade was divided into two new teams, namely the No. 8 and No. 11 teams of the Zhigang Brigade.

1981   The three teams in Ji village and two production teams in Qin village were separated from the six teams in Su village to form the Qindian Brigade. The No. 11 team of the Zhigang Brigade became the No. 5 team of the Qindian Brigade.

1984   The No. 5 team of the Qindian Brigade was renamed the No. 5 Group of Qin Village.

Preface

THE DOCUMENTARY sources for this study came primarily from Qin village of Dongtai municipality (Dongtai county before 1987) in Jiangsu province. These materials recorded the economic and political activities in the community under agricultural cooperatives in the 1950s and under production teams in the following two decades. Among them were the various account books that detailed the collectives' revenues and expenditures as well as labor remuneration and income distribution for individuals; records of different kinds of meetings in the collectives; village cadre notebooks; and official documents about government policies and regulations that had been distributed to the local collectives. The importance of these firsthand documents is evident; they are more reliable for understanding the realities of day-to-day operation of the rural collectives than any kind of official publications on national or regional conditions that were manipulated more or less to reflect the government's purposes.

Unfortunately, despite their exceptional value for studying rural China, such village-level materials have been increasingly scarce in most communities throughout the country since the abolition of the collective system in the early 1980s because they became "outdated" and "useless" in the opinion of the villagers; almost all of them, therefore, were recycled in local paper mills or burned as firewood for cooking, a fact that I realized during my fieldwork in Dongtai and Songjiang. Local county archives also made no effort to collect and preserve them because these documents were so large in volume and so "trivial" in the eyes of the archivists that it was practically impossible and "unworthy" for them to keep them. Likewise, Chinese researchers, concerned mainly with the issues of the reform era and at the regional or national levels, paid little attention to such local-level sources, nor were Western-language studies of collective-era China able to systematically use the original data of the local collectives, due to the problem of accessibility. I hope that readers will be convinced of the indispensability of the original village data for understanding rural China after reading the chapters on agricultural collectivization in the 1950s, the problem of cadre privilege and abuse, cadre-peasant relations, the collective economy, and household income.

In addition, this study also uses a variety of documents from local county and township government archives that cover the period from the 1950s to the 1970s; they reveal the situation of the entire county or the township (formerly the people's commune) during the successive political campaigns and the condition of the collective economy and sociopolitical relations under the collective system. These materials allow me to delineate the larger contexts in which the activities of individual villagers and the events of the community took place. Therefore, they nicely complement the materials from the village. Many of the problems revealed by the archival materials were never mentioned in official publications or village records and made known to the villagers.

The villagers' oral narratives are as important as the documentary materials for this study. Growing up in Qin village until age 15 when I left for college, my experience in, and memory of, the community life in this locality was largely limited to the collective era. Though I was able to update myself with the developments in the village and refresh my acquaintance with the villagers during my subsequent annual visits to the village (until I left China for my doctoral study in the United States in 1993), to know systematically what had happened to the community in the past five decades entailed a more serious effort. With a research agenda about the village in my mind, I returned to Qin village seven times in the summers of 1994, 1995, 1996, 2002, 2005, 2006, and 2008, when I studied at UCLA and then taught at the University of Missouri–Columbia and the University of Texas at Austin. Each time I stayed there for a few weeks or up to a few months. As a native of the village, I felt free to stroll around the community and chat with the villagers whenever possible. Many of my informants were those in their sixties and seventies, who lived through the entire collective period. I found that the best time for me to converse with them was in the evening after supper when they continued the old habit of "enjoying the cool" (*chengliang*) outside their houses, unlike the youngsters in the village who preferred to stay inside watching TV or playing mahjong. I visited with them from household to household on different evenings for a chat that often lasted for hours and attracted villagers from neighboring families. The number of people who joined the chat thus varied from a few to more than a dozen. Our casual conversations often began with their curiosities about my family and life in the United States and then moved to my questions about their experiences and recollections of different events from the early 1950s to the present.

While turning to the elderly for answers to questions about the collective era, I spent more time with young and middle-age villagers on various questions about their life and recent changes in the village since the 1980s. Many of them were my childhood friends and classmates, who made a living as farmers, small business owners, cadres, contractors, and so forth. Their conversations with me were much more informative than the limited statistics and documents from the village government office. After the collapse of the agricultural collectives, detailed and reliable records of the economic activities of individual households and of the village as a whole were no longer available. As the accountant of the village government admitted, the annual reports he compiled about the local economy, especially the income of individual households, were based on his gross estimates, because most villagers were unwilling to tell him how much they had earned. In the opinion of many villagers, even the village government's records of its own economy were questionable, such as those about its payments to individuals for using their labor or resources; the rents it received from villagers for using the village's public land, pond, and other resources; and other sources of its revenue. By contrast, many of the villagers with whom I talked knew their neighbors and their economic conditions better than the cadres did, and they did not hesitate to share with me their thoughts about the cadres and others in their neighborhood when we talked individually.

But this study is not limited to Qin village. In my examination of local reactions to agricultural collectivization in the 1950s, I expanded the scope of my investigation to the larger Dongtai county as well as Songjiang county in southern Jiangsu (now part of Shanghai municipality), in order to show the contrasts between areas of different socioeconomic settings in the evolution of village-state relations during the critical years when an institutional foundation was laid for further developments in the following decades. All other chapters in this book, while concentrating on Qin village, frequently refer to the conditions in the township or the entire county and view them against the backdrop of nationwide political and socioeconomic trends.

This project originated in 1994 when I first wrote about the work-point system in Qin village. That initial attempt convinced me of both the promising prospect for conducting research of this sort and the necessity of tracing the transformation of rural society and village-state relations in contemporary China back to the pre-1949 period. My first book, *Village Governance in North China, 1875–1936* (Stanford University Press, 2005), therefore, is about North China villages during the late Qing and Republic years. This book is a sequel to that title not only in terms of the time period it covers but also because it addresses the same kind of issues and employs the same approach as does my first book. Both projects examine the patterns of peasant behaviors and the complex relationship between the state and village from a micro-historical perspective. Both focus on individual villagers and perceive their choices in a social, historical milieu in which the values, norms, and practices indigenous to the peasant society interplayed with the systems and demands imposed by the state to shape their motives and actions in local economic, social, and political activities.

Over the years in which this project evolved, I have received support from many individuals and institutions that was essential for completing the book. I acknowledge the University of Texas at Austin for a Dean's Fellowship, a research grant, and a summer research assignment; the University of Missouri–Columbia for a summer research fellowship and two Research Council grants; the University of Missouri system for a research grant; and the Universities Service Center for China Studies at the Chinese University of Hong Kong for a visiting scholar grant. For their comments and suggestions on the entire book manuscript or various draft chapters, articles, and conference papers that have been incorporated into this book, I thank Kathryn Bernhardt, Lucien Bianco, Devika Bordia, Tom Brass, Kathryn Edgerton-Tarpley, Susan Flader, Daniel Little, Gail Minault, Christopher Reed, Edward Rhoads, Helen Siu, Ralph Thaxton, and Roger Thompson. I am indebted to Philip C. C. Huang and Yunxiang Yan, who have been a great source of intellectual stimulation and moral support for me. I am particularly grateful to Jonathan Unger for his perceptive comments and detailed suggestions, which greatly helped me turn the manuscript into its current form. I would like to express my sincere thank to James Scott and participants in the Agrarian Studies Colloquium at Yale University, and to James Lee and participants in the University of Michigan Center for Chinese Studies Noon Lecture Series, for their questions and comments that helped sharpen my arguments in chapters 3 and 8. Some chapters of this book were discussed in my graduate seminar on the history of contemporary China at the University of Texas at Austin. For their helpful comments, I thank Anthony Bonville, John Harney, James Hudson, Linlin Wang, and Xiaoping Wang. My fieldwork in China benefited from the generosity and hospitality of many of my friends at Nanjing University, Jiangsu Province Academy of Social Sciences, and Jiangsu Province Gazetteer Compilation Office, including, to name only a few, Han Pogen, Jie Xiang, Lu Xiaopo, Zhan Renshan, and Zhang Hua. Chapters 3, 8, and 9 contain material previously published in my articles in *Twentieth Century China* (vol. 33, no. 2, 2008), *The China Journal* (no. 54, 2005), and *The Journal of Family History* (vol. 30, no. 1, 2005), respectively. I thank the publishers for granting me the permission to include them in the book.

I owe my greatest gratitude to my fellow villagers, who never treated me as an outsider when I visited them on many summer evenings. Most helpful in my completion of this project was my father, Li Weixiang, who served as the accountant of a primary cooperative and then of the advanced cooperative in Qin village in the 1950s, and subsequently as the accountant of the brigade and a production team in the same community until he retired from the position as the head of the brigade in the early 1980s. He not only made available to me all the materials of the former collective organizations in the village, but never failed to answer my questions with patience and care whenever I asked him in person while in China or picked up the phone for an international call from my home in the United States. Thanks finally to my wife, Guiyun, and our two children, Daniel and Cathy, for their invariable support and the warmth of family throughout the years of writing.

H. L.
Austin, Texas
October 2008

VILLAGE CHINA UNDER
SOCIALISM AND REFORM

CHAPTER 1

Introduction

Contrasting Views on Chinese Villagers

The six decades in post-1949 rural China can be divided roughly into two halves: the first half, from the 1950s to the 1970s, when villagers lived under different forms of collective organizations; and the second half, after 1980, when a series of reform policies led to the rise of family farming and subsequent changes in the countryside. So different were the agrarian institutions and government policies before and after the reform that people have tended to accentuate the contrast and discontinuity in rural economic conditions and sociopolitical relations between the two periods. For instance, it is widely held that the *peasants* under the collective system were subservient and powerless under the socialist state, with little leverage to challenge the state's policies that aimed to extract rural resources for its vigorous program of industrialization at the expense of the villagers. On the other hand, the independent *farmers* of the 1980s and the 1990s are widely believed to be the vanguards of the economic reform, who spearheaded the spontaneous, bottom-up process of decollectivization and shaped the orientation of the state's policies that were increasingly favorable to the rural population.[1]

The juxtaposition between the collective and reform eras is also evident in the conventional wisdom on village politics. Agricultural collectivization in the 1950s, it is thought, made Chinese peasants completely dependent on local collectives and submissive to the cadres who controlled the resources; they had to seek protection from the "native emperors" (*tu huangdi*) or risk being victimized by them. By contrast, the farmers' economic independence after decollectivization presumably made them politically active and innovative, as evidenced in their initiation of the democratic election of village officials, which led to the nationwide implementation of the self-government program in the countryside.[2] Their growing awareness of legal rights also purportedly enabled them to combat relentlessly and fruitfully against the corrupt cadres and unpopular government polices.[3]

In a similar vein, studies of rural economy in contemporary China have underscored a disjunction between the two periods in the villagers' behavior. It is assumed that the cultivators under the collective were shirking in agricultural production, owing in part to the state's agricultural policies that failed to link effort with reward and in part to the difficulties in labor monitoring, which are supposed to be a problem intrinsic to collective agriculture. On the other hand, the farmers of the reform era are described as self-interested, rational actors, whose strong incentive to maximize the returns of their family farms was arguably a key factor leading to the economic "miracle" that occurred immediately after the reform.[4]

There are obvious reasons why these assumptions have prevailed in reform-era China and found echoes in scholarly interpretations in the West. To justify the necessity, and to prove the success, of the reform policies that they have promoted since the early 1980s, for example, reformers in the Chinese government and pro-reform scholars in China have tended to describe the collectivized agriculture as a complete failure and have emphasized the stagnation of the rural economy and the poverty of villagers under the collective system. Meanwhile, it is obligatory for them to attribute the significant increase in agricultural output and improvements in rural living conditions in the 1980s and 1990s solely to the implementation of a series of reform programs, and to interpret such programs as a radical break with the pre-reform socioeconomic institutions.

Some social scientists, especially economists, inside and outside China have also contributed to those stereotypes with their works that emphasize the formal institutions imposed on the villagers by the state, such as different social organizations, economic systems, and policies on farming, marketing, income distribution, and family reproduction. When explaining the functioning and effectiveness of those institutions in the countryside, researchers have generally regarded the villagers as goal-directed, rational actors, able to respond to different systems and policies with different strategies for maximizing their self-interest. The different economic performances during the collective and reform years thus are interpreted as a function of the farmers' varying motivations for production under the ever-changing systems and policies. What is often missing in their accounts is the subinstitutional social basis of the formal structures, especially the indigenous social relations, customs, work norms, collective consciousness, and identities that conditioned the villagers' behavior in the formal institutional context. I shall argue that such informal and often invisible institutions were no less important than the obvious, formal institutions in shaping the villagers' perceptions of the self and the community and determining their consequent choice of action. Based on an empirical investigation that takes into account both the formal and informal structures, the conclusions contained in this study will necessarily depart from those obtained from an analysis of the formal institutions.[5]

Some Preliminary Findings

This book sheds light on the complexity and diversity of the motivations and actions of Chinese villagers within different institutional settings, and it addresses from a new vantage point some of the basic issues about contemporary rural China, including the relationship between state and village, the relationship between grassroots cadres and ordinary villagers, and the problems of economic incentives and farming efficiency under the collective system, as well as the new developments during the reform era. Let us begin with the issue of village-state relations during the collective and reform years.

Village-State Relations

Agricultural collectivization in the 1950s no doubt deprived the peasants of their basic means of production and turned them into dependents of the cooperatives and later of the production teams. This should not lead us to infer, however, that they were weak and vulnerable to the manipulation of the ostensibly all-powerful socialist state and that the latter was able to impose on the former whatever means of control and extractions it wished. Quite the contrary: the villagers played a decisive role in shaping the state's rural policies through their persistent and unrelenting resistance. My examination of agricultural collectivization in the 1950s shows that the villagers used a variety of strategies to articulate and to defend their interests in that process. To resist the

unpopular state policies that jeopardized their subsistence, the villagers first appealed to the indigenous values and practices, including traditional ethical norms (primarily the right to survival), community relations, and popular cults that were powerful and easily available to them.
However, as the state established its administrative and ideological
control in the countryside, the villagers increasingly turned to the legitimate means allowed by the government and couched their requests in
the language of official discourse to make their actions "rightful" (i.e.,
legal) to the state. Their resistance, in the form of either hidden, everyday noncompliance or overt, collective defiance, forced the state to make
substantial adjustments of its rural policies in the wake of widespread
unrest against collectivization in the 1950s and later again in the early
1960s immediately after the disastrous Great Leap Forward (1958–1960).
Aimed at protecting the economic interests of the peasants and providing them with necessary incentives for production, these revised or
newly introduced policies remained largely unchanged throughout
the collective era. The introduction of the household responsibility system in the early 1980s is best seen as a further and logical step in the
state's readjustment of its rural policies that had lasted since the 1950s
in response to the popular protest.

The state's accommodation to peasant demands is also evident in its
strategies to handle rural discontent during the collective and reform
periods. In the early 1950s, the central government as well as local cadres initially treated all forms of resistance to grain procurement and
collectivization as signs of opposition from their traditional "class enemies" (*jieji diren*, i.e., former landlords, rich peasants, and counterrevolutionaries) and violently suppressed them. However, they soon
turned to the nonviolent method of "persuasion and education" (*shuofu
jiaoyu*) to deal with such problems, which, as the government eventually admitted, fell into the category of "contradictions among the people"
(*renmin neibu maodun*) because the majority of the resentful were ordinary villagers rather than the class enemies. These patterns of discontent and government treatment continued to shape the ways in which
the farmers interacted with the state in the 1980s and 1990s. As the burden of taxes and fees on individual households escalated and as local
cadres' abuse of power and corruption increased, the farmers' rightful
protests resurfaced as the dominant form of discontent in many localities, in which the villagers justified their claims and actions with government policies and regulations.[6] The state, likewise, reemphasized
the use of nonviolent means in dealing with the unrest, which was

again defined as manifestation of the "contradictions among the people."

Cadre-Villager Relations

The villagers' relationship with grassroots cadres was more complicated than the dichotomous construct of domination/subordination implies. Unlike an insulated community in the imperial times, where interpersonal relations were subject primarily to the regulation of endogenous social hierarchies and shared values, state making in twentieth-century China exerted a profound impact on power relations in the villages through the vigorous expansion of the formal government system into the countryside and the diffusion of new, national-level values among the rural dwellers. The externally imposed systems and assumptions, together with the locally embedded values and practices, at once empowered and constrained the elites as well as ordinary villagers (H. Li 2005a, esp. chapters 7, 8, and 10). Despite the Communist Revolution and the subsequent collectivization of agriculture that fundamentally changed the economic and social structure in rural China, state penetration of the village, a process that had begun from the early twentieth century under the late Qing and Republican governments, continued and reached an unprecedented level during the collective era. Agricultural collectivization not only enabled the state to extend its reach down to each household but also resulted in the creation of millions of grassroots cadres; so huge were the ranks of the cadres that they were practically out of the government's direct control. To discipline the cadres, the state could only rely on the initiatives of ordinary villagers through two means: the imposition of various institutions that allowed the "masses" (*qunzhong*) or ordinary people to supervise the cadres from the bottom up, and the making of a new discourse that empowered the masses by assuming the political correctness of the "poor and lower-middle peasants" (*pingxiazhongnong*) and their supremacy over the corruptible cadres. My examination of the villagers' activities in political participation shows the varying degrees of the effectiveness of such institutions. Throughout the collective era, the villagers repeatedly challenged the abusive cadres by writing "people's letters" (*renmin laixin*), by making complaints to higher authorities, or by participating in the periodic account-checking meetings and recurrent political campaigns. To be sure, not all villagers had equal access to such officially promoted means; more often than not, the latter remained a tool for the literate and the informed to articulate their interests. Nevertheless, the bottom-up supervision by the masses, I will show, produced a constant pressure on the cadres and effectively curtailed their potential abuse of power. The villagers' extensive experiences in using the legitimate means to deal with the cadres under the collective system prepared them to participate in the new program of "self-government by villagers" (*cunmin zizhi*) from the 1980s onward, which not only continued some of the disciplinary measures of the collective era but further allowed the villagers to elect the cadres.

It should be emphasized that the vigorous penetration of the state in the countryside after 1949 did not necessarily erode and eliminate pre-revolutionary social relations and practices. This book will show that, despite the recurrent political campaigns in the countryside, traditional community ties based on kinship, neighborhood, and friendship, together with the calculation of self-interest, continued to shape interpersonal relations in the village, causing hatred and discrimination as well as favoritism and factionalism to the relationship between the villagers and cadres. It was therefore the inherent practices and assumptions in the peasant community, in combination with the imposed, formal institutions and discourse, that conditioned the way the villagers expressed themselves and interacted with the cadres.

Decollectivization after 1980 weakened the state's presence in the countryside. Consequently, some of the old customs and community relations, which had atrophied under the collective system, were revived. Although the economic autonomy and prosperity that the farmers gained through the reform offered them greater strength and a willingness to defend themselves against cadres' abuses that *directly* harmed them, their interest in supervising the cadres through the formal channels attenuated, which in turn explained the cadres' corruption and malfeasance that have become more rampant than in the collective era. Making the newly introduced direct election of village cadres an effective tool to discipline the cadres, rather than a means for the rich and powerful to amass their political strength by manipulating the traditional social ties, remains one of the major challenges in rural China.

Economic Incentives and Constraints

The villagers' economic motivations were as diverse and complex as their political behavior. Official economic policies, especially the labor remuneration system, no doubt influenced the morale of farm workers under the collective system, but the villagers' choices were more than a function of the imposed policies and organizations. As this book will suggest, a team member's actual strategy for collective production reflected one's gender and changing status in his or her life cycle, the availability of work opportunities, his or her role in the collective, and most of all, the team leader's abilities of labor management. Local cadre leadership played a key role in shaping farm workers' behavior. Their rational planning of farming activities, fair labor payment, effective monitoring, and good reputation were central to the villagers' attitude toward team production. Therefore, the performance of individual workers and the team as a whole changed significantly under different leaders. Overall, as demonstrated in this book, the economic and social identities among the cadres and workers in a collective enabled them to maintain necessary constraints against shirking in farm production and management, which in turn explained the substantial growth in grain yield and improvements in the living conditions of rural residents during the 1960s and 1970s. What limited the potential of rural collectives for further developments, I shall argue, is primarily the state's measures of extracting agricultural surpluses rather than the low morale of farmers. More rapid economic growth was possible in the reform years not only because the collectives had provided the newly created family farms with a solid technological basis but also because the state has loosened and finally removed all of the measures of extraction that it had imposed on the collectives.

The Micro-historical Approach

Characteristic of the approach used in this study, therefore, is a *micro-level* analysis of the villagers as both individuals and a group in the rural community. Past studies on the rural economy in Maoist and reform China have tended to emphasize the decisive roles of formal institutions (namely the externally imposed organizations, systems, and policies) in shaping the villagers' motives and actions. In contrast, this study shifts its attention to individual villagers and looks at their attitude and behavior in a historical context in which the formal institutions coexisted and interacted with the informal institutions indigenous to the local community. My emphasis is on the informal factors, such as the villagers' identities with the collective and the community; their shared assumptions about authority, reputation, and legitimacy; gender roles, family relations, kinship ties, and group commitments; customs and established practices in economic and social life; various ways of social sanction against deviation from group or community norms; and the language, symbols, and rituals in expressing their interests and concerns. Unlike the obvious, formal institutions structured by official policies and universally implemented throughout a region or the entire country to serve primarily the interest of the state, the informal constraints were invisible, local, and varying from village to village to serve the everyday needs of individuals and their communities. They constituted the micro-foundations on which the formal institutions operated. Peasant behavior, I will suggest, was not merely a result of the functioning of organizations and policies created by the state, but rather an outcome of the interaction between the formal systems imposed from above and informal institutions embedded in the rural communities.

This study also departs from past studies on rural China in its use of a *historical* approach to examine peasant behavior and the patterns of social and political changes in the countryside. The rural economy and society under the collective system was once a central topic for social scientists in the China field. A large amount of scholarly literature was published from the 1950s to as late as the early 1990s, covering a wide range of issues about the agricultural economy, social and political organizations, and village-state relations under the collective system.[7] Since decollectivization in the 1980s, however, China scholars have gradually shifted their attention to new issues arising in the course of economic and political reforms, such as rural industrialization, village election, and popular discontent. By contrast, the collective era serves only as a backdrop against which the issues of the reform era are investigated in the more recent studies. Not surprisingly, what informs the depiction of the collective era in most of such studies is primarily the knowledge that the earlier generation of scholarship on rural China has produced. Few have paid serious attention to the issue of how the economic, social, and political legacies of the collective era influenced the new developments during the reform period.

As a historical study of post-1949 rural China, this book covers both the collective and reform periods and emphasizes the continuities as well as the discontinuities between them. The collective era from the early 1950s to the beginning of the 1980s witnessed drastic social, economic, and political changes, including the land reform, the enforcement of state's unitary grain procurement and sales, the successive waves of collectivization, and the Great Leap Forward in the 1950s as well as the Socialist Education movement, the Cultural Revolution, and the campaign of "Learning from Dazhai" in the 1960s and the 1970s. All these events deserve a close examination. The three chapters in Part One of the book thus look at the villagers' encounters with the state in the 1950s, ranging from their involvement in creating agricultural cooperatives to the disastrous communization.[8] The three chapters in Part Two explicate local politics under the collectives, focusing on both the villagers' participation in "formal" political processes and their daily engagement in the "informal" social and political relations. Part Three uses three chapters to discuss the villagers' participation in collective production and the impact of imposed economic campaigns and policies on their family income as well as the collective economy as a whole. Compared to the collective period that witnessed incessant and dramatic changes, the reform era from the early 1980s onward, which is covered by the three chapters of Part Four, appeared relatively "quiet"; except for the periodic reelection of village government officers, there were no more political events that agitated the villagers. Nevertheless, profound changes took place silently in their economic, social, and family life, which are examined in this book by frequently comparing to the developments during the collective era in order to highlight the connections and differences between the two periods.

Qin Village

As an "administrative village" (*xingzhengcun*) of Qindong township, Qin village, the focus of this study, had an area of about 1.25 square kilometers and a population of 1,260 in 2005. The 362 households in the village belonged to six "villagers' groups" (*cunmin xiaozu*). The largest group (No. 5) had 89 households and 276 people.[9] Members of this and other two groups (No. 4 and No. 6) resided in the original Qin village, a natural community that had borne its current name for centuries, while groups No. 1 and No. 2 historically belonged to a separate community called Ji village.

Geographically, Qin village and the rest of Qindong township are part of the Lixiahe region in middle Jiangsu province. Originally a bay between two alluvial plains of the Yangzi and Huai rivers and later an inland lake separated from the East China Sea by sediments along the coast, the Lixiahe plain, an area of about 13,500 square kilometers, emerged about 7,000 years ago when deposits from the various branches

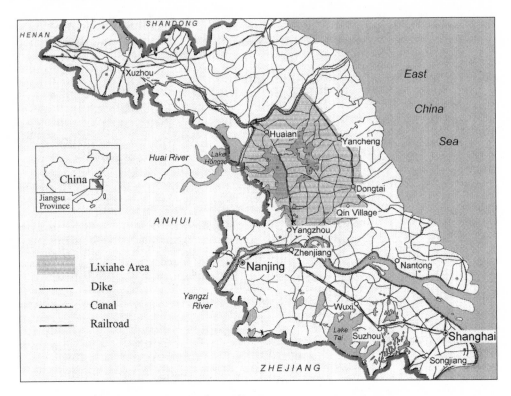

MAP 1. Jiangsu province in the early 1950s.

of the Yangzi and Huai rivers caused the lake to silt up. Therefore, to-day's Lixiahe region, still crisscrossed with rivers, rivulets, lakes, and ponds, is lower than all surrounding areas. Located at one of the lowest parts of the region, most of Qindong township is less than two meters above the sea level, and some areas are under one and a half meters (*Qindong gongshe shezhi* 1981: 2). Not surprisingly, before the 1950s, about 46 percent of the township's total area (about 60,000 mu) was marsh-land covered with reeds (*Qindong gongshe shezhi* 1981: 65) (see Map 1).

Qin village was neither prosperous nor poor by local or national standards. Income distribution under the collective system in this community, for example, ranged between 75 and 95 yuan per capita during most of the 1970s, only slightly higher than the regional and national levels.[10] In 2005, the villagers' annual net income increased to about 5,500 yuan per capita, which was 69 percent higher than the national level but lower than the municipality's average level and only slightly higher than the provincial level.[11] By and large, we may take the economic condition in this village as indicative of the rice-growing regions of eastern China.

Land Ownership and Cultivation Before 1949

Most farmland and marshland in Qin village and the neighboring areas before the Communist Revolution belonged to a widowed landlord of Ma village, about 20 miles from Qin village. Therefore, almost all peasants in the village were tenants. Among the 77 households of the community in the late 1940s, six were semi-tenant households that owned a total of 40 mu of farmland, or about 6.67 mu per household. All others were completely landless. Altogether, the 77 households (421 people) worked a total of 570 mu of land, or about 7.4 mu per household. The most well-to-do were the two Meng brothers, who worked 18 mu and 20 mu, respectively. The poorest had only two or three mu per household. A tenant household that rented a large piece of land from the landlord also had the privilege to use the landlord's waterwheels or windmills and to live in a "tenant house" (*dianfang*) provided by the landlord free of charge; there were six such houses in Qin village (QD2 2003).[12]

The farmers grew crops twice a year: wheat or barley in the winter and rice or cotton in the summer. The first cropping, from sowing the seeds of wheat or barley in late September or early October to harvesting the following June, yielded about 180 catties of wheat or 280 catties of barley per mu on average. The second cropping, beginning with the transplantation of the rice seedlings in June, yielded an average of 420 catties of the crop per mu in September. Alternatively, the villagers planted cotton instead of rice in late April or early May and gained about 60 catties of ginned cotton per mu in October and November.

The methods of cultivation in Qin village and the rest of the Lixiahe area in the 1940s were traditional. Oxen played a critical role in farming. Most households had an ox to plow and rake the earth for sowing and transplantation or to pull a stone roller over crops for threshing. Another important tool was a man-powered waterwheel or a windmill, which pumped water from a pond or creek to a paddy field to grow rice seedlings in the early summer or to a low-lying, single-cropping field that did not grow wheat or barley during the winter to keep it waterlogged for growing rice the next summer. There were 30 waterwheels and 28 windmills in the village in the 1940s. Boats were as important for the farmers in this area as carts were in North China;

they were used for shipping fertilizers and crops, for transporting goods to sell, for dredging river mud, and so forth. To fertilize their farms, the villagers turned to manure, firewood ashes, bean cakes, and the mud from riverbeds; no chemical fertilizers were available in the 1940s and earlier.

In the absence of modern inputs and labor-saving tools, cooperation among different households was necessary for the completion of some tasks during the busy season. To prepare a field for transplanting rice shoots, for example, farmers had to fill the field with a large amount of water and then use an ox to plow and level the soaked earth. Together, these tasks were called *kaitian* (literally, "opening the field"). A household usually needed at least six adults to pump water into the field; four of them would tread on the pedals of a waterwheel continuously for hours while singing a work song, while the other two, waiting alongside to replace any pedal walker who needed a break, beat a bronze gong to synchronize the walkers' pace.

In another instance, to transplant rice seedlings to a field, a household needed 4 to 10 workers, depending on the size of its field, to ensure that the job was done in a single day. Otherwise, if the family did the task over a number of days on its own without helpers, the rice seedlings transplanted on different days would grow differently, causing inconvenience later in irrigating and harvesting the crops. Therefore, it was essential for the different families to cooperate in rice cultivation by doing the same task for each other for the same number of days without payment, which they called *bangong* ("mixing the labor"). Alternatively, a household would hire a number of needed laborers to do the task and pay each of them two *dou* (28 catties) of grain a day while serving them good meals. So expensive was the hired labor for "opening the field" and transplanting rice shoots that it cost a household about a half or more of its income from a single cropping on the same field.

Drought, locusts, and flooding were the major threats to agriculture in the area. As one of the lowest parts of the Lixiahe region, Qin village and the surrounding area were especially prone to flooding. From 1522 to 1949, for instance, 95 severe floods hit Dongtai county, averaging about once every four years. During the Republican years (1912–1949), this county suffered four major floods (*Qindong gongshe shezhi* 1981: 71–73). The most devastating one occurred on August 26, 1931. On the morning of the day when the flood occurred, the water level rose at about five centimeters per hour. All villagers rushed to their own fields to cut their rice crop, whether the crop was ripe or not. By the afternoon, the flood had drowned all of the fields and the villagers had to harvest the crop in the water. The next day, the water level increased to more than a meter above ground level, and the villagers could row or pole a boat freely over the fields. Many of them used a rake to gather crops from deep in the water and no one cared to whom the field belonged.

Living Conditions

Tenants in Qin village typically paid about 50 to 60 percent of their harvest to their landlords as rent. The annual rent in the area and the surrounding region was customarily three *dan* (420 catties) of grain (rice or wheat) per mu for regular, double-cropping farms and two dan (280 catties) for low-lying, single-cropping land during normal years when there was no severe natural disaster (QD2 2003).[13] In addition, the tenants were responsible for paying taxes on behalf of their landlords. After receiving a notice from the landlord about the amount of tax on the rented land, a villager had to deliver the tax to the county government before a deadline. He then presented the receipt of tax payment to the landlord when paying rent to deduct the tax from the rent.

The income from farming after rent payment was insufficient for most families to make ends meet. With an average of only about 235 catties of grain per capita for self-consumption, the 71 tenant households in the village had to seek extra income from other activities, such as dredging river mud as fertilizer for well-to-do farmers in the winter and early spring for a pay of five to eight catties of rice per day, cutting reeds for marshland owners for a wage in the form of 16 to 20 percent of the reeds harvested, or transporting the bundles of reeds to a neighboring market town for a pay of 4.5 catties of rice for each dan (140 catties) of reeds shipped. Alternatively, the villagers hired themselves out to cut rice for large farm owners in local or surrounding areas for one dou (14 catties) of rice a day during the harvest season or do other jobs for half a dou a day during slack season. Many of them also traveled in groups to the coast to cut rice crop for about a month, earning six to seven catties of rice a day.

To supplement their limited amount of grain, Qin villagers enriched their food by catching fish, shrimps, crabs, and clams in the ponds and creeks in their spare time. Almost every household grew water chestnuts in the nearby water and could collect hundreds of catties of chestnuts a year. In addition, each family had a tiny plot to grow bok choy, eggplants, chives, onions, peppers, pumpkins, carrots, cucumbers, and the like. And every household raised some chickens and ducks for eggs and meat. Due to the dearth of fodder, only the few tenant families with large fields raised pigs for extra income and, more important, for manure as fertilizer; to maximize their rent income from the land, the landlord also encouraged the tenants to raise pigs by giving those who had more than two pigs five catties of barley a month for each pig.

Most households, therefore, lived barely above the subsistence level. During normal times, they ate three meals a day, including porridge in the early morning and evening, and steamed rice blended with vegetables as well as stir-fried vegetables and sometimes fish or other aquatic products as lunch. During slack seasons and years of poor harvest, they ate only two meals a day. The villagers ate pork only during the lunar New Year and important events such as weddings, funerals, or anniversaries of the death of a deceased parent or grandparent when the pork was part of the sacrifice to the dead. Most houses in Qin village were small huts with thatched roofs and adobe walls.

In addition to the 71 tenant households, there were six households in Qin village that owned a total of 40 mu of land and at the same time rented a total of 31 mu of land. On average, each of them had 11.8 mu of farmland and 4.5 mouths, and each mouth had 1,005 catties of grain for self-consumption after rent payment. These households, as well as some large tenant households that rented more than 10 mu of land, were relatively better off. They usually hired one or two long-term laborers to do farm work. Some of the well-to-do households had a house with brick walls and a partly tiled roof, which were the best in the community.

The Land Reform

Various military forces, including the pro-Japanese Nationalists under Wang Jingwei, the anti-Japanese Nationalists under Chiang Kai-shek, the Communist guerrillas, and rogue bandits, competed for control of Dongtai county and the neighboring areas in the early 1940s. Each of them harassed Qin village by drafting adult males by force, by collecting taxes, and by forcing the villagers to provide boats and laborers for rear service. After the Japanese surrender in 1945, villages in this area witnessed a constant seesaw battle between the Nationalist army and its paramilitary organizations on one side and the Communist guerrillas (still known to the villagers as the "New Fourth Army") on the other. Before 1948, the Communists kept their activities underground in the village; they furtively visited individual households at night, providing free food and clothing to attract villagers into their ranks. But most villagers had a profound fear of the Communists as well as all other military forces; they avoided siding with any of them, worrying about the retaliation from its enemy.

In October 1948, at the time of harvesting marshland reeds, the entire Dongtai county came under the control of the Communist force, which soon dispatched an officer, named Xia, to Qin village for a mass meeting. Still fearing the possible compulsory drafting, no adult males in their prime attended the meeting; only the elderly, women, and children showed up. Xia told the villagers that the days of "Nationalist bandits" were numbered—they were just like "standing on the melting ice"—and that the Communists would soon "liberate" the entire country and distribute land to the villagers. Timid and skeptical, no villagers responded to his announcement. Xia then kindly bent over to ask Meng Jinfa, one of the old villagers, what he thought about the idea of receiving free land. Meng's reply was honest: "I don't dare receive it." "Why?" Xia asked. "Because it would be even more troublesome for us to figure out the rent we would owe to our boss," Meng explained. "The landlords will soon be overthrown, so what do you still worry about?" Xia asked again. Meng was still doubtful: "Well, I would accept the land if you, the New Fourth Army, do not leave and stay here forever."

The Communists stayed and the Nationalists never came back. The Communists soon established new government organizations at the district and village levels. Qin village and other two communities formed a *xiang* (a local administrative unit), and its head was Wang Zhiquan, a native of the neighboring Ji village, who had joined the Communist Party in 1947 (TG1 1949; TG2 1951). The first action of the new government was implementing a rent reduction program that required the landlords to reduce rent by 25 percent. Wang and his comrades also worked hard to mobilize the villagers to support the Communist army that was to cross the Yangzi River. Qin village provided a boat and two adult males to the army. Every adult woman was asked to make three pairs of shoes for the soldiers, using the materials supplied by the new government. By that time, the villagers had built a trust in the Communists and wanted them to win. Thus, in late April 1949, when the Communist force was to launch the campaign of crossing the Yangzi

River, almost every family in the village voluntarily prepared *zongzi* (cooked glutinous rice wrapped with reed leaves) as sacrifice to Bodhisattvas and burned a handful of incense, praying for the Communist force's safe operation. Later, when the army successfully crossed the river, the villagers set off firecrackers to celebrate.

The land reform started in the area in the winter of 1950. An initial step was creating a "peasant association" (*nongmin xiehui*) in the village with the help of a work-team member from the county government. The association consisted of 14 members, one chosen from every 30 villagers, to conduct a land survey. The next step was determining each household's class status according to its land ownership. Households owning 10 to 20 mu of land and farm tools, such as boats, waterwheels, and windmills, were classified as "upper-middle peasants." Those having up to 10 mu of land and at the same time renting extra land from landlords belonged to "lower-middle peasants." Households living entirely on rented land were "poor peasants." "Rich peasants" were those who had more than 30 mu of land and hired laborers to cultivate their land or leased out part of their land for rent income. "Landlords" were large landowners who did not cultivate the land by themselves but instead rented it out for income. Qin village had only one upper-middle peasant household that owned 12 mu of land and five lower-middle peasant households that had five or six mu of land. All others in the village were poor peasants cultivating farmland under tenancy. There were no rich peasants or landlords in the community.

Class structure in the larger Qindong district, which comprised 7,058 households and a population of 30,529, was more complicated. About 53 percent of the households were made up of poor peasants, who had 2.38 mu of land per household on average and 10.24 percent of all land in the district. About 31 percent of the households were made up of middle peasants, who owned an average of 9.66 mu of land per household or 24.39 percent of all land. The 336 landlord households (less than 5 percent) in the district possessed almost 53 percent of the land, or 137.7 mu per household; most of them concentrated in the west and southeast of the district where most of the land was well cultivated. The 387 rich peasant households (5.48 percent) owned more than 10 percent of the land or 23 mu per household (TG3 1951: tables 2 and 3; *Qindong xiang nongye qingkuang* 1987: 3–4).

After confiscating the land, houses, farm tools, furniture, animals, and grain from all landlord households and some rich peasant households, the district and xiang governments started redistributing them to poor and middle peasants.[14] The redistribution plan in Qin village allowed every villager to receive two "standard mu" of land, which was equivalent to two mu of "first-grade land" that was well cultivated and able to grow crops twice a year (rice in the summer and wheat in the winter), or four mu of "second-grade land" that could also grow crops twice a year but was low-lying and prone to flooding, or six mu of low-lying and infertile "third-grade land" that could only grow rice in the summer and had to be waterlogged in the winter, or 12 mu of "fourth-grade land" (i.e., the reed-growing marshland). To make sure that all households had enough food and reed stems as firewood for cooking, each one received some cultivated land and some marshland. As a result of the reform, every household in Qin village owned 7.4 mu of cultivated land and 35 mu of marshland on average, or about 1.35 mu of cultivated land and 6.5 mu of marshland per person. After the land reform, the village government still kept about 300 mu of marshland, which was leased out to some households to generate the needed income as salaries for village cadres and their office expenses.

The land reform in Qindong district encountered various problems in the course of land confiscation and redistribution, especially in villages where the landlords concentrated. On the eve of the reform, for example, some landlords clandestinely sold their land off or gave it to their friends and relatives, in order to lower their class status to "half landlords" or rich peasants. Some landlords dismantled their houses and sold off the building materials, furniture, and farm tools to preserve their wealth in cash. Some underreported their landholdings or "pretended to be enlightened" by giving fake land deeds to the peasant associations to reduce their loss during the upcoming land reform. Some bribed the peasant association leader and village cadres with grain, cigarettes, wristwatches, or gold rings, or "seduced" them into having sex with "pretty women" in order to have their protection in determining their class status. As a result, the district government found that "a minority of the Party members showed favoritism to landlords and deviated from the correct stand, and the vast majority of village cadres have the problems of corruption and illicit sex" (TG4 1951). In Beitao xiang, for example, except for a female Party member, all other Party members and all village cadres were involved in "collective corruption and protecting the landlords." As a result, 10 landlord households in this place were incorrectly classified as "half-landlord type" rich peasants, or rich peasants who had leased out part of their land for rent income (TG4 1951).

Nevertheless, under the guidance of the district government, every village in the district that had landlord households held a "struggle meeting" (*douzheng hui*) to mobilize the peasants and openly condemn the "unlawful" landlords. The district government's survey shows that 8,693 villagers in different places of the district attended a total of 31 such meetings in the spring of 1950, who denounced 164 landlords. After the struggle meetings, 74 landlords were arrested for their maltreatment of peasants or other crimes, 8 of them were put to death, 13 of them were sentenced to death with a reprieve, 23 of them were imprisoned, and 43 of them were put under custody (TG4 1951). Therefore, all other landlords in the district were intimidated. It was reported that many of them, who had been arrogant and reckless in their communities, stayed home all of the time and were never seen on the streets. When they did come out and encountered a cadre or a peasant association activist on the street, they would stand aside and yield to them while bending over to say greetings. The landlords trembled whenever they heard that the villagers were setting up a stage for a struggle meeting (TG4 1951).

The land reform completely reversed the landholding structure in Qindong district. After the reform, the 338 former landlord households owned only 3.6 percent of the land in the district or about two mu per person, which was only about one-fifteenth of their landholding before the reform. In contrast, the 3,754 poor-peasant households owned 55.8 percent of the land or 2.95 mu per person, which was more than five times their landholding before the reform. Middle peasants also benefited slightly from the reform, whose landholding increased by 10 percent, from 2.48 mu to 2.74 mu per person. Meanwhile, the reform moderately infringed on the interest of the 387 rich-peasant households, whose per capita landholding decreased from 4.44 mu to 3.16 mu (TG3 1951: tables 5 and 6). These results reflected the purposes of the Communist Party's land reform policy, namely: relying on poor peasants in the countryside, uniting with middle peasants, eliminating the landlord class and rent exploitation in agriculture, preserving the rich-peasant economy to stabilize and increase agriculture production and ensure the rich peasants' neutral stand toward the reform (TG6 1951; see also Du Runsheng 1996: 281–296).

After the reform, each family received a land deed from the county government, which specified the size, location, and boundaries of the plot and its owner. Affixed with the red seals of the county, district, and xiang governments, the document looked sacred to the villagers.

Many of them placed the deed in front of the family god (normally the Guanyin Bodhisattva, God of Fortune, God of Kitchen, or God of Earth) while setting off firecrackers and burning incense before hiding the document in a safe place.

In the following few years, the villagers' livelihood improved remarkably; most households grew enough crops on their private plot to feed themselves and earned extra cash income by selling the reeds from their private marshland. During the lunar New Year, all families were able to cook steamed buns and glutinous cakes and buy enough pork and fish to celebrate the festival. An indispensable part of the celebration was posting red-paper couplets on the two sides of the gate of one's house to express their wishes for the coming year. Traditionally, the villagers had favored such phrases on the couplets: "Money trees grow in front of the gate; silver ingots flow into the house" (*men qian zhang de yao qian shu; dou da yuan bao gun jia lai*). Now the most popular ones read: "Listen to Chairman Mao, whose words are indeed true; Follow the Communist Party, whose road is always broad" (*ting Mao zhuxi hua ju ju zhen yan; gen Gongchandong zhou tiao tiao da lu*). The villagers were thankful to the Communists and optimistic about their future.

PART ONE

Deference and Defiance in the 1950s

CHAPTER 2

Interest, Identity, and Ideology:
The Collectivization of Agriculture

SHORTLY AFTER the land reform, the state started another campaign, the collectivization of agriculture. To organize all cultivators into collective groups right after the land reform, according to the state, was like "hammering the iron while it is hot" (*chen re da tie*) (Liu Ruofeng 1997: 243). In other words, it would be relatively easy to collectivize the villagers who had recently obtained land from the government and still had a warm feeling toward the government before the emergence of a new class of rich peasants who would oppose the movement, a lesson that the Party leaders had learned from the history of the Soviet Union.

From 1952 to 1957, collectivization in rural China underwent three stages, in which different levels of collectives prevailed in succession: "mutual aid teams" (*huzhuzu*), "primary cooperatives" (*chujishe*), and "advanced cooperatives" (*gaojishe*). This chapter examines the process of collectivization in Qin village and the remainder of Dongtai county. It shows that the government's vigorous campaigning and local cadres' activism, rather than initiatives from ordinary villagers, explained the rapid transition from mutual aid teams to the advanced co-op. It is further demonstrated that the effect of these collective organizations on agricultural production depended on two factors: the extent to which members of those organizations shared a common interest in collective production, and the extent to which they shared a sense of identity that enabled them to sanction shirking in cooperative activities.

Mutual Aid Teams

A nationwide drive to establish mutual aid teams started in 1952, immediately after the Chinese Communist Party (CCP) central committee's promulgation of the "Resolution on mutual aid and cooperation in agricultural production" on December 15, 1951. That resolution emphasized two principles guiding the creation of mutual aid teams: "being voluntary" (*ziyuan*) and "being mutually beneficial" (*huli*). It warned against two possible mistakes in the campaign. One was "coercion and commandism" (*qiangpo mingling*), which disregarded peasants' attitudes and their property right—a tendency likely to occur at the beginning of the movement. The other was a noninterference (*fangren ziliu*) attitude, more likely to appear in the later course of the movement when middle peasants dominated agricultural production, causing the growth of rich peasant economy (GNW 1981a: 95–105). The Party planned in 1952 to organize 80 to 90 percent of peasants into the mutual aid teams in two years in "old liberated areas" and three years in "newly liberated areas" (GNW 1981a: 78).[1]

The campaign started in Qindong in February 1952, when local leaders announced the Party's resolution to all cadres of the district (DT2 1952). In three months, the district established 274 mutual aid teams (DT3 1952). By the end of 1954, the mutual aid teams increased to 332, mostly seasonal ones (DT10 1954). In the entire Dongtai county, 10,634 teams were created by the end of 1954, admitting 95,437 households, or 61.8 percent of peasant households in the county. Likewise, 70.5 percent of the mutual aid teams were seasonal and loosely organized (Dongtai xian nongye ju 1987a: 3.4.2).

Qin village founded four mutual aid teams in the autumn of 1952. Each team was based on a neighborhood or a hamlet. The nine households of the Li Hamlet, for instance, formed the Li Weigen Mutual Aid Team, named after its head. The team head's duties were to bring together team members and coordinate their farming activities. The head himself was an "activist" (*jiji fenzi*), whose service was completely voluntary and without compensation from team members. The team members voluntarily helped each other when transplanting rice seedlings or harvesting wheat, as they had customarily done so before. These households did not have to pay each other if they worked the same days for each other. However, if a household lacked enough hands to do so, it had to pay the helpers for the extra days. Typically, the household paid one dou (14 catties) of barley per person for one day's help during the busy season or half a dou during the slack season. During the busy season, all households of the team worked as a group for each of them in turn, but they often disputed with each other or argued with the team head over the sequence of the households they worked for and over the number of laborers or workdays each household provided. Almost every family wanted the group to work its own farm first. As a compromise, the head had to divide the group into several subgroups and let members of the subgroup cooperate with one another to reduce their disputes. To make the mutual help fair to each participant, the team appointed an educated young man, Li Weixiang, as the bookkeeper, who volunteered to record the number of days each household had worked for others. Households that worked less for others had to pay them according to the aforementioned custom. A few households that had many members also hired out the additional laborers to families outside the team for extra incomes during the busy season (QD1 2000). Cooperative activities became increasingly rare in late autumn when the season was over, and recurred the next spring during the time of plowing and sowing. A saying thus went among the mutual aid teams in the district: "get organized in the spring and break down in the autumn, and then start over the next year" (*chun zuzhi, qiu kuatai, kai guo nian lai you chong lai*) (DT7 1954; DT8 1954).

It is worth noting that most villagers joined the mutual aid teams voluntarily because the mutual help and the way they were compensated had long been a tradition in their community. The only difference from the past was that the cooperation under the mutual aid team became more regular during the busy season, and the mutual obligations among team members were more strictly observed because of the team head's monitoring and more accurately measured by the bookkeeper. By contrast, before they joined the mutual aid team, some households had been reluctant to help their neighbors or relatives precisely because the latter were unable to help them the same way or to pay them. In other words, the regulated cooperation under the mutual aid team was more effective than the informal help before.

Although the district and xiang cadres rarely turned to coercion when promoting mutual aid teams, they worked hard to maintain the mutual aid teams, which they called "buds of socialism" in agriculture. In order to demonstrate the "superiority" of the mutual aid teams and win more peasants into the team, they took several measures to help team members increase their output. To fight insect pests in wheat fields, for example, the district government promoted the use of pesticide and atomizers, and invited villagers to visit model teams for a demonstration. Another measure was to introduce new strains of crops to team members. Through its marketing co-op, the district government sold the peasants 15,855 catties of *nantehao* rice seeds, 27,000 catties of improved cotton seeds, and 10,000 catties of improved wheat seeds. The government further provided them with technical support, so that they knew how to fertilize, irrigate, and drain the fields at appropriate times. To control floodwater, the district government urged the villagers to build dikes or to widen and heighten the existing dikes surrounding low-lying paddy fields (DT10 1954). These measures, coupled with the more effective cooperation among households under mutual aid teams, explain the steady increase of annual grain output in the district and Dongtai county in the early 1950s.[2]

Villagers in Qindong district and the county on the whole showed no resistance to the mutual aid teams. For one thing, as explained earlier, in most communities, there had been a long tradition for the cultivators to help each other in farming activities. Thus, it was not difficult for them to cooperate within the mutual aid team, where the team head's and bookkeeper's involvements only made their mutual help more organized and efficient, while their individual property rights on the land, farming tools and animals were untouched by the team, and each member of the team also had complete control of its crop. For another, most villagers in this locality had long lived barely above subsistence because of poor natural conditions and low farm yields. They thus wanted to improve their livelihood by joining the mutual aim teams when the government tried to convince them the advantages of "getting organized" (*zuzhi qilai*) through the aforementioned measures to increase grain yields. Moreover, the new state had successfully won the villagers' "unlimited trust" (*wuxian xinren*) during the land reform only a few years earlier. Many of them were readily willing to accept any new program proposed by the government, which was supposed to be necessarily beneficial to the poor (DT9 1954).

The creation of mutual aid teams in Dongtai was smooth also because of the low stratification of the rural population in the county. After the land reform, landlords as a class completely disappeared. In many villages, former landlords and rich peasants did not exist at all. In the entire county, rich peasant households, accounting for only 5 percent of rural households, were only slightly better off (2.78 mu per capita) than poor peasants (2.69 mu per capita) (Dongtai xian nongye ju 1987a: 3.1.3). The average landholding of middle peasants in the county

(2.52 mu per capita) was also close to that of poor peasants. The gross homogeneity of peasant households made it relatively easy for them to cooperate under the mutual aid teams. Not surprisingly, local cadres generally tolerated rich peasants' participation in the mutual aid teams, provided that the latter met three conditions: they joined the labor force, they abided by the principle of "exchange at equal value" (*dengjia jiaohuan*), and they respected the team head's leadership (DT3 1952).

To understand how different ecological and social settings affected the attitudes of villagers of different economic standings toward mutual aid teams and the local governments' changing strategies for promoting the cooperative organizations, a comparison of Dongtai county to Songjiang county in southern Jiangsu province is in order. At first glance, the development of mutual aid teams in Songjiang was no different from that in Dongtai. The first team, called the "Wang Menglai Permanent Mutual Aid Team," came into being in January 1952 in Chengdong district, attracting a few households from Zhongjiaqiao village, a community of 33 households and 127 residents. By the end of that year, peasants in the county had created 6,298 teams, comprising 48,492 households, or 61.3 percent of all peasant households. Most of them, however, were seasonal or temporary teams; permanent "year-round mutual aid teams" (*changnian huzhuzu*), 1,892 in total, accounted for only 30 percent of all teams in the county, with 22 percent of peasant households (*Songjiang xianzhi* 1991: 9.1.3).

However, unlike villagers in the poverty-stricken Dongtai county who willingly accepted government measures that would improve their livelihood, peasants in the prosperous Songjiang county were content with their current situation and skeptical to any imposed systems that would change their traditional methods of cultivation. Those who had joined the mutual aid teams showed no willingness to maintain them after the autumn harvest or to revive them the next spring. In Chengdong district, for example, although the government had created 780 teams that had 7,382 households by 1954, only 727 teams survived in the spring of 1955, and their total membership dropped to 6,684 households (SJ1 1954). The government thus had to play a more aggressive role than its counterpart in Dongtai to bring the villagers into mutual aid teams; their use of coercion became unavoidable from time to time under the fearsome slogan: "Eliminate independent households!" (*xiaomie danganhu*). Some village leaders intimidated the households unwilling to join the team by refusing to offer them certificates to obtain loans from government-sponsored credit co-op or to buy grain husks, a major source of pig feed, from the marketing co-op. They further branded the independent households as "backward elements" (*luohou fenzi*) and condemned them as "unwilling to listen to Chairman Mao" and "refusing to take the socialist road." Therefore, those who stayed outside the mutual aid teams complained that they had "seven fears." They feared that they would be ridiculed as being backward; unable to buy husks; unable to get loans; unable to find helpers from other households for farm work; unable to pay the helpers at a higher wage rate; unable to borrow farm animals or tools from other households; and repeatedly summoned by the government to attend meetings for ideological education. The county's Party committee admitted that "many independent households were forced to join the mutual aid teams" in 1954, resulting in the mushrooming of new teams. "The xiang and village cadres," continued the report, "were only interested in the numbers [of the mutual aid teams], rather than their actual results and qualities. Many mutual aid teams were thus perfunctorily created and soon collapsed after the autumn harvest" (SJ1 1954).

Furthermore, unlike the low-yield farms in Dongtai county, where any improvements in farming techniques and organizations could easily result in significant increase in output, farmlands in Songjiang county had already benefited from a highly developed irrigation and drainage network and sophisticated farming methods. Local government leaders in Songjiang thus found it difficult to drastically increase agricultural production. Throughout the years under the mutual aid teams, annual grain output in Songjiang remained relatively stable, increasing at 2.7 percent annually, which contrasted sharply with the rapid and steady growth (14 percent a year) in Dongtai county (*Dongtai shizhi* 1994: 236).[3] Therefore, peasants in Songjiang who had joined the mutual aid teams were much more sensitive to any increase or loss in their farming incomes and much more concerned with the balance between their contributions to, and benefits from, the mutual aid teams. Any unfair handling of their relationship with the team or fellow members could easily result in disputes and resentment among the villagers. Some of them were dissatisfied with the evaluation of their work for individual team members because the team leader usually only paid attention to the quantity, rather than the quality, of their work, and only took into account their contribution of labor and farm cattle, ignoring their sharing of farm tools. Some teams failed to square accounts and balance the mutual contributions among team members. Households that contributed more labor to others than they received found it difficult to have their extra labor contribution paid, while those who worked less for others were unwilling to make up their deficit. Likewise, almost every member wanted the group to work for himself first, and no one was willing to compromise. Unable to agree on the sequence of the team's work for individual families, many mutual aid teams broke down or existed in name only (SJ1 1954).

Moreover, unlike the peasants in Dongtai whose gross homogeneity made it easier for them to cooperate under the mutual aid teams, the high differentiation of rural households in Songjiang explained their different motivations to join the teams. The landholding of middle peasant households, averaging at 3.40 mu per person, were 35 percent more than those of poor peasants (2.52 mu per person) in the county (*Songjiang xianzhi* 1991: 9.1.2). Therefore, many of them were willing to join the team because the help they would receive from other team members could significantly reduce the cost of hiring additional laborers to work their large farms. Lu Dingrong of Yangjing village, for example, used to hire laborers to work his farm for 35 days and pay them 2 yuan a day, thus spending 70 yuan in total. After joining the mutual aid team, he only needed the laborers' help for 15 days and paid them 1 yuan a day, saving 55 yuan a year (SJ2 1954). Poor peasants in the team, to be sure, also benefited from middle peasants' participation because the latter brought into the team large-sized farm tools and animals that the poor peasants lacked. Therefore, the government encouraged middle peasants to join the team and warned against poor peasants' intentions to "scrounge" (*kaiyou*) at the expense of the middle peasants (GNW 1981a: 135).

The situation of rich peasants was very different. Unlike their counterparts in Dongtai whose landholding was only slightly higher than poor peasants' and who had no difficulties to join mutual aid teams, the rich peasants in Songjiang were strictly prohibited from being team members in accordance with the state's policy (GNW 1981a: 58). From the government's point of view, if the rich peasants joined the team, they could easily dominate poor peasants and exploit their labor because their landholding, averaging 5.76 mu per person, was more than twice that of poor peasants. The rich peasants in Songjiang thus were left with only two options. One was to clandestinely join the team by bribing team leaders, such as lending money to the leader or raising cattle together with him, or by changing their class status from rich peasants to middle peasants. An alternative was to compete with the team for laborers. Rich peasant Jia Guilou of Gusong village, for example, successfully won over a villager named Chen Yaming from a mutual aid team. His words were appealing to the poor man: "When working for the team, you have to prepare your own meals yet receive no wages. Come work for me. You'll eat well and earn more money." After paying Chen 10 yuan in advance for helping him transplant rice seedlings, the rich peasant persuaded Chen to quit his team membership and become his permanent laborer. Other rich peasants attracted members from local mutual aid teams with sharecropping. Wang Yonggen of Changyu village thus abandoned his job as head of a mutual aid team, concentrating on a six-mu farm offered by rich peasant Zhang Fushou for sharecropping. Some mutual aid teams eventually collapsed after their leaders or key members left (SJ3 1954). But such "sabotage" activities by rich peasants and their impact on the entire campaign should not be exaggerated. After all, the rich peasants in Songjiang accounted for only 2.19 percent of all rural population. The government generally tolerated their economy (GNW 1981a: 95).

Clearly, villagers in Dongtai and Songjiang responded to mutual aid teams in different ways. Whereas the widespread poverty and the government's successful efforts in advancing crop yields explained their enthusiasm for the new organizations and techniques in Dongtai county, the limited growth and even stagnation of land output under the mutual aid teams in the prosperous Songjiang accounted for the villagers' reluctance in joining the teams and the government's use of coercion in the campaign. Moreover, whereas the gross equality of landholdings in Dongtai explains local mutual aid teams' tolerance of the already deprived rich peasants, the disparity in landownership between the rich and ordinary peasants in Songjiang made it necessary for the local government to adopt a strict policy against the rich peasants. Despite such differences, however, villagers in both counties generally accepted the mutual aid teams and showed no resistance to the program, as did peasants in the remainder of the country in the early 1950s, when local governments left the private landholdings of peasant households untouched. There was no sign in the entire country of drastic decline in peasant income after the introduction of mutual aid teams.

Cooperativization

The next step of collectivization was to create "agricultural production cooperatives" (*nongye shengchan hezuohe*). A co-op differed from the mutual aid teams in that its members, about 30 households on average, had to turn in their farms to the co-op for collective use while they still legally owned the land and therefore earned "land dividends" (*tudi fenhong*) from the collective. In most cases, land dividends accounted for 45 percent of a household's income from the co-op, while labor contribution to the co-op accounted for the remaining 55 percent (GNW 1981a: 222).

A nationwide drive to found co-ops started in the spring of 1954, when the state cautiously planned that about 35,800 co-ops would be established in that year, and each county in the "newly librated areas" (mostly the eastern, southeastern, and southwestern regions) had to limit the numbers of co-ops to one to three (GNW 1981a: 277). However, a fever of cooperativization soon swept the country, resulting in the creation of 480,000 co-ops that year, which admitted a total of 12,700,000 households, or about 40 percent of all rural households (GNW 1981a: 589). The rapid development of the co-ops and the introduction of the grain procurement program in 1954 caused disorder in rural communities and disruption of farming activities (Li 2006). The state had to put the brakes on the drive and reduce the number of existing co-ops. In Zhejiang province, for instance, over 15,600 co-ops were dissolved in a few months in early 1955 (Lin Yunhui and Gu Xunzhong 1995: 157). However, dissatisfied by the conservatism that prevailed in local provinces and among the Party's leading members responsible for rural work, Mao called for a "high tide of the socialist mass movement" in the summer of 1955, ridiculing the conservatives as "women with bound feet" (GNW 1981a: 360). The movement resurged afterward, bringing the total number of co-ops to more than 1,900,000 by the end of the year, when more than 70 millions peasant households, or 60 percent of rural households, joined the co-ops (GNW 1981a: 589).

The Top-Down Movement

The development of agricultural cooperatives in Dongtai was no different from the national trends. By the spring of 1954, 1,063 peasant households, or 0.7 percent of all households in the county, had joined 38 co-ops. The co-ops increased to 143 by the end of that year and 3,297 in 1955, comprising 58.4 percent of all rural households (Dongtai xian nongye ju 1987a: 3.4.3).

However, the peasants were reluctant to join the co-ops at the beginning of the movement. Those who had lived on the sidelines, burning bricks, grinding cotton, and making bamboo baskets, worried that they would lose the freedom to do off-farm jobs and their income would decrease after joining the co-ops. Well-to-do households with plenty of good-quality farms but fewer hands were concerned with their disadvantage in sharing the co-op's income in relation to those having less land but more workers. Elderly peasants without children to support them in their old age and families with limited labor force were especially worried about their livelihood after cooperativization because they were unable to earn enough workpoints or unable to work for the co-op at all. In general, the peasants, especially middle and rich peasants who had been satisfied with their existing living conditions, felt uncertain about the future of their lives after joining the co-ops. They used various excuses, such as waiting until their sons or grandsons got married or until their children graduated from school, for their refusal to be a co-op member (DT6 1954; SJ2 1954).

Aware of the widespread skepticism toward cooperativization, the state cautioned against "blind impetuosity" and "adventurism" in establishing cooperatives at the beginning of the drive. A fundamental principle that guided the drive "anywhere and anytime," according to a resolution passed by the CCP central committee in December 1953, was the peasants' voluntary participation. It admonished local cadres to strictly avoid using coercion and commandism in organizing poor and middle peasants into the co-ops and using the method of deprivation in collectivizing their means of production. The only way to make the peasants "voluntarily get organized" was "persuasion, demonstration, and government assistance" (GNW 1981a: 218, 232).

Abiding by this policy, Qindong district created only one cooperative, called the Taiping Agricultural Cooperative, in the spring of 1954. Based on the former Zhu Baojun Mutual Aid Team and other two teams in Luocun village, it had 29 households. In the autumn, two more cooperatives were set up in Fanshen and Kaixiang villages, respectively. In the spring of 1955, six more cooperatives were established, bringing the number of co-ops in the district to nine, which attracted 218 households, or 3.6 percent of all households in the district (DT14 1955; DT15 1955).

However, local cadres soon gave up the cautious approach in the summer of 1955 when a nationwide campaign against "rightist conservatism" (*youqing jihuizhuyi*) in cooperativization swept the district. In the following months prior to the season of "autumn sowing," 137 new cooperatives emerged in the district, which, together with the nine existing co-ops, comprised 5,664 households, or 55.32 percent of all households of the district (DT15 1955). Many of them were set up in haste. Three of them took only 5 or 6 days to put up; another 21 co-ops used 7 to 10 days; 47 co-ops used 11 to 15 days; and the remaining 66 co-ops used 16 to 25 days. The district government later found many problems among the co-ops that were created in less than 10 days and had to ask them, among other things, to rewrite their "co-op regulations" (*shezhang*) to include proper provisions on labor remuneration. Because of the lack of regulations on compensations for using farm tools of peasant households, some co-op members did not allow other members to use their boats or windmills (DT15 1955). Some village cadres thus had to turn to coercion in dealing with this issue. Zhu Hongdao, head of the Fansheng co-op, for example, took away the farm tools from Shen Xingfa without the latter's consent and blamed Shen for "intending to take the capitalist road" when the peasant attempted to stop him (DT12 1955).

Local Initiatives

But the district government's pressure alone cannot explain why so many co-ops were set up almost overnight in all villages. Equally important was the quick response from village activists. Take Qin village, for example. In June 1955, Meng Yougen, head of the village, started the first co-op in the community (later named as the No. 9 Cooperative of Suqin xiang) and successfully attracted 26 households, mostly from the Zhangs, the Wangs, and the Mengs. The xiang government soon named it as one of the few model co-ops. Zhang Qianyuan, a long-time adversary of Meng, initiated another co-op three months later. Zhang, however, was an ordinary villager making his living by trading reed; therefore he was not fully qualified to be the head of the co-op, so he invited Jiang Changgui, a Party member, to be the head, and named himself as the vice head. Zhang also invited Li Weixiang, a 20-year-old man, to be the accountant. All other households in the village, 24 in total, that had not joined the No. 9 co-op thus automatically became members of the new No. 10 co-op (QD1 2000).

Village cadres, Party members, and activists thus played a key role in starting the co-ops. In the opinion of the local government, these people were the "backbones" (*gugan*) in cooperativization because "they are the leaders of the peasant masses, they are able and just, they have the support of the masses, they have a high reputation among the masses, and they are able to work for the masses. Without relying on the cadres and activists, a co-op cannot be run well and consolidated well" (DT15 1955). In November 1955, the district government gathered 580 such co-op backbones to train them in the Party's ideologies and policies. The backbones were enthusiastic in cooperativization because they could not only use their positions in the co-op to enhance their influence in the community but also receive workpoint subsidies (DT11 1955).

Qin villagers showed no open resistance to the creation of the primary co-ops. When asked why he joined the co-op, a Qin villager answered the question by quoting an old saying: "people follow the law of the state just like grass bends with the wind" (*ren sui wangfa cao sui feng*). In the eyes of the villagers, collectivization was a wind sweeping across the country, so they just followed suit when all others inside and outside the village were joining the co-op. Another reason was that the villagers did not feel they were losing anything when joining the co-op because they still owned the farm that they had turned in to the co-op, and they would be rewarded land dividends from the collective at the end of a year according to their shares of land in the co-op (one share equals two mu of land). By the regulations of No. 10 co-op, for example, income distribution in the co-op was based on both land shares (accounting for 45 percent of the total income distributed) and labor contribution (55 percent) (QD1 2000). Thus, even the households that never worked for the co-op still received payment from it for their land shares; their property right, in other words, was well acknowledged by the co-op.

Local initiatives explained not only the mushrooming of the primary co-ops but also their deviation from state policies in many aspects. Although the state allowed no rich peasants to join mutual aid teams or cooperatives (GNW 1981a: 268), many co-ops in Qindong district admitted rich peasants and even landlords. Taiping Cooperative, the very first co-op of the district, for example, included a rich peasant, a "reactionary," and a former soldier of the Nationalist army (DT12 1955). In two other co-ops, rich peasants filled the position of co-op accountant (DT15 1955). In Luocun village, four rich peasants, one landlord, and four "impure elements" (*buchun fenzi*) or former *baozhang* (officer for local security under the Japanese occupation or the Guomindang government) were co-op members (DT12 1955).

Some co-op leaders failed to adhere to the policy of relying on poor peasants as the major force of cooperativization. They were unwilling to accept poor peasants because the latter were destitute, lacking able workers and the necessary means of farming, and therefore were treated as a burden. Meanwhile, they worked hard to attract middle peasants, especially upper-middle peasants, despite their attitude to remain independent, because such households "have boats, pushcarts, oxen, good farms, and literate persons" (DT16 1955). In some villages, "the rich seeking the rich" and excluding the poor from the co-op became a severe problem (DT12 1955). To make sure that poor peasants played a dominant role in co-ops, the district government announced a policy in November 1955 that co-op heads had to be poor peasants while middle peasants could only serve as vice heads (DT16 1955). It also made efforts to purge rich peasants, landlords, and "impure elements" from local cooperatives (DT12 1955).

Without any training or experience in managing the newly established co-ops, some local cadres had difficulties in planning team-farming activities, rewarding the workers, and handling financial matters. Among the 137 new co-ops in Qindong district, for example, seven or eight co-op leaders proved to be unable to perform their duties. Disappointed by the inefficiency and unfairness in collective farming, some members, especially middle peasants, wanted to withdraw from the co-op (DT12 1955; DT13 1955; DT16 1955).

Co-op Consolidation

To stabilize the newly founded co-ops and increase their production, the government of Qindong district took a number of measures to improve labor management, collective finance, income distribution, and farming techniques. The first was improving the method of labor remuneration. The official method promoted by the Party in December 1953 was *pinggong jifen* (literally, "appraise the work and record points") (GNW 1981a: 221). By that method, every co-op member was assigned a fixed number of workpoints beforehand for his or her labor contribution per workaday according to his or her overall working abilities; this standard number of points constituted a basis for appraising his or her daily points. The worker's actual points on a specific day was then publicly discussed according to the quantity and quality of the task that he or she had finished, which could be a bit more or less than his or her standard points. This method thus was also called *siding huoping*, or "fixed assignment but flexible appraisal" (GNW 1981a: 221). Qin villagers had strong interest in this method during the first one or two months after they created a co-op. Every night after supper, they gathered together to discuss each member's points for that day. The co-op head usually let everyone assess his or her own points and then asked others to discuss. The villagers actively joined the discussion and seriously evaluated each other's effort. A member who worked harder or finished more than others received more points than his or her standard points, and vice versa. However, as time went on, the co-op members increasingly felt bored by such repeated discussions that lasted for hours and even as late as to the midnight. Many of them complained of insufficient sleep and kept yawning the next morning. Even worse was that the villagers quarreled more and more over the appraisal of each other's workpoints, which harmed their relationships. As a result, they gradually lost interest in such evaluations and were unwilling to utter a word when the co-op head asked them to discuss. Thus, whenever a man tried to say something on this occasion, his wife would quickly stop him with her elbow. When the head attempted to offer different points to people who had done the same task, however, the one who received "even half a point less than others" would argue with the head and ask him "hundreds of whys" (QD1 2000). Therefore, the co-op head could only give each of the members who did the same job the same points. The villagers saw no reasons to work harder.

The state soon realized the problems with *pinggong jifen*, criticizing this practice as "both time-consuming and unable to correctly reward co-op members according to their actual labor," and instead promoted the piecework system (GNW 1981a: 494). To implement that system, the two co-ops in Qin village formulated a long list of standard workpoint rates and quality requirements for all kinds of tasks, including farming and sideline activities. The rate for sowing wheat seeds, for example, was 10 points per 20 mu. To receive the full points, a team member had to sow the seeds evenly and limit the number of seeds to the required amount. In reality, the co-op cadres seldom strictly adhered to those requirements, unwilling to cause arguments with those who did a poor job. Nevertheless, the piecework system offered a strong incentive for co-op members to increase labor input; some of them could earn as many as 17 or 18 points a day (QD1 2000).

The second measure was to help co-ops create an effective accounting system. In November 1955, Qindong district government required that each co-op set up "three accounts and one book," namely, the general account, the account of daily transactions, the account of workpoints, and the register of fixed assets (DT16 1955). To receive intensive training in accounting skills, all co-op accountants in Dongtai gathered at the county seat in the late autumn of 1955. Li Weixiang, the accountant of the No. 10 Co-op of Suqin xiang from Qin village, thus joined a two-week program together with other 10 accountants from the same xiang. According to his recollection, each of them had to demonstrate his ability to use the abacus to multiply or divide three-digit numbers before being issued an admission ticket. The first three days focused on political study, when they listened to and discussed county leaders' reports on cooperativization. Beginning with the fourth day, the training course consisted of several sessions, each lasting three days and focusing on a particular type of account. They usually spent the first day attending a large class of hundreds of people, where the teacher demonstrated accounting skills step by step, using four huge chalk boards full of different forms. The second day was for group study and discussion. The third day they took a test in the morning and had free time after lunch. The program ended with a graduation ceremony, where accountants from each xiang took turns answering a question by drawing lots and singing a song for entertainment.

The third had to do with the management of the means of production, especially oxen, boats, and windmills. Without sufficient funds and hence unable to buy oxen, the newly founded co-ops in Qindong district often rented oxen from private owners outside the co-op. The rent for using their oxen was 0.70 to 1.00 yuan per mu for the first round of plowing, 0.40 to 0.60 yuan for the second round, and 0.40 to 0.50 yuan for the third. Co-op members using their private oxen for the collective were rewarded 1.5 to 2.5 workpoints per mu. Older co-ops usually had their own oxen, and the government enforced its regulations to ensure their proper maintenance (DT16 1955). As a result, unpaid and irresponsible use of privately owned oxen, boats, and windmills became increasingly rare and peasants' property rights were thus protected.

The district government and co-op leaders paid particular attention to measures for increasing agricultural production, which was believed fundamental to stabilizing and expanding the co-ops. One of these measures was introducing new varieties of crops, such as Nante rice, which was first grown on 460 mu of land in the autumn of 1954 and quickly expanded to 1,037 mu in 1955. Even more popular was Liying No. 3, which was introduced in 1955 and soon expanded to 5,262 mu of rice fields. Local co-op leaders were also enthusiastic in adopting new farming techniques. The cadres of the No. 7 Co-op of Suqin xiang, for example, were praised for soaking wheat seeds in water blended with pods of locust trees. Some peasants were skeptical of this new method because the seeds turned black and smelled foul when soaked that way for a few days. Nevertheless, it turned out that these seeds germinated in as few as three days and were resistant to pests. Other co-ops and independent households soon accepted this method; such soaked seeds covered more than 800 mu of farms in the xiang (DT15 1955).

These measures explained a significant growth of farm yield and peasant income in most co-ops in Qindong in 1955 and 1956. Among the nine co-ops in the district that were created in 1954 and the spring of 1955, the average grain output in the summer of 1955 was 263 catties per mu, or 24 catties more than their output in the preceding year, and 49 catties more than the average output of independent households in the current year. Among the 155 poor peasant households in the nine co-ops, 151 households (97.5 percent) had an increase of 137.60 yuan per household on average, and among the 64 middle peasant households of the nine co-ops, 62 (97 percent) had an increase of 141.50 yuan per household. Compared to independent households, the co-ops showed their advantages in their first year when the peasants just joined them. The co-op members witnessed not only a significant increase in their income but also the higher efficiency of collective effort than independent farming. It was reported that the co-ops generally finished "autumn sowing" a few days (and even as many as six to eight days) earlier than mutual aid teams or independent households. Many peasants agreed that the co-ops did four things faster than non–co-op households: watering paddy fields, plowing and leveling the field, sowing seeds, and germinating seeds. As a result, some households that had been hesitating toward cooperativization willingly applied for co-op membership (DT15 1955).

To sum up, the co-ops in Qindong district fared quite well and did not encounter much resistance from peasants in their first year, a situation no different from the overall process of cooperativization in the rest of rural China. Three factors explained the smooth development of the co-ops. First, for personal gains and/or political aspirations, village cadres and activists were generally enthusiastic in initiating and stabilizing the co-ops. To win a great number of independent households, they worked hard to improve the efficiency of co-op production and to increase the income of co-op members. Second, the government took critical measures in institutionalizing the co-ops, such as training co-op accountants, introducing various systems of co-op management, and promoting new farming techniques. Third, peasants saw no reason to resist because the co-ops guaranteed their property rights under the arrangement of land dividends and rents or workpoints for using their farming tools. As new co-op members, the peasants generally had a faith in the government and local cadres, anticipating a secured and improved livelihood under the co-ops.

Advanced Cooperatives

By the beginning of 1956, most rural households in the country had joined the primary cooperatives. Although the rush to set up co-ops and the enforcement of grain procurements had caused chaos and disruption to local social and economic orders, most co-ops survived and functioned reasonably well, for reasons just examined. However, in the view of Mao Zedong, the primary co-ops were only semi-socialistic in nature because they still allowed the private ownership of means of production. What he wanted was the fully socialist advanced cooperatives (Mao Zedong 1955a, 1955b). The advanced co-ops, as the Party defined, were agricultural organizations that collectivized land and large-sized farm tools. Members of the advanced co-ops, about 250 households per co-op, received income only according to their needs and labor contribution, rather than the private ownership of means of production. Therefore, they were completely socialist in nature (GNW 1981a: 564–588).

But the peasants were practical. When local cadres in Dongtai propagandized the transition to advanced co-ops in 1956, the villagers once again aired their doubts and reluctance. The primary co-ops, in their eyes, were newly set up and had not yet been firmly established. To merge them into a large advanced co-op right away, in the words of peasant Liu of the No. 1 Co-op of Nanzhuang xiang, was like forcing a toddler, who was still learning to walk, to run. Middle peasants with a great deal of land and a large number of farm tools, such as Zhu Ruqing of the No. 3 Cooperative of Taiping xiang, were particularly unwilling to join the advanced co-op, saying that they would rather be independent again if their primary co-ops were merged into an advanced co-op (DT17 1956).

Despite the resentment of well-to-do peasants, the transition to advanced co-ops proceeded swiftly throughout the country in the spring of 1956 and continued to the end of the year, when 87.8 percent of all rural households in the country joined the advanced co-ops (GNW 1981a: 590). However, the rapid transition soon caused decline in grain

production in many co-ops and the consequent wave of peasant protests in many parts of the country. Frustrated by their decreased income and hunger, peasants in many areas beat up co-op cadres and
petitioned to the government for withdrawal from the co-ops (see the
following chapter for details).

In Dongtai county, the transition began in January 1956 when the
county's Party committee created five model advanced co-ops in separate districts. By the end of March, the county had created 559 advanced
co-ops within three months, covering 144,596 households, or 88.5 percent of all peasant households in the county (Dongtai xian nongye ju
1987a: 3.1.4). In the same year, peasants in the county witnessed a widespread decline in grain yield after four years' consecutive growth that
reached 458 catties per mu in 1955. In 1956, the county's grain production fell to 347 catties per mu, or 24 percent less than the previous year's
level. Wheat output decreased by 36 percent, from 137 catties per mu in
1955 to 87 catties per mu in 1956. Rice output also fell by 30 percent,
from 311 catties per mu in 1955 to 217 catties per mu in 1956 (Dongtai
xian nongye ju 1987b: 116–123).

Qindong district created three advanced co-ops in early 1956 and
21 more in the fall of the same year, which included 6,008 households, or
about 90 percent of all households in the district (DT17 1956). The transition to advanced co-ops in this district thus was seven or eight months
later than that in the county, and its effect on agricultural production did
not fully occur until 1957, when grain yield in the district fell by 28 percent, from 351 catties per mu in 1956 to 252 catties per mu in 1957 (*Qindong gongshe shezhi* 1981: 152–153). Qin village experienced a similar production decline after creating a single advanced co-op on the basis of its
two primary co-ops and another two primary co-ops of the neighboring
Ji village in the fall of 1956. Its grain yield fell to 270 catties per mu in 1957,
or 17 percent less than its 1956 level (324 catties per mu) (DT21 1957).

To understand why agricultural production decreased and why
peasant resistance prevailed after the transition to advanced co-ops,
we need to examine the issue of peasant incentives for production under
the advanced co-op, and the changing roles of co-op cadres and their
relationship with the villagers.

Inefficiencies in Production

First of all, villagers' identity with the collective and their concern with
its well-being greatly weakened after joining the advanced co-op. Under

the mutual aid teams and primary co-ops, the villagers were generally responsible when tilling the farms or using the oxen, boats, windmills, or other farm tools because they still owned those means of production and their ownership was well recognized by the dividends they received from the collective. Even when working a farm or using a tool that did not belong to himself, a farmer still had to pay attention to his job and take care of the tool he was using because the villager normally worked with other members of the team or the co-op and therefore was subject to their surveillance. As a group, the farmers knew well which farm, boat, or ox belonged to whom and paid close attention to one another to make sure that their property was properly maintained or taken care of. They were able to use various forms of collective sanctions, such as public denunciation, deduction of payments, and even expulsion from the co-op, to prevent irresponsible use of their private properties. In the words of some Qin villagers, they still had a strong sense of "being the master" (*dangjia*) of their co-ops; they called their co-op a "big family" (*dajia*), a term they borrowed from government propaganda, which nevertheless made sense to them because they still owned all the farms and tools that they had pooled together for collective use. They thus described joining the primary co-ops as "merging small families into a big family" (*bing xiaojia wei dajia*) (QD1 2000). Moreover, living in the same community, the co-op members usually had kinship ties or friendship with one another, which further enhanced their solidarity.

After the transition to advanced co-ops, however, the villagers lost their land and tools. Now they treated co-op cadres as the true masters of their co-op, who controlled all resources of the collective. Working only for workpoints, the co-op members merely paid attention to the quantity, rather than the quality, of their jobs. They no longer treated the farms or tools as their own properties and no longer paid attention as closely as before to each other's work performance and use of tools. Farming quality and efficiency deteriorated.

Another problem had to do with the scale and organization of the advanced co-ops. On average, an advanced co-op in Dongtai county, for example, had 259 households, or nine times larger than a primary co-op, which had only 29 households.[4] Unlike the original primary co-op that was based on a hamlet or a neighborhood in a village, an advanced co-op typically comprised several natural villages or hamlets that were several *li* apart. Furthermore, unlike primary co-op members who interacted closely with one another as neighbors, kinsmen, or friends and were able to discipline themselves with shared sense of identity and interests, members of the advanced co-op did not necessarily know each other if they did not live in the same community. In the absence of close ties among co-op members from different villages, it was difficult for them to foster a sense of identity with the new collective. And it made no sense for the villagers to work hard when they had to share with people from other villages the fruit of their effort. To further understand this point, we need to look at how the workers were organized and rewarded within the advanced co-op.

An advanced co-op was divided into a number of production teams, which were identical to the original primary co-ops in most cases. The production teams were necessary because the co-op leaders, only a few in number, were unable to assign tasks for hundreds of co-op members and personally supervise their activities. The advanced co-op thus had to divide itself into several teams for the convenience of labor management and let each team decide for its members what to do and how to supervise and reward them. Nevertheless, a production team was not an independent economic unit. It could not control its own products and determine the cash value of its members' workpoints. Instead, the advanced co-op functioned as the basic accounting unit. It put together the output of all teams and determined the total amount of payments in kind and in cash to all its members after deducting from its total output the total farming costs of all teams as well as taxes and public funds. The co-op then determined the cash value of each workpoint by dividing its total income for distribution with the total workpoints earned by all members of the co-op. In other words, regardless of which production team they belonged to, all households shared the co-op's distributable income. How much grain they could receive and how much their workpoints were worth were not determined by a team's own output but by the co-op's overall performance. The link between a farmer's labor input and his or her income from the collective thus was greatly attenuated when compared to that under the former primary co-op, which was an independent accounting unit.

To arouse individual teams' incentive to increase production, the state nevertheless promoted a number of measures. The "Exemplary Regulations of Advanced Agricultural Production Cooperatives" promulgated by the National People's Congress in June 1956 provided that a co-op may contract with its production teams to set a fixed output and reward those teams that surpassed the production target (GNW 1981a: 572).

Later these practices were developed into the so-called "three contracts and one reward" (*sanbao yijiang*), including "contract for fixed workpoints" (*baogong*), "contract for fixed output" (*baochan*), "contract for fixed cost" (*baoben*), and rewards for surpassing production targets (GNW 1981a: 727). According to Li Weixiang, the former accountant of the advanced co-op in Qin village, to put a cap on each team's total workpoints was absolutely necessary because the team would otherwise have given excessive workpoints to its members and hence shared more of the co-op's total income. In his co-op, the fixed workpoints for each of the four teams ranged largely between 110,000 and 120,000, depending on the actual number of workers in each team. If the team offered more than the fixed workpoints to its members during the year, the team's accountant had to cut each team member's total annual workpoints by a standard rate at the end of the year so that the team's total workpoints met the fixed amount. On the other hand, he may increase each member's annual points if the team's total workpoints were less than the fixed amount. This fixed amount of workpoints was also linked with the team's predetermined fixed output. The team would be rewarded by the co-op if its actual output exceeded its target while its total workpoints and/or cost of production were less than their original targets. The reward was usually 50 percent or 60 percent of the increased output.

These practices, however, only offered limited incentives for team leaders to improve labor management and farming efficiency. Unlike the production teams after the Great Leap Forward, which eventually became independent accounting units and had complete control of their output after fulfilling agricultural taxes and grain procurements, the production teams under the advanced co-op lacked the basic level of autonomy: they had no right to decide what and how much to produce, and they had no control of what they had produced—the power of production planning and income distribution for each team remained in the hands of co-op leaders. According to Li, among the "three contracts and one reward," only the contract for fixed workpoints had some effects on his production teams because the team leaders were able to control the amount of workpoints they rendered. However, they were largely unable to control the cost and output of production to meet the contracted targets because how much they had to spend on farming and how much they could produce were not merely determined by human efforts, but more often than not by weather; a long-lasting drought in the spring or flood in the summer could make a huge difference to the team's input and output.

Moreover, the purpose of "three contracts and one reward" was only to stimulate team leaders' interest in improving farming efficiency; none of them made sense to ordinary team members, who did not care about the team's contracted total workpoints, production costs, or output at all. What they cared about was only their daily workpoints. The method used by production teams to remunerate their members remained the piece-rate system. Male and female farmers usually worked as separate groups and received workpoints from the team according to the quantity of their work. However, the adoption of the "contract for fixed workpoints" in effect offset the incentives offered by the piece-rate system because although this system allowed the members to maximize their labor input and earn as many points as they could, as a group the farmers understood that the more points they earned, the more likely the team's annual total workpoints would exceed the contracted amount allowed by the co-op and therefore would be cut down at the end of the year. And they knew well that no matter how hard they worked, the increased output they had produced did not belong to their own team and could not directly increase the cash value of their workpoints because the value of workpoints was determined by the overall performance of all teams in the co-op. With the link between the farmers' individual efforts and returns greatly weakened under the advanced co-op, their interests in labor input and work quality deteriorated in comparison to the situation in the small, independent primary co-ops. The result was the immediate decrease in farm output during the year under the advanced co-op.

Problems of Co-op Cadres

Cooperativization also resulted in a significant change in the role of rural cadres and their relationship with ordinary villagers. During the time of primary co-ops, especially when the majority of local households remained independent, the cadres made every effort to attract them into the co-ops. They worked hard to increase co-op members' incomes in order to stabilize the co-op and prevent the members' withdrawal from it. After the transition to the advanced co-ops, however, the peasants completely lost their land and large tools. It was no longer possible for them to quit the co-op; they became completely dependent on the collective. Therefore, the co-op leaders' attitude toward co-op members changed. Instead of seeking consensus with the villagers, they gradually turned to "coercion and compulsion" (*qiangpo mingling*) in carrying out their decisions or instructions from above. The Party's central committee well observed this problem in November 1956: "After agricultural cooperativization, coercion and commandism has become increasingly prevalent among rural grassroots cadres. Many of them believed that the peasants have become members of the socialist collectives and everything has become easy to do and easy to promote. When leading co-op members in production or dealing with issues pertaining to their everyday lives, they consciously or unconsciously give up patient persuasion and education, and substitute them with simple administrative orders" (GNW 1981a: 640). Many co-op cadres "have become arbitrary and peremptory" (*duduan zhuanxing*), who never "consult the masses and listen to their opinions" and instead made decisions by the will of a few or even a single person. In Dongtai county, 44 cadres from five districts were found to have the severe problems of "coercion and compulsion," involving beating and shouting at people, although the county Party committee's report provided no details about such abuses. The same report noted that these phenomena were "rare and isolated," occurring only to a minority of grassroots cadres, but nevertheless they incurred strong resentment among the masses (DT18 1957).

Co-op cadres also alienated themselves from the rest of the villagers by certain privileges that they had obtained. The most obvious were their nonparticipation in collective farm work and the workpoint subsidies they received from the co-op. According to Article 35 of the aforementioned Exemplary Regulations, a co-op should reward its "management personnel who could not directly participate in productive work" with a certain number of workdays according to their duties and workload. A co-op head's yearly workdays "normally should be higher than the yearly workdays earned by a medium-grade laborer," and the total number of workdays received by the management personnel should not exceed 2 percent of the co-op's total workdays (GNW 1981a: 573; see also 494). The final account of the advanced co-op of Qin village in 1957 shows that in 1956 eight co-op cadres received a total of 870 workdays (1 workday=10 workpoints) as their subsidies, which accounted for 4.75 percent of the co-op's total workdays. In 1957, the co-op's 12 cadres received 1,230 workdays in total as subsidies, or 4.22 percent of the co-op's total workdays, far surpassing the limit allowed by the Exemplary Regulations. Among the 12 cadres, the head, the vice head, and the accountant of the co-op each received 180 workdays, and the head and accountant of the four production teams each received 70 to 80 workdays as subsidies (DT23 1957).

In addition to workday subsidies, each co-op cadre also earned workpoints by performing their duties daily. A team head, for example, received workpoints when he spent time assigning tasks to team members, traveling between fields to monitor their activities, or attending a meeting. An accountant earned workpoints when he measured the field, laid out lines for digging water drains, or counted each team member's workload. On occasion, they also joined team members to do some light manual work, such as cleaning up the threshing ground or drying straw in the sun. Normally, however, they did no manual work. Realizing the widespread problem of co-op cadres' nonparticipation in production, the Party urged the cadres to "use every possible moment" to do farm work and thereby arouse team members' enthusiasm for production (GNW 1981a: 675). This notice seemed to have little effect on local co-ops. Throughout the collective period, the rural cadres' nonparticipation in farm work remained the norm in Qin village.

The biggest problem with co-op cadres was their possible malpractices in managing co-op business and handing public accounts. As the Party's central committee observed in March 1957, local cadres tended to monopolize the power in all co-op affairs, such as the distribution of produce, the deposits in a bank, the government's advance payments for agricultural products, the prepayment to co-op members, and the handling of government relief funds. In addition, they seldom publicized co-op accounts to let co-op members know how they had handled financial matters. As a result, the co-op cadres' excessive privileges, use of coercion in dealing with co-op members, and mishandling of co-op accounts became widespread in the countryside (GNW 1981a: 674). Co-op cadres in Dongtai county were not free of corruption and malpractices as well. Among the 19 co-op and team cadres in Sitang Cooperative of Chengdong district, for example, 7 were found to have treated co-op members with "coercion and compulsion," 10 sought undue privileges and illegal incomes, and 11 team cadres admitted that they had recorded a total of 4,897 unearned workpoints to themselves. They also had never publicized the collective's account for one full year since its founding (DT18 1957; DT19 1957).

In summary, one of the major consequences of cooperativization in rural China in the 1950s was the creation of co-op cadres as a privileged group in the village society. Before the transition to advanced co-ops, many of them had been veterans of the Communist Revolution or backbones and activists in the land reform, in the formation of mutual aid teams, and in the early stage of cooperativization. They had won villagers' respect for their hard work, austerity, and intimacy with the masses. After the completion of cooperativization, however, they soon alienated themselves from the rest of the community because of their privileges; they received plenty of workpoint subsidies and, without doing much work, they earned more income than most strong laborers did. They controlled all aspects of the co-op economy, including the assignment of work opportunities, the awarding of workpoints, the distribution of agricultural products, and management of co-op finance. In addition, they engaged in various forms of corruption and malpractice.

Conclusion

Two basic factors determine the effectiveness of cooperative organizations. One is the "shared interest" among participants in the cooperation: their collective effort is fruitful when they all have a willingness to cooperate in order to produce what they cannot obtain individually, and when their individual input in producing the collective good is directly and fairly linked with their respective share of the output (Hechter 1987, 1990). Equally important is the "shared identity" among the producers: they not only agree on their mutual duties and rights in the whole course of cooperation, but also share certain forms of social connections and territorial ties that allow them to enforce both formal regulations and informal forms of collective sanction against defection and free-riding in producing and consuming the public good (Mayhew 1971).

The interest and identity of the villagers under examination varied remarkably as they underwent different stages of cooperativization in the 1950s. After joining the mutual aid teams, they continued their old practice of mutual help during the rush periods in a new form. When well managed, all members of different economic status could benefit from the cooperation: well-to-do households enjoyed the labor of poor households while the latter took advantage of the farm tools of the former. As acquaintances or relatives living in the same neighborhood, the limited number of team members could closely monitor each other's performance and prevent free-riding during the cooperation. But the more members and activities involved in the team, the more difficult it was to manage the group and achieve a balanced partition of duties and benefits among the participants. Therefore, large-size, permanent mutual aid teams were more difficult to organize and maintain than the small, seasonal ones.

Under the primary cooperatives, the interests of different households were much less congruent than under the mutual aid teams. Middle peasants were unwilling to join the co-op or allow poor peasants to join them, when their share of the co-op's goods was much less proportional to the land and farm tools they contributed under the state's policy that allowed for higher labor share of the collective income; the poor peasants welcomed the co-op precisely because they contributed less but could receive more from it. But the incongruence of interests decreased as poor peasants came to dominate the co-op in most instances. Moreover, the primary cooperatives displayed a remarkable degree of efficiency in production, owing to some important consensuses of co-op members. First of all, to attract more independent households into the co-op and prevent the withdrawal of existing members, co-op leaders as well as the majority of co-op members, who were poor peasants and beneficiaries of the cooperation in most cases, had a strong incentive to increase the co-op's output by improving farming techniques and labor management. Second, all co-op members exercised a sense of responsibility when working the farms and using the farm tools, which remained the private property of individual households. Third, as fellow villagers, all co-op members were aware of their personal or their family's standing in the community and were sensitive to others' opinions on themselves. Therefore, social sanction in the form of public opinion remained an effective tool against dereliction in cooperative production.

After they joined an advanced cooperative, however, the villagers lacked both a shared interest and a shared identity. No matter how hard they worked, members of a production team had to share their harvest with other teams of the same co-op, and each member's labor input was poorly linked with his income from the co-op. As residents of different villages, the co-op members paid little attention to the well-being and opinion of other teams, and it was difficult for the different teams to coordinate their activities in production and labor remuneration. The identity was also absent between co-op cadres and ordinary members. After they joined the advanced co-op, co-op members lost not only their land ownership but also the right to exit the co-op. The cadres therefore lost the incentive to please the members by increasing their income and maintaining a good relationship with them. A chasm inevitably emerged and widened over time between the leaders and the members because the former increasingly turned to coercion and even abusive measures in dealing with the latter. All these reasons accounted for the low morale of the farmers and the decreased farm output in Qin village and other areas of rural China under the advanced cooperatives.

To recapitulate, the agricultural collectivization in the 1950s, especially the transition to advanced cooperatives, was far from a successful story as the conventional wisdom suggests (e.g., Bernstein 1967; Shue 1980: 275–333; Lin 1999). Serious problems existed with the methods of collectivization and the ways villagers were organized and rewarded for participation in production, which explain the significant decline in crop yield and popular resistance observable at both national and local levels, as shown in the next chapter. Although the government appealed to the self-interest of the majority of peasants when formulating its policies regarding the establishment of mutual aid teams and primary cooperatives, it increasingly resorted to administrative measures and the political compliance of local cadres to carry out the program of socialist transformation in the countryside. What accounted for the swift transition to the advanced cooperatives, in a word, was the state's compulsion and local cadres' ideological commitment, rather than the material incentives offered by the state's policies. This will become clearer when we move to peasant resistance to collectivization in the next chapter.

CHAPTER 3

"People's Disturbances": Resistance
to Agricultural Collectivization

IN RESPONSE to the Party's call for a "high tide of socialism" (*shehui-zhuyi gaochao*) in the winter of 1955, collectivization in rural China accelerated at a rate far exceeding the government's original scheme, turning nearly 90 percent of peasant households into members of agricultural cooperatives in just one year. What was totally unexpected to the optimistic Party leaders, however, was a wave of unrest that swept many provinces and involved millions of peasants, persisting until the summer of 1957. Discontented with the sharp decline in their income, the corruption of co-op cadres, and the poor management of collective economy, the villagers harvested collective crops for themselves, took back their oxen and farm tools that had been collectivized, beat up abusive cadres, and petitioned for quitting the co-ops.

Beginning with a depiction of the events in Qin village, this chapter examines the nationwide turmoil in the mid-1950s and the reasons behind peasant grievances. Focusing on the poverty-stricken Dongtai county and the prosperous Songjiang county, it shows how different economic and social settings affected peasant claims during the unrest. My examination of the major events in the two counties further sheds light on two basic patterns of peasant contention, which in turn reflect the changing relationship between the socialist state and the populace in the 1950s. One is what we may call *righteous resistance*, which was rooted in the values and shared assumptions innate to the villagers, as manifested in their sense of right and wrong, collective memories, popular cults, folklore, or social practices, and therefore was believed to be moral and just in their opinions. Before the Communists came to power, it took the form of either collective violence, such as riots and rebellions that openly challenged the state or local power holders, or everyday resistance, in which the individuals vented their anger against, or sought protection from, the powerful with "weapons of the weak" (Scott 1985), including rumors, curses, and sabotage, or, alternatively, bribing, illicit sex, fictive kinship, and so forth.[1] The villagers continued their "righteous" actions after the Communist Revolution, as seen in the campaign of "unified purchase and sales" (*tonggou tongxiao*) of grain in the early 1950s, when the villagers resisted the program by either underreporting their harvest, hiding their grain, bribing grassroots cadres to reduce their duties in grain procurement, or openly gathering together to protest against the program and demand food supplies from the government.[2] The same kind of actions recurred during the collectivization drive in Dongtai and Songjiang, when the protesters, mostly ordinary peasants, surrounded government offices for more food, beat up or cursed the unpopular cadres, and illegally distributed the grain or harvested the crop of the collectives when the reduced crop yield and grain ration threatened their livelihood. In those events, the villagers defended their action with the oldest yet strongest reason: their right to subsistence. As the vulnerable in the community, women, the elderly, and children were among the most active in such unorganized actions. When organized, the peasants would demonstrate their strength and defy government authorities by turning to popular cults or celebrating traditional community events. Though denounced by the government as backward and superstitious, in the eyes of the peasants, their actions were morally well grounded and no different from what they had learned from the past.

Yet, this chapter also sheds light on the new methods and appeals that the villagers employed in their resistance to collectivization in the 1950s. We will find that, as the socialist state established its control of the villages through economic reorganization, social restructuring, and ideological indoctrination, the villagers gradually changed their strategies for dealing with the state. In Qin village and both counties, the peasants increasingly turned to the ideologies and channels promoted by the state itself to articulate their interests. Those who were most active in the resistance were usually the "elite" members in a community, such as teachers, retired soldiers, family members of soldiers in active service, former village leaders, doctors, or Party members. With access to newspapers, broadcasting, or other forms of public media, the elite were familiar with government policies and events outside their immediate communities. They were able to use the language that they had learned from the official media and take advantage of the channels allowed by the government to make their actions appear legal and justifiable. Therefore, the elite villagers never openly challenged the policies or systems imposed by the state; instead, they focused their attacks on local cadres who had abused their power in carrying out government policies or running the collectives, especially through favoritism in income distribution, malfeasance in managing co-op finance, and inability to increase production and food supplies. Even when petitioning to quit the co-ops, an action that was officially allowed, the villagers promised to fulfill their tax duties and abided by state laws while excluding landlords, rich peasants, and other "bad elements" from their ranks. Their activities, therefore, spearheaded the *rightful resistance* (O'Brien and Li 2006) that prevailed in rural China the 1980s when the increased burden of taxes and fees and rampant cadre abuse again drove the villagers to act collectively in defense of their interests.

Resistance in Qin Village

Qindian Advanced Cooperative, created in the autumn of 1956 on the basis of four former primary co-ops in Qin and Ji villages and with more than 200 households, underwent a significant decline in production in 1957. Its 381.5 mu of wheat yielded only 70,656 catties in the summer of 1957, or 185 catties per mu, which was 24.5 percent less than that in the previous year. Consequently, the grain ration for each member of the co-op for the entire year decreased to 411 catties, or 14.4 percent less than the level of 1956. The villagers' annual labor remuneration from the collective was only 68.39 yuan per person, 23.8 percent less than that in 1956 (DT22 1957; DT23 1957). Therefore, many villagers lost interest in working for the co-op; their income from the collective was much less than what they earned from family sidelines such as fishing in the reed marshes in the summer or selling reeds as firewood to the townspeople in the winter. The villagers complained of their decreased income after joining the advanced co-op with a newly invented doggerel (*shunkouliu*):

> Independent households bought meat;
> Mutual aid team members ate bean curd;
> Co-op members had nothing else to eat
> But rice porridge and pickled vegetables.[3]

To prevent the escalation of popular discontent, the government required local cadres to avoid the use of coercion in dealing with the
resentful villagers. The head of the Qindian cooperative, Mr. Wang,
thus explained that policy to fellow cadres: "if co-op members beat us,
we should never fight back. If they curse us, we should never shout
back. And even if they spit on our face, we should only clean it by
ourselves and never spit back in anger." The cadres' adherence to the
state's policy, however, only encouraged the villagers' unrest. In July,
some of them started organizing the Green Crop Club (*Qingmiao hui*).
Traditionally, they did so to raise funds for a ceremony in the spring to
pray for a bumper harvest or in the autumn to celebrate the harvest.
After 1949, the government condemned the custom as superstitious
and wasteful, and had prohibited it for years. Now the villagers revived the club, holding the ceremony in the middle of summer, rather
than spring or autumn, for a different purpose: to show their collective
strength and defiance to the cadres. Two club organizers thus collected
contributions from individual households at one yuan per person. On
July 20, the club set up a tented stage on the north side of the village. At
the center of the stage were four tables, on which they placed the stat-
utes of a bodhisattva and the God of Earth that they had removed from
local temples. On the side of the stage were colorful banners written
with words such as "Flourishing crops and bumper harvest," "Calamities disappear when Great Peace arrives; disasters go away when Good
Fortune descends," or "The God of Literacy and Prosperity blesses the
longevity of children." In front of the stage was a 10-foot, pagoda-shaped
tower consisting of many layers of bundled incense. Next to the incense tower was a butchered pig with burning incense in its mouth.
The club organizers invited several storytellers and folk singers to perform on the stage with drums and gongs. They also set off firecrackers
from time to time, attracting more and more spectators from local and
neighboring communities.

The cadres of the co-op knew well that the event was "superstitious"
and that the government had banned it. Afraid of being cursed and
beaten up, however, none of them dared to intervene. Eventually,
Mr. Wang, the one-eyed co-op head and a political counselor of the
district, appeared, trying to disperse the crowd. One of the club organizers, named Zhang, warned him not to step in. Wang ignored him
and jumped onto the stage, trying to take down the tent. Zhang immediately followed him, grabbed him around the waist from behind, and
threw him three meters away from the stage. Humiliated and furious,

Wang shouted at Zhang and threatened to seek help from the district government.

At about 11:00 p.m., the villagers saw many flashlights flickering in the distance and gradually approaching the other side of the river, north of the village. They soon realized that the district cadres were coming. The local co-op cadres used a boat to ferry the district people to the village. A total of 36 cadres arrived, including Zhou Baishou, the Party secretary of the district, who carried a pistol with him. Zhou, a man from southern Jiangsu with a strong accent, asked the co-op cadres to gather all co-op members in a house by the river. Most villagers were already in bed by that time. However, when the local cadres knocked on their door to tell them that the "cadres from above" were assembling them for a meeting, they all went out. In no time, the house was full of male villagers. All of them were waiting for Zhou's scolding. To their surprise, Zhou greeted them kindly and then explained government policies on collectivization, persuading the villagers to "unite and take the socialist road." It was only in the last minute that he reminded the villagers that "it's better not to continue the Green Crop Club." He blamed nobody and had the district cadres leave the village immediately after the meeting.

The activities of the Green Crop Club continued for the following two days and culminated in the afternoon of the third day when the club organized a parade. To prepare for the event, the villagers put the bodhisattva's statue on a chair, which was tied with red silk bands and decorated with bamboo branches and leaves. Two 10-foot long bamboo poles were attached to the chair for people to carry it on shoulders. The parade lasted for about two hours, when the villagers carried the bodhisattva, beat drums and gongs, and marched around the village. They stopped by each home and let the statute of the bodhisattva face the home for a short while to "bless" the family. After receiving coins and rice from the family, the club organizers painted two big red characters on the wall of the home: "*tai ping*" (great peace), and left a yellow slip written with four characters; "*xiao zai jiang fu*" (calamities disappear and good fortune descends). More than 200 villagers joined the parade.

After that event, the Green Crop Club organizers became more confident. Their next action was to withdraw from the co-op. One night at the end of July 1957, they gathered about 30 co-op members to meet in a cottage in the reed marsh outside the village, where they wrote an agreement to quit the co-op. When one of the organizers asked the villagers to sign their name and leave a fingerprint on the paper, however, no one dared to be the first because any person who signed his name first would possibly be identified later by the government as a leader. So they put a bowl upside down to draw a big circle on the paper, and then each put his name and fingerprint around the circle. Together, their fingerprints looked like a sunflower. After the meeting, more and more villagers refused to work for the co-op. Some of them harvested the co-op's crops and reeds for themselves, despite the cadres' warning. Those who refused to turn their boats in to the co-op pulled the boats to the bank and destroyed them to make furniture.

It was at that moment that the Anti-Rightist campaign started and soon swept the entire country. The district government sent a cadre to Qin village, who worked with the co-op cadres to investigate the activities of "sabotage against socialism." Meng, who had initiated the secret meeting and drafted the "sunflower agreement," was detained and sentenced to two years in a labor camp. Zhang, the man who threw co-op head Wang off the stage, was sentenced to one and a half years in a labor camp. A man who dismantled his boat received the same punishment. Two others who attacked co-op cadres were detained for 15 days. All the villagers were intimidated. Open protests disappeared following that episode (QD1 2000).[4]

The Nationwide Disturbance

Qin villagers were not alone in protesting cooperativization. According to a report by the Rural Work Department of the Party's central committee, at least 1 to 5 percent of peasant households in provinces such as Liaoning, Shaanxi, Henan, Hebei, Anhui, Jiangsu, Zhejiang, Jiangxi, Sichuan, and Guandong successfully quit their co-ops, and up to 20 percent of households wanted to withdraw around the "autumn harvest" in 1956 (GNW 1981a: 655).

The nationwide disturbance continued into 1957. In Jiangsu, peasant unrest took place in northern counties such as Xuyi, Yancheng, Binhai, Ganyu, Xinyi, Dafeng, Hai'an, Qidong, and Shuyang and in southern counties such as Yixing, Wuxi, Wujiang, and Chongming. The most severe riot occurred in Tai county, involving more than 30,000 households (or one-sixth of all households in the county) in 73 xiang (82 percent) and 502 co-ops (47.4 percent). The protesters looted a total of 37,500 catties of grain from their co-ops and beat up 224 local cadres. A total of 6,400 people petitioned the county government within five days in

May, and almost 10,000 households successfully quit their co-op membership (GNW 1981a: 686–687; Lin and Gu 1995: 213).

Peasant Grievances

Several reasons explain the widespread resentment in rural China following the "high tide" of cooperativization. First, some peasant households, especially the well-to-do, found that their income declined significantly after joining the advanced co-op. The central government estimated at the end of 1956 that in general about 10 to 20 percent of co-op members in each province saw a decrease in their incomes, and most of them were prosperous middle peasants, petty traders and peddlers, and skilled craftsmen. These households wanted to quit co-op membership for a simple reason. "Cooperativization," in their opinion, was "to let the rich support the poor and to let the strong support the weak." In short, it involved "a great leveling" (*da laping*) (GNW 1981a: 653).

However, participation in these incidents was not simply limited to the well-off peasants. In Guangdong, for instance, some poor and lower-middle peasants also wanted to withdraw from the co-op because of decreased production and family incomes. In Jiangsu, poor peasants in need of food and support were active in demanding grain and money from the government. In the hilly Zhejiang province, independent peasants had previously been able to make 0.70 or 0.80 yuan a day cutting firewood; after becoming co-op members, they earned only 0.30 to 0.40 for a workday. About 80 percent of peasant households in Xianju county received no money at all from their co-ops and instead owed money to their collectives (GNW 1981a: 650, 687, 694).

Second, the villagers were disgruntled because of the unfair distribution of the co-op's income among the various production teams. As the reports from Henan and Jiangsu provinces indicate, it usually happened in larger co-ops that comprised several villages, where the co-op adhered to a universal standard of income distribution to all co-op members without considering the different conditions and performances of individual teams or villages. Rich villages or production teams thus felt it was unfair that the co-op took away their "surplus land, farm tools, animals, and grain" to support other villages or teams in need. Disputes also took place between different xiang or different co-ops about controlling water resources, fertilizing plants, or fishing rights (GNW 1981a: 662, 687).

Third, the villagers widely complained of their loss of freedom after cooperativization. The Party's Rural Work Department admitted at the end of 1956 that co-ops throughout the country imposed "overly strict" requirements of work hours on co-op members, and the farm work for the co-op was "excessively strained." According to its report, "Peasants had no time to engage in family sidelines, and it was difficult for them to make pocket money for daily expenses; nor did they have time to do household chores. Some of them could not even find time to wash and sew clothes or to grind grain. Some felt extremely exhausted." The report mentioned several complaints from peasants in Liaoning province: "The co-ops may be good; but you have to put up with the restraints, oppression, and bullying," and "To join the co-op is no better than staying in a labor camp; after all, the labor camp allows a Sunday." For many villagers, to join the co-op only caused "increases in sufferings rather than income" (GNW 1981a: 656).

Finally, the peasants were very upset with the co-op cadres' irresponsibility in managing accounts and the coercion in dealing with co-op members. Without much experience or skills in accounting, cadres of the newly established co-ops often paid little attention to the management of the collective's finance and individual members' labor contribution. They failed to set up reasonable criteria for awarding workpoints and fairly distribute workpoints among different teams or workers of different abilities. They spent public funds carelessly and failed to maintain and publicize co-op accounts. Embezzlement of co-op monies and the theft of collective properties abounded. Even more intolerable to co-op members was the cadres' rude manner in treating them. Cursing, beating, tying up, and hanging were among the many methods they used to deter and punish disobedient peasants (GNW 1981a: 677, 687, 695). Peasants also complained of the contrasting attitudes of the cadres before and after the cooperativization: "Before joining the co-ops, the cadres made lots of empty promises, saying that no difficulties could not be resolved. Now they are treacherous and ruthless. Instead of resolving problems for co-op members, they treated them with a tongue-lashing" (GNW 1981a: 656). The harsh attitudes only made the peasants, who had already suffered hunger and disappointment over their decreased income, even more resentful.

Domestic Politics

The rise and decline of rural disturbances in late 1956 and early 1957 also reflected the changing situations of domestic politics. For Mao Zedong, 1956 and 1957 were "troubled times" (*duoshi zhi qiu*) (Mao Zedong 1977:

339). In response to Nikita Khrushchev's de-Stalinization in the Soviet Union in February 1956 that triggered liberalization and mass riots in its eastern European satellite states, Mao implemented the "hundred flowers" policy in April 1956 and later the campaign of "free airing of views" (*daming dafang*). Aimed at pacifying the resentful intellectuals, these measures only incurred their harsh criticism of the Party's policies as well as petitions, strikes, and riots by workers and students in the cities. Mao reacted to these developments with his famous speech, "On the Correct Handling of Contradictions Among the People," in February 1957. Mao argued that after the completion of socialist transformation of all economic sectors in China, massive, violent class struggles were over. Most conflicts that remained in the society were "contradictions among the people," which were rooted in the gap between the advanced relations of production and the backward forces of production. These contradictions, Mao proposed, should be handled with the approach of "unite, criticize, and unite" and should be distinguished from the "contradictions between ourselves and the enemy," which had to be settled with coercion and suppression (Mao Zedong 1977: 363–402).

The emergence of peasant disturbances in the same period should be understood in this context. Although the poor management of the cooperative economy and the decline of peasant income were major reasons leading to the unrest, the political atmosphere in the cities no doubt encouraged many informed elites in the villages to take action. In addition, the nonviolent approach to the handling of "contradictions among the people" also encouraged the discontented peasants to air their resentment and act freely.

The Anti-Rightist campaign that started in June 1957, however, soon brought the political liberalization to an end. The Communist Party now claimed that "the struggle between proletariats and capitalists, and the struggle between the socialist and capitalist roads, remain the major contradictions in the country," and that suppression remained necessary to handle such contradictions (Liu Shaoqi 1958). Consequently, hundreds of thousand intellectuals who had criticized the Party were branded "rightists," and many of them were imprisoned or sent to labor camps. In the countryside, the government increasingly treated the activists in peasant disturbances as enemies of the socialist system, and had them sentenced and punished. Peasant protests lasted for a year and swept most of the country, eventually vanishing after the summer of 1957.

Although peasants throughout the country showed similar discontent over their decreased incomes, the poorly managed accounts, and

the corruption and harsh leadership of co-op cadres, there were significant differences between different regions in the major reasons leading to their resentment. To show how different social and economic
settings caused the regional variations, let us first look at the situation
in Dongtai county.

Dongtai County

Located in the poverty-stricken "Inner lower rivers" (Lixiahe) region,
Dongtai county was known for its harsh environment and low yield.
Agricultural output of the county was usually 20 to 30 percent less than
the level of Songjiang county. In 1956, the county's land yield averaged
only 347 catties per mu, or 41.6 percent less than that of Songjiang. During the mid-year distribution in 1957, 30 to 60 percent of households in
different co-ops of the county received no payment in kind or in cash
from the co-ops and instead owed money to the collectives. Some
households, therefore, had no grain at all and had to eat vegetables as
their three meals. Their most common complaints were "we've suffered enough" or "we are starving to death!" For many of them, to exit
the co-op was the only way to avoid starvation. They compared their
withdrawal to "being compelled to go to Liangshan" (*bi shang Liangshan*) (legendary rebels of the Song dynasty who had their stronghold
on Liangshan mountain) (DT18 1957).

The peasants in Dongtai showed their discontent in two ways: by
dividing the co-op's crops and by withdrawing from the co-op. During
the summer harvest in 1957, 205 incidents took place, in which the villagers "illegally divided" and "stole" a total of 211,200 catties of grain
from their co-op. Members in the Tangwang Cooperative of Xixi district, for instance, divided 17,700 catties, to prevent their co-op from
paying too much grain as taxes to the government. Among the 489 production teams in the county who were required to provide free "surplus grain" to other teams, 358 teams faced strong resistance from their
members, who beat up co-op cadres and looted the grain being transferred to other teams. A wave of withdrawals from the co-ops took
place in the county during the short period from May 25 to June 5. It
started with the Sitang Cooperative of Chengdong district, where 45
households tried to get out of the co-op, and soon spread to 30 co-ops
of seven xiang in the district, involving 654 households. In response,
villagers in neighboring districts demanded independence from their
co-ops as well. Throughout the county, 328 co-ops (53 percent of all

co-ops) reported incidents in which a total of 2,209 households (1.35 percent of all households in the county) attempted to quit the co-op. The scale of those incidents varied. According to the county Party committee's report, 239 co-ops had incidents involving fewer than 10 households, 67 co-ops suffered disturbances involving 10 to 30 households, and 12 co-ops had incidents involving 30 to 50 households. Two co-ops saw collective actions of 50 to 70 households and one had more than 70 households involved (DT18 1957).

Dividing the Harvest

The harvesting of the co-op's crops and distribution of the collective grain without the cadres' permission frequently took place in Dongtai county. It was reported that 737 households in different co-ops harvested a total of 902.5 mu of collective wheat fields from May 25 to June 5, 1957. To guard themselves and fend off intervening cadres, the 147 villagers from three co-ops of Chengdong district, for example, displayed their "weapons" such as shoulder poles, pitchforks, and buckets of manure on the field where they were cutting wheat. The head of the Xinqin Cooperative, Haiyan xiang, thus was showered with a bucket full of manure, and the head of the same xiang suffered a bite and a lash of a shoulder pole by angry villagers when he was trying to "persuade" the latter to stop cutting (DT18 1957).

One event from the Zaoxi Cooperative was even more illustrative of this kind of peasant discontent. The Zaoxi co-op, located in Zaodong xiang of Chengdong district, had 380 households and a population of 1,400, including 169 households with poor-peasant status, 144 middle-peasant households, 19 rich-peasant households, and 4 landlord households. With 2,711 mu (80 percent of its fields) growing cotton and 442 mu growing peppermint, the villagers had been better off before joining the advanced co-op in January 1956. Since then, however, crop failures in the collective had reduced its members' grain rations to as low as 330 catties per person that year. During the wheat-harvesting season, 12 instances of illegal harvesting and distribution took place. The most dramatic one occurred on May 31.

On the afternoon of that day, more than 10 hungry villagers from the No. 2 team entered the co-op's fields to pick broad beans on their own. Soon, more than 100 people from the No. 1 team joined them. In response, members of other teams wanted to cut the co-op's wheat for themselves. To pacify the villagers, Zhang Yongsheng, head of the xiang, decided to distribute 10 catties of wheat that were on the threshing ground to each co-op member. Many peasants complained, however, that 10 catties were far from enough. In addition, without proper preparation and explanation, the distribution turned out to be chaotic. People scrambled to sack grain for themselves and quarreled with each other when weighing their shares. Some put additional grain in their sacks after weighing them; others carried away their stuffed sacks without weighing in at all. Realizing that the situation was out of control, Zhang and some team leaders stopped the distribution and walked away in anger, leaving the wheat unattended. The villagers decided to continue distributing it by themselves, and more than 700 catties of wheat was distributed in an orderly manner. In addition, they gave each household two dou of vegetable seeds; more than 900 catties of vegetable seeds were thus distributed.

Zhang and other cadres came back to the threshing ground in the evening to find that the wheat and seeds were gone. They interrogated Bi Baoqia, the grounds watchman. Bi refused to tell what had happened and in turn blamed the cadres who had failed to affix the pile of grain with lime stamps (a way to prevent stealing and tampering) before leaving there. A quarrel thus started and escalated when Zhang pulled the screaming Bi to the xiang office. Upon seeing this, Bi's son rushed out from his home and yelled to the neighborhood: "Catch the thieves! They're beating people to death!" He soon gathered more than 60 men. The crowd quickly surrounded Zhang, tied him up, and beat him soundly. After venting their anger, the villagers left the xiang leader standing alone on the ground, in order to punish him further. They then went home and Zhang soon fled to the xiang office.

Afterwards, the county's Party committee and the prefectural Party committee sent a joint "work team" (*gongzuo zu*) to the co-op to investigate. Frustrated, Zhang insisted on arresting the most active persons in the incident, especially Bi and his son: "If nobody is arrested, the masses will be out of control, and it makes no sense for me to stay in office." The vice head of the co-op also threatened to resign: "Having worked [for the co-op] for years, the xiang head earned nothing other than a beating. We won't work any more. Better to go home and be a good co-op member." Other cadres shared their feelings: two of the three co-op accountants and two of the nine team leaders wanted to quit their jobs and all others felt frustrated and pessimistic about the future of the collective. The work team, however, declared the incident a "contradiction among the people" and arrested nobody. They only asked the Bis and the other two who had tied up or beaten the xiang head to "make a self-criticism" and "admit their mistakes" at a meeting, and to visit the xiang head's home with an apology. Meanwhile, the work team conducted an investigation of the illegal distribution, and asked all households involved to return the grain and vegetable seeds that had been distributed. Alternatively, they could count what they had received as advance payment, which would be deducted from future distributions. These measures, according to the county Party committee's report, were satisfactory to both the cadres and the villagers, who allegedly worked even harder after the incident and finished the summer sowing 10 days earlier than they had in the previous year (DT20 1957).

It should be noted that throughout the county, the private distribution of collective harvests was not limited to ordinary villagers. Sometimes co-op leaders were also involved. When weighing the grain being distributed, for example, some cadres deliberately tampered with the scale so that the weight shown on the scale was always less than the real weight of the grain. Alternatively, they prepared two versions of accounts, one for their own records and the other for the superior authorities to examine. Meng, the vice head of the Qindian co-op in Qin village, whose family had eight members and therefore was in desperate need of food, encouraged the head of his team to secretly distribute the team's grain. The team head and his assistant thus poled a boat to deliver grain to every household of his team in the night at the rate of 20 catties per family member. Later, however, this illegal action was uncovered, and Meng lost his candidacy for Party membership.

Withdrawing from the Co-op

A more threatening form of resistance was organized withdrawal from the co-op. The county's Party committee noticed an important feature of peasant actions in this regard that made them different from earlier mass protests: "in the past, disturbance took place in a scattered and unorganized manner. The recent troubles, however, were well organized, with a plan and leadership, and were seriously done. Some of them had a representative, who was elected to bargain over the terms [with the government], and others involved secret meetings and the signing of agreements" (DT18 1957). Among the 554 households of different co-ops in Chengdong district who wanted to leave their co-ops, for example, 315 participated in such organized activities. The leading members of the Nanxin co-op planned their actions so well that they always shot a flame into the night sky as a signal to gather team members for secret meetings in the neighboring reed marshes. The discontented villagers agreed at one of the meetings to treat the cadres of different levels in different manners. To cadres at the district level and above, they would behave nicely, admitting to them that government policies were good. At the same time, however, they would blame local co-op and team cadres for their failure to carry out those policies and for the hunger that the masses had suffered. Members of other co-ops voluntarily raised money and food to support their representative's travel to the county or prefectural seat to complain about corrupt and abusive local cadres. Meanwhile, they dispatched people to the neighboring districts and counties to check the situations in those places. The activists also assigned to each of themselves a couple of households, persuading those households to join their efforts (DT18 1957). To illustrate how the villagers organized themselves to get out of the co-op, let us consider the example of the Sitang Cooperative.

The Sitang co-op, located in the Chengdong district next to the county seat, was founded in February 1956 and included 103 households from four former primary co-ops and 154 independent households. Ninety-nine households (38.5 percent) were poor peasant status; the remainder were middle peasants (149, or 58 percent), rich peasants (eight, or 3 percent), or landlord (one household). Because of local cadres' poor management, the co-op, with about 2,000 mu of land, produced only 504,132 catties of grain in 1956, or 252 catties per mu, which was 35 percent less than in the previous year. The grain ration for co-op members was as low as 355.5 catties per person. Dissatisfied with the limited food and co-op cadres' poor performance and crude manner in dealing with them, two co-op members, Xia and Zhou, gathered 45 households to collectively withdraw from the co-op in May 1957. Among them were 37 middle-peasant households and 8 poor-peasant households, including one cadre, one veteran soldier, the wife of a soldier in active service, two Youth League members, and two subteam group leaders. They requested a grain ration of 600 catties per person and termination of co-op membership for reasons such as the co-op cadres' "undemocratic style of leadership," the muddle of collective accounts, and the hardship of their lives.

To make their action more defendable and successful, the villagers held three secret meetings, in which they decided to pay grain taxes to the government in a timely manner, to exclude rich peasants and the landlord from their activities, and to take care of households in poverty. They also enforced an agreement to prevent any participant from giving up and to punish the "traitors" by removing the straw from the roofs of their houses. The peasants had a strong sense of acting within the bounds of government policies and regulations.

To make the participants confident in their actions, Xia claimed that 13 co-ops in the neighboring district had broken down and that the yard of the prefecture's government office was full of petitioners seeking to quit the co-op. He also collected 0.10 or 0.20 yuan from each participating household as funds to file a complaint against the co-op cadres. Xia further assured his followers: "With your support, I have no fear at all. If someone has to be beheaded, I'll go first." Because of his efforts, 51 more households showed their willingness to join his action. ·
As many of them admitted later, they joined Xia only because they worried about the possible retaliation from him and his followers or ridicule from the rest of the team members for the futility of their efforts.

As a major step in their plan to withdraw, the 45 households all refused to work on May 26. Instead, they cut the wheat on fields that had belonged to them before cooperativization and immediately divided among themselves what they had harvested. Threatening to beat any intervening cadres, the participants cut 26 mu of the co-op's wheat on that day. Other co-op members lost confidence in the collective. Seventy-four percent of them failed to work for the co-op that day. Three households took back the oxen that they had turned in to the co-op. In the following two days, no one worked at all for the co-op, despite the urgent tasks of cutting wheat, weeding the peppermint field, replanting cotton seedlings, or sowing the maize seeds.

The co-op cadres' initial reactions were mixed. Some were sympathetic to the villagers; three of them even wanted to quit their jobs. Others wanted to suppress the "troublemakers" by arresting at least the most active individuals as quickly as possible. They all knew, however, that without the government's support, they alone were unable to deal with their disgruntled fellow villagers, who were well organized.

A "work team" appointed by the county's Party committee soon came to the co-op. It first gathered all of the 15 co-op and team cadres, asking them to conduct a "self-criticism" for possible faults and mistakes, while assuring the cadres that the work team would side with them to deal with the troublemakers. On the work team's instruction, the local cadres agreed to treat the disturbance as a "contradiction among the people," to be settled by "education and persuasion" rather than punishment as they had expected. The work team then gathered the discontented villagers, asking them to complain of their difficulties and the cadres' problems. After two such meetings, in which the angry members were gradually placated, the work team assigned a couple of households that had participated in the incident to each of the local cadres. The cadres visited those households and apologized for their rude manners in treating the villagers and for mistakes in managing the co-op.

The next step was to hold a meeting of both the households that had participated in the disturbance and those that had not. Both groups of households were urged to unite and to avoid any ridicule or discrimination against each other. To encourage the disgruntled villagers to rejoin the co-op's labor force, the work team asked all co-op and team cadres to take the lead in doing farm work. Most co-op members thus reportedly resumed farm work in a few days. As a final step in its mission, the work team selected 14 co-op members, including the two leading troublemakers, to form a group responsible for investigating and clearing the co-op's and teams' accounts. The incident was completely resolved when the group finished its task and publicized the co-op's accounts. To improve the relationship between co-op cadres and members, the work team nominated 13 candidates for the election of new co-op and team cadres (DT19 1957).

The cases just examined show both the continuities and changes in peasant resistance following the Communist Revolution. The villagers' unauthorized cutting of co-op crops and distribution of collective grain were not too different from their looting of wealthy households and smashing of rice shops in the old days, to the extent that those actions were driven by hunger and backed by a shared understanding of the "right to survival"—the claim to available community resources for the very basic need of subsistence. And the co-op members beat, cursed, and humiliated local cadres who blocked their actions in the same way that they had dealt with the unpopular village heads (*baozhang*) and rent collectors before. However, as seen in Dongtai county, the unrest during cooperativization, especially the collective actions to withdraw from the co-op, showed significant changes. Not only did their organizers try to limit their activities within a scope allowed by the government and even to justify their claims by citing state policies, but the state also avoided using coercive measures to deal with the discontented villagers. This conciliatory relationship, in fact, reflected a subtle balance of power between the two sides in the course of collectivization. While the state's growing influence in the countryside through land reform, ideological indoctrination, and the unprecedented effort of administrative reorganization forced the villagers to accept its new legitimacy and therefore make their own actions rightful, the state had to be cautious in handling the protests of the disgruntled peasants and, whenever possible, satisfy their demands in order to stabilize the existing co-ops and absorb more households into the co-op. However, once collectivization was finished and the villagers lost their means of production, the balance would tilt in favor of the state, allowing its termination of the placation policy.

Songjiang County

Songjiang was one of the core counties in the high-yield Yangzi delta, where peasants had long enjoyed a relatively high standard of living. Before the widespread creation of advanced co-ops, agricultural output in Songjiang had reached 594 catties per mu or 902 catties per capita in 1956, high above the national levels (188.5 catties per mu and 620 catties per capita in 1956) (*Songjiang xianzhi* 1991: 9.1.3; Guojia tongjiju 2000: 40, 79). Although the full-scale transition to advanced co-ops caused a significant decline in the county's land yield in 1957 (491 catties per mu or 732 catties per capita), most households had no problems supporting themselves with grain rations from the co-op (419 catties per capita, or 13 catties more than the national level, but 26.7 percent less than the county's 1957 level) and their own grain reserves from previous years (SJ5 1956; Nongyebu zhengce yanjiushi 1979: 105).

What dissatisfied Songjiang villagers was not hunger or the absolute shortage of food as seen in Dongtai but that they had received much less from the co-op than what they had expected. To pacify the peasants and stabilize the co-op, many cadres paid grain or cash to co-op members in advance so frequently that by the time of mid-year distribution many households found that they had been overpaid, and instead of receiving further payments, they actually ran into debt with the co-op. Dissatisfaction thus often occurred because of the early overpayments followed by nonpayments and indebtedness at the end (SJ12 1957; SJ14 1957; SJ17 1957; SJ19 1957). Because of the gap between their expectations of the co-op and the limited income they actually received, the peasants were particularly sensitive to, and intolerant of, the embezzlement of co-op grain or funds by the cadres, the uneven division of co-op income shared by different teams, and the unfair use or possession of their land, water, and other resources by neighboring co-ops or teams.

The Party committee of Songjiang county reported on June 4, 1957, only 24 incidents of "mass disturbance" (*qunzhong naoshi*) in the county during the preceding 12 months, including 9 incidents to withdraw from the co-op; 11 disputes between members of different teams or co-ops for disputes over the ownership of land and other properties or the right to use water, to fish, and to gather weeds in border areas; 2 collective petitions against local cadres' maltreatment of co-op members or indifference to their hardship; and 2 collective protests or strikes against co-op cadres' coercion, corruption, and mishandled accounts. Those who wanted to cancel co-op membership ranged from 30 to 85 individuals; turf wars between neighboring collectives often involved dozens or as many as hundreds of people; and collective protests or petitions also attracted dozens or even up to hundreds of participants (S15 1957; SJ19 1957).

The county's Party committee report, however, was far from complete. Many more incidents took place in local districts. During the few months from March to July of 1957, for example, Fengjing district reported eight "collective disturbances" (*jiti naoshi*) in the form of group quarrels, strikes, feuds, and withdrawal from co-ops, involving 15 out of its 43 co-ops and 2,080 participants (SJ14 1957). In Chengdong district, 32 incidents took place from late 1956 to April 1957, involving 10 co-ops and 1,036 people (SJ9 1957). In Tiankun district, 1,890 members from 24 co-ops participated in 51 incidents, with the largest one involving about 800 people (SJ6 1957). Sijing district reported 65 incidents during 1956 and early 1957, mostly collective withdrawal from the co-op, protests against co-op cadres, or quarrels (SJ7 1957). The Sheshan district listed nine incidents in its report of "people's disturbances," including eight conflicts between different co-ops and one that involved more than 50 villagers wanting to exit the co-op (SJ17 1957). There is no doubt that in addition to these five districts, the other four districts had similar instances of disturbance, though no documentation about those districts is available. The total number of incidents that occurred in the entire county in the second half of 1956 and the first half of 1957 might have been around 200.

Demanding More from the Co-op

The Xinwu Cooperative, located in Xinwu xiang, comprised five administrative villages, 6,146 mu of land (averaging 2.29 mu per person), and 595 households, mostly poor-peasant households. It was one of the few large co-ops with more than 500 households (the average size of advanced co-ops in the county was 248 households). The co-op consisted of 16 teams, originating from 15 former primary co-ops, most of which had been set up as late as the autumn of 1955 and had not experienced any collective production activities before merging into the advanced co-op in January 1956. Nevertheless, owing to the hard work of 22 co-op cadres and activists, including 28 Party members and 57 Youth League members, the co-op performed quite well in 1956: its agricultural production yielded 603 catties per mu, a bit higher than the county's average level (594 catties). In addition to distributing 535 catties of grain to each co-op member as their "basic ration" (*kouliang*), the co-op kept 43,000 catties as reserves. Its sidelines also developed well: it raised 120 pigs and 1,300 ducks, which contributed to 20 percent of the co-op's total income. In addition, individual households owned 116 tools to make straw sacks for building dikes and 63 tools to make straw ropes. More than 30 percent of the households engaged in bird hunting during slack seasons. Overall, most members in the co-op lived a life above the average level of the county. And they were definitely well-to-do by national standards.[5]

However, the co-op did a poor job in financial management. Since May 1957, the individual teams of the co-op regularly distributed the rationed grain and money to its members every 10 days, on the first, eleventh, and twenty-second days of each month by a co-op–wide standard. The villagers called the grain thus distributed as "customary grain" (*xiguan liang*). Over time, they became dependent on their respective teams for any amount of grain they needed. They also turned to the co-op for small loans on any pretext. One member, named Qian, for instance, borrowed from the co-op five times simply to buy a wok. Another person borrowed eight times with the excuse of curing a tiny ulcer on his leg. Once they obtained the money, however, the borrowers never planned to repay the co-op. The cadres yielded so easily to their demands because they allegedly had "five fears": they feared the co-op members' curses, strikes, accusations, starvation, and exit from the co-op. This was especially true after they were instructed to treat the "mass disturbances" as "contradictions among the people" in February 1957 (GNW 1981a: 671).

Because of the repeated loans from the co-op, however, many households failed to pay off their debts with the workpoints they had earned. According to the co-op's original scheme of advance distribution scheduled for July 10, its 16 teams should have distributed a total of 8,813.97 yuan of income in kind and in cash to its members. However, because of the numerous loans and repeated distribution of the "customary grain," the co-op had only 2,600 yuan available for distribution. About 80 percent of households were to receive no money, and many of them in fact owed money to the co-op instead. Therefore, on the night of July 10, when the co-op head announced the actual distribution plan, many members protested: "What will we eat tomorrow if we're overdrawn households and get nothing from the co-op?" "You told us that lots of fields have grown crops for the summer harvest and the yields will be high. So we've been waiting for the summer distribution day after day. How could we have nothing left? What's wrong with you cadres?" The cadres explained but to no avail. The audience argued with them for a long while and then left in anger. The co-op cadres knew that something bad was going to happen the next day when the villagers expected the distribution of grain and money from their teams.

In the early morning of the next day, July 11, Wu Jinyun, a man from the No. 8 team of the co-op, built a dike to block the drainage of water from the paddy field so that nothing could be done in the deep water after a rain. He then warned fellow team members: "If anybody goes to work today, then that means he has grain, and let's all go to his home to eat." As a result, none of the team members came out to work for the team, and they all gathered at the team's office asking for their "customary grain." Under pressure, the team leader distributed five catties of grain to each team member, which was two catties more than the team's customary level. This action encouraged people of other teams, who wanted their team leaders to do the same. When their team leaders refused, about 70 or 80 villagers gathered at the xiang government office and surrounded the xiang cadres, shouting: "Is there grain and money? If not, pay us for our straw sacks and contributions to pigsties!" Some complained: "With only one cropping a year we ate fish and pork before; now there are two croppings a year but we live a hard life." "You've taken over our farms, controlled our grain, and held all the money in your hands. Do you want us to starve to death?" Three or four villagers announced that they wanted to withdraw from the co-op. Three desperate women from the No. 4 team dragged the co-op head to a nearby creek, saying that they wanted to drown themselves together with him. Meanwhile, a boat from the No. 4 team, loaded with wheat that was to be sold as "surplus grain" to the government, passed by. A group of men quickly blocked the boat, saying in anger: "We're struggling to find food to eat. Why is there surplus grain to sell?" They dispersed only when the vice head of the co-op intervened and warned: "This is the state's grain! Dare any of you touch it?"

The news of the gathering, however, soon spread to all other teams of the co-op. About 100 more villagers had joined the protesters by 9:00 a.m., and everyone carried a shoulder pole and sacks to get grain. The crowd, now made up of more than 200 people, became even more agitated. They kept shouting at the cadres and threatened to beat them up. Some of them cursed the cadres as bandits, "stubborn and unyielding," "worse than the xiangzhang and baozhang before." They did not break up until 4:00 or 5:00 p.m. when the cadres finally promised to borrow 750 yuan from different units of the township for distribution five days later to the 13 teams whose members had joined the protest. The remaining three teams promised to make distributions the following day. Because of the gathering, farm work in most teams of the co-op stopped on July 11.

The county's Party committee dispatched a work team to the co-op that same night. The team members were mostly Mandarin-speaking "cadres-down-to-the-south" (*nanxia ganbu*), who came from North China and migrated to the southern region when the Communist Revolution expanded there. The work team first investigated the incident by having several meetings with the cadres of the co-op and then with the cadres and activists of different teams. Villagers responded to their arrival by changing their supper from the typical steamed rice to porridge, a way to show their dearth of food. They believed that, once the "people from above" arrived, there would be a solution to the problems of grain and money. On the night of July 14, the work team and co-op cadres divided into several groups to visit each team and gathered team members to offer them an opportunity to complain. The villagers remained resentful of the limited grain they had received from the co-op and refused the cadres' suggestion to save on food: "We already live under socialism. Does it still make sense to speak of frugality?" "We only want to have enough to eat and care about nothing else!" "The socialist happy life is coming to an end; it's just like beating a gong with a cucumber—the longer you beat, the shorter the cucumber becomes." Many women, beating with chopsticks on their bowls filled with porridge, grumbled to the cadres: "Look! We farmers are eating porridge. Don't you feel guilty?" A veteran soldier stood up and shouted: "Why did you set the grain ration to as low as 520 catties? I ate twelve *liang* [1.32 lbs.] of rice a day and had fishes and pork every day when I was a soldier. Now I no longer have meat and enough rice to eat." Others chimed in: "Yes, how could we farmers eat only one catty of rice a day! You cadres never work yet have meat to eat every day. How unfair it is!" Unable to pacify the disgruntled villagers, the cadres ended the meeting without a resolution. The villagers also left the meeting place disappointed: "We supposed that the northerners had come here with a solution. It seems now that they are helpless as well." "Better not to have them here. We used to get grain and money every 10 days. Now after the quarrel we only got the steadfast word of frugality." Nevertheless, they were waiting for the coming of July 16, the day to distribute grain and money that the co-op cadres had promised five days earlier.

Worried about the possibility of trouble on that day, the work team and co-op leaders met on the night of July 15 and decided to do two things early in the next morning: to summon the most active 50 "troublemakers" to the xiang office for a meeting and to let each team leader drive co-op members to work as early as possible. In the early morning of July 16, however, only about 10 of the troublemakers attended the meeting, and they continued to quarrel with the cadres. Others were more cautious; they reminded each other: "Watch out! The outsiders are carrying pistols. The rafters that jut out rot first: better to stay home and watch things going on around us." Nevertheless, they encouraged women to go out and ask the cadres for grain. More than 100 women from different teams, all carrying a sack, thus assembled at the xiang office. To their disappointment, none of the co-op cadres who had made the promise appeared. Only the work team members were greeting the women. Unable to get money and grain, the women were angry, shouting and cursing the work team members: "What a sort of people you northerners are! Unable to understand our dialect, how could you know our sufferings?" After a few hours' protests, they left the xiang office around 11:00 a.m. with empty sacks.

The protests in Xinwu Cooperative eventually subsided. Farm work resumed in all teams on July 17, and the attendance rate bounced back to 90 percent under pressure from the work team. The work team then started a thorough investigation of the actual situation of grain shortage in each team. They first tried to get information with the help of the local co-op and team cadres, but soon found that those cadres themselves had a number of economic problems. The information they provided was often unreliable: according to the xiang leaders, 80 percent of households, or more than 470 households, in the xiang were short of food. The work team adopted the approach of "mass line" (*qunzhong luxian*), turning to Party members and peasant activists in the co-op for information, and found that only 222 households were indeed in need of food. The work team then divided the 16 teams of the co-op into three categories: six teams had enough grain and could be self-sufficient; four teams were short of grain and needed supplies of grain from other teams; six other teams had surplus grain and would have to supply grain to the aforementioned four teams. All in all, they believed that there was no need for the co-op to ask for additional grain supplies from the state. By July 26, the work team had successfully asked the six teams with surplus grain to provide 5,780 catties of grain to the four teams in need.

Meanwhile, after organizing a meeting in each team in which the villagers reportedly confessed their mistakes during the riot, recalled their distresses before Liberation, and expressed their gratitude to the Communists for their "happiness" under the new government, the work team terminated the practice of distributing the "customary grain" and began a program to save on food. At the same time, the co-op drastically reduced the loans to its members. Before the incident, the co-op normally loaned at least 50 yuan a day. During the 17 days from July 11 to 27, however, it loaned only a total of 45 yuan. Unable to borrow money and grain from the co-op, nine households of the No. 11 team had to sell their rice straw and several chickens and ducks to buy food. They also began eating porridge twice a day (SJ12 1957).

"Contradictions Among the People"

The incident of the Xinwu co-op was illustrative of the many instances of peasant resistance in Songjiang in 1956 and 1957. The villagers protested against co-op cadres' poor management of the collective finance, especially their embezzlement of public funds, failure to publicize accounts, and unfair allocation of the collective's grain or funds that benefited only a few. The main way of airing their anger was demanding grain and money, cursing the cadres, and refusing to work for the team. In another incident, 11 members of the Xingming co-op, dissatisfied with their cadres' misappropriation of public funds, requested the distribution of rice seeds and stopped working for more than 10 days in March 1957. When asked to resume farm work, they replied to the team leader: "if you want us to work, prepare three good meals a day for us." Some even threatened the cadres with the demand for withdrawal from the co-op. One co-op member, Yang Jiyun, thus pulled the ox that had belonged to him before cooperativization back to his home, and even cut two boats of vetch grass (used as forage or organic fertilizer) from the co-op's field. Following his example, three more households tried to take back their oxen, and 13 households wanted to quit their co-op membership (SJ8 1957). However, many admitted later when the disturbance was over that they had not really intended to withdraw from the co-op; they were well aware that doing so was difficult and almost impossible. What they really wanted was only more grain and money from the co-op, and the reason was not that they actually ran short of food or money (SJ14 1957). The aforementioned Yang, for instance, had received a total of 3,308 catties of grain for the seven members of his household in 1956. He had also raised 13 piglets, 1 sow, and 5 chickens. The real purpose behind their demands was that they thought it unfair that the cadres had embezzled the co-op's funds or allowed some favored or resourceful fellows to obtain additional grain or money from the collective.

Nevertheless, some middle peasants, unhappy with their decreased income, were indeed determined to withdraw from the co-op. Take the four middle-peasant households from the Minzhu Cooperative of Zhongsheng xiang, for example. Before joining the co-op in early 1956, the four households were relatively well-off. After becoming co-op members, however, three of them found that their incomes fell by 20 to 100 yuan that year. What made them even more dissatisfied was that, unlike the poor peasants in their co-op, they were not qualified for loans or advance payment from the co-op, nor could they engage in sidelines such as making straw sacks for two to three yuan a day. Worried about their incomes, the four households acted together to withdraw from the co-op, complaining that "the co-op was good only for poor peasants." They stopped working for the co-op and attending team meetings, and visited the tea house in the neighboring town each day, where they said "bad words" about the co-op (SJ10 1957; SJ11 1957). Unable to obtain the co-op leaders' permission to quit, some middle peasants even turned to the county's prosecutor's office for help (SJ9 1957).

In most instances, however, participants in rural disturbances were not limited to the middle peasants, but included all kinds of co-op members. This was especially true in situations in which all the co-op members suffered from the local cadres' misconduct and poor management—but those who started or led the protests were rarely the simple villagers. A report on the riot in the No. 2 team of the Guang-ming Cooperative, Sheshan xiang, reveals the background of the riot leaders. The team had 63 households and their grain ration was 560 catties per person, which was relatively high in Songjiang county. Unable to obtain more grain or receive anything from the co-op during the advance payment because of their debt and insufficient work-points, 25 members of the team quarreled with co-op cadres and even wanted to withdraw from the co-op. Among the most active individuals, three had family members in government offices or state-owned factories, two had family members working as doctors, one was a primary-school teacher, and three were peddlers traveling between Songjiang and Shanghai. All of these people had wider social connections than the ordinary villagers had and were well informed of the political situation outside the village: "They learned the news from newspapers and knew about the campaign of 'free airing of views' (*daming dafang*) in the cities. They thus were encouraged and spoke freely" (SJ13 1957).

The county Party committee's report on handing the eight incidents in the Fengjing district describes the leading individuals in such events as follows: 15 of them were former cadres who had failed to be reelected or had been dismissed and therefore were resentful of the current cadres who took over their jobs; 13 were veteran soldiers who were dissatisfied with the government's assignment of their jobs; 35 of them were team or co-op cadres, including 11 Party members, who were "selfish, indifferent, and difficult to get along with," and 2 were family members from landlord or rich peasant backgrounds. The report concluded that "only a few of them were really in need of grain or money or had other difficulties" (SJ14 1957).

Because the majority of the leaders and participants of the disturbances were current or former co-op cadres or their family members, retired soldiers, or Party members, as well as ordinary peasants, and because former landlords, rich peasants, and counterrevolutionaries were rarely involved, the government treated their discontent primarily as a manifestation of "the contradictions among the people," resulting from co-op cadres' poor performance or decreased income. Therefore, it emphasized the use of "persuasion and education," rather than forceful crackdowns, in dealing with the disgruntled villagers. In Song-jiang county, the government and Party leaders usually handled the disturbance with several steps. The first was dispatching a work team to the area. Members of the work team had to be experienced "competent cadres" (*deli ganbu*), capable of dealing with complicated and capricious situations, sometimes including the county Party committee's secretary himself and his direct subordinates. The next step was to "stabilize the masses' emotion" and to make them resume work. The work team normally allowed the discontented co-op members an opportunity to complain and fully vent their anger through a public meeting, then explained to them the Party's policies of cooperativization, criticized what they had done, and persuaded the peasants to accept government policies by asking them to compare their lives before and after the Liberation. In addition, the work team had special meetings with individual leading members of the incident, and "from time to time successfully turned them into activists to help calm down the turmoil" (SJ14 1957).

To placate the villagers, the work team always did something to solve the problems that had caused their resentment. If the incident resulted from poorly maintained accounts, the work team would help consolidate them, and even organize a "financial clearing committee," which included co-op members, to clear and publicize the accounts. The cadres had to apologize to co-op members if they had angered the latter by their coercive or arbitrary style of leadership (SJ14 1957). Cadres who embezzled or engaged in some form of corruption had to return the illicit gains before a certain deadline (SJ18 1957). Production teams that had awarded excessive workpoints to their members and had caused other teams' frustrations had to cut back their points (SJ16 1957; SJ19 1957). Households that had been overpaid had to return the difference to the co-op while those actually requiring help were allowed to keep what they had been paid (SJ17 1957). Those who truly wanted to withdraw from the co-op, such as the three households from the No. 7 team of Xinmin Cooperative, were allowed to go (SJ19 1957).

Peasant protests in Songjiang thus showed a pattern similar to what we have seen in Dongtai despite the two counties' different ecological and economic settings. Though much better off than the Dongtai villagers who lived in absolute poverty, the ordinary villagers in Songjiang turned to the "right to survival" as well to justify their claims for additional grain and money from the co-op when their income decreased or lagged behind their expectation after becoming members. They showed their anger and frustration by beating and cursing the unpopular cadres who failed to meet their demands. Their *righteous* actions, in other words, were essentially no different from what they had done with the much-hated tax or rent agents or usurers and rice-shop owners who had threatened their livelihoods before the Communist Revolution. However, like the elite villagers in Dongtai, the most active in the protests in Songjiang were among the most privileged and informed in their communities. They knew state policies and nation-wide situations well and therefore acted tactically to make their appeals and actions *rightful*. The local government, likewise, adopted the same approach for the same reasons as seen in Dongtai county—"education and persuasion" instead of coercion and punishment—in handing the unprecedented protests.

This similarity in state-peasant relations between the two counties should be seen as a result of the encounter between a peasantry that had yet to lose all of its means of production and still adhered to its traditional ethic of subsistence and the socialist state that had successfully established its legitimacy in the countryside but had yet to completely control the rural population and resources. The same kind of relationship between the state and the peasants revived in the reform era of the 1980s for similar reasons: the peasants regained a degree of economic autonomy after decollectivization but faced flourishing abuses and injustices that threatened their subsistence, while the state still maintained its legitimacy in the peasant society but had lost much of its control of the latter after the collapse of the collective system. Thus, what we have seen in Dongtai and Songjiang, two vastly different areas, was by no means accidental; the two locales both reflected a particular form of village-state relations that was common in rural China under the conditions prevailing before and after the period of collectivized agriculture.

Conclusion

It has long been held that agricultural collectivization in China, beginning with the creation of mutual aid teams and culminating in the transition to advanced-stage cooperatives, encountered little resistance from poor and lower-middle peasants, owing in large part to the government's economic and financial measures that benefited the majority of rural residents and to the effective working of the Communist Party's grassroots organizations (e.g., Bernstein 1967; Shue 1980; Teiwes 1987; Madsen 1991; Lin 1999). The resistance, if any, came from the "class enemies" in the countryside, namely landlords and rich peasants. Perry (1985), for example, shows how the landlords and rich peasants, who controlled various kinds of local sects, prevented their followers from joining the collectives or instigated them to rebel against local governments. The realities in both the country on the whole and the localities under examination contradict the received wisdom because not only did resistance to collectivization occur widely, but the vast majority and the most active of the participants in the resistance came primarily from ordinary peasants rather than their class enemies.

Two different cultures shaped the patterns of peasant resistance in rural China in 1956 and 1957, which in turn reflected the changing village-state relations in the course of collectivization. One was the traditional peasant culture that survived the Communist Revolution. Embedded in the rural community, this culture was characterized by the peasants' taken-for-granted acknowledgment of the supremacy of the survival ethic in their everyday lives and in dealing with authorities inside and outside their community. The "right to survival" was superior to anything else, including imposed systems and assumptions, to defend one's actions, whenever any forms of calamities or ill arrangements had threatened his or her livelihood. The hungry villagers in the cooperatives thus felt justified to cut the collective's crops or divide its grain for themselves without the co-op cadres' approval when crop failures and the reduced grain ration drove them to the verge of starvation; in some instances, even co-op cadres themselves had to conspire with the peasants to divide the harvest in secret. To demand grain or money from the co-op, the villagers usually let women, the elderly, or children act first because they were the most vulnerable in the community, and their actions were most defendable by the survival ethic shared by all community members.[6]

Also characteristic of the traditional peasant culture was the villagers' use of the symbols and languages conveniently available from popular cults to mobilize themselves, air their grievances, and defy external authorities when the latter had not yet fully established their legitimacy in the community. The villagers felt it natural and acceptable to gather together under the Green Crop Club, to ridicule the unpopular collectives with work songs and newly coined adages, and to fight the cadres inside and outside the community who infringed upon their interests. Needless to say, such "righteous" actions were possible only when the state had not yet fully penetrated the peasant society, institutionally and symbolically, and when the villagers still retained a degree of autonomy, evidenced in their private ownership of land and other resources before full collectivization, the legal right to withdraw from the co-op until the middle of 1957, and the survival of the traditional peasant culture.

Equally evident in the rural disturbances, however, was a new culture growing among the "elite" villagers, including current or former co-op cadres, retired soldiers, Party and Youth League members, and other literate individuals, who increasingly accepted or acknowledged the legitimacy of the imposed systems and ideologies. What they challenged during the unrest was not the collective system or Party leadership but instead the co-op cadres' malfeasance and incompetence. Their demand to exit the co-op was allowable by government policies and therefore legal. To make their endeavors politically correct, they wisely excluded former landlords, rich peasants, and counterrevolutionaries from their participants.[7] Their actions, in other words, were presumably legitimate and rightful. To be sure, in many instances, the *rightful resistance* was not clearly distinguishable from the *righteous resistance* discussed earlier. The hungry peasants who joined unorganized gatherings in defiance of co-op authorities could not totally ignore government policies. Conversely, those who wanted to act within the bounds allowed by the government could not completely keep their actions rightful; dividing co-op harvests or beating co-op cadres often were mingled with the efforts to legally withdraw from the co-ops.[8]

In fact, not only did the peasants change their strategies in dealing with the socialist state; the latter, too, adjusted its methods in handling rural discontent. In its early attempts to curb the unrest in grain procurement and cooperativization, the government tended to use the same methods that they had used during the preceding campaigns of land reform and suppressing counterrevolutionaries to treat those involved in the disturbance. They presumed any action against the campaigns to be a manifestation of the "antagonistic contradiction" (*diwo maodun*) between the communist state and its traditional enemies in the countryside (i.e., landlords, rich peasants, and counterrevolutionaries), and dealt with them with violent suppression and punishment. However, as the government soon realized, those who opposed the state policies were rarely the conventional enemies; instead, resistance came primarily from ordinary villagers, including poor and middle peasants, who had allied with the state during the earlier years of the Communist Revolution and land reform. The increased inapplicability of its old conception of rural problems to the new realities caused the state to adjust both its representation of the new issues and strategies for handling them. Instead of suppressing the discontented villagers with violence, the state redefined their grievance as "contradictions among the people" and emphasized the use of persuasion and education to handle the problem. To pacify the villagers, local government leaders openly censured the grassroots cadres for their mistakes and malfeasances, removed the unpopular village leaders from office, or asked them to make self-criticism at a meeting.

The state itself also made significant adjustments of its rural policies regarding financial management, income distribution, and local cadres' participation in labor work. It was during the heyday of the popular unrest that the state promulgated a series of policies to address the problems that the peasants most resented. On September 12, 1956, for example, the Party required all co-ops to distribute 60 to 70 percent of their incomes to co-op members to ensure that 90 percent of them increased their income; on November 30, 1956, it warned against rural cadres' use of coercion and compulsion in dealing with co-op members; on March 15, 1957, it asked all co-ops to publicize their financial revenues and budgets in a timely manner; on September 14, 1957, it allowed co-op members to criticize the cadres' mistakes at co-op meetings and to choose co-op cadres through a "bottom-up election" instead of the Party branch's "top-down appointment"; and on September 25, 1957, it urged co-op cadres to join co-op members in production and limited the cadres' workpoint subsidies to 1 percent of a co-op's total workpoints (GNW 1981a: 613, 640, 675, 724, 738). All these remedies, introduced during peasant protests in 1956 and 1957, later became part of the regular policies to govern rural collectives, as promulgated by the state in the "Working Regulations for Rural People's Communes" (GNW 1981a: 474–491). Contrary to the assertion that Chinese peasants were "almost powerless" in dealing with the state after the Communist Revolution (Kelliher 1992: 19–25), they played a pivotal role in shaping the Party's agrarian policies in the formative years of the collective system.

To conclude, the process of agricultural collectivization not only witnessed the continual confrontation between the state and the peasantry but also occasioned their mutual accommodation, in which the peasants, while remaining righteous in their resistance, began to accept the legitimacy of the increasingly penetrative state and tried to make their protest appear rightful by avoiding direct challenge to its policies, and the state, too, avoided the use of violence in dealing with the dissatisfied peasants at a time when the latter still retained a degree of economic autonomy. This conciliatory relationship, no less important than any other factors, explains why agricultural collectivization in China, as swift and massive as it was, did not develop into a nationwide disaster involving a drastic drop in agricultural output and widespread rebellion as seen elsewhere in the world.

CHAPTER 4

The Great Leap Forward and Its Aftermath

THE GREAT Leap Forward (1958–1960) was one of the most dramatic moments in the history of socialist China.[1] As a hallmark of the Leap in the countryside, the "people's communes" (*renmin gongshe*) were widely created in place of the preexisting advanced cooperatives. Comprised of thousands of households, the commune was hailed as a bridge leading to communism: it promised to offer all commune members free food and comfortable living conditions, and its gigantic scale would presumably facilitate the mobilization of manpower, the mechanization of agriculture, and the construction of large-scale projects.

The three-year experiment of the Great Leap Forward turned out to be disastrous. Villagers lost their private properties in the "wind of communization" (*gongchan feng*); the collective economy verged on collapse in the "wind of blind command" (*xia zhihui feng*); and tens of millions of people died in a widespread famine. In the end, the Party had to give up not only the ambitious production plans but even the basic institutions and policies of the former advanced cooperatives, and instead revived many economic practices of the original primary cooperatives that had existed prior to the advanced co-ops. What occurred after the "winds" of the Great Leap Forward thus was a true "Great Leap Backward."

There were obvious reasons behind the failure of the Leap in the rural area, as some scholars have explained, such as the consecutive natural catastrophes during those three years, which the Party leaders persistently emphasized to excuse their mistakes (Chen Donglin 2004); the lavish consumption of food under the free supply system at the beginning of the Leap that caused severe shortages later (Yang 1996; Luo Pinghan 2000; Wang Xiao 2001); the massive mobilization of labor forces for projects that turned out to be unproductive and wasteful (Madsen 1991); and the exaggeration of crop yield by local leaders that led to the state's excessive procurement of grain from the countryside and the shrinking size of crop farms (Lardy 1987; Zhang Shouchun 1996). This chapter instead focuses on the inner workings of the people's commune by examining the collective organization, agricultural production, and income distribution in Qin village during the Great Leap Forward years. In addition to the trans-village organizations and the newly introduced methods of farming that caused inefficiency in agricultural production, this chapter demonstrates that what accounted for the bankruptcy of the Leap is primarily the state's extortionate procurement of grain and the attenuated link between effort and reward under the free supplies and wage systems that resulted in the low morale of commune members in collective farming.

The People's Commune

The movement to create the people's commune first emerged in Henan province in July 1958 and quickly swept the entire country in September after the CCP central committee announced a decision of communization (GNW 1981b: 69). By the end of that month, a total of 23,384 communes had come into being, involving 112,174,651 households, or 90.4 percent of all households in rural China (GNW 1981b: 84). Completed in just two months, the process of communization was much swifter than the earlier transition from primary to advanced co-ops, which took more than a year. In fact, however, what rural cadres did during communization was merely to "set up a framework" (*da jiazi*), or to finish the administrative organization of the communes (GNW 1981b: 107), which was indeed much easier than the establishment of advanced co-ops that involved the collectivization of private land and farm tools.

The Qindian Cooperative of Qin village joined the newly created Shiyan People's Commune in August 1958. In Dongtai county, 11 communes, comprising 151 brigades and 308,984 workers, were founded on the basis of 609 advanced agricultural co-ops, 14 fishing co-ops, and 7 salt-producing co-ops. Those 11 communes were soon reorganized into 23 smaller communes in February 1959 (Dongtai xian nongye ju 1987a: 3.4.5). As a result, Qin village, which had been a company (*zhongdui*, a military unit), joined 21 other companies to separate from the Shiyan commune and formed the Qindong People's Commune, which had a population of 29,165 and 178 production teams under 12 brigades. Qin village and the neighboring Su village formed the Suqin Brigade, which had five production teams and a population of 1,958 (QD4 1959).

The people's communes were characterized in official propaganda as being "big and collective" (*yi da er gong*). They were "big" because each commune had, on average, 4,797 households, which was more than 30 times the size (164 households) of an average former advanced co-op (GNW 1981b: 84, 110; Ling Zhijun 1996: 59);[2] they were "collective" because the commune controlled to varying degrees all the resources and production within its boundary. However, since a commune normally consisted of more than 20 brigades and each brigade further had more than six teams, as seen in the case of Dongtai county, it is necessary to examine the triangular relationships among the commune, the brigade, and the team in resource sharing, production, and income distribution, in order to understand how "collective" the commune system actually was.

The drive to set up the people's commune came with the "wind of communization" that prevailed throughout the country. According to the "Exemplary Regulations" of Chayashan People's Commune in Henan province, which was revised by Mao in person and promoted as a model for all communes in the country, "all public properties" of former co-ops as well as the private properties of individual households, such as the lots of their houses, farm animals, trees, and, most importantly, their private plots, had to be turned in to the commune (GNW 1981b: 95). It thus was legitimate for local communes to appropriate both the public properties of former co-ops and peasants' private belongings, such as their houses, furniture, utensils, and animals, for whatever projects under the commune's name. Villagers living in scattered houses had to dismantle their homes in order to build new houses in the designated residential areas. So fanatical were some cadres and enthusiasts during the "the wind of communization" that, according to a popular saying, they "seized money, took over goods, dismantled houses, and carried away grain on shoulder, upon seeing any of them" (Ling Zhijun 1996: 69). In Fengxian county of Shanghai municipality, the communes dismantled 2,147 houses for relocation, 3,188 houses for water-control projects, and 1,823 houses and 1,345 storehouses simply for killing pink bollworms in cotton fields. So devastating was the "wind" that, in the words of the municipal Party committee's report, it was no different from the Japanese army's "mopping-up" operation in the late 1930s and early 1940s: "broken tiles and dilapidated walls, as shocking and miserable as they were, meet the eye on every side" when one looked around from a high place of the county seat (Song Liansheng 2002: 289).

The same wind hit Qin village. To construct the three rooms of the commune's agricultural middle school, the Suqin Brigade provided 18,000 bricks, 21,000 tiles, 288 rafters, and other materials as well as workers. Together, they were worth 1,519.44 yuan (QD4 1960). In addition, the brigade contributed 100 yuan in cash to the school, six desks (worth 36 yuan), 12 pigs (worth 96 yuan), a boat (worth 210 yuan), and an ox (worth 350 yuan); it also contributed 7,000 yuan to the commune's plant propagation project, seven boats (worth 1,521 yuan) to its transportation station, a fishing boat, and 5,145 yuan of its income from selling marsh reeds to the commune. Together, these contributions equaled 14,803.50 yuan (QD4 1961), or 7.89 percent of the brigade's gross income in 1958. A victim of the commune's merciless appropriation, the brigade also showed no mercy in taking over its own members' properties for its projects. To construct a storehouse and an office building, for instance, the brigade dug out an ancient tomb located within its boundary and further asked all households to provide additional materials. The most unfortunate among them was the Huang family, who had just bought enough bricks, tiles, and lumber to build a new house; all of these iems were "communized" without compensation. An estimate made in March 1961 showed that the goods that the brigade had appropriated from its five production teams were worth 3,081.26 yuan in total, averaging 1.57 yuan per person (QD4 1961).

Production and Management

Another important part of communization during the initial months (from 1958 to early 1959) was the so-called "militarization" (*junshi hua*), "battle-like operation" (*zhandou hua*), and "large-scale cooperation" (*da xiezuo*) in production and labor management, which originated from the model communes in Henan province in late 1958 and soon prevailed nationwide (GNW 1981b: 86). By those methods, all workers in a commune formed a "regiment" (*tuan*); each brigade a "battalion" (*ying*); each production team a "company" (*lian*), which was divided into several platoons each consisting of workers of different labor grades, named as "the youth skyrocket platoon," "the adult leaping forward platoon," "women's shock platoon," or "the juvenile pioneering platoon"; and the platoons were further divided into several squads (Song Liansheng 2002: 165). The commune members were required to act like soldiers, who had to "get up, eat, sleep, work, and discharge in unison" (Kang Jian 1998: chapter 5). The entire commune was divided into a number of "theaters of operations," and all units, from the regiment to the hundreds of squads, were subject to the commune leader's unified command. Regardless of where they were from, commune members of different battalions were often appointed to a designated "theater" for a specific "battle." It was not uncommon, therefore, that tens of thousands of villagers from different places gathered together to do the same job, such as weeding the cotton fields or killing sparrows, which were considered pests. The purpose of the militarization was to break the boundaries of different localities and to concentrate manpower and speed up tasks. This new method of organization made the traditional workpoint system obsolete for measuring individual workers' labor input and the "three contracts and one reward" systems that defined the relations between a brigade and its production teams (see Chapter 2). Instead, as will be explained, new methods were introduced to enthuse the teams and individual workers (GNW 1981b: 86).

The militarization of production was accompanied by the "wind of blind command." When planning farm activities, local commune leaders only carried out the policies or instructions of superior authorities or made decisions on their own, ignoring local conditions and traditional farming techniques. Take the plowing of fields, for example. Traditionally, farmers used a plow drawn by an ox to turn the earth over and to prepare the soil for sowing the wheat seeds in the autumn. Believing an exaggerated report from Shandong province that plowing the earth to the depth of half a meter could double the yield, Mao required that all farmland in China had to be plowed at that depth. Local cadres thus competed to turn the earth over as deeply as possible. Instead of using a plow and an ox, which were obviously unable to perform the job, a commune usually mobilized thousands of people to work day and night. In some extreme cases, they reportedly dug the earth as deep as four meters, or fully 13 feet (Song Liansheng 2002: 84)!

Qin village was not free of the national craze for deep plowing. The brigade organized its adult male and female workers into two separate companies; each was divided further into several platoons and many more squads. The heads of the companies, platoons, and squads wore a red armband with a different number of yellow lines to identify their ranks. These armbands pleased some women activists, who were proud of their leading status and therefore worked exceptionally hard. Their enthusiasm helped keep the other women in high spirits. Almost all young women in their late teens through their thirties in the village participated in the deep plowing. Women from other brigades also joined them under the slogan of "socialist grand cooperation" (*shehuizhuyi da xiezuo*). To keep their morale high, the brigade decorated the work site with colorful flags and banners written with slogans. It also appointed a music teacher to lead the young women singing work songs while they were working. In the night, the brigade lit a number of gas lamps around the site when the women worked on deep plowing. After partly finishing the brigade's own task, all of them moved to a neighboring village a few miles away to do the same job. The female villagers thus constituted the major labor force in deep plowing (QD1 2000).

Another example of this "blind command" concerned a water-control project. After sowing wheat in the winter of 1958, all adults in Qin village (except pregnant women) were required to join a project in the coastal area about 50 miles away, together with hundreds of thousands of laborers from other communes. The task was digging a canal, which involved the strenuous work of removing the earth with a shovel, putting it into a basket, and moving the earth away on a shoulder pole. Each day the villagers got up in the chilly early morning, wearing straw sandals that were frozen for a time before the warmth of their feet thawed the straw. Women, especially the younger mothers, had a particularly difficult time. Many of them brought their babies with them, and the babies cried during the night, making it difficult to sleep. In the daytime, they had to travel between the work site and the child-care place to breastfeed their children. Even more frustrating was that their husbands, although working at the same place, could not help them. The men and women were separated, sleeping in different work sheds in the night.

To raise the laborers' morale, each brigade had to find a model worker, or to "launch a satellite," as the cadres called it. The cadres and workers from Qin village launched two "satellites," a man and a woman. The man, nicknamed "Wang the Big Shovel," reportedly dug so fast that he alone was able to serve as many as 40 laborers who moved the earth away. In fact, to help Wang, many of his coworkers filled the cart by themselves or let him fill only half the cart. The female "satellite" was hailed as an "anonymous heroine," because she alone allegedly dug 50 cubic meters of earth in a single night without letting the cadres know. In fact, she and her 20-odd coworkers worked the night to finish the job. Later each of them was allowed to take a break for a day when the cadres learned what they had done (QD1 2000).

In the next two winters, Qin villagers continued to travel to the coast for different projects. Later they learned that some of the canals along the coast proved to be useless because of their poor designs, which were done in haste during the height of the Great Leap Forward, and had to be refilled. After years of hunger and toil, many men and women were exhausted and even lost their ability to work because of various illnesses and starvation.

Dividing the Harvest

"The Wind of Exaggeration"

In addition to the "wind of blind command" that debilitated the villagers, the Great Leap Forward also involved the local cadres' unrestrained exaggeration of the local harvest, or the "wind of exaggeration" (*fukua feng*). Hence the state's dramatic increases in grain procurement, in combination with widespread crop failure, threatened the villagers' livelihood.

An important factor leading to the "wind of exaggeration" was the unrealistically high targets of agricultural yield set by the central and local government leaders before and after they launched the Great Leap Forward. Mao required in October 1957, for example, that the grain output had to reach 2,000 catties per capita in China within five years. The following year, the central government further required that the country's total grain output had to increase by 60 to 90 percent—to 600 to 700 billion catties (or about 1,000 catties per capita) in 1958—and further to 1,500 billion catties (about 2,000 catties per capita) in 1959. Many county governments accordingly proposed to increase their output of wheat to 1,000 catties per mu in 1958 and further to 2,500 per mu or even more in 1959 (Song Haiqing 2000: 383, 394–395). To meet those goals, local cadres had to inflate their yield by several and even hundreds of times. Those who wanted to report their output honestly ran the risk of being denounced as "rightist conservatives" or "bound-feet women," a phrase Mao coined to ridicule the cautious economic planners in the central government (Mao Zedong 1955c).

The "wind of exaggeration" began with reporting the wheat yield of local experimental fields in different areas in 1958, which allegedly reached 3,530 catties per mu in a co-op in Henan, 4,353 catties in a co-op in Hubei, 5,103 catties in a co-op in Hebei, and finally, according to *Renmin ribao* (People's Daily) of July 23, to 7,320 catties in a co-op in Henan. The yield of rice in the summer of 1959 reportedly reached 15,361 catties per mu in Xiaogan county of Hubei and, according to *Renmin ribao* of August 13, 1959, to 36,956.7 catties in Macheng county of the same province. Finally, a commune in Huanjiang county of Guangxi boasted on September 18 that its rice output reached 130,434 catties per mu! Under the pressures from above and their peers, local cadres competed to boast not only the yield of the limited number of experimental fields but also the total output of their farms. In general, they reported a bumper harvest of several thousand catties of rice per mu. These numbers, of course, were wild exaggerations. The scientists from the Chinese Academy of Science produced only 900 catties per mu on their experimental farm in June 1959. After several decades of experiments, agronomist Yuan Longping finally generated a new variety of rice, the "Super Rice," that yielded 2,393 catties per mu in September 2001 (Song Liangsheng 2002: 108–123).

At first, the cadres of Qin village were skeptical when they heard from commune leaders that the model co-ops in other provinces had produced 7,000 catties of wheat per mu or more because the yield of wheat or rice in their own co-op was only 200 to 300 catties per mu. Later they found from *Yanfu dazhong bao*, a local newspaper published by the prefectural Party committee, that the "high-yield satellites" (*gaochan weixing*) also took place in the neighboring counties. A co-op in Sheyang county reportedly produced 9,328.12 catties of wheat per mu, and another co-op in Xiangshui county produced 12,000 catties of rice per mu. To make readers believe the story, the newspaper reported that the county's Party secretary, together with two other supervisors, were at the site to supervise the weighing of the grain. Soon the neighboring Baozhuang village "launched" its own "satellite": its experimental field yielded 30,000 catties per mu! Qin village had several experimental fields as well, which had been deeply plowed, intensively seeded, and heavily fertilized. Knowing that the commune leaders would visit the village to examine its experimental fields the following day, the cadres ordered team members to cut the wheat from other fields and in the night secretly shipped the wheat bundles to the experimental fields. The next day, the commune cadres arrived and took a look at the fields, and then all the bundles were shipped to the team's threshing ground for a measurement. It turned out that the yield was only about 5,000 catties per mu, which dissatisfied the commune leaders. By that time, the cadres of Qin village had learned the trick of other satellite launchers: gathering the crop of other fields and moving it to the experimental field to inflate its yield, or "merging the fields" (*bing tian*), as known to all cadres everywhere. Still, no one was willing to tell the truth and hence be labeled as a conservative.

When the autumn harvest was over, Li Weixiang, the general accountant of the Suqin Brigade, was required to report his brigade's total yield to the commune government. Earlier, about 18 or 19 cadres from the village attended a "meeting of ten thousand people" at the county seat in July, where, under the pressure of the commune leaders, they promised to produce 4,000 catties per mu. Now, however, the general accountant had to be honest when reporting the brigade's actual output of the year because that figure would be linked with the government's procurement of grain. The actual output of rice in the brigade was only 416.4 catties per mu in 1958. The accountant forced himself to be bold enough to report a yield of 500 catties per mu; later he likened this action to "a sparrow using all its strength to lay a goose's egg." Disappointed and annoyed, the commune's Party secretary publicly censured the accountant as "a frog looking at the sky from the bottom of a well," meaning that he had a very narrow view, and told him in a stern manner: "How could you still have a conservative mind at this moment when you're coming here to report your output? Don't enter anything into the form if you don't want to report at least four or five thousand catties per mu!" The accountant thus entered 4,000 catties per mu after he learned that all other brigades had reported 4,000 or as high as 7,000 catties per mu (QD1 2000).

Grain Procurement

The wild exaggeration of grain output led to the state's high demand of grain procurement. The central government estimated in early December of 1958 that the total grain output in the country would be about 850 billion catties and no less than 750 billion catties (GNW 1981b: 104–105). In fact, the actual output in that year was only 395.3 billion catties. Based on the inflated total output, the state procured a total of 117.5 billion catties in 1958, or 29.7 percent of the year's total output and 22.1 percent more than the grain procured in 1957 (96.2 billion catties, or

24.3 percent of the year's total output). During the next three years (1959–1961), the average grain output in the entire country was 82.76 billion catties less than that in 1957, but the average amount of grain procured was 9.58 billion catties more than that in 1957, accounting for 34.4 percent of the three-year average amount of total grain output. The grain procured in 1959, in particular, amounted to 67.4 billion catties, or 39.6 percent of the year's total output (Caizhengbu 1994: 244; Chen Donglin 2004).

Natural disasters during the Great Leap Forward years worsened the situation in the countryside. In the spring and summer of 1959, the major agricultural areas in North and Northeast China suffered a long-lasting drought, whereas repeated typhoons, heavy precipitation, and floods ravaged the southeastern provinces. Together, these disasters affected 97.7 million people (2.87 times the average number between 1949 and 1958) and 42.67 percent of the country's farming land. The next year again saw widespread drought in the north and unrestrained floods in the south, which affected 129.8 million people and 62.42 percent of the farmland. In the third year, natural disasters further affected one-third of the country's population and 59.77 percent of its farmland (Guojia tongjiju 2000: 29; Chen Donglin 2004). The natural calamities, coupled with the failures of the Great Leap Forward, caused sharp decreases in agricultural production throughout the country: from 395.3 billion catties in 1958 to 339.4, 287.7, and 273.0 billion catties in 1959, 1960, and 1961 respectively (Guojia tongjiju 2000: 37). As a result, the amount of grain available for the consumption of rural population after the state's procurement decreased greatly: from 409 catties per capita in 1957 to 312 catties in 1960 and 307 catties in 1961 (Guojia tongjiju 1980: 336).

The natural disasters and the exorbitant procurement also afflicted Qin villagers. The flood in the summer of 1960, for example, inundated 1,610 mu or 65.5 percent of the brigade's rice fields, including 247 mu that were completely ruined. The same flood also submerged 833 mu or 67.4 percent of the brigade's cotton fields, including 209 mu that had no harvest at all (QD4 1960). Because of the recurrent floods as well as the deteriorating work efficiency, grain output in the brigade decreased from 403 catties per mu in 1958 to 329, 219, and 238 catties per mu in 1959, 1960, and 1961, respectively, or 81.6, 54.3, and 59.0 percent of the 1958 level. While the grain output decreased, the amount of grain procured by the state increased from 359,800 catties in 1958 or 24.9 percent of the brigade's total yield in that year to 664,638 catties in 1959 or 56.3

percent of the year's output. So huge was the increased procurement that it greatly cut into the villagers' rations and threatened their livelihood; later the government had to sell 275,476 catties back to the brigade. The net amount of grain procured by the state in 1959 thus was 389,162 catties, or 33 percent of its total output, still much more than that in the preceding year. In 1960, Qin village witnessed the poorest harvest since cooperativization, and the government nevertheless procured 71,400 catties from the brigade. As a result, the grain ration for each Qin villager decreased from 447.5 catties in 1958 to 352.5 catties in 1959 and 304 catties in 1960 (QD4 1961).

In response to the severe food shortage and the state's overprocurement, villagers everywhere in the country hid their grain and refused to sell it. According to a talk by Mao in February 1959, virtually all brigades and production teams were involved in "cheating on the yield and privately dividing the harvest" (*manchan sifen*); "discontent" (*fengchao*) over grain, oil, pork, and vegetables took place "almost everywhere" in the country and on an unprecedented scale in late 1958 and early 1959. "To protect their products," noted Mao, "the brigades and production teams stored them deeply in cellars and guarded them with lookouts and patrollers" (GNW 1981b: 141–143). In fact, not only did the brigades and teams hide their products from the government, individual households also hid their grain from the search by local cadres. They concealed small amounts of grain in straw piles, cowsheds, toilets, walls, bellows, coffins, tombs, and even in nests in the trees (Kang Jian 1998: chapter 7). To meet the unrealistic goal of grain procurements, commune and brigade leaders in the Xinyang Prefect of Henan province launched a vigorous campaign against grain hiding and sent "grain-search teams" (*souliangdui*) to villages, where they were free to tie up, hang, beat, slap, and torture team leaders and peasants who failed to surrender their grain. Violence, in their understanding, was a necessary way to show their loyalty to the Party; a person being kind to the peasants ran the risk of being labeled as a conservative rightist. The result of the campaign was disastrous: during the nine months from November 1959 to July 1960, the local police in Xinyang arrested 1,774 people and detained 19,720 people; 707 of them died in prison or while in custody (Song Liansheng 2002: 299). Later the provincial Party committee described the situation of most peasant households after the rapacious grain search as, using traditional Chinese idioms, "nine houses out of ten are stripped bare" and "utterly destitute" (*shishi jiukong, jiaping ruxi*). People who died of starvation or beating numbered to 80,000 in Zhengyang county and almost 100,000 in Xincai county. In the Chayashan commune of Suiping county, the first people's commune in the country, nearly 4,000 people, or 10 percent of its population, died; in some of its production teams, the death toll amounted to 30 percent of the population. So tragic was the situation in the prefect that the provincial authority described it as "a world of terror and darkness" (GNW 1981b: 421).

Such tragedies, to be sure, did not spread everywhere in the country. Several in Qin village recalled that their commune and brigade leaders were conciliatory in dealing with local teams and few used violence in grain procurement—nor did the villagers hide their grain in a manner as their counterparts in Xinyang did. Nevertheless, the Qin villagers suffered as much as peasants in most other communes in the nationwide, man-made disaster that was unseen in China's past in terms of the scope of the famine and the number of deaths.

The Mess Hall

One practice symbolic of the people's commune and also the most controversial during the Great Leap Forward was the public mess hall, where hundreds of commune members in a village ate together. For millions of Chinese peasants, the introduction of the mess hall once kindled their imagination of a communist paradise and aroused their passion for a new way of life that promised to do away with poverty for good. The horrible hunger and imminent death that they soon experienced, however, also made the mess hall the most dreadful memory in their lives.[3] The eventual dissolution of the mess hall in the wake of mass starvation symbolized the complete failure of the Great Leap Forward and the end of a time of suffering and desperation for millions of helpless peasants.

Before the introduction of the commune, it had long been a custom in many parts of China for different households to cook and eat together when they helped each other during the busy season. The villagers continued this tradition under the advanced cooperatives. They voluntarily cooked and ate together during the busy times, and everyone ate what he or she contributed to the shared meals. Alternatively, the participants steamed rice together but each brought his or her own side dish and ate separately. When the "wind of communization" (*gongchan feng*) started, however, the acute, ideologically minded cadres in provinces such as Hunan and Henan soon identified this voluntary, temporary cooperation in cooking as "buds of communism" and turned it into permanent, regular mess halls, which spread quickly to the rest of the country under the government's ardent promotion (Song Liansheng 2002: 179–185).[4] To persuade villagers to join the mess hall, government propaganda named many of its benefits: people who attended the mess hall could synchronize their meal times and would not have to wait for each other for work, meetings, and study; free of family chores, more women would join the labor force; couples and female in-laws in the same household would no longer quarrel with each other because there would be no more cooking at home; the people who ate at the mess hall by the same standard no longer quarreled for more grain from the collective; and so forth (GNW 1981b: 40). For most villagers, the mess hall seemed particularly attractive because it provided free meals. To make that possible, all communes in the country implemented the "free grain supplies" system (GNW 1981b: 65, 98). "To eat free" (*chi fan bu yao qian*) thus became the most popular slogan at the beginning of communization. Indeed, during the first few months of their existence, most mess halls in the country allowed diners to eat as much as they could. Many of them offered three meals of steamed rice, rather than only one meal (the lunch) of steamed rice and two meals of rice porridge as most households customarily had. In some provinces, such as Hubei, the mess halls did not limit their service to the three meals, but provided food to eaters whenever they came by, no matter whether they were local commune members or passersby (GNW 1981b: 208). Because the mess hall provided free meals to all households, it was supposedly no longer necessary for families to keep their private plots for growing vegetables or to raise pigs, goats, or other animals; such practices were denounced as "remnants of private ownership" that had to be completely eliminated (GNW 1981b: 89).

Qin village, as a single production team (No. 5) of the Suqin Brigade, set up its mess hall in October 1958. Five villagers were appointed to run it, including a "representative of poor and lower-middle peasants" (*pingxiazhongnong daibiao*) as a supervisor, an accountant from a neighboring village who supposedly had no connections with local villagers and therefore was free of nepotism, a cook, and two helpers for burning firewood and washing. Because of its limited space, the mess hall, located in a villager's house, had no tables or benches for villagers to dine there. Instead, each family used a bucket to get food from the mess hall and then ate at home. Like in all other places, all households in the village turned over their private plots to the production team, destroyed their private stoves, and surrendered their cooking utensils to the collective for iron smelting, another important task during the Great Leap Forward. The mess hall provided two kinds of staple food at the beginning: steamed rice and rice porridge. To limit team members' consumption, it issued food stamps to the villagers and allowed everyone to eat one catty of rice a day.

The mess hall itself received grain from the brigade. The brigade had five production teams and each had a mess hall. Each month, the brigade allocated grain to each hall according to the team's total number and by a universal standard of ration. The ration was based on the brigade's total population and its estimated total amount of grain for consumption during the entire year. However, the estimate made at the beginning of a year was often higher than the actual amount of grain available, owing to the unpredictability of the year's actual yield and the state's procurement of grain. The mess hall in Qin village, for example, allowed one catty of rice for each team member during the first few months but quickly reduced the ration to 0.75 catties per person in the spring of 1959 (QD4 1959). The brigade also had to consider the team members' actual needs of food during different seasons when determining the monthly rations. The ration for slack seasons had to be lower than that for busy seasons.[5]

Because people of different ages had different food needs, the actual allocation of grain ration to each team had to consider its members' ages. The brigade divided all team members into five grades according to their ages. The first four grades were members at ages 1–2, 3–6, 7–9, and 10–13; people at and above 14 belonged to the same group and received the same ration.[6] Because of the different age compositions of its members, the average per capita ration of each team varied. The No. 3 team, for example, had the highest level of ration, 100 catties for the first five months of 1961, or 20 catties per month on average (QD4 1961).

These rations, of course, were far below the team members' daily need. Beginning from the spring of 1959, the mess hall in Qin village stopped serving steamed rice because of the severe food shortage and provided only rice porridge to its members. To cook as much porridge as possible with the limited rice, the workers usually baked the rice first and then add 18 catties of water for each catty of rice (QD1 2000). Because of the shortage of food and the rapidly decreasing number of pigs and fowls in early 1959, a situation that prevailed throughout the country, the state once again ordered local communes to allocate private plots to peasant households in May (GNW 1981b: 222). In Qin village, the private plots were limited to 0.04 mu per person for people to grow vegetables and later increased to 0.1 mu per person in late 1959. The brigade had a total of 198.8 mu (4.6 percent of its total acreage) as private plots to individual households (QD4 1959), which was well within the limit of 5 percent allowed by the state (GNW 1981b: 222). To alleviate the nationwide food shortage, the state encouraged peasants to grow vegetables, melons, and fruits to supplement the limited grain. Mao also recommended local communes to produce starch from the roots and stems of plants as a food supplement (GNW 1981b: 294). So that they could cook vegetables at home, Qin villagers were allowed to rebuild a private stove at home. They mixed the vegetables with the extremely watery porridge that they got from the mess hall as their regular meals.

All these measures, however, had only limited effect in relieving the nationwide famine that worsened in 1960. Hunger edema occurred almost everywhere among the starved villagers, and millions of them died as a result. In Qin village, 149 people, or 7.6 percent of its population, had the symptom of dropsy and had to stay in a local clinic, called "the patients' house" (*bingfang*), for an average of 29 days in March 1961, where they received special treatment, including 2,049 catties of rice (0.76 catty of rice a day per person), 288 catties of soybeans, 72 catties of oil, and 72 catties of sugar. In the next month, 76 people were sent to the house, where they received a total of 1,029 catties of rice, 144.5 catties of soybeans, 36.1 catties of oil, and 36.1 catties of sugar (QD4 1961). Sugar was believed to be especially effective for patients who had eaten too many vegetables and had the symptom of cyanosis. With a cup of sugary water, the patient could quickly recover. Many people thus survived in 1960, the worst year of the long-lasting famine that ran from 1959 to 1961 (QD1 2000). Still, in the Qindong People's Commune, to which Qin village belonged, about 4,470 people, or 15 percent of the commune's population, "died of disease and hunger" during those years (*Qindong gongshe shezhi* 1981: 35).

There are no official statistics available about the deaths in Qin village. The brigade's population in 1959 was 1,958. It decreased to 1,955 by the end of 1960 and further to 1,952 by the end of 1961 (QD4 1961). Under normal conditions in the 1960s (i.e., without famine and birth control policies), the brigade's population grew from 2,036 in 1963 to 2,662 in 1969, or 4.56 percent a year. We may suppose that, had there been no famine, the population in the brigade should have grown at the same rate, from 1,958 in 1959 to 2,047 in 1960 and 2,140 in 1961. There is a gap of 188 between the projected and actual populations of the brigade in 1961, which was 9.6 percent of the brigade's actual population in that year. Both the increased mortality rate during the famine and a re-duced fertility rate could have contributed to this loss of population. In the entire country, the high mortality and low fertility resulted in a loss of at least 30 million and possibly 50 million in rural population from 1959 to 1961.[7]

Income Distribution

Changes in National Policies

The distribution of collective incomes under the people's commune in-volved two critical issues. The first is the level of the "basic accounting unit" (*jiben kesuan danwei*), at which the collective income was distrib-uted to members of the unit at the same rate. When the commune was the basic accounting unit, all of the 4,700-odd households of an average commune received the same amount of grain ration per capita and their labor input was remunerated at the same rate, irrespective of the differences in performance and output among different brigades or production teams. Low-yield teams and brigades thus benefited from this arrangement while the better ones suffered; none of them had the incentive to improve their performance because their output was to be shared by all other brigades or teams. By contrast, when the pro-duction team was the basic accounting unit, which had only 10 to 30 households, team members had a strong willingness to increase their output. Of course, the villagers would have the strongest incentive when each household was responsible for its own production and had the complete control of its products. During the Great Leap Forward, all of these four levels (communes, brigades, production teams, and individual households) were tried in sequence, beginning with the com-mune as the basic accounting unit and ending in the production team as the permanent accounting level. In most of the Leap period, how-ever, the brigade was the dominant accounting unit, while in some desperate circumstances the individual household contract system was temporarily allowed to let the starving peasants survive the famine.

The second issue is the ratio between the part of collective income distributed according to the commune members' consumption needs, or free supplies, and the part distributed according to their labor input, or wages. The communist principle, in the official propaganda, was "to distribute according to need" (*anxu fenpei*), which allowed no discrimination toward any member regardless of his or her work abilities. The socialist principle was "to distribute according to work" (*anlao fenpei*); people who work harder should earn more from the collective and vice versa. Since the people's commune was hailed as the "bridge" to communism, there was a strong urge among Party leaders and grassroots cadres to increase the part based on need in order to move closer to communism. The villagers, however, were practical. They had the strongest incentive to work for the collective when labor input was the only basis for income distribution, and they had the least interest in work when labor input did not count. Finding an optimal ratio between the two factors—free supplies and wages—in income distribution thus was another major concern of government leaders.

At the beginning of the Great Leap Forward, the state allowed either the commune or the subcommune brigade to be the unit for income distribution, and to let each province make the decision (GNW 1981b: 108). It also let each commune decide its own ratio between free supplies and wages (GNW 1981b: 119). In actual practice, local cadres, eager to show their enthusiasm for communism, tended to accept the commune as the basic accounting unit and set the ratio of free supplies to wages at 6:4 or even 7:3. It should be noted that the wage paid monthly or quarterly to a commune member was based on his or her wage grade (the government allowed six to eight different grades; see GNW 1981b: 119) as well as the worker's attendance or number of workdays. It had nothing to do with either the quality or the quantity of the daily work that he or she actually did. Because of the weak link between work and payment, commune members soon lost interest in collective production. It was reported, for instance, that "four increases and four decreases" prevailed in Xinhui county, Guangdong province, after the first payment of their wages: "those who ate free meals increased while those who worked decreased; those who pretended to be sick increased while those who took medicines decreased; those who were lazy increased while those who were industrious decreased; and those who read books increased while those who worked decreased" (GNW 1981b: 127–128). In some communes, the attendance rate decreased by 50 or 60 percent after the wage payment. The villagers also lost interest in improving work efficiency. For instance, those who had carried two baskets of fertilizer on a shoulder pole for more than 200 trips a day before did so now for only 50 or 60 trips. Many individuals who had been able to carry two baskets by themselves on a shoulder pole now worked with another person to carry only one basket of fertilizer. The load of the fertilizer also decreased from 100 catties to 50 catties per pair of baskets. The peasants' complaint was straightforward: "people who work harder cannot earn more; it makes no difference to do more or less" (GNW 1981b: 128).

This sharp decline in work efficiency immediately caused great concern among Party leaders. The Party's politburo announced a regulation on the "management system" of the people's commune in February 1959, which defined the brigade as the basic accounting unit (GNW 1981b: 147). Mao himself publicized a letter addressed to the Party on March 15, in which he proposed to "firmly use the former advanced cooperatives or the current brigades as the basic accounting unit" (GNW 1981b: 157). To offer incentives for production teams to improve their production, the government further revived the "three contracts and one reward" system that had existed under the former advanced cooperatives, including contracts with teams for a fixed amount of workpoints, fixed output, and fixed costs, and rewards for greater output and less workpoints and costs than the fixed levels (Chapter 3; see also GNW 1981b: 134, 149, 191). In reality, local cadres pushed the policy further to allow the production team as the basic accounting unit and even restored the traditional "independent production" (*dangan*) by individual households (GNW 1981b: 250). So that the villagers were able to raise pigs and poultry on their own, the state once again allowed local production teams to allocate "private plots" to individual households, which had been cancelled at the beginning of communization (GNW 1981b: 222, 223).

Meanwhile, the government required that the wages paid to commune members had to be raised to 60 or 70 percent of their total income from the commune while the free supplies be reduced to 30 or 40 percent, the reverse of the earlier practice in many localities (GNW 1981b: 221). Furthermore, the amount of a worker's wage had to be linked with his or her performance. The team leaders again had to record workpoints for each member according to his or her wage grade as well as the person's daily workload (GNW 1981b: 195). Because of the effective implementation of those measures, by the summer of 1959, the brigades and production teams had appeared no different from the preceding advanced co-ops and teams, except for their obligations to support the projects of the people's commune.

A turning point of the Great Leap Forward was the two consecutive meetings of Party's politburo and central committee at Lushan, known together as the Lushan Conference, in July and August 1959, in which Peng Dehuai (1898–1974), Minister of Defense, harshly criticized Mao's rural policies, causing Mao's fierce counterattack of Peng's "rightist opportunism" and ousting him from the top leadership. All the measures just mentioned were halted or reversed in the second half of 1959. Instead of delegating the basic accounting unit to production teams, the Party proposed to move it up to the commune at the end of the year (GNW 1981b: 275). The "wind of communization" once again swept many areas (Song Liansheng 2002: 283). These radical policies, coupled with natural calamities in both the northern and southern regions of the country, caused further decline in agricultural production in 1960 and the worsening of a nationwide famine that had persisted since 1959. The Party thus had to reconsider moving the basic accounting unit back to the brigade level (GNW 1981b: 313), and again promoted the "three contracts and one reward system" in production teams and urged them to pay wages to commune members according to their workdays rather than wage grades (GNW 1981b: 316). Eight months later, the Party's central committee reaffirmed that the policy of brigade as the very basic accounting units would not change for "at least seven years" beginning from 1961 (GNW 1981b: 378). It also reasserted in May 1960 that the free supply of grain should be no more than 40 percent and no less than 30 percent of the total income distributed to commune members (GNW 1981b: 333). Later in September, the Party further fixed the free supplies at only 30 percent of the income distributed from the brigade (GNW 1981b: 359, 382).

The Suqin Brigade

To illustrate the actual implementation of the national policies in local collectives and the real problems of the commune system during the Great Leap Forward, an examination of income distribution in the Suqin Brigade is in order. Since the birth of the Shiyan People's Commune in August 1958, the Suqin Brigade had been the basic accounting unit, with five production teams as subunits for day-to-day operation. The brigade had 1,952 people in 1961, of which more than 820 were laborers, divided into five grades according to their work abilities. Under the "three contracts and one reward" system, the brigade contracted with each production team to limit its total workpoints. The contracted number of total workpoints for the 176 workers of Team No. 1, for example, was 268,940 at the beginning of 1961, averaging 1,528 points per person. Later, the brigade adjusted the contracted number of workers to 151 and their workpoints to 217,200, or 1,438 points per person. In fact, however, only 129 workers participated in collective production, indicating a decrease in both the number of workers owing to the continued famine in 1961 and their willingness to work for the collective. The same situation was also true for the entire brigade, where the actual workers were less than the adjusted number of workers and even fewer than the original contracted number (QD4 1961).

It is interesting to note that the number of workers decreased at a rate corresponding to their labor grades. The total number of first-grade workers in the brigade fell to 91 percent of their original number; the workers of the second to fifth grades fell to 76.3, 74.2, 68.1, and 50 percent, respectively (QD4 1961). The reason behind the decreasing percentages of workers of different grades is that those of higher (the first and second) grades were usually in their prime (twenties through early forties) and therefore strong enough to survive the famine and able to work throughout the year, whereas workers of lower grades were either teenagers or the elderly, who were more vulnerable and less willing to work for the team.

Now let us look at how the villagers received income from the collective. The year under examination is 1960, the most difficult year in the Great Leap Forward. The total amount of the brigade's revenue for distribution to its members in that year was 102,145.79 yuan. It consisted of three parts: free supplies, totaling 27,024.60 yuan; wages, totaling 74,476.30 yuan; and rewards, totaling 644.89 yuan. The reward was paid to Team No. 5 only; the other four teams had only two parts in their income distribution: free supplies and wages. The amount of free supplies varied from 24.5 percent (Team No. 2) to 29 percent (Team No. 5) of the total income distributed to individual teams and accounted for 26.46 percent of the total income distributed in the entire brigade, well below the 30 percent limit allowed by the state. The free supplies were distributed free of charge, mostly in the form of rationed grain (QD4 1960).

Workpoint (or "wage") was another important source of household income from the collective. The 630 "full laborers" and another 630 "auxiliary laborers" earned a total of 1,441,600 points or 144,160 workdays in 1960, and each workday was worth 0.516 yuan in cash value (74,476.30 yuan in total as wages divided by the number of workdays). Individual households also earned income by contributing their manure, ashes, and other kinds of wastes as fertilizers to the team, which totaled 6,205.67 yuan, or 6.07 percent of the brigade's total income distributed.

In addition, the brigade offered varying numbers of workdays as subsidies to certain villagers. In the midst of crop failure and famine, individual production teams also grew 207 mu of carrots, worth 8,280 yuan, which were distributed to individual households free of charge (QD4 1960).

What needs to be further discussed is the method by which the brigade distributed grain rations to its members. The brigade's total yield in 1960 was 1,007,386 catties (146.8 catties per mu, or 515.28 catties per capita). After paying the state 164,671 catties as agricultural taxes and other deductions, the brigade was left with 785,060 catties, of which the brigade sold 71,400 catties to the state to fulfill its procurement quota, and reserved 112,808 catties as seeds and 6,532 catties as fodder for collective pigs and oxen. The grain left for distribution was only 594,320 catties, 59 percent of the brigade's total yield, which were to be shared by 1,955 people, rendering the average grain ration at 304 catties per person. Instead of giving each member of a production team the same amount of grain (304 catties), the brigade divided the 1,955 people into three groups and distributed each of them a different amount of grain. Of these grain rations (594,320 catties in total), only 357,042 catties (or 60 percent) were distributed as free supplies, as the state policy required (QD4 1960).

Finally, let us look at the total income the villagers annually received from the brigade between 1957 and 1961. The per capita income distributed to individual members of the brigade increased steadily from 42.65 yuan in 1957 to 55.81 yuan in 1961. Those numbers seem counterintuitive because the brigade's distributable grain sharply declined during those years, from 1,443,520 catties in 1958 to 785,060 catties in 1960, and the villagers' grain ration also declined from 447.5 catties per capita in 1958 to only 304 catties in 1960 (QD4 1959–1961). Li Weixiang, the former general accountant of the brigade who produced the numbers, confirmed that the numbers were true. The superior authorities, he explained, required that all brigades show in their annual accounting reports an increase in the brigade members' per capita income, in order to demonstrate the "superiority" of the people's commune. Indeed, throughout the Great Leap Forward period, the state repeatedly required local collectives to do their best to ensure an income growth for more than 90 percent of commune members (GNW 1981b: 136, 332, 381). To meet this goal, it instructed local cadres to "keep less and distribute more" (*shaokou duofen*) by cutting down the collective's management and production costs and reducing its "accumulation fund" and "public welfare fund" (GNW 1981b: 194, 381). In the Suqin Brigade, the amount of revenue kept as accumulation funds was reduced from 20,454.26 yuan in 1958 to only 4,000 in 1959 and none in 1960. The taxes paid to the state also decreased from 17,809.04 yuan in 1958 to 13,205.94 yuan in 1959 (QD4 1959–1960). Meanwhile, the brigade increased its revenue from sideline ventures, especially by selling marsh reeds, to offset the decreases in agricultural output. These efforts thus produced a paradoxical phenomenon during the Great Leap Forward years: the continual declines in farm yields and the worsening shortage of food among the commune members, and at the same time a moderate yet steady increase in the peasants' per capita income.

But the income increase was false for two reasons. First, because of the decreased farm yield, the brigade did not have enough grain or cash to pay its households. The result was the so-called "emptiness in distribution" (*fenkong*). In the Suqin Brigade, 372 households (83 percent of all households in the brigade) thus were underpaid in late March 1961 for the preceding year and became *fenkong* households to whom the brigade owed a debt. To reduce the number of such households, the brigade created many new deductions from payments to the households, such as the "advance cash payment," "stipends for dropsy patients," "roofing reeds," "purchase of carrots," and so forth. As a result, the *fenkong* households were reduced to only 138, while "overdrawn" (*chaozhi*) households, which owed a debt to the brigade, increased from 76 to 291 households (QD4 1961)!

Second, the few households (only 19 in the entire brigade) that did receive a small cash payment from the brigade found that the money was much less valuable than it was before or after the Great Leap Forward. For example, in 1960, when the famine was the most severe, the price of rice in the black market (or private trading between local households) was fully two yuan a catty, whereas the same rice was normally sold to or by the state at only 0.12 yuan a catty, or 6 percent of the black market price. For Qin villagers as well as the millions of peasants elsewhere, what was true was their absolute shortage of food and life-threatening hunger during the Leap, despite the falsified increase in their nominal income from the collective.

Conclusion

This chapter has focused on the operational realities of the Great Leap Forward policies in labor remuneration and income distribution, an issue that has received little attention in past studies. It sheds light on how those policies failed to link the villagers' work effort with their income from the brigade or the commune in the following three aspects. First, during the initial period of the Leap, the government abolished the workpoint system and replaced it with the so-called wage system that paid the villagers according to their fixed wage grade or the year-end appraisal of their general performance. The quality and quantity of a commune member's daily effort did not directly affect his or her income from the collective. Second, after the state reinstated the workpoint system, the workpoints awarded to the villagers were almost worthless because of the unavailability of grain from the brigade to "cash" the workpoints and because of the extremely low purchasing power of the limited sum of cash paid to the few. Third, under the free-supplies system, most of the rationed grain was distributed free of charge to commune members according to their needs. Therefore, the link between labor input and income distribution was weak during the Leap; the villagers found no reason to work hard for the commune. It was small wonder that Qin villagers only asked for an extra spoon of porridge from the mess hall, rather than extra workpoints, when they were assigned a heavy task (QD1 2000).

Party leaders, who had experienced many crises on their way to power, were reluctant but eventually compelled to abandon or adjust the Great Leap Forward policies to survive the new crisis. In March 1961, Mao gave up his insistence on the mess hall, the very "stronghold of socialism in the countryside," allowing villagers to freely withdraw from it and thus actually accepting its demise (GNW 1981b: 463, 484). As a way to help the villagers survive, the government restored private plots in May 1959 and increased its size to 7 percent of the collective's farmland in January 1961 (GNW 1981b: 222, 436). They also gave up the wage system and revived the workpoint system in April 1959 and reduced the portion of free supplies from 50 percent of total distribution to 30 to 40 percent in May 1959 and further limited it to 30 percent in September 1960 (GNW 1981b: 108, 221, 333, 359). The government switched the basic accounting unit from the commune to the brigade and finally to the production team in October 1961 (GNW 1981b: 147, 157, 378, 518), and further reduced the size of communes, brigades, and production teams in 1961 (GNW 1981b: 492). Instead of the brigade, the production team, normally having 20 to 30 households, now became the basic accounting unit. The Great Leap Forward practice of large-scale cooperation among different brigades gave way to the traditional "three contracts and one reward" under production teams and finally the "total contract" (*dabaogan*) in September 1961 (GNW 1981b: 134, 436). By the autumn of 1961, when the Leap was over, the collective organization and its labor management and income distribution systems had been essentially no different from what had prevailed under the primary cooperatives in 1955 and earlier, except for the absence of land dividends for individual households since they no longer had private land. The Great Leap Forward, beginning with the Party leaders' utopian schemes, ended in a "Great Leap Backward." All the remedies that prevailed in the wake of the Leap remained largely unchanged in the following two decades of the collective era. Some of the measures, such as the "household contract" (*baochan daohu*) system, later became the point of departure for Deng Xiaoping and his supporters to start another round of agricultural reforms in the early 1980s.

PART TWO

Power and Control Under Socialism

CHAPTER 5

"Rightful Weapons": Political Participation Under the Collective

THROUGHOUT THE collective era, one of the state's central concerns with the rural collectives was how to put grassroots cadres under its effective control. When collectivization was finished, the state found that the cadres, including about 7 million at the brigade level and more than 15 million at the production team level, were too numerous to include into the regular government system.[1] Unlike the "state cadres" (*guojia ganbu*) at the commune level and above, who received salaries and other welfare benefits from the government, the cadres at the brigade and team levels had to participate in production and make a living on workpoints just like ordinary villagers. Nevertheless, these local cadres played a key role in the relationship between the villagers and the government. They carried out state policies in their collectives, planned economic activities, and controlled all kinds of local resources. How to regulate the rural cadres and ensure their conformity with government policies, therefore, was one of the biggest challenges to the state after collectivization.

Given the large number of grassroots cadres, it was impossible to count on the few state cadres to supervise them from above. Instead, the state adopted the "mass line" (*qunzhong luxian*), that is, to turn to ordinary members of rural collectives to supervise them from below. From the early 1960s to the end of the collective era, the state employed three means to control the cadres. The first was the recurrent political campaigns against cadre corruption and malpractices, including "Free Airing of Views" (*daming dafang*) in 1957–1959, the Socialist Education ("Four Clean-Ups") in 1963–1965, the Cultural Revolution in 1966–1969, and the "Three Attacks and One Anti" in 1971–1973. The most important among those campaigns was the Socialist Education; the ideologies and methods used in that event shaped all other movements that followed. The second was letting villagers write "people's letters" (*renmin laixin*) to higher authorities to expose local cadres' wrongdoings. The third was the villagers' participation in production teams' day-to-day "democratic management of finance" (*minzhu licai*). This chapter examines the actual participation of Qin villagers as well as their counterparts in the rest of the commune or the county in those activities, the strategies used by the villagers as well as the cadres for dealing with each other, and the extent to which the state was successful in using the peasants to combat the wrongdoing of the cadres.

The Socialist Education

The "Socialist Education" (*shehuizhuyi jiaoyu* or *shejiao*), as a campaign against abusive cadres, started in 1963 when the country was just recovering from the disastrous Great Leap Forward, and ended in 1965 on the eve of the Cultural Revolution. Known also as the "Four Clean-Ups" (*siqing*), the movement was intended to "clean up" local collectives' workpoint records, accounts, property, and inventory.[2] According to the Party's propaganda, this movement was necessary because "a severe and intense class struggle" existed in society, in which the former landlords and rich peasants attempted to "corrupt the cadres and usurp their leadership," and, as a result, many cadres became "degenerate elements" embezzling, stealing, illegally trading collective goods, and colluding with the landlords and rich peasants to commit all sorts of crimes (GNW 1981b: 684). Conflicts between ordinary peasants and the "unclean" cadres thus became a "major contradiction" in the countryside. The unclean cadres themselves, according to the Party, fell into two categories: those with minor problems and still belonging to the people, and those committing severe crimes and therefore becoming enemies of the people (GNW 1981b: 791). The purpose of the movement was to mobilize the "poor and lower-middle peasants" (*pingxiazhongnong*) to fight the unclean cadres and help them "wash hands and take a bath" in order to "settle the abnormal relations between many cadres and the masses that had lasted for many years" (GNW 1981b: 686).

The Socialist Education campaign achieved impressive results in Qindong People's Commune. A survey of the results of the campaign in 1964 and the beginning of 1965, dated January 26, 1965, shows that 1,000 or nearly 72 percent of all cadres in the commune had the problems of "four kinds of uncleanness" (*si buqing*).[3] Their wrongdoings fell into four categories: "excessive eating and taking" (*duochi duozhan*), "embezzlement and theft" (*tanwu daoqie*), "overdrawing and misappropriation" (*chaozhi nuoyong*), and "speculation and profiteering" (*touji daoba*). The total value of the goods or funds unlawfully obtained through these channels by the 1,000 cadres amounted to 104,830.53 yuan, or 104.83 yuan per person, which was more than twice the annual income a villager earned from the collective (averaging 50.72 yuan per person in Qindong commune in 1965) (SQ7 1965; see also *Qindong gongshe shezhi* 1981: 128–129).[4]

Interestingly, the surveys of both the commune and the county show similar patterns. In both cases, the misconduct that involved most cadres was the first type, excessive eating and taking. This was most common because the cadres who recorded workpoints were likely to give themselves more daily workpoints or more year-end workpoint subsidies. They also had many chances to eat or take more than allowed, such as when distributing the collective's goods, attending a meeting outside the village, or when treating a visiting leader from above. The vice team leader and the warehouseman of a team of Baozhang brigade, for example, embezzled five catties of cooking oil that should have been distributed to team members. To hide their wrongdoing, they blended five catties of varnish into the oil, causing vomiting among members from 36 households, some of whom had to stay home for a couple of days to recover (SQ3 1965). Compared to the other three types of "uncleanness," however, "excessive eating and taking" was believed to be the lightest, and the per capita amount involved was also the lowest. Most cadres, therefore, were willing to confess this kind of wrongdoing.

The wrongdoing that involved the smallest number of cadres was the fourth type, "speculation and profiteering." Unlike private traders or peddlers, few cadres had the time or abilities to engage in this unlawful activity. Their status as cadres also prevented them from openly getting involved in this crime.

The wrongdoing that involved the highest per capita amount in both the commune and the entire county was the cadres' "overdrawing and misappropriation." It happened to many cadres whose family had many mouths but few workers. Unable to earn enough workpoints to cover the distribution in kind from the production team, many of them became "overdrawn households" in debt to the team, or had to illegally "borrow" money or grain from the team for private use. Strictly speaking, overdrawing was not a crime because it happened to many families with similar difficulties, and it could not be hidden from the team's accounts; everyone in or outside the team also well knew each cadre household's work abilities and economic situation. Therefore, the amount of grain or money involved in this category was the highest. On the other hand, embezzlement and theft, as outright crimes, had to be done clandestinely and concealed. Although the number of cadres who admitted this kind of crime were about the same as the overdrawn cadres in the county or even more in the commune, the per capita amount they admitted was much less than that involved in the third type.

The government uncovered the cadres' misconducts through two basic channels: villagers' accusation and cadres' self-confession. Before examining their respective strategies in those activities, let us look at how the government created a new discourse in the rural society to redefine peasant-cadre relations.

The Discursive Supremacy of Poor and Lower-Middle Peasants

For many years, the Party relied on grassroots cadres to carry out its policies in the countryside. Recruited mostly from Party members and peasant activists, the cadres supposedly had stronger class consciousness and loyalty to the Party than ordinary villagers; therefore, their tasks were educating the people and mobilizing them to join the campaigns of land reform, grain procurement, and collectivization. When collectivization was finished, however, the state found that the grassroots cadres' corruption and malfeasance had been the major problems in the collective economy. Unable to incorporate the village cadres into the formal bureaucracy and put them under its direct control, the only alternative available to the state was using the peasants themselves to check their power. "The cadres," in the words of Party leaders, "should be subject to supervisions from above and below, primarily the supervision of the masses" (GNW 1981b: 827). To do so, the Party first had to redefine the relationship between the cadres and the masses, from the one in which the former acted as pioneering revolutionaries leading the latter to the one in which the politically correct masses supervised the corruptible cadres. According to the Party's new propaganda, poor and lower-middle peasants, or *pingxiazhongnong*, were eligible to supervise the cadres because their status as "proletariats and semi-proletariats in the countryside" made them "the most active supporters of the socialist road and the collective economy" during the land reform and cooperativization. With correct class consciousness, the peasants continued to be the major force in the countryside upon which the Party had to rely for the "socialist transformation and construction" (GNW 1981b: 685).

To effectively supervise the cadres, the Party advocated the creation of peasant organizations in local collectives, including the annual conference of *pingxiazhongnong* representatives at the communal and brigade levels, and the *pingxiazhongnong* committees or associations. According to a regulation enacted by the CCP central committee in September 1963, the peasant organizations had the right "to assist and supervise the cadres at commune, brigade, and production team levels." The latter had to consult those organizations before making a decision on the major issues of the commune or local collectives, and they had to invite peasant representatives to attend their discussions (GNW 1981b: 705). Articles 12 and 13 of the "Regulations on the Organization of *pingxiazhongnong* Associations," promulgated by the Party on June 25, 1964, further provided that the peasant organizations at all levels "shall help and supervise cadres at all levels to ensure their correct implementation of the policies of the Party and the state"; "should sincerely and kindly propose suggestions and criticism to cadres who had shortcomings and mistakes and help them correct"; and "should supervise the management committees and cadres at all levels to ensure their strict conformity with financial management regulations." The peasant organizations, by Article 13, "have to promptly criticize and expose misconducts such as excessive eating and taking, extravagance and waste, self-profiteering and fraudulence, graft and embezzlement, and destruction of public properties, and contact relevant government offices for serious handling of severe crimes" (GNW 1981b: 725–726).

One way to cultivate the peasants' loyalty to the Party and justify their role in the Socialist Education campaign was speaking of the histories of their families, villages, and collectives. Recalling history, especially "speaking bitterness" (*suku*) or telling about the sufferings that they had endured before the Communist Revolution, would purportedly arouse the peasants' class consciousness and hatred toward their class enemies (landlords, rich peasants, and other evil elements), and would build their confidence in the socialist system (GNW 1981b: 671). In the Suqin Brigade (including Su and Qin villages), several team members were picked as activists in "speaking bitterness." Xue, one such activist and a Communist Youth League member, thus described the past of his family:

For three generations my family has worked for landlords and rich peasants to make a living. We never had enough to eat and to wear. My grandparents died from working as year-round laborers for the landlords. Unable to pay taxes and levies, both of my uncles were arrested by the landlords' restitution corps. One of them was shot dead, and the other was badly wounded and soon died at home. Now liberated and standing up under the leadership of the Party and Chairman Mao, we have rice to eat, clothes to wear, and money to spend. My father is a team leader, my brother a storehouse-keeper, and I am an accountant. The history of my family is the one of bitterness and glory. . . . We have to listen to the words of the Party and Chairman Mao. Who else would join the revolution if we, the children of poor and lower-middle peasants, did not take the lead? (SQ3 1965)

Another villager, named Huang, told the story of his family as follows:

In the old society, we *pingxiazhongnong* suffered economic exploitation and political oppression [by landlords]. For generations, my family had no house to live in. My parents died when I was very young. We three siblings were separated from one another. I had to herd the ox and watch fish hawks for a rich peasant when I was nine, and I suffered bullying and hunger each day. Now we stand up as masters after Liberation. Our bitterness in the past was indeed as deep as the sea, and our happiness today is as abundant as a mountain. We should never forget where we are from. (SQ1 1965)

Because of their sufferings in the past and happiness after Liberation, the *pingxiazhongnong* were supposed to be more revolutionary than other elements in the society. The young *pingxiazhongnong* activists in the Suqin Brigade, therefore, organized themselves into "groups of redness and expertise" (*hongzhuan xiaozu*) to study Mao's essays, such as "Serve the People" and "Get Organized." They took the lead in abandoning traditional customs, such as the traditional wedding and funeral ceremonies that were deemed wasteful and superstitious, and mounted Mao's picture on the wall of their living rooms in place of the portraits of family gods or bodhisattvas. They excluded the children of former landlords and rich peasants from the local militia to ensure its political purity. These actions supposedly demonstrated their unparalleled loyalty to the Party. Not surprisingly, the term *pingxiazhongnong* became the most frequently used expression on public occasions during the Socialist Education period and the following Cultural Revolution years; it was associated with the right class status, correct political consciousness, loyalty to the Party, and support to socialism. By promoting a discourse that juxtaposed the politically correct *pingxiazhongnong* with the corruptible cadres, the state intended to empower the ordinary villagers and use them to supervise local cadres and keep their possible abuse in check.

The discursive superiority of the *pingxiazhongnong* is best seen in their respective roles in the annual conferences of cadres and *pingxiazhongnong* representatives. At the meeting during January 1–14, 1965, for example, the 605 peasant representatives of the Qindong commune reportedly "conducted a tense and uncompromising ideological battle with the cadres." They "proposed suggestions and criticisms freely and in all manners." As a result, "the cadres' rightist ideas and wrong behaviors were exposed and sharply criticized. They voluntarily confessed their mistakes and promised to improve their ideological consciousness" (SQ1 1965). To prevent the cadres from making further mistakes, the peasant representatives proposed "eight supervisions": to supervise the cadres in (1) carrying out the Party's policies and guidelines, (2) taking the right side, (3) actively performing their duties, (4) shunning speculations and manipulations, (5) avoiding excessive eating and taking, (6) actively participating in collective production, (7) staying away from illicit sex, and (8) managing the collective diligently and thriftily (SQ1 1965). The cadres, on the other hand, had "three fears"—one of which was the peasant representatives, especially their ungrounded criticism (the other two were their fears of the indiscriminate criticism and pressure from above) (SQ4 1965). It was reported that more than 90 percent of the brigade cadres who attended the meeting "expressed to the *pingxiazhongnong* representatives their willingness to carry out their plans of rectification and improvement" and the representatives "felt satisfied" (SQ4 1965).

There is no doubt that the political superiority of *pingxiazhongnong* offered the peasant representatives a degree of confidence and courage to criticize the cadres and vent their grievances. Nevertheless, it did not change the basic fact that throughout the Socialist Education campaign most cadres remained in power within their collectives, who planned everyday farming activities and controlled all aspects of the collective economy, including the distribution of income in kind and in cash to individual households. The peasants, including the *pingxiazhongnong* activists, remained under the actual dominance of the cadres. As shown below, this simultaneous coexistence of the peasants' discursive dominance with their everyday subordination shaped the strategies of both the villagers and the cadres in exposing or confessing the problems in their teams or brigades.

Peasant Strategies

It was reported that 75 percent of the 639 members who attended the Qindong Commune's first meeting of *pingxiazhongnong* representatives in January 1965 actively criticized the cadres. Because of their criticism, 373 cadres confessed their involvement in the "four kinds of uncleanness," by which they unlawfully obtained a total of 58,557.68 yuan of collective funds or illegal profits and 74,064 catties of grain in total (SQ1 1965).

There is no doubt that some of the peasant representatives were indeed active in criticizing the cadres; they used the meeting as a perfect opportunity to air their complaints against the cadres they disliked. A member from the Luoer Brigade, for example, reportedly worked "day and night" during the meeting on his accusing materials. After criticizing many cadres from his brigade, he felt satisfied: "I never dreamed that I could attend such a meeting. For years, I kept my grievances to myself and never dared to vent them. Today I eventually had the chance to speak out." A young man from the Zhouhuang Brigade, in another instance, was praised for his frankness and enthusiasm. He criticized all cadres from his brigade, including his brother-in-law, a production team leader, and he never returned home during the meeting, even when his wife gave birth to a child (SQ1 1965).

The *pingxiazhongnong* representatives from Qin village also exposed some of their cadres' "uncleanness." According to their accusations, for example, the Party branch secretary of the brigade discriminated against one of the villagers by offering him a subsidy of three yuan for his sickness, which was two yuan less than the standard amount he had given to other patients. The deputy secretary of the brigade was charged with being arbitrary in appointing cadres and assigning tasks to production teams. The financial director of the brigade allegedly offered relief funds to two of his mother's brothers who were unqualified for the relief (SQ8 1965). In most cases, the peasant representatives criticized the cadres because the latter failed to satisfy their personal or their team's requests; the charges were relatively light, mostly limited to problems with the cadres' "work style" (*gongzuo zuofeng*), or the ways they performed their duties, rather than their personal wrongdoings.

In fact, the peasant representatives had a difficult time at the meeting: as a requirement, they had to give some complaints against their brigade cadres; the cadres also expected the peasants from their brigades to make some "appropriate" criticisms so that they could safely get through the ordeal. The villagers thus were very cautious, using tact and discretion when criticizing the cadres from their own community. They could only pick some minor shortcomings of their cadres and avoid mentioning any grave ones, so that they could meet the government's requirements while making no offense to their cadres. The peasants and the cadres had some kind of tacit agreement at the meeting, each knowing well the other side's intention, choice of action, and its possible consequences on both sides.

The main reason that the *pingxiazhongnong* representatives were unwilling to expose their cadres' major wrongdoings at the meeting was their fear of the cadres' possible retaliation after they returned home. Thus, although the commune government's announcement of the Party's policies on punishing retaliating cadres incurred a "surge of criticisms" against commune leaders, once they were asked to move their attention to the "uncleanness" of brigade- and production team cadres and help them "wash hands and take a bath," the peasant representatives "showed low spirit and fear of future retaliations, saying that the higher [the cadres are], the easier it is [to criticize them], and the lower the more difficult" (SQ1 1965). The reason was obvious to them. The commune cadres, though more powerful than brigade and production team cadres, were after all the people far above, who did not directly lead them in everyday production. The brigade and production team cadres, in contrast, were people living in the same village or even the same neighborhood as the *pingxiazhongnong* themselves. The production team cadres, in particular, were the ones who assigned them tasks and awarded them workpoints each day. In the words of the *pingxiazhongnong* representatives, the team cadres were the people they "have to get along with in the days to come" (*jinhou haiyao guo rizi*) (SQ1 1965). Therefore, their general strategies were to expose "the obvious problems rather than the hidden ones"; "the minor problems rather than the severe ones"; "problems that took place in the remote past instead of the recent ones"; "problems of the collectives instead of the personal ones"; "problems of the cadres who have retired instead of those who are still in office"; and "problems concerning misappropriation and overdrawing instead of embezzlement and theft" (SQ2 1965; SQ4 1965).

It was no wonder, therefore, that the cadres' embezzlement of collective funds, a grave crime, as revealed at the meeting of the commune's *pingxiazhongnong* representatives and cadres in December 1965, involved

only about 100 yuan in the *entire* commune, whereas their misappropriation, a relatively light offense, amounted to 3,452 yuan. Likewise,
their embezzlement of collective grain was as low as 97.5 catties, whereas
their "wasteful consumption," again a minor offense, was as much as
9,519 catties (SQ4 1965). Instead of a heated argument and fierce confrontation between the cadres and peasant representatives as the state
expected, what occurred at the annual meetings was often their "mutual understanding and keeping on good terms with everyone" (SQ2
1965). In fact, as the commune leaders found, many of the so-called
pingxiazhongnong representatives were the team or brigade cadres'
"own men" (*si ren*), who were picked by the cadres to help them survive
the meeting (SQ2 1965).

To be sure, not all peasant representatives were the cadres' followers
and were satisfied with the way they interacted with the cadres at the
meetings. Villagers from the Gaoqiao Brigade complained, for example,
that they "had a full belly of resentment but dared not to vent" and
that "the lord's trees were too big to remove," meaning that the cadres
and their local networks were too powerful and deeply entrenched to
challenge. Unable to make complaints at the meeting, three members
of the No. 2 production team of the Luoyi Brigade, in another instance,
visited the commune government office after the meeting, upset that
their team leader had failed to eliminate the workpoints that had been
inappropriately awarded to certain team cadres and members, including more than 400 points of subsidies to unqualified households (SQ2
1965). Despite such widely harbored resentment among the villagers,
however, few of them were willing to openly criticize the cadres and
fully expose their wrongdoings on formal occasions because they not
only had to save the cadres' face but also feared the cadres' possible
retaliation.

Cadres' Reactions

Just like the peasant representatives who imagined themselves as the
rightful monitors of corrupt cadres, the cadres unanimously depicted
themselves on public occasions as "sick men" who had various kinds of
"uncleanness" and therefore needed to "wash hands and take a bath"
and "cure the disease" with the help of the peasants. Remarking on his
personal experience at the *pingxiazhongnong* meeting in January 1965,
Zhang, head of the No. 5 team of the Suqin Brigade, said: "This meeting has been the one to 'cure the disease and save the patient.' Had I not

attended the meeting, my illness could not have been cured and would have been even worse. To leave the meeting with a clean and healthy body, I have decided to return what I have illegally obtained from the team by selling my pigs, coats, and woolen sweater." Another "reformed" cadre thus described his feeling toward the movement: "We [the cadres] have been members of the new society and received the Party's education and support for more than ten years. I have been a cadre because of the masses' love and the Party's trust in me. We should have taken the lead in adhering to the socialist road and become the model for the masses. It is too bad that we have embezzled and excessively taken the collective's goods and have beaten and cursed at people. It would be too dangerous if we do not take the correct road hereafter" (SQ3 1965). Expectedly, all of the cadres expressed their gratitude to the peasants who had criticized them and promised to work harder and correct all of their mistakes thereafter.

However, there was always a gap between the cadres' oral commitments and their real actions. When it came to "self-examination" (*ziwo jiantao*), for example, many cadres only confessed the mistakes that were minor or already known and denied those that were severe or unknown, a tactic no different from the peasants' criticism of their mistakes as just discussed. Sun, the accountant of the No. 10 team of the Luoyi Brigade, for instance, only admitted embezzling 300 catties of barley that the government had subsidized the team in 1963, a fact that had been well known, but denied other charges about his misappropriation or theft. Li, the Party branch secretary of the Zhouhuang Brigade, denied any accusation of his wrongdoings at all. Later, it was found, however, that he had underreported as many as 80,000 catties of the brigade's yield to the commune and illegally distributed more than 8,000 feet of cloth coupons (SQ1 1965).

To force the cadres to confess their mistakes as much as possible, the leaders of the Qindong Commune employed the approach of "pressing from above, squeezing in the middle, and pushing from below" (*shang ya, zhong ji, xia ding*). "Pushing from below" means to let the peasant representatives criticize the cadres and expose their wrongdoings, a method discussed earlier. To "press from above," the commune leaders usually provided a list of the major mistakes that they expected local cadres to admit when asking them to conduct self-examination; the commune leaders knew some of their mistakes beforehand through channels such as "people's letters" and verbal complaints from ordinary villagers or other cadres. To "squeeze in the middle," the commune leaders asked the brigade and team cadres to accuse each other of their mistakes. The cadres knew each other's wrongdoings better than the ordinary villagers because they had access to the brigade's or the team's accounts, and sometimes they committed wrongdoings together.

There were two methods of mutual accusation among the cadres. One was "face to face" (*mian dui mian*), or open criticism at group meetings. Understandably, few cadres were willing to fully expose each other's misdeeds for fear of coming under scrutiny themselves. The other was "back to back" (*bei dui bei*), or informing in secret any cadre's mistakes to the commune, a method presumably more effective than face-to-face criticism but in effect more troublesome to the commune leaders because they had to spend a lot of time verifying the charges and forcing the wrongdoers to admit their mistakes. Once the commune leaders received a secret accusation, they would invariably ask the cadres involved to make an "additional examination" (*buchong jiancha*).

Obviously, these methods exerted tremendous pressure on the cadres, who claimed that they had "three fears": they feared punishments because they had too many mistakes; they feared that the amount of money or goods involved in their "uncleanness" was too large for them to repay; and they feared that they would lose the trust of superior leaders (SQ2 1965). Because of the pressure, some cadres did provide a long list of their mistakes to the commune authority. One production leader, named Wang, listed in his "Revolutionary Self-Examination" twenty-five instances of economic "uncleanness," nine mistakes in class struggle, five mistakes in carrying out the Party's policies, and eight mistakes pertaining to his work style. "All these," stated the team leader at the end of his self-examination, "were only [results of] my preliminary examination. I am asking the *pingxiazhongnong* representatives to continue to give me help, which would be the most precious gift to me. I shall be subject to punishment by state law if I take any action of retaliation" (SQ5 1965).

Tuipei, or repaying the collective what they had unlawfully taken, was a necessary step for the cadres to correct their mistakes and to show their determination to reform themselves. At the *pingxiazhongnong* and cadres' meeting in January 1965, for example, all local cadres who had admitted their mistakes of uncleanness made a *tuipei* plan, and the plan was individually verified and approved by the peasant representatives. The same day, they started *tuipei*. To take the lead in doing so, the deputy Party secretary of the Baozhuang Brigade took off his Swiss watch and gold ring as repayments for what he had embezzled

TABLE 1

"Unclean" Cadres in Dongtai County, 1965

Cadres	"Unclean" cadres		Percent of total unclean cadres	Per capita *tuipei* due (yuan)	Actual *tuipei* amount	
	number	percent			yuan	percent
Commune cadres	389	81.04	1.47	126.85	64.69	51.00
Brigade cadres	3,109	87.18	11.79	154.87	78.63	50.77
Team heads and accountants	8,170	93.84	30.97	98.63	50.68	51.38
Other team cadres	13,735	74.01	52.07	24.41	12.59	51.58
Total	26,377	80.46	100	67.79	33.88	49.98

SOURCE: SQ7 1965.

from his brigade. A Party branch member of the same brigade took off his winter coat and sweater. He also allowed his team to take a sow and seven piglets from his home as repayment. Together, the 1,000 "unclean" cadres in the commune had returned a total of 32,621.88 yuan of goods (32.62 yuan per cadre), or 64.9 percent of their dues by January 20, 1965 (SQ7 1965).[5]

As Table 1 shows, production heads and accountants who directly controlled the economy of the local collectives had the highest percentage of "unclean" individuals. Next were brigade cadres, whose per capita *tuipei* liability was the highest among the cadres of all levels because of their greater authority than team cadres and their easy access to collective funds and goods. Commune cadres had a lower percentage because of their stronger ideological commitment and fewer opportunities for wrongdoing. "Other team cadres" such as subteam group leaders and workpoint recorders had the lowest percentage of people involved in uncleanness and the smallest *tuipei* amount because of their limited influence within the team and therefore limited opportunities for abuse.

Production team and brigade cadres, therefore, suffered the most, mentally and materially, during the consecutive Socialist Education movements. Because of the immense pressure from both above and below, about 70 percent of production team leaders in the Qindong Commune wanted to quit their jobs at the *pingxiazhongnong* meeting in January 1965 (SQ1 1965). The government well understood the consequences of their resignation: the production team leaders were usually the most reputable and competent individuals in local communities.

Their experiences and organizing skills were indispensable for the teams to remain functional each day. To let so many of them quit their jobs would have paralyzed the collective organizations. Therefore, the government's general principle in dealing with the "unclean" cadres was "to change one's mind rather than to change the person" (*huan sixiang bu huang ren*) because few team members had the necessary abilities and reputation to take over the roles of the existing cadres (SQ1 1965). Thus, instead of treating the abusive cadres as enemies to be eliminated, the Party asked peasant representatives to deal with them with "class feelings" (*jieji ganqing*), or to treat them as people of the same class. Consonant with the Party's instruction, the peasant activists claimed that the purpose of their criticisms was to "pull the cadres back to the bank, rather than to drown them in water" and that they should "unite with the cadres and work together to increase production" (SQ1 1965). Only in rare cases did the commune consider changing the current brigade and team cadres who proved to be too notorious among the peasants (SQ3 1965). The cadres knew well their importance to the collective and the superior authorities. Many of them, therefore, became so-called "thick-skinned persons" (*lao lianpi*) or "old campaigners" (*lao youtiao*) over the course of the recurrent Socialist Education campaigns, who repeatedly confessed their mistakes but never felt embarrassed; they delayed their *tuipei* again and again or returned only a small portion of the amount due. Disappointed, some peasants in the Qindong Commune complained that "every year there was a fuss against the four kinds of uncleanness, but every year the cadres only paid lip service to it" (SQ3 1965).

Because of the villagers' reluctance to openly criticize the cadres and the difficulties in replacing the grassroots cadres and getting their repayment, the Socialist Education movement lost its momentum in late 1965, when the atmosphere of the annual meeting of *pingxiazhong-nong* representatives and cadres totally changed. In the words of the attendees at the meeting, the Socialist Education campaign this time had become "civilized" (*wen de*), having fewer conflicts and criticisms, unlike the previous years when it had been "militant" (*wu de*), and it focused on the "inside" (*litou*), or one's incorrect ideas, rather than the "outside" (*waitou*) or economic problems. The approach of the Socialist Education also switched from that of "pushing" (*ya*), or forced criticism and confession, to that of "learning" (*xue*), or studying the Party's documents. The peasants knew how to talk at group meetings: in their words, "you are free to praise a person with thousands of words, but

you can easily annoy a person with only a few words." Many of the attendees openly remarked: "there seems to be no pressure this year and
we do not want to criticize [the cadres]" (SQ4 1965). The cadres, on the
other hand, reportedly had "three toughnesses" (*san ying*) this time:
first, they had fewer problems of uncleanness and therefore were more
confident in themselves; second, they had paid attention to the problems of the peasant representatives in the preceding year and were
better prepared to deal with the peasants; and third, the Party's new
document, known as the "23 articles," redirected the targets of the movement from the "unclean" rural cadres to "capitalist power holders" at
higher levels (GNW 1981b: 819–828), thus offering the grassroots cadres
a relief after three years of strained Socialist Education campaigns. Instead of exposing the cadres' personal "uncleanness," the meeting held
in December 1965 focused on three issues: examining how the cadres
had dealt with class enemies or former landlords and rich peasants,
discussing how to handle the problem of "overdrawn households" that
owed money to the collectives, and making production plans for the
coming year (SQ4 1965: 3–5). The Socialist Education movement came
to an end with this meeting.

"People's Letters"

Writing "people's letters" was another way for the villagers to expose
the misconduct of local cadres and to vent their resentment. Unlike
open criticism at public meetings, where the speaker had to think twice
before saying anything about the cadres because of their possible retaliation, writing letters avoided the face-to-face conflict between the
writer and the accused. It allowed the writer to fully express his views
and reduced the possibility of the cadres' revenge because the letter
could be anonymous and, if signed, his identity had to be kept confidential by government authorities. For those who really wanted to
bring the cadre's malfeasance to the government's attention, writing a
people's letter was obviously preferable to open accusation. The Party
leaders, too, encouraged the writing of these letters, promoting it as an
effective means to expose and curb the problems of cadres at all levels
and an "important channel to link the Party and the state with the
masses" (Mao Zedong 1977: 72–74). The Party paid particular attention
to the people's letters during the Socialist Education movement and
subsequent political campaigns, and required government agencies to
set up a special office to handle such letters.

The Qindong Commune received about 60 or 70 letters a year in the 1960s and 1970s. About one-third of them were forwarded by higher authorities, primarily the county government, and the remaining two-thirds were directly addressed to commune leaders (LX2 1965). After receiving a letter, the commune authority normally assigned one of its cadres to investigate the matter exposed by the letter. The investigator then visited the brigade or the production team from which the letter originated and talked to local residents individually to verify the charges contained in the letter. If the charge was about a production team cadre, the investigator usually did not let the brigade cadres know what his mission was to prevent them from getting involved in his investigation and possibly protecting the team cadre involved in the case. After secretly talking to enough local residents to clarify the facts, the investigator would have a formal talk with the accused and invite the brigade's leader, normally the Party branch secretary, to join them as a witness. He then submitted to the commune authority a report of investigation about the matter, based on his personal investigation and the accused cadre's confession, and suggested a proper solution to the case or further steps to investigate the matter. Because of the secretive manner in which the investigator handled the case, the cadre did not know the charges and possible results until the very end of the commune cadre's investigation. The pressure that he faced throughout the process was much greater than what he would experience during open criticisms on public occasions.

To examine the letter writers' motives, the effectiveness of letter writing, and interactions among all parties involved in the process from writing the letter to concluding the case, let us focus on three letters from the Suqin Brigade (including Su and Qin villages), all having to do with team cadres.

Letter from the No. 4 Team

In June 1963, the secretary of the Qindong Commune's Party committee received a signed "people's letter," fully 11 pages long, from the storehouse-keeper and the workpoint recorder of the No. 4 team of the Suqin Brigade, who were brothers of the A family. The letter accused the team's vice leader, B, of many misbehaviors, such as stealing more than 100 catties of immature cotton from the team's field; violating state regulations on village election by asking other team members to vote him in 1963; having sex with a landlord's daughter and another woman; exploiting team members by using them to work his private plot for more than 15 workdays without payment; gambling several times in- and outside the brigade; showing favoritism toward the landlord, who treated him with poached eggs at home; and embezzling more than 6,000 catties of straw, 300 catties of reeds, and a piece of lumber from the team.

The writers not only signed their letter but also affixed a personal stamp or put a fingerprint on each fact they stated about B, to make their charges credible. They stated their purpose of writing the letter at the beginning: "we the commune members do so not because we have any personal hatred towards him. Nor is it because we want to be a cadre in his place. Instead, we just make some accusations about the mistakes he has committed out of our sincere purpose of helping him and making the Party's policies more brilliant in the countryside."

Jiang, director of the commune's veterinary station, was appointed as an investigator of the case. After interviewing four individuals, he realized the true purpose of their letter. The A brothers, as it turned out, had been B's close friends and had aided him in many acts of wrongdoing, such as secretly dividing the team's grain and other goods. They also lied to help B hide some of his crimes, such as stealing the team's cotton. Later, however, the A brothers quarreled with B for unknown reasons. B thus excluded them from his circle, especially when having "feasts" (including eggs, fish, and alcohol) with other team cadres, despite the A brothers' threatening words that such "extravagant eating and drinking" violated the official regulations, known as the "Sixty Articles." To make the A brothers even more upset, B told them: "I don't care if it is 60, 61, or 62 articles. We enjoy the feasts here because we are in our capacity to do so. You are not in such a position and can only watch us eating. Go and accuse us. You'll be able to eat here in our stead if you win."

Unfortunately, although most of their accusations about B's economic problems were true, the A brothers did not win. From his talk with B and the team head's testimony, Jiang learned that B had returned most of the grain and other goods to the team that he allegedly "borrowed." Furthermore, B admitted honestly that he did have illicit sex with a woman from 1958 to the autumn of 1959, but he denied that he had affairs with any other women. The investigator thus concluded in his report to the commune that "there are only a few problems that remain unverified, such as his adulterous affairs. All other unresolved problems will be left for the upcoming campaign of Four Clean-Ups"

(LX3 1964). In fact, B successfully kept his job as a team leader during the following years of the Four Clean-Ups movement.

Letters from the No. 5 Team

The Party committee of the Qindong Commune received four anonymous "people's letters," dated January 5, 7, 8, and 9, 1964, from the No. 5 team of the Suqin Brigade, all targeting the vice team leader, C. Born in 1925 in a poor peasant family, C founded a primary cooperative in 1955, and the next year, when the co-op joined a newly established advanced co-op as the No. 5 team, C automatically became the team head. However, he soon lost that job because of his embezzlement of collective grain. In the spring of 1960, C was appointed as the head of the Suqin Brigade's pig farm and remained in that position until 1962 when he was reappointed as the vice head of the No. 5 team.

According to the four letters, C gambled with at least four team members, spending more than 30 yuan as stakes; when serving as the pig farm's head, he slapped a farm worker, named Wang, who had stolen a dead piglet from the farm, causing Wang's vomiting of blood and subsequent death; he bribed the brigade's Party branch secretary with 80 catties of the team's rice in exchange for the secretary's favor; he had illicit sex with a young woman (unnamed in the letter) in his team; and he never did farm work for the team yet received 500 workpoints as his subsidies from the team.

Realizing the close relationship between the vice team head and the brigade's secretary, the writers requested at the end of the last letter: "we hope that the higher authorities never ever send this letter back to the brigade. Once returned to the brigade, the letter will be destroyed. Hope that the Party committee directly handles it."

On January 9, the same day when the last "people's letter" was written, the vice Party branch secretary of the brigade also wrote a letter to the secretary of the commune's Party committee, in which he confirmed several of the charges, especially C's adultery with the woman of his team, whose husband was a soldier in active service. In response, the commune leaders once again appointed Jiang, the director of the commune's veterinary station, as investigator of the case. Jiang visited the brigade on January 17 and April 13, and talked to 19 people individually. As the records of these talks show, the writers of the four letters were a Party member, a subteam group leader, and two villagers.

They wrote the letters not only out of their own resentment of the vice team head's many problems but also because they received support from the team head, who had long been the vice head's adversary. The team head in turn was backed by the deputy secretary of the brigade's Party branch. The vice head, on the other hand, was backed by the Party branch's secretary, who was the sworn enemy of the Party branch's deputy secretary. It was small wonder, therefore, that the deputy secretary encouraged the woman who had illicit sex with C to accuse him of rape and to personally write a letter to the commune Party committee's secretary to confirm the charges included in the letters. Writing the "people's letter," in other words, continued the factional struggle between the brigade's power holders.

Jiang's investigation confirmed the letters' charges about C's gambling and embezzlement of collective goods. Of all the charges included in the four letters, the two most severe ones were C's alleged rape of the soldier's wife, a crime severe enough for a death penalty at that time, and his beating of the pig farm worker and the latter's subsequent death. While the woman repeated her story of C's alleged rape and two failed attempts, her brother-in-law only confirmed C's two unsuccessful attempts when interviewed by Jiang. Another female team member who talked to Jiang only confirmed that C's wife quarreled often with him because of her suspicion of his extramarital affairs. But none of the two personally witnessed C's having sex with the woman. The eight team members who were interviewed on April 13 for C's beating of the pig farm worker all confirmed that C slapped the worker twice, the first time with his hand and the second time with his shoe, and that the worker died about a month later, indicating no direct link between his beating and the worker's death. In his report to the commune's Party committee, Jiang summarized C's wrongdoings but remained uncertain if C's alleged rape of the soldier's wife was true. He did not mention C's beating of the pig farm worker at all. At the end of his report, Jiang concluded that C "does have severe problems, such as making vindictive attacks on those who had offended him, fawning on the superiors, and bullying the subordinates," and that the team members "requested to discharge C from his vice team head's post."

A few months later, C lost his job in an election of team cadres. The commune authorities' final decision on the case, as stated on the cover of the file dated September 22, 1964, was that "[C] failed to win the election; [therefore] no punishment to be rendered" (LX4 1964).

Letter from the No. 1 Team

In January 1964, the Party committee of the Qindong Commune received two anonymous letters from the No. 1 team of the Suqin Brigade,
complaining of team leader D and team accountant E, respectively. Unlike the letters in the preceding two cases, which were written neatly in
cursive handwriting and using the official language (indicating the
writers' good educational background), the two letters in this case
were written in vernacular, full of incorrect words, with awkward
handwriting, and on poor-quality paper, suggesting their writers' poor
literacy. According to one of the letters, D, though still in his early forties, had never done farm work for the team yet his workpoints were
more than those of two strong laborers combined; he received 700 catties of grain from the team, which were 200 catties more than allowed;
and he smoked expensive cigarettes imported from Albania, but his
limited income could not explain how he had afforded to buy them.
The other letter charged accountant E with tampering with the team's
accounts to increase his family's workpoints; illegally obtaining 100
catties of rice and 120 bundles of reeds from the team in the previous
year; and embezzling other goods of the team, such as bricks, lime-
stone, iron nails, iron wires, hemp ropes, and tung oil.

The commune soon sent a cadre, named Yu, to the brigade for an investigation. According to his records of interviews with 19 team members and cadres, the team leader, the accountant, and the storehouse-
keeper acted together in 1962 to illegally divide 120 catties of the
team's wheat, each receiving 40 catties. In 1963, the three cadres together
embezzled 290 bundles of reeds and 280 catties of "surplus grain" of
the team. The three cadres also gave themselves a total of 3,630 unearned workpoints, including 1,230 points to the leader, 1,200 to the
accountant, and 1,200 to the storehouse-keeper. Furthermore, according to the interviewees, the team leader had a bad temper and often
shouted at team members, especially those of "households in difficulty" and incompetent workers, therefore earning the nickname "big
cannon."

After clarifying the facts, Yu held a formal talk with the team leader
and the accountant respectively. The team leader admitted almost all
the wrongdoings exposed by the letter and the interviewees, saying
that he had "excessively received" the team's reeds, grain, and workpoints and that he had been "venomous" in dealing with team members. The accountant, too, admitted his mistakes and remarked that,

"born into a rich peasant's family and deeply influenced by [the bad habits of] the old society," he "never participated in production and spent most of [his] time reading books and loafing about." In his report to the commune Party committee, the investigator listed all of the two team cadres' mistakes that he had verified and asked the committee for a decision. He mentioned that both cadres had been cooperative with his investigation, and had frankly admitted their mistakes and repaid the team what they had improperly taken. Probably because of their voluntary *tuipei* actions, the Party committee did not punish the two cadres (LX5 1964).

Overall, most writers of the people's letters, as seen with these examples, were either team or brigade cadres or activists with the cadres backing them. They were not only literate and hence able to use the letters to serve their purposes but also familiar with the wrongdoings of their targets. Some of the accusers, as the case from the No. 3 team shows, were directly involved in the misdeeds of the accused, and knew almost every detail of their opponent's activities. They wrote letters or encouraged others to write when they strongly resented their long-standing adversaries or when their friends became enemies after a quarrel. In such cases, the letter worked only as a tool for the cadres of different factions to vent their hatred toward each other, rather than as a weapon for the people, or poor and lower-middle peasants in the countryside, to defend themselves and fight the abusive cadres as the state intended.

This is not to say, however, that ordinary villagers were inactive in this respect. The writers of the two letters from the No. 1 team, as explained earlier, were likely such ordinary villagers, as the poor handwriting, the dialectal words, and the many incorrect characters used in the letters suggested. However, unlike the cadres who knew well the wrongdoings of their peers, the ordinary team members, without access to the team's accounts and decision-making process, derived their knowledge of the team cadres' mistakes mainly from hearsay; what they accused thus was much less accurate and complete than what the commune cadre's investigation later revealed. Furthermore, ordinary villagers seldom had the willingness to write people's letters, not only because they were illiterate and unable to express their resentment in writing but also because of the ineffectiveness of this option for many of them. In their respective instructions on the prompt handling of people's letters, both the county's and the commune's Party committees complained in 1965 that some offices of the county or commune authorities adopted a bureaucratic, "master-like" attitude toward the letters. They either left the many envelopes unopened for months or simply delegated the letters to lower levels of government agencies for handling. In many cases, the letters, after being delegated to lower levels several times, ended up in the hands of the cadres whom the letters accused, only incurring the cadres' stronger retaliation against the writers (LX1 1965). Not knowing how to write the letter, to whom the letter should be addressed, and how to keep the letter confidential after being mailed, villagers usually did not think writing the people's letter to be a good idea for them. It is no wonder that the Qindong Commune, with a population of more than 31,000, received only 35 letters during the first 10 months of 1965 (LX2 1965).

The Democratic Management of Finance

"Checking the Account"

A regular means to check the grassroots cadres' abuse of power was the team members' periodic participation in the "democratic management of finance" (*minzhu licai*) in their production team, a practice that lasted from the early 1960s to the end of the collective era.[6] Changing the basic accounting unit from the brigade to the production team in 1961, as one of the many measures to reverse the radical Great Leap Forward policies, no doubt offered the teams an incentive to improve their production. But it also let the grassroots cadres control their own finances and therefore opened the door for them to engage in self-profiteering activities. So numerous were the teams in a people's commune that it was practically impossible for the few commune cadres to personally monitor or audit each team's day-to-day financial transactions. The only way to put the team cadres under control, therefore, was to rely on the initiatives of ordinary team members; that is, to supervise the cadres from below. In addition to mobilizing the villagers for participating in the recurrent political campaigns such as the Socialist Education and encourage their writing of people's letters, the government asked each team to form a *"pingxiazhongnong* group for the democratic management of finance," consisting of several members, who periodically examined the team's financial accounts and complained of any problems that they had found from the accounts.[7]

The *minzhu licai* members, by government requirements, should be chosen from those who were literate, able to use the abacus and understand different kinds of accounts, and most importantly, politically reliable. The actual selection of the members, however, was more complicated. The basic and foremost qualification was, of course, one's literacy. In the early 1970s, for instance, the head of the financial group in the No. 11 team of the Zhigang Brigade in Qin village was a young woman, who graduated from a middle school in the late 1960s and was the most educated among all team members at that time. However, education was not the only consideration when the team members nominated a *minzhu licai* member; they tended to favor those who were outspoken in team member meetings or in dealing with the team cadres. The team leader, to be sure, did not like those who were "nitpicking" and "troublemaking" in their eyes; what they favored were those "easy to get along with" or subservient to them. Nevertheless, to avoid the team members' strong resentment and possible complaint to brigade cadres, he had to appear to be open to the public opinion and accept the results of their nomination.

Kinship was another factor the villagers considered when nominating a candidate. In general, they favored a candidate from their own lineage. Descent groups that had no people serving as team cadres especially wanted to have one of their members to represent them in the *minzhu licai* group and "supervise" the cadres from other descent groups. As a result, four of the *minzhu licai* members in the No. 11 team, named Chen, Huang, Jiang, and Zhang, each represented one of the four dominant surnames in the team; the fifth member, named Yuan, was chosen because he was particularly good at using an abacus, though his personal family was the only one that bore his surname.

The five *minzhu licai* members, together with the team cadres, usually met after supper, on the fifth day of each month in the team's office. During the peak season, when all team members were busy with farm work, the meeting had to be delayed until the season was over. The meeting normally lasted about an hour but could go as long as two or three hours if the *minzhu licai* members had not met for several months or if they debated with the cadres about any problems they had discovered. All attendants would be rewarded three to five points, depending on the actual hours they spent on the meeting.

The meeting usually had three tasks. The first was checking the team's records of transactions with team members or external individuals or organizations and verify its monthly income and expenses in cash and kind. To do so, the *minzhu licai* members carefully examined each receipt provided by the accountant, asking him to explain the purpose and amount of the transaction, and affixed the *minzhu licai* group's seal on it when they felt satisfied with his explanation. Then one of the members would use an abacus to calculate the total amount of the team's monthly income and expenses to see if the results tallied with the accountant's report. The second task was checking the team's workpoint records. The members primarily paid attention to the workpoints of the team cadres and their family members. They particularly cared about how many days the cadres actually did farm work or were away from the team for meetings or other business, if their daily points were higher than those of the first-rate male laborers, and if their daily points did not tally with their total monthly workpoints as the accountant reported. Finally, the members and cadres would discuss the team's anticipated revenue and expenditures in the coming month and agree on a monthly budget. Without such a budget, the team would find it difficult, or even impossible during the early 1960s when the state practiced strict economic policies, to withdraw its deposit from the commune's credit cooperative.

The members found no problems with the accounts and thus stated in the monthly *minzhu licai* record that "the examiners have no objection." They frequently complained about things that they felt were unsatisfactory. At the meeting in January 1973, for example, they made the following comments (LC 1972):

1. The transactions were not recorded in a timely manner.
2. The public welfare funds were used without a discussion among the masses.
3. The subsidy workpoints were awarded without a discussion among the masses.
4. Public goods were not managed strictly.
5. Workpoint accounts were not squared.
6. [Undue] subsidies were awarded to someone for traveling to Luocun to buy diesel oil.

The cadres had to address these complaints during the following month and fix the problems that the *minzhu licai* members had pointed out. The next month, when they met again, the first thing the members asked about was how the cadres had handled the issues that they had complained about last time. If the cadres repeatedly ignored their criticisms, the members would threaten the cadres that they would refuse to attend a meeting or would refuse to affix the *minzhu licai* group's seal on the monthly record of the meeting—and the members indeed refused to affix the seal on May 3, 1976, when the cadres failed to handle their complaint on the improper use of the team's accumulation funds (LC 1976). The cadres thus had to yield to their pressure and make the corrections as well as they could. This was necessary because the brigade persistently required that the team accountants had to submit their monthly *minzhu licai* records together with their monthly financial reports to the brigade for examination, and the regular *minzhu licai* meeting and the cadres' prompt handling of the questions raised at the meeting accounted for about 30 percent of the cadres' annual merit evaluation. The brigade-level examination was conducted by team accountants, who mutually reviewed each other's records and reports under the supervision of the brigade's financial counselor. However, unlike the *minzhu licai* members, who were usually captious and contentious when examining the accounts, the team accountants tended to be lenient, only raising a few insignificant questions so that they could survive each other's scrutiny.[8]

Complaints on Workpoints

At the monthly meeting, the *minzhu licai* members complained most often about two issues: workpoint records and the team's financial management. When recording the team members' workpoints each day in the late afternoon or evening, the team leader used a mimeographed copy of the standard form that listed all workers' names, so he simply needed to enter each person's points to the space next to his or her name. The leader then delivered the form to the accountant, who transferred the team members' daily points to the monthly bulletin, which showed each member's daily points over the month. The bulletin was publicly displayed in a frame on the wall of the team's office and covered with transparent film to prevent possible tampering with the workpoints. Ideally, the accountant should transfer all team members' workpoints to the bulletin each day shortly after he received the daily record from the team leader, so that the next day people were able to check if the points they had earned on the preceding day were accurately recorded.

All team members checked the bulletin frequently. Some women checked it almost every day to make sure that their hard-earned points were credited. Barely literate, they were nevertheless able to identify their name on the form or at least remember the line where their names were located. They also had no problem reading Arabic numerals and therefore could check their workpoints for any date. From time to time, the team members felt frustrated when they found that their points were missing or incorrect. It was no wonder that the *minzhu licai* members often complained at the meeting that "too many workpoints are missing" (e.g., LC 1979). Once a team member found that his or her work was not credited, the person would immediately complain to the accountant and request a correction. To make sure that the worker did in fact take part in the task that had not been recorded, the team leader always asked his or her co-workers to give testimony to the person's attendance. Once verified, the accountant would add the missing points.

Therefore, what made the villagers most resentful about the workpoints was the accountant's failure to update their daily points on the monthly bulletin. The *minzhu licai* members, for example, blamed him for not squaring and publicizing their workpoint records at their meeting on January 31, 1973. A month later, on February 28, they complained again at the monthly meeting that "the workpoints are not timely recorded and publicized." On August 31, the members continued to complain at the meeting that "the workpoints have not been cleared up for a long time" (LC 1973). At their meeting in October 1976, the members blamed the team cadres as usual: "The workpoints are not recorded timely. The [daily records of] workpoints have usually been locked in the desk for more than ten days [before being publicized]" (LC 1976).

The reasons behind the delayed publicizing of workpoints varied over time. In the 1960s and early 1970s when there were recurrent political campaigns, the team cadres had to attend various meetings or study groups at the brigade, commune, or county level, which lasted for days or even one or two weeks. Therefore, they were unable to update and publicize the workpoints when they were away from the team. The cadres also might delay the task during the peak season when they were preoccupied with farming for both the team and their private plots, as mentioned earlier. By and large, in the 1960s and early 1970s when the successive campaigns produced a strong pressure on the team cadres, delays in updating and publicizing workpoint records were relatively rare. However, in the late 1970s, when the Cultural Revolution was over and the pressure lessened, the cadres became increasingly arbitrary in running the *minzhu licai* meeting and performing their duties in recording and publicizing workpoints. It was no wonder that the members complained at the meeting in August 1979 that "the workpoints have not been entered into the account and publicized for months" (LC 1979).

Team members had the strongest resentment over the cadres' favoritism in recording workpoints. At the meeting on May 5, 1977, for example, *minzhu licai* members complained: "there has been the problem of unfair recording of workpoints; different points are given to different people" (LC 1977: 5). Two months later, at the meeting on July 10, they wrote again: "recording workpoints has been unfair; certain people have been deliberately favored, who did nothing but earned the same points [as others]" (LC 1977: 7). As a former team leader admitted, when awarding workpoints, he did have different attitudes toward different people. To those who were "easy to get along with" (*chu de lai de*) and "listen to [his] words" (*tinghua*), he tended to be lenient and flexible. On the other hand, he would be rather strict in dealing with those who were "hard to get along with" (*chu bu lai de*) because they often argued with him over workpoint rates, appeared picky in job assignment, or complained too much in public meetings. When there was a new work opportunity that came with more points, the team leader would consider a candidate whom he liked, if he was no less qualified than others. Not surprisingly, the three tractor operators of the team all came from the "easy-to-get-along-with" group. Chen, a trouble-making *minzhu licai* member, thus complained at the meeting on July 10, 1977: "The production team [cadres] appointed laborers as they pleased. Some people who have friendship with them received special arrangements without the team committee's discussion. For example, three strong laborers were appointed to operate machines. Other workers slacked off upon seeing them loafing around" (LC 1977).

It should be noted, however, that such favoritism, though occurring from time to time, could never be overt and excessive. The team leader, for example, could not award different points to different workers who did the same job and finished the same quantity. And he could not always assign labor-saving and high-point jobs only to his friends, family members, or relatives. He had to find a reason or at least a proper excuse when he intended to do so. Open protection or discrimination would give his opponents a reason for accusations and hence subject him to brigade or commune leaders' censure. Whenever possible, the team cadres had to appear to be compliant with official regulations and to keep favoritism, if necessary, in a subtle form and limit it to a level tolerable to the resentful team members and forgivable to superior authorities.

Complaints on Team Finance

Another problem that the *minzhu licai* members often complained about was the production team's improper handling of transactions with team members or outsiders and poor maintenance of collective properties. Since the early 1960s, production teams in the Qindong Commune had adopted a strict practice in financial management: "those who keep books do not keep money; those who keep money do not spend money; and those who spend money do not deposit money." According to the instructions of commune authorities, the team accountant could not charge any expense to the team's account "if the procedures are not complete"; "if the transaction is not finished"; and "if the money and goods involved in the transaction do not meet relevant regulations" (QD4 1974). In managing the team's grain, an established practice was that the accountant was responsible for recording the transaction, the storehouse-keeper weighing and handing over the grain to a payee, and a *pingxiazhongnong* representative keeping a key to the door of the storehouse and affixing white lime stamps on the surface of a grain pile after the payment. Three locks were placed on the door of the storehouse, and the three keys were respectively in the hands of the team leader, the storehouse-keeper, and the *pingxiazhongnong* representative. When paying grain to a team member, all those three persons, plus the accountant, had to be present. In case one or two of the cadres were away for a meeting or for any other reason, payment had to be postponed until they returned. Alternatively, they would leave the keys to a team cadre, and the latter had to invite all other available cadres to open the storehouse and pay grain to the team member. The *minzhu licai* members, however, were suspicious of this irregular practice. So a complaint at the meeting on August 30, 1979: "The grain was not paid timely. No witness was present when making grain payment. There were back-door deals" (LC 1979).

There were many other complaints over favoritism involved in the team's transactions. On August 31, 1972, for example, *minzhu licai* members complained that the team cadres had favored certain team members who sold old and inedible yam vines to the team as pig fodder while keeping the fresh and tender vines for their own animals. On May 5, 1977, the *minzhu licai* members criticized the team cadres for another problem pertaining to the team's pig farm: "[The team cadres] sold the piglets of the team's pig farm just as if they were selling green vegetables and carrots, freely giving the team's piglets [to somebody] as gifts without a reason. [They also] reduced the weight and price when selling the piglets to acquaintances" (LC 1977). Among the buyers of the team's piglets, for instance, was a policeman's father from a neighboring commune. Like soldiers, police officers enjoyed a particular status in society. To show their respect to the police officer, the team cadres reduced the price of the piglet sold to his father. Some team members thus were resentful. A rumor quickly circulated among them: the cadres sold the piglet cheap to the police officer's father because they wanted to please the officer, so that the officer would not tie them up too tightly when arresting them for their economic crimes later!

The improper spending of collective funds and poor maintenance of collective properties was another concern of the *minzhu licai* members. They found, for example, that "there have been too many non-productive expenses" (LC 1977); "too much kerosene has been used; 8.3 catties were spent for ten days" (LC 1973); "the team's hemp ropes were taken home by a certain individual"; "the public funds were used without a public discussion"; "the public funds were used wastefully; the plows are repaired every year, each time spending tens of yuan without calculating the costs"; and "too many batteries were bought" (LC 1973). They urged the team cadres to "demand the repayment of the team's grain that has been lent to outsiders"; "to be strict in using the collective funds"; "to clear up the team's properties" (LC 1972); and "to be as frugal as possible" (LC 1977).

Conclusion

Throughout the collective era, brigade and team cadres in rural China were under constant pressure from above and below. They repeatedly had to confess their mistakes to superior leaders and face open criticisms from their colleagues and peasant representatives during the successive political campaigns. At normal times, they worried about "people's letters" from known or unknown enemies who accused them of various kinds of wrongdoings. The cadres were subject to team members' supervision and *minzhu licai* representatives' regular examination in their day-to-day management of the collective. Indeed, it is no exaggeration to state that, compared to their counterparts in both the pre-revolutionary and post-collective periods, the grassroots cadres in the Maoist era faced the strongest political constraints and had the least room for corruption and abuse. As this chapter has shown, various abuses in team management no doubt existed, but they had to be hidden and limited to a "safe" level so as to avoid the cadres' total discredit and loss of job. In localities where the reach of the state was limited, there were certainly unscrupulous team or brigade leaders who acted like a "local emperor" (*tu huangdi*), overtly abusing their power and bullying ordinary villagers, but they did not represent the overall picture of the grassroots cadres under the collective system as some observers have assumed, given the disciplinary mechanisms widely instituted in the countryside despite their varying degrees of functionality.

The villagers' participation was critical to the effective functioning of the different means in disciplining the cadres. Not all team members, to be sure, had access to those means or were interested in using them to guard themselves against cadre abuse. Nevertheless, the most active of them, such as *pingxiazhongnong* representatives and *minzhu licai* participants, did play a part in monitoring the cadres and exposing their wrongdoings. This chapter has shed light on two major factors behind their activism. One is a public discourse shared by all members in the rural collectives, which presumed the political correctness of the *pingxiazhongnong* and justified their role as supervisors of the corrupt and abusive cadres. It was not uncommon among Qin villagers that whenever they felt resentful about a cadre's wrongdoing or unfair treatment, some of them would be bold enough to shout to the cadre: "Don't be so arrogant! Wait for the next campaign!" The villagers said so not only to vent their anger but also to express a shared assumption among themselves: they had the unalienable right granted by the state and legitimized by its ideology to condemn the cadres during the campaign. Not surprisingly, outspoken members who frequently complained of the cadres often received support from ordinary members and thus became their representatives at the brigade- or commune-level *pingxiazhongnong* conference or at the team's *minzhu licai* meeting. The other factor is the team members' identity of interest with the collective. All team members well understood that the team was the major source of their family income; how the cadres managed the collective economy directly affected their personal interest. Therefore, they criticized not only the cadres' immoral conduct but also their improper maintenance of collective properties and spending of funds that would affect the well-being of all team members.

All these facts contradict the traditional view about the general ineffectiveness of the formal channels of interest articulation and political participation in rural China under the collective system and the
reluctance of Chinese peasants to use those formal means to challenge
village leaders owing to their "dependence" on the latter who controlled rural resources critical for the peasants' lives (Burns 1988: 174;
Oi 1989: 8, 151). After all, despite their roles in assigning tasks, recording workpoints, and other activities pertaining to work opportunities
and income distribution, the team leaders were by no means comparable to the landed elites before the Communist Revolution, who privately owned the land and other means of production on which the
landless and land-poor made a living. The cadres could neither de-
prive the team members of their right to work nor openly discriminate
against them. The villagers, in other words, were much less economically dependent on, and politically submissive to, the cadres than their
predecessors before 1949 had been to the landlords. They were always
in a position to use, directly or indirectly, the formal as well as informal channels to protect themselves whenever injustice occurred to
them.

Nevertheless, the effectiveness of those formal means in constrain-
ing the cadres cannot be overestimated. Although the *pingxiazhongnong*
were supposed to have the correct political consciousness and be politically superior to the cadres, the production team and brigade cadres
maintained their actual dominance over the former through their everyday roles in managing collective properties and funds, and in determining team members' task assignment, labor remuneration, and
income distribution. Moreover, despite the team members' repeated
criticism, the cadres rarely lost their jobs when their wrongdoings remained within the scope allowed by the state because what the state
sought in the recurrent campaigns was to correct the cadres' thinking
rather than to change the personnel. Worried about the cadres' future
retaliation, the villagers had to be cautious when criticizing the cadres
on public occasions; many treated such criticism only as a formality
rather than a true means to fight the abusive cadres. Writing "people's
letters" offered some villagers a chance to bring the abusive cadres to
the government's attention, but it was not available to all team members, and not all members who were able to write considered this
method to be safe and effective. More often than not, the people's letters
turned out to be a tool for cadres and peasant activists of different factions to fight with each other, rather than a weapon for ordinary team

members to defend their interest. In the final analysis, the officially promoted methods, including political campaigns, people's letters, and the regular checking on an account, exerted tremendous pressure on cadres and effectively limited their malpractices, but the existing social ties and power relations in the village community greatly curtailed their functionality.

CHAPTER 6

The Cultural Revolution:
A Multifaceted Experience

THE CULTURAL Revolution was initially and predominantly an urban phenomenon, involving almost every youth and adult in the cities in political agitation and violent conflicts between different factions. By contrast, most villages were quiet at the beginning but soon became involved in the nationwide turmoil, causing agitation, unrest, and even bloody confrontation (Baum 1971; Unger 1998; Walder and Su 2003). In Qin village, the situation at the height of the Cultural Revolution in the late 1960s was as turbulent and dramatic as the situation at the time of the Great Leap Forward. However, unlike the Great Leap Forward, which aroused excitement among the villagers at the beginning but soon tormented them with hunger and desperation, thus lingering as a horrible nightmare for years, the Cultural Revolution remained as a memory of amusement and excitement to many Qin villagers three decades later when they talked about it.

Part of the reason that the villagers had a different feeling toward the Cultural Revolution lies in the fact that their livelihood was basically secure and few suffered famine or death in those years, thanks to a lesson that the state had learned from the Great Leap Forward and its subsequent policy that stressed the stability of agricultural production during the Cultural Revolution. Another reason has to do with the way the villagers participated in the mass mobilization. Unlike the Great Leap Forward that exhausted almost all farmers in the wasteful and inefficient economic activities because of the arbitrary leadership at all levels, the Cultural Revolution was basically a political event, which had little to do with the organization of agricultural production, except for the introduction of a new labor payment system, as will be explained shortly. In Qin village, almost all adults were involved in the Cultural Revolution as members of different Red Guard organizations. The most active of them initiated or participated in the seizure of power against existing village leaders, while ordinary villagers joined the everyday routines of political activities characteristic of the Cultural Revolution, such as studying Mao's teachings and attacking old customs and culture. Focusing on the most chaotic years of the Cultural Revolution (1969–1970) in Qin village, this chapter depicts the event as a process encompassing three realities: a power struggle that continued the preexisting rivalry for dominance between different factions of village elites; mass participation in ideological propaganda that showed a gap between the representation and actual purposes of the villagers' public actions; and a campaign against traditional customs that incurred both compliance and defiance among the villagers. In all these areas, this chapter argues, the Cultural Revolution in the countryside showed remarkable differences in its meanings and consequences from the same event in the cities.

Power Struggle

The Communist Party had different strategies for conducting the Cultural Revolution in the cities and in the countryside. Whereas the Party's top leadership encouraged urban youth to join collective actions in attacking local government officials and creating "Red Guard" organizations, it cautioned against uncontrolled social, political turmoil that would interrupt agricultural production in the rural areas. On September 14, 1966, and February 20, 1967, for example, the CCP central committee required all commune members and cadres to concentrate their energy on farming activities during the "Autumn Harvesting" or "Spring Plowing" seasons (GNW 1981b: 861, 865). To ensure the stability of local government systems, a precondition for the normal functioning of agricultural collectives, and to avoid their paralysis as what had occurred widely in the cities, the Party repeatedly assured that the vast majority of rural cadres at all levels were "good or relatively good" and that those who had mistakes "should be allowed to correct their mistakes" (GNW 1981b: 865, 867). In its notice on March 7, 1967, the Party clearly required all brigade and production team members "not to engage in the struggle for power" during the busy season (GNW 1981b: 867). On September 14 and December 15, 1966, and December 4,

1967, the Party's central committee repeatedly ordered that no "work teams" should be sent to the villages to mobilize the peasants and that no urban students, workers, residents, or cadres should go to the countryside and no peasants should go to the cities for mobilization purposes. It warned against any attempts to "instigate one group of the masses to fight another" and any kinds of factionalism or armed conflicts (GNW 1981b: 861, 862, 869–870). Obviously, the Party had learned a lesson from the chaotic and disastrous Great Leap Forward that had badly hurt agriculture and caused nationwide famines.

These policies seemed to be effective in the Zhigang Brigade (formerly the Suqin Brigade), which comprised Qin and Su villages. The villagers did not create their own Red Guard organization until the end of 1966 when the fall harvesting was over. The organization was named *weidong bingtuan* (literally "guarding [Mao Ze]dong corps"), with members mostly from the six production teams of Su village, about a mile away from Qin village. The most active of them were a few teachers from the brigade's primary school and some literate men in their twenties or thirties; the head was Ai Guolong, a machinery technician of the brigade. Among them were also some Qin villagers, who soon found that that they were too few and their voice too weak to rival the Su villagers who dominated the corps. Therefore, on April 15, 1967, the Qin villagers formed their own organization, "67415 Headquarters," named after the date of its establishment. Almost all members of the five production teams in Qin village joined the Headquarters. Each of them clipped a rectangular badge made of red cloth, with the organization's name in yellow on it, to the upper left part of one's clothing, to distinguish them from corps members who wore a red cloth band on their left arms.

The Headquarters' leader was Zhang Qianyuan, who created one of the two cooperatives in the village in the early 1950s. Later in 1957, when the co-ops were organized into a single advanced co-op, Zhang failed to become its head and rejected an appointment as a production team head under the co-op. Disappointed, he gave up working for his team and instead engaged in private trading of marsh reeds, for which he was censured by Party branch secretary Zhu of the brigade. Zhang, however, fought back by writing a people's letter to the county's Party committee, which accused Zhu of many wrongdoings, causing the county to send an investigation group to the village and temporarily terminate Zhu's job (WG4 1979). In 1962, Zhu resumed his position as the village's Party leader when it turned out that most of Zhang's accusations were false or exaggerated. Living in frustration and isolation for years, Zhang found the advent of the Cultural Revolution a perfect opportunity for him to stage a counterattack. Using his remaining influence among some villagers and the mobilizing skills that he had already displayed in the 1950s, Zhang turned himself into a leader of "rebels" (*zhaofanpai*) in the village. All of the Qin villagers became members of his Headquarters because to join the "rebellion" against "power-holders" (*dangquanpai*) was the only way for them to show their support to the Cultural Revolution and because there were no other organizations of rebels in the local community for the villagers to choose.

Once the Headquarters was organized, he decided to ally with the corps to deal with Zhu and other brigade leaders. Several times the two organizations worked together to gather thousands of villagers, where they denounced many of the former and existing brigade cadres as "capitalist power holders" (*zouzipai*), and forced them to stand on the stage together with former landlords, each wearing a tall paper hat as a sign of humiliation. Zhu remained the nominal Party branch secretary during the heyday of the Cultural Revolution (1966–1969) but completely lost his influence in the brigade, just like his counterparts in many other brigades. Therefore, the most powerful persons in the brigade were Ai and Zhang, one responsible for the six teams in Su village and the other for the five teams in Qin village. Their major task was "taking charge of revolution" (*zhua geming*) or overseeing political activities in their respective teams. All team leaders had to consult them and obtain their approval when making an important decision. The commander of the brigade's militia battalion was responsible for "boosting agricultural production" (*cu shengchan*) in the brigade, whom each team's accountant had to contact for economic issues, such as the sales of crops and the distribution of income in kind or in cash within the team.

Although the two organizations maintained a cooperative and peaceful relation for most of the three peak years of the Cultural Revolution when their primary target was former or current brigade leaders, conflicts took place from time to time between them because of their different views toward former brigade leaders or over issues that pertained to the interests of different teams. The biggest conflict erupted on a night in December 1967, when the leaders of the two organizations argued over the location of the construction of an electric pumping station. People on each side wanted it to be built in their own village. Their argument eventually developed into a fight, when they threw furniture and other objects in the brigade's meeting room at each other, and some of them were injured. Quarrels also occurred within each organization. Many members of the Headquarters in Qin village, especially those who were sympathetic to Zhu, were discontent with Zhang's arbitrary leadership. With support from the corps, they accused Zhang of "instigating one group of the masses to fight another" in the winter of 1968 and planned to convene a brigade-wide meeting to denounce him. Zhang quickly fled from Qin village to avoid the attack. The next morning, a slogan was posted on the wall of the brigade's office: "Down with Zhang who absconded to avoid punishment!" Zhang, however, sneaked back to the village the next night to take down the slogan, and traveled to the county seat, where he displayed the slogan in the front yard of the building of the county's Cultural Revolution committee, and accused Zhu of "making vindictive attacks on Red Guards." In response, the country sent a "workers' propaganda team" of three members to conduct a "study session" in the brigade, in which Zhu was finally dismissed from his position as Party branch secretary. Huang, a Youth League branch secretary, became the brigade's new Party leader. Afterwards, both the corps and the Headquarters basically ceased their activities, as the nationwide turmoil of the Cultural Revolution gradually subsided (QD1 2000).

Studying "Mao Zedong Thought"

Learning Mao's Teachings

Social life and agricultural production in Qin village were orderly in general during the height of the Cultural Revolution. Nevertheless, the propaganda of radical ideologies and the nationwide worship of Mao stirred up many villagers and brought obvious changes to their everyday lives. For all members of the No. 11 team, for example, a central task during those years was studying "Mao Zedong thought," especially Mao's quotes contained in the "Red Treasure Book" (*hongbaoshu*) or *Mao zhuxi yulu* (Quotations from chairman Mao), which were distributed to each adult team member free of charge. In addition, many villagers purchased a book called *Lao san pian* (Three Constantly Read Essays), which included Mao's three famous essays: "Serve the People," "In Memory of Norman Bethune," and "The Foolish Old Man Who Moved a Mountain." Some families also bought the four-volume *Mao Zedong xuanji*

(Selected Works of Mao), to display them in the "treasure book case" (*baoshutai*), an elaborate wooden structure in red lacquer, which was placed at the center of the shrine desk in the living room, together with a plaster statue of Mao. Even more important than the quotes of the "little red book" were Mao's "latest instructions" (*zuixin zhishi*), which were broadcast through a network of wired speakers that connected each family. There were usually several "latest instructions" by Mao each month during the first three years of the Cultural Revolution.

For many villagers, the biggest barrier in studying Mao's quotes or instructions was their illiteracy. Each production team thus appointed a young, literate team member as a counselor (*fudaoyuan*), whose duties were leading the team members in singing revolutionary songs, reciting Mao's sayings, and explaining their meanings at the routine gathering each day before farm work. In addition, each of the team cadres, including the leader, the accountant, and the storehouse-keeper, was responsible for supervising a group of team members in studying Mao's thoughts when taking a break from a task.

The villagers worked hard to memorize Mao's sayings. Unable to read the little red book by themselves, many women could only memorize Mao's words by repeating what they had learned from the counselor or team cadres. Each morning, silently or aloud, they recited to themselves from memory Mao's words while sitting behind the stove to cook breakfast. When working together as a group or taking a break, they helped one another recall a quote or a "latest instruction" that they had just learned, each contributing a sentence so that they could piece together a complete saying of Mao. The most intelligent of them were able to recite from memory a complete saying of Mao after following the counselor two or three times and even an entire piece of the "Three Constantly Read Essays," which has thousands of characters. On the other hand, there were also a few who had a hard time memorizing the quotes. The counselor personally had to repeat Mao's words to them more than 20 or 30 times before they were able to recite the saying (WG5 1969).

In addition to learning Mao's published quotes and new instructions, the team members were encouraged to sing songs in praise of Mao, such as "The East Is Red," "Counting on the Helmsman When Navigating in the Sea," and "There Is a Golden Sun in Beijing." By 1969, when the turbulence of the Cultural Revolution subsided, most team members were able to recite from memory 20 to 30 quotes of Mao and about 10 to 20 songs.

It should be noted that learning the quotes or songs themselves did not lead to workpoint rewards, nor was there any mandatory requirements on the number of quotes or songs to be learned. However, all team members felt a pressure to recite or sing them. Each day at the morning gathering, the counselor or team cadres would ask the villagers to recite a quote of Mao that had been taught last time; those who failed to do so would be censured and even labeled as "backward elements," while those who performed well could be praised as a "pacemaker" (*biaobing*) at the team's or brigade's meetings and hence awarded a higher score in labor remuneration.

The study of Mao thoughts was inseparable from the use of certain rituals and symbols, which made it tantamount to a cult. To show one's loyalty to Mao, a villager had to clip one or more badges bearing Mao's likeness to the upper left part of his or her coat or shirt. Many villagers were fond of collecting as many badges as they could and putting them together on a piece of cloth, to be displayed above the portrait of Mao on the wall of the main room of their house. Equally important was the little red book. Each team member had to put it into a special "treasure book bag" (*baoshudai*) and take it with him or her when going to work. Before work started, all team members, consisting of two female groups and two male groups, had to gather on the threshing ground in front of the team's office building, where they did the "four first things" (*si ge shouxian*) while facing a big portrait of Mao with the little red book in their hands and four red flags on two sides: singing "The East Is Red"; reciting in unison "We sincerely wish Chairman Mao a boundless longevity! A boundless longevity! And a boundless longevity! We sincerely wish Vice Chairman Lin a good health! And a lasting health!" and then bowing three times to Mao's portrait; reciting in unison Mao's saying: "Be firmly resolved and never afraid of sacrifice, overcome all difficulties, and strive for a victory!" while waving the little red book in their right hands; and finally singing "Counting on the Helmsman When Navigating a Sea." When the "four first things" were done, the team leader would assign tasks to the different groups and dispatch them to different worksites.

Celebrating the release of Mao's "latest instruction" was another routine event in the village. Whenever a new instruction from Mao was to be released, a notice would be announced several hours beforehand, and all villagers were required to gather around the speaker in their house and listen to the broadcasting of the instruction at the scheduled time. Once broadcast, all adult and young villagers would come out to celebrate by setting off firecrackers and joining a gala parade for about an hour; the participants proceeded with many red flags while beating drums and gongs and shouting slogans. Sometimes Mao's instruction was announced as late as 8:00 or 9:00 p.m. when it was already dark; nevertheless, the active villagers would still gather together and parade for a time to show their loyalty to Mao (WG5 1969).

One thing that seemed truly exciting and amusing to the villagers was the "Mao Zedong Thought Propaganda Group" that each production team created at the beginning of the Cultural Revolution. The No. 11 team's propaganda group included five or six girls in their late teens or early twenties, who were good at singing and dancing, and about the same number of young men, who were able to play musical instruments (WG1 1969). The group's primary task was putting on a show at frequent team- or brigade-level meetings and other events such as seeing off young villagers to join the army, or sending off laborers to join water-control projects at a distance from the village. The show included singing revolutionary songs and performing dramatic plays. The two most popular plays that the team performed were "Sending Off the Son to the Army," in which an old-age couple sent their only son to the army, to show their loyalty to the Party, and "The Unforgettable June Second," in which a poor peasant was forced by his landlord to sell his last piece of land and hence lived a life as a beggar, wandering about together with his little child, a play intended to arouse the audience's hatred against the class enemies (landlords and rich peasants) and to show gratitude to Mao for liberating the poor. The propaganda group members showed great interests in rehearsing and performing the programs because doing so not only gave them an opportunity to show off their talents in music and performance but also turned out to be more enjoyable than doing farm work, while the workpoints they received were no less than those for farm workers of the same gender and labor grade.

Putting Mao Thought into Action

Studying Mao Zedong thought, according to government propaganda, should not be limited to reciting Mao's sayings or singing revolutionary songs; people should practice Mao thought in everyday life. A popular term describing this approach was *"huo xue huo yong"* (active learning and active application). The best way to practice Mao thought was "to be a good person and to do good things" (*haoren haoshi*). In other words, people should give up selfish ideas, show sincere concern for the interests of the collective, and voluntarily help others without seeking reward. It was no wonder, therefore, that many "anonymous heroes/heroines" (*wuming yingxiong*) emerged in Qin village. In the late 1960s, members of the No. 11 team were divided into four groups, including two women's groups and two men's groups. Among the 12 women of the No. 1 group, five or six were quite active in practicing Mao's thought. Every month or so, they would meet in the late afternoon to work out a plan for acting as "anonymous heroines." After they ate supper and finished the family chores at about 8:00 p.m. when it was already dark, each of them would carry a sickle and sneak to a preplanned destination, where they cut crops for two or three hours. Whenever somebody passed by, the women would quickly lay down so that the passerby would not notice them. They thus cut about five mu of the crop and bundled them before going home. The next morning, when the team leader found or was told that the crop had been harvested in the night by certain "anonymous heroines," he would make an "investigation" to see who they were. Once the heroines were identified, the cadre used a large piece of red paper to write a "commendatory letter" (*biaoyang xin*) and post it on the wall of the team's office building, which listed their names, described what they had done, and praised their love of the collective and loyalty to Mao. Later, the team leader would not only praise the "good people and good deeds" at the team's meeting but also report them to the brigade and therefore have them praised once again at the brigade meeting (WG7 1969).

Such "good people and good deeds" were not limited to the No. 1 group; women in the No. 2 group did the same and so there tended to be a competition between the two groups. When asked if they did the "good things" for workpoints or for other personal gain, my village informants denied it, saying that they did not receive any points at all because doing good things was meant to be selfless. The only motive for doing so, they explained, was to receive praise from the cadres at the meetings. They quoted a saying, which was popular at that time: "To have a pile of grain as high as the roof at home is no match to being praised at a mass meeting." What mattered most to the team members during those years was not so much workpoints or other forms of material gain as their social and political standing.

The workpoint system itself was also an area in which Mao Zedong thought had to be practiced. By 1968, most teams in the country had adopted the "Dazhai-style workpoint system," named after a model brigade in Shanxi province of North China, which implemented the system as early as in 1961 (GNW 1981b: 877). The state vigorously promoted this new system as a way to cultivate the peasants' consciousness of working for the "public" (*gong*) and to fight their concern with the "self" (*si*). Under that system, a production team no longer recorded workpoints for its members according to the hours or quantity of the work they had finished daily. Instead, it let each member appraise his or her own overall performance in collective production on a scale of 1 to 10 to determine the worker's "base score" (*jiben fen*), and then asked other team members to discuss and adjust the person's base score. Usually the team member would give himself a score a bit lower than he expected to show his modesty and selflessness, and then others would raise the score a bit. Such "self-appraisal and public discussion" (*zibao gongyi*) was usually conducted once or twice a month or every two or three months. Once a team member's base score was determined, then the team only needed to record his or her actual days of attendance in collective production during a certain period, and calculated the person's total workpoints at the end of the period by timing the number of his workdays with his base score. This method, therefore, terminated the team leader's daily assessment of the team members' work and eliminated their disputes over the recording of daily workpoints. People were concerned only with their participation in team production rather than with the number of points they earned each day. The Dazhai system, in official propaganda, was "to arm the farmers with Mao Zedong thought and to revolutionize the minds of both the cadres and commune members." Therefore, it was purportedly "conducive to arousing the commune members' incentives in collective production, promoting the unity between the cadres and commune members and the shared prosperity of commune members" (GNW 1981b: 872). The traditional piece-rate and time-rate systems, by contrast, only cultivated the peasants' mentality of "farming for workpoints" (*zhongtian wei gongfen*) and therefore were condemned as "workpoints in command" (*gongfen guashuai*) and "material incentive" (*wuzhi ciji*) (GNW 1981b: 874).

The No. 11 team adopted the Dazhai method in mid-1967. The team members met in the team's office every 15 days to determine each one's base score. At the meeting, the leader first let the members study Mao's quotes and asked each to make a self-examination, telling the audience what he or she had done to show his or her love for the collective and what kind of selfish ideas remained in his or her mind that had to be eradicated. Then it was time for self-appraisal. Everyone had to pretend to be unselfish and propose a low score for him- or herself. During the next few minutes of public discussion, others would try to say something good about the person and increase the score by half a point or one point. In general, however, most male "full laborers" received the full score of 10, and most female "full laborers" 8.5 or 9. The scores ranged between 5 and 6 for "half laborers" and between 3 and 4.5 for "auxiliary laborers" (QD1 2000). The gap of workpoints between team members of the same category was minimal under the Dazhai system.

Despite the utmost importance of political consciousness, personal relations played a key role in the public appraisal of one's basic score. If the person had many friends, he or she never worried about the result of the appraisal because there were always people speaking for him or her. However, there were always a few who were shy and never opened their mouths at the meeting; in that case, the team leader had to offer a score for him or her and then let the others discuss it. There were also a few who had no friends at all and found nobody speaking for them. Quite the contrary, there could be even criticisms from the audience on his or her selfishness and carelessness in production. The team leader could not help if nobody spoke for the person being discussed and if the blame sounded reasonable; he could only comfort the person by saying, for example, "you should sincerely accept the help from other comrades and work harder in the days to come for a higher score." Dissatisfied with the score, some team members openly argued with the leader, and a few frustrated women even wept at the meeting after receiving a low score, totally forgetting that they had just studied Mao's quotes on unselfishness (QD1 2000).

"Learning Mao Zedong Thought Activists"

During the heyday of the Cultural Revolution, as in the many movements before, to find and give publicity to "activists" (*jiji fenzi*) was an indispensable part of mobilizing the people. Once identified, local cadres would help the activists prepare a speech on how they had studied and practiced Mao's teachings. These people would then repeatedly speak at mass meetings of different levels, known everywhere in the country as *jiang yong hui* ("a meeting for propagating and practicing [Mao thoughts]"). Three such Qin villagers were selected to represent their brigade at the commune's meeting in May 1969. One of them was Meng, a bachelor from the No. 8 team. According to his speech, Meng had been so preoccupied with studying Mao thoughts that he kept doing so even when "eating, sleeping, walking, and taking a break." As a result, he was able to recite from memory Mao's "Three Constantly Read Essays" and more than 100 quotes. Later, when assigned the task of maintaining the brigade's network of wired speakers, he hesitated at first because he had stammered since his childhood and the job entailed verbal communication with various people inside and outside the brigade. However, he soon changed his mind and accepted the job when he was allegedly enlightened by Mao's saying: "What is work? Work is struggle. There are difficulties and problems in those places for us to overcome and solve. We go there to work and struggle to overcome these difficulties. A good comrade is one who is more eager to go where the difficulties are greater."

Meng also described the good deeds that he had done. For example, one night when there was a thunderstorm, he passed by the team's pig farm and found in a nearby creek a boat fully loaded with carrots, which was about to sink. So he decided to move the carrots to the bank and finished the task at 2:00 a.m. The next morning, when the team leader learned that the carrots had been unloaded and tried to identify the "anonymous hero," nobody knew who the hero was, including the watchman at the pig farm, until Meng's mother revealed the secret several days later.

In another instance, Meng found that the neighboring No. 10 and No. 11 teams lagged behind his own team in preparing the rice seedling bed, when he recalled Mao's saying: "We are from different parts of the country yet we get together for the same revolutionary goal. . . . All people of the revolutionary rank should take care of each other and help each other." So one day he invited 15 young men of his team to help the two neighboring teams make their beds and worked there until midnight (WG6 1969).

The second activist, named Zhou, was a young mother of three from the No. 10 team. Though illiterate, Zhou was able to recite from memory all of the "Three Constantly Read Essays" after overcoming her illiteracy and other difficulties. One day, according to her speech, when the team leader allowed all adult women to take a break from work, she decided to stay on the farm reciting to herself Mao's "In Memory of Norman Bethune" while all other mothers returned home to breast-feed their babies. Later when those mothers came back, Zhou realized that she had forgotten to feed her own baby! In another instance, Zhou was reciting Mao's essays early in the morning while sitting behind the stove to make pancakes. So engrossed was she in remembering Mao's words that she forgot she was making breakfast until the pancakes were burnt.

Zhou also mentioned in her speech many of the good things she had done. One night, for example, she and two other women spent hours cutting grass on the team's plot and shipped the grass to a different place for fertilization. The team leader, who had planned to assign four members for that task on the following day, was surprised by their good deed and wanted to record an entire workday for each of the three women. Zhou refused the award, quoting a saying by the villagers of the famous Dazhai Brigade: "It is not for workpoints that we work; we would not work if it is for workpoints." She further added that "we did the night work voluntarily, without the intent to seek public praise. We did so only to show our loyalty to the reverent Chairman Mao."

Likewise, Zhou found that the neighboring No. 8 team suffered a shortage of labor, which reminded her of Mao's teaching: "One should show utter devotion to others without thinking of oneself." Therefore, one night, she invited 11 women and traveled to the neighboring team, where they moved its dried sludge to a rice seedling bed for fertilization.

Zhou admitted in her speech, however, that she had been unpopular among the women of her team. After quarreling with a woman, she had not spoken to her for six years, and she also had not spoken to six other women for two years. After studying Mao's instruction that "there is no fundamental conflict of interest within the working class," Zhou realized that all those women were her "class sisters" or "melons of the same stem," so she took the initiative to restore good relations with all of them (WG6 1969).

Unlike the preceding two activists, who were ordinary team members, the third, named Huang, was an accountant from the No. 4 team. In his speech, Huang first criticized his own "indifference to politics" before studying Mao thought. As an accountant, he used to stay in his office all the day, only to "deal with the abacus and get along with the kerosene lamp," and never visited a farm or did any manual work together with other team members, causing their strong resentment against him. He then completely changed his work style after learning Mao's teaching: "To be responsible for the people is our duty. All our working cadres, regardless of the rank of their positions, are servants of the people." He thus participated in collective work and did accounting only at night. However, unlike the other activists who, as ordinary team members, did many voluntary tasks in helping their own or neighboring teams, Huang emphasized his role in propagandizing Mao Zedong thought. He and his family all joined their production team's "Mao Zedong thought propaganda team," and he was responsible for directing the team's performance. They rehearsed their programs whenever taking a break from work or in the evening, and put on a show frequently inside and outside the village, often returning home as late as midnight. In addition, he helped the neighboring No. 6 team rehearse their programs, to show his unselfishness and collectivism (WG6 1969).

To the extent that each team member was involved in the cult of Mao and the study of Mao's teachings, the state was indeed unparalleled in Chinese history in infiltrating its ideology into the village society. Unlike the official ideology of the Cultural Revolution that emphasized a persistent struggle between socialism and capitalism in policy making within the Party and in economic life, however, what prevailed in the village was simple, consisting of two major components: the loyalty to Mao, and the denial of "self" (*si*) in serving the "public" (*gong*). The Cultural Revolution was successful in cultivating the villagers' loyalty to, or worship of, Mao through the intense study of Mao's instructions and the use of many symbols, rituals, and slogans. Mao's status, therefore, was sacred to all villagers; they had to avoid any words that would vilify the "great leader." A woman in Qin village was condemned in public and paraded around the community for hours with a humiliating "tall paper hat" on her head, simply because she had mispronounced "*mao xuan*" (Mao's Selected Works) as "*mao wan*" (food container for cats) (QD1 2000). When discarding useless papers, the villagers had to make sure that the papers did not contain Mao's name or portrait. Their feeling toward Mao was a mix of fear and awe.

Altruism was another part of the Cultural Revolution ideology. Qin villagers had to pretend to be selfless on public occasions and enthusiastic in doing "good things." But a gap existed between their words and deeds. When doing something as anonymous heroes or heroines, the villagers never wanted their actions to remain unknown to the public forever. They expected praise from the cadres for their "selfless" deeds, which would enhance their status in the public appraisal of their base scores. Doing "good things" and becoming "activists" in studying Mao's teachings appealed especially to certain team members who wanted to improve their standing in the team. Unlike other means of achieving fame and honor, which entailed certain qualifications unavailable to the ordinary and disadvantaged villagers, "being a good person and doing good things" was easy to practice and open to anyone who dreamed of being a hero or heroine. It is no wonder, therefore, that the two "studying Mao Zedong thought" activists chosen from ordinary Qin villagers were a bachelor with speech difficulties and a woman who once had many enemies in her team. For these people and many other villagers who shared the same dream, the Cultural Revolution was a time of hope and aspiration; a quarter century later, they still recalled their experiences in those years with pride and joy.

Wiping Out the "Four Olds"

Aside from studying Mao thoughts, an integral part of the Cultural Revolution was attacking the "Four Olds" (old thoughts, old culture, old custom, and old habits). Shortly after the beginning of the movement, Red Guards in Qin village (mainly young team members who had received several years of education, local school teachers, and students) visited each household to take down the pictures of the "family god" (*jiashen*) from the wall of the main room in each house. The god could be the Guanyin bodhisattva (Goddess of Mercy), Rulai or Tathagata Buddha, Guandi (God of War), God of Fortune, or simply a wall scroll with the single character "shen" (god) on it. Some village cadres and Party members had removed the picture of such deities in the early 1960s during the Socialist Education movement. Most households, however, did not do so until the outbreak of the Cultural Revolution at the Red Guards' demand. They also took away the incense burner and the candlestick from the family-god chest and moved the chest from the middle to either side of the main room. It was only after 1967 that they moved the chest back to the original position and placed on it Mao's mini statute and the "treasure book case."[1]

During the initial years of the Cultural Revolution, there was also a strict ban on "superstitious" activities in the countryside. Qin villagers traditionally offered sacrifices to their ancestors three times a year. On the Qingming Festival (April 4, 5, or 6), they paid a visit to their ancestors' tomb, where they added new dirt to the top of the grave, displayed some food as a sacrifice on the ground next to the grave, and burned paper sheets. The Red Guards strictly prohibited such visits. Those who had secretly added dirt to a grave top in the night, once discovered, had to remove it at the order of the Red Guards. Almost all households gave up the custom of offering sacrifice to ancestors on the fifteenth day of the seventh month (Festival of Ghosts) and the day before the eve of the lunar New Year. Traditionally, on those two days, a family displayed on the square dining table in the main room many dishes that were surrounded with a certain number of bowls filled with rice (depending on the actual number of the father's deceased parents up to his great-grandparents) and the corresponding pairs of chopsticks, as well as burning incense and a shining candlestick on the family-god chest, while the family members performed kowtow to the dining table before burning fake paper money. To avoid being detected by Red Guards who inspected each home at the lunch time on those two days, a few families who insisted on the custom made the offerings early in the morning while keeping the door of the house closed.

The Spring Festival, or the lunar New Year, was the most important day of the year. From 1966 to 1970, the government promoted a "revolutionary Spring Festival." On the eve of the lunar New Year, all young people in Qin village had to gather at their team's pig farm to eat a poor meal (the so-called *yikufan*) that was only slightly better and cleaner than the coarse fodder that was fed to the pigs. This was a way for the young people to recall the sufferings before Liberation. Each family was allowed to put up couplets (*duilian*) on the two sides of a door, but the couplets had to avoid traditional words about good fortune and family prosperity and instead use quotes from Mao's poems or revolutionary phrases. On the night of New Year's Eve and the early morning of New Year's Day, people could no longer set off firecrackers or wear new clothes. When greeting each other on that day, they were to say "good morning" rather than "wish you happiness and prosperity" (*gongxi facai*). Instead of celebrating the New Year for about 15 days, visiting relatives and enjoying good food, the villagers had a break of one day only and had to resume collective farm work on the second day of the New Year. Team cadres could not celebrate the New Year at all; they had to attend a meeting at the commune seat for 10 days. After 1970, such meetings were delayed for a few days after the New Year but the cadres had to be on the night shift during the break, patrolling the village against possible "sabotage" activities by "class enemies" and "bad elements." Ordinary villagers enjoyed more days of the festival. The traditional methods of celebration gradually revived. Many villagers, mostly males, secretly gathered together once again to play poker and gamble, a traditional form of entertainment, despite the government's repeated warning and prohibition.

Marriage was another area where significant changes took place during the Cultural Revolution. Traditionally, Qin villagers observed elaborate etiquette when proposing a marriage, providing betrothal gifts, arranging a wedding, and rewarding the matchmaker. In the late 1960s and early 1970s, the government propagandized against arranged marriage and betrothal gifts. Although a matchmaker was still indispensable when proposing a marriage, and parental consent was still a precondition for a successful marriage, the children who grew up during the Cultural Revolution became more and more independent. Parents could rarely impose a marriage on them without their agreement. At mass gatherings, local cadres repeatedly warned against arranged marriage, often quoting a hearsay about a daughter in such-and-such a village who committed suicide after she had argued with her parents over a proposal she disagreed with. Few parents openly provided betrothal gifts to the family of a prospective daughter-in-law in the amount and kind according to customs. The wedding itself was also simpler than before. The groom's parents would only invite their closest relatives to their home for one meal, rather than the traditional three meals a day for three consecutive days. When the Cultural Revolution ended in the mid-1970s, traditional rituals and formalities regarding betrothal and wedding soon resurfaced, but arranged marriages that were made against the will of the young couple became increasingly rare because youths were not only more educated than their parents but also economically independent, having earned as many workpoints as their aging parents. Improvement in the villagers' economic conditions, therefore, was more effective than the imposed policy to change their marriage practices.

It is worth noting that, despite the government's suppression of the Four Olds during the Cultural Revolution, old customs such as witchcraft and fortune-telling remained alive in the village, though they took place surreptitiously in a villager's house. When a family member fell ill, for example, villagers usually considered three solutions before 1949: seeing a doctor; visiting a temple and praying for help; and, if these methods did not work, seeking help from a sorcerer or witch. In the 1950s, all temples and simple shrines in the neighboring villages and towns were dismantled or changed into schools; to visit a temple was no longer an option. While they still burned incense and said prayers to the Guanyin or Rulai at home, the villagers invariably visited the village's clinic or, at the clinic's referral, a hospital in a neighboring town for medical treatment. Since the 1950s, the commune had installed a simple clinic in each village, which was staffed with one or two "barefoot doctors" who had received basic training in Chinese and Western medicine and were able to treat ordinary illnesses. Thus, seeing a doctor was always the villagers' first choice. Nevertheless, there were occasions when medication did not work and the villagers would turn to sorcery for help. Among the amateur sorcerers/sorceresses was a native villager, nicknamed "the Hunchback," who was known for drawing a talisman on a yellow paper to heal patients, and an old lady, known as "the Grandaunt," from the neighboring Shen village, who from time to time was invited by the villagers to "expel ghosts" at their homes. In the 1970s, a woman named Meng from the No. 10 team of the brigade was believed to be able to perform a certain kind of witchcraft and cure strange and inexplicable illnesses that doctors had failed to handle. One father thus described what happened to his 14-year old daughter in 1975. For more than a week, the girl had persistent headaches and fever despite the use of medicine provided by the village's clinic. So the parents brought her to the hospital in a neighboring town. After a careful checkup, the doctor told them that everything was normal with her, and indeed the girl's fever and headache disappeared. However, once they returned home, all her symptoms recurred. Perplexed, the parents invited Meng to their home for help. Asserting that the girl's soul had left her body, the woman used a broom to draw an invisible circle on the floor of the living room. She worked hard to stand an egg on a kitchen knife and eventually succeeded, which meant, she explained, that the daughter's soul finally came back. Before she left, Meng instructed the father to make a certain number of paper *yuanbao* (a shoe-shaped gold or silver ingot) and burn them at a designated place 45 steps northwest of the house, a way to thank Earth God, who had sent the soul back. The father seriously did the work in the night. To the parents' amazement, their daughter's illness vanished completely.

The villagers' attitudes toward such activities varied. From time to time, at meetings when talking about "wiping out the Four Olds," the village cadres condemned them as "superstitious." However, neither the cadres nor ordinary villagers strictly banned those activities in their community, for they knew that those who sought help from the Hunchback, the Grandaunt, or Meng were usually the illiterate, elderly villagers, especially women, who belonged to the category of "backward masses" (*luohou qunzhong*) rather than that of bad elements or counterrevolutionaries, and who were their neighbors or team members. It made no sense for them to be too serious to deal with such ignorant folk, as long as the latter kept their superstitious activities underground. Everyone knew that there was a difference between what should be said in public and what should be allowed in everyday life.[2]

Conclusion

As we have witnessed, the Cultural Revolution in the countryside involved three simultaneous processes, which both resembled and differed from the same event in the cities. First, as in the cities, the Cultural Revolution in the village also took the form of mass mobilization that culminated in the seizure of power by Red Guards from the hands of preexisting village/brigade leaders. However, the way the villagers organized themselves deviated significantly from the formation of Red Guard factions in the cities. In the urban area, according to a classical interpretation, people joined different political organizations according to their different economic and social backgrounds, resulting in the bifurcation and confrontation between the conservative factions comprising primarily members who had benefited from the preexisting economic and political arrangements and the radical factions whose members came mainly from the disadvantaged and marginalized groups (Lee 1978; see also Schurmann 1968; Rosen 1982). Obviously, this "interest group" approach is inapplicable to the situation in the countryside because almost all participants of the Red Guard organizations were members of the production teams, and there were no institutionalized differences among them in work opportunities and subsequent differentiation in social status and income distribution. The team members' task assignment and labor remuneration, to be sure, varied from person to person, depending on their gender, labor grade, work abilities, and personal relationship with team cadres, as the following chapters will show, but such differences did not produce a social disparity as striking as that between, for example, the regular workers of state-owned factories and contract or temporary workers in the cities. Therefore, what determined the villagers' affiliation with a specific Red Guard organization, as seen in this chapter, was their residential location, rather than economic or social status. The Red Guard leaders, likewise, drew the core members or activists of their organization mostly from those within their personal networks, including their friends, relatives, or fellow team members. In other words, the traditional social ties that bound the villagers together continued to dictate their political choices during the years of radicalism.

Second, despite the traditional boundaries that defined the scope and options of their political actions, the Cultural Revolution offered ordinary villagers a new opportunity to express themselves and advance their interests. Unlike the urban residents' frequent involvement in militant confrontation and even bloody strife between different factions, the villagers' participation was limited primarily to political studies and ritualized propaganda. One of the official purposes of their involvement was cultivating their awareness of "class struggle" in the countryside. However, unlike the land reform in the late 1940s and early 1950s that indeed triggered a heightened moment of class struggle between the landed and the landless or land-poor and allowed the latter to benefit materially from that process, the Cultural Revolution in the countryside saw a disjunction between the political discourse of class struggle and the social realities in the countryside, for there no longer existed true landlords or rich peasants after the land reform and collectivization (P. Huang 1995). Without much economic interest involved, this kind of class struggle rarely aroused the villagers' enthusiasm. What interested them were their demonstration of loyalty to Chairman Mao by studying Mao's teachings and doing "good things" because such activities could help them become a model team member, achieve higher scores of labor payment under the Dazhai system, and improve their standing in the collective. Thus, rather than a heightened struggle between different factions as widely seen in the cities, what predominated in the countryside during the Cultural Revolution was primarily an ideological campaign that forced the villagers to show their political conformity and at the same time offered them an opportunity of self-representation and elevation.

Finally, the campaign against the Four Olds had different meanings in urban and rural China. Whereas in the cities it focused mainly on destroying religious idols, ancient books, arts, and buildings that represented the "feudal" culture, rather than banning traditional customs, habits, and faith, much of which had been dampened or wiped out after the Communist Revolution, the reverse was true in the countryside. Without many material symbols available for destruction, the rural Red Guards attacked mainly the "superstitious" practices associated with ancestral worship, witchcraft, and popular cults, as well as the old customs in weddings, funerals, and traditional festivals that were condemned to be wasteful and backward. Although their efforts were far from successful and long-lasting, the Four Olds nevertheless lost their legitimacy in the rural communities during the height of the Cultural Revolution. For the first time in twentieth-century China, the efforts to combat "feudal superstition" (*fengjian mixian*) and "feudal thoughts" (*fengjian sixiang*), which had begun in the early twentieth century but remained limited largely to the cities, swept the entire countryside and exerted a tremendous impact on the mentality of the villagers; many of them, especially the young generation grew a disdain of old customs and a rebellious mind toward the authorities in the family and community. For the rest of the villagers, however, the attack on the Four Olds deprived them of the most meaningful part of their lives in the family, the community, and the spiritual world. All in all, the Cultural Revolution in the countryside was at once a time of great turbulence involving fierce competition for power among the rural elites and a process of discursive engagement and cultural transformation open to ordinary villagers.

CHAPTER 7

The Reach of the State: Rural Control During the Cultural Revolution

A TURNING POINT of the Cultural Revolution was the September 13 Incident in 1971, when Lin Biao (1907–1971), the minister of defense and vice chairman of the CCP, together with his family members and followers, died in an airplane crash on their way to the Soviet Union, fleeing the country after an aborted assassination attempt on Mao. Handpicked by Mao as his successor, Lin initiated the nationwide craze of worshipping Mao during the height of the Cultural Revolution from 1969 to 1970. He was also responsible for many other radical economic and social policies during those years. Therefore, after the incident, Mao and the Party took measures to eliminate Lin's influence and reverse his "ultra-leftist" policies, such as terminating the ritualized worship of Mao, reviving some economic practices in rural collectives that had prevailed before the Cultural Revolution, and reintroducing certain forms of material incentives in team production. At the same time, Mao strived to safeguard the socialist economy by indoctrinating villagers with socialist ideologies, launching new political campaigns against abusive grassroots cadres, and tightening the government's control of the collective agriculture and individual households. However, as we will find in Qin village, in the wake of the turbulent Cultural Revolution, it was even more difficult than before for the government to achieve its goals when the political pressure from above lessened and mass agitation subsided. The state thus faced a dilemma in overcoming the Cultural Revolution radicalism while maintaining its socialist orthodoxy, a situation that remained unsolved until the state decided to dissolve the collective system and revive family farming in the early 1980s.

Regulating Team Members

Ideological Indoctrination

After Lin Biao's death, the ritualized worship of Mao came to an end in Qin village and the rest of the country. Nevertheless, the Party insisted on "politics in command" (*zhengzhi guashuai*) or the priority of political study and conformity with the Party's policies in everyday life. Team members in the village attended endless brigade-wide meetings to listen to the announcement of *zhongyang wenjian* (CCP central committee's documents) and to join the repeated sessions studying and discussing such documents and newspaper editorials, usually in the team's office building or at a team members' house after supper. In 1972 and 1973, their political study focused on condemning Lin and the ultra-leftist policies of the preceding years. A model team of the brigade held 14 meetings in a few months (QD4 1974). Speakers at such meetings were usually the literate adult males, who often linked the radical policies with their own experiences. At a meeting of the No. 11 team in Qin village on February 23, 1973, for example, a member named Yuan thus complained: "Lin Biao carried out impractical policies even during the busy season of Autumn Sowing and Harvesting. How much time we have wasted on singing and dancing! We were required to carry the 'quotes bag' [*yülu dai*, a tiny bag to hold the book of Mao's quotations] all the time, even when we were doing farm work; how clumsy it was!" Another team member Pu followed: "The scoundrel Lin Bao played deceptive politics. He required us to do the Four Firsts and to recite [Mao's] quotes even when we were walking or eating. While cheating on us to win our trust, he attempted to assassinate Chairman Mao. What a double-dealer he was!" To their remarks, team member Jiang added: "Lin Biao was really an evildoer. He said that the busier our farm work was, the more attention we had to pay to politics. How could we make a living on saying words without doing work? Lin was indeed deceitful" (QD4 1973).

Beginning in early 1974, the political meetings in the village shifted from condemning Lin to "criticizing Lin and Confucius" (*pi-Lin pi-Kong*), in response to a nationwide campaign. At the meeting on February 14, 1974, for example, the leader of the No. 11 team assigned each of the team's eight activists a saying of Confucius for them to criticize (QD4 1974). However, such sayings were no longer relevant to their personal or collective experiences. They attended the meeting only for workpoints; each time they received three points per person. Later in 1976, when the campaign of "criticizing Deng and fighting the rightist wind of reversing verdicts" (*pi Deng fanji youqing fan'an feng*) started nationwide, the team no longer held the traditional meetings to criticize Deng Xiaoping (1904–1997), who had been in charge of the government in 1975 but gone too far in reversing Mao's Cultural Revolution policies. Instead, the team responded to the campaign only by displaying posters on the wall of the team's office.[1]

Although the team members lost interest in political study, they showed genuine enthusiasm for attending the "political night school" (*zhengzhi yexiao*), which was created in each production team in the late 1960s and persisted until the end of the Cultural Revolution. All illiterate villagers had to attend the school that was open in the winter and housed in the team's meeting room. It taught new songs and new techniques of farming, especially the use of pesticide or chemical fertilizers, and the cultivation of new strains of crops. What really benefited the team members was the literacy class. To encourage their attendance, the No. 11 team distributed a textbook, a pencil, and an exercise book to each attendant free of charge. The texts that they learned were popular slogans, Mao's sayings, and various verses. In addition, the class also taught the team members how to read and write their own names, the names of ordinary farm tasks, Arabic numerals, and arithmetic. The night school ended with a test; those who passed the test received a certificate of literacy (*saomang zhengshu*). As a result of their attendance for several winters, most team members, male and female, were able to check the team's workpoint accounts or keep their own daily work records. Some villagers who owned a store or factory in the 1990s attributed their abilities to keep books or operate machines to the night school that they had attended 30 years ago.

"Cutting the Capitalist Tails"

Another significant change in the collective economy in the early 1970s was the abolition of the Dazhai workpoint system and the revival of the time-rate and piece-rate systems in labor remuneration, which supposedly did away with egalitarianism and best represented the socialist principle of income distribution: "from each according to his ability, to each according to his needs" (*ge jin suo neng, an lao fenpei*) (GNW1981b: 898). As we will see in Chapter 8, this policy was effective in stimulating team members' labor input and increasing the team's output. Most families in the No. 11 team, who had been "overdrawn households" under the Dazhai system in 1968 and 1969, gradually paid off their debts to the team in the following years and received an increased amount of payment in cash at the year-end distribution. At the same time, the government also promoted "equal pay for equal work between men and women" (*nannü tonggong tongchou*), to encourage women's full participation in collective production. Cadres in Qin village tried hard to narrow the gap between men and women in workpoint earnings and hence became a model brigade in promoting the equal pay policy in the county. In actuality, however, as Chapter 8 will show, the cadres could only apply that policy to a selected group of team members and for a limited time when the government's pressure was strong. The difference between adult men and women in their physical strength as well as the traditional notion of gender roles continued to dictate task assignment and labor remuneration in team production.

In addition to regulating the collective economy, the state attempted to put the private economy of rural households under its strict control. From the beginning of agricultural collectivization in the mid-1950s, the government had allowed all households of a cooperative or a production team to keep a small piece of land, known as "private plot" (*ziliudi*), which they received from the collective free of rent. The private plot was necessary because the crops and vegetables that a household grew on it were the major source of fodder for domestic animals and important supplements to the household's food from the team. Although a household never owned the plot, it had the right to decide what to grow on the plot and had complete control of its yield. Therefore, the villagers had a strong incentive to work the plot well and maximize its output; the crops growing on private plots were invariably better than those on collective farms. To ensure that the team members concentrated most of their energy on the collective farms, however, the state had to limit the size of the private plot. Before communization, the total size of private plots in a cooperative was limited to 5 percent of the co-op's total farmland (GNW 1981a: 484). As a remedy to the devastated agriculture and widespread starvation during the Great Leap Forward, the state increased the size of private plots to 7 percent of a collective's total farmland in early 1961 (GNW 1981b: 436). Later, the state limited the private plots to "five to seven percent," which remained the official policy until the end of the collective era (GNW 1981b: 983). Qin village seemed to conform to the policy in the 1960s. The No. 11 team's private plots totaled 26.1 mu in 1966, or 6.94

percent of the team's farmland, and remained so until 1971 when they increased to 32.6 mu, while the team's total farmland also increased to 479.6 mu, owing to the reclamation of marshland (QD4 1966; QD4 1971).

The state allowed the private plots, ridiculed as "the capitalist tail" (*zibenzhuyi weiba*), even during the heyday of the Cultural Revolution; obviously it had learned a lesson from the devastating communization during the Great Leap Forward—the cancellation of private plots in 1958 and 1959 was an important factor leading to the nationwide famine. After the Lin Biao incident in 1971, grassroots cadres were less and less scrupulous in reallocating private plots to individual households when the intense political pressure was over. By late 1975, the problem of excessive allocation of private plots had developed to such a degree that the state had to instruct all production teams to conduct a survey and take back the extra portion of private plots from team members (GNW 1981b: 919). The No. 11 team surveyed its private plots in August 1976. The result was surprising. The 50 households of the team occupied a total of 41.371 mu of private plots, or 8.77 percent of the team of total farmland. In addition, they also used a total of 30.07 mu as their vegetable gardens. The size of the collective land for private use thus amounted to 71.441 mu, or 15.16 percent of the team's total arable land, which was more than double the limit allowed by the state. Instead of taking back the undue proportion of the private plot from each household, the team only asked the latter to compensate the team by reducing its grain to be distributed from the team. For every 0.1 mu of extra plot used by a household, the team deducted 80 catties of grain from its distribution, including 30 catties during the summer harvest and 50 catties during the autumn harvest (QD4 1976).

The government also tried to limit the villagers' family sidelines, especially the raising of domestic animals, which were again treated as a "capitalist tail." By an official regulation, for example, each household in Qin village and the rest of Dongtai county was allowed to have one or two pigs, so that the household and the team could use the manure for fertilization when the availability of chemical fertilizer in the early 1970s was limited. The household usually sold the pigs to a government-sponsored purchasing station for cash income. In fact, to encourage the household to raise pigs, the government linked the size of its private plot to the number of pigs it raised: in addition to 0.11 mu per person, a household was allowed 0.2 mu for each pig. A family of five members and one pig, for instance, was officially allowed

0.75 mu as its private plot. If the family sold the pig to the state, it would be allowed to buy 140 catties of barley from its team as the fodder it had spent on the pig. However, the government strictly prohibited a household to raise more than two pigs or a sow to give birth to piglets for profits because that would lead to a "spontaneous capitalist tendency" (*zifa de zibenzhuyi qingxiang*) in the countryside and the pigs would compete with human beings for food. Likewise, the government also limited the number of domestic fowl, including chicken, ducks, and geese, to 30 per household for the same reasons. These regulations were largely effective in Qin village. The villagers seldom raised pigs and poultry more than the official limits because they did not have much fodder to feed the animals. Thus, although the government allowed each household to raise up to two pigs, 47 out of the 50 households in the No. 11 team raised only one, and the remaining three households raised no pigs at all. And most households raised only a few or up to 10 chickens (QD1 2000).

The activities of the "five kinds of craftsmen" (*wujiang*), including carpenters, bricklayers, lacquerers, coppersmiths, blacksmiths, and the like, were also subject to the government's regulation. The No. 11 team had two carpenters, a coppersmith, a bamboo product maker, and six fishermen. As a universal policy in the county, the team required those people to work for the team for a minimum of days. When a craftsman was away from the team to make money in his trade, he had to pay the team one yuan in cash for every 10 workpoints so that he could join other team members to receive grain rations from the team because the grain from the black market was more expensive than the grain rations and at times unavailable at all. The actual value of a workpoint in the early 1970s was about 0.04 to 0.06 yuan. To charge the craftsmen at one yuan per 10 points was a way to discourage them from leaving the team. Two of the fishermen, who were entirely absent from collective production on the excuse of being crippled or having a chronic disease, had to pay 350 yuan and 450 yuan to buy 3,300 and 3,800 points, respectively, from the team (QD4 1974). Nevertheless, the craftsmen and the fishermen accepted the terms because they could earn two or three yuan a day when working in their own trade, whereas a first-rate male farmer earned only about 10 to 20 points or 0.50 to one yuan a day.

To stabilize its labor force, the team enforced a countywide policy that prohibited young men under 19 to apprentice with any kind of craftsmen in the early 1970s and threatened to punish violators by discontinuing their grain rations and straw supply and taking back the private plots. Once a man was over 20, he would find it increasingly costly to be an apprentice because he was already a full laborer and had to earn workpoints to support his family, whereas being an apprentice for years received no compensation from his master at all. Therefore, few team members had the opportunity to engage in off-farm activities at that time. Later, the leader of the No. 11 team himself violated the policy, allowing his eldest son to apprentice with a carpenter, and therefore was ridiculed by team members as a person with a "long arm" who grabbed too much for his own family. In general, however, villagers who engaged in full-time noncollective activities were few; the government was quite successful in curbing the "capitalist tails" and maintaining the dominance of the collective economy in the countryside until its dissolution in the early 1980s.

Reaching the Households

In addition to family sidelines, domestic matters of individual households were also open to the government's intervention. In the early 1970s, for instance, commune leaders required all households to rebuild their kitchen stoves according to a style it recommended. The new style had a smaller burning area and a shorter distance between the wok and the bottom of the stove than a traditional one and arguably met the requirements of "three tens," namely, to boil 10 catties of water in 10 minutes with 10 *liang* or one catty of straw. Promoting the "straw-saving stove" was supposedly necessary because there was an increasing shortage of cooking straw in the 1970s when local population increased steadily while the supply of straw decreased owing to the reclamation of marshland. Therefore, each production team had to send a member to the commune's seat to learn how to build the new-style stove and then to teach his fellow team members the new method. As a result, all the households in Qin village rebuilt their stoves. The new-style stove indeed saved straw. However, many people complained that it did not save their time. With the traditional stove, a villager could put a big bunch of straw into the burning space and then walk away for a short while doing something else. When using the new stove, however, he or she had to sit with it and keep adding additional straw. Therefore, when the campaign of promoting the straw-saving stove was over, most households restored their stoves to the traditional style.

Another example had to do with raising chickens. Traditionally, a household set free its chickens in the early morning and called them back in the evening, locking them in a tiny brick-made coop and thus guarding them against yellow weasels. In 1971 and 1972, the government promoted the new method of raising chickens in an enclosure for three official reasons: to prevent the chickens from eating crops, to keep one's house and yard clean, and to protect the chickens from being killed by predators. To promote the new method, the commune gathered all team cadres to a model brigade, where all households had confined their chickens. At the commune leader's instruction, the No. 11 team in Qin village assigned a few strong laborers to pull out the fence from each household's vegetable garden, so that the household had to confine its chickens or the vegetables would be ruined by the pecking of the chickens. This way, the new method was enforced universally in the village almost overnight. However, many villagers soon complained that they had to spend a lot of grain feeding the confined chickens, and the chickens were less healthy and laid fewer eggs than before. Therefore, when the drive was over, most households again set free their chickens and rebuilt their garden fences. Nevertheless, some families who wanted to keep their house and surroundings clean did voluntarily accept the new method and confined their chickens for good.

Although the state's attempt to intervene with the domestic life of individual households rarely succeeded, the villagers would unanimously and voluntarily accept an imposed measure when it met their needs. A case in point is the construction of earthquake shelters in 1976. On August 19, at about 10:00 a.m., a broadcast by the county government shocked all villagers: an earthquake would take place within the next two or three days! The government required all urban and rural residents to build simple shelters in open places at least 20 meters away from water and to sleep only in the shelters at night. In response, the Zhigang Brigade instructed its production teams to stop farming activities and to let each household build a shelter in the afternoon. By the evening, most families had finished setting up a shelter with a simple stove attached to it. To make sure that an earthquake alarm could reach every villager in case the wired broadcasting network failed to work, a number of villagers stood guard at night at a distance of about 100 meters from each other along the routes from the brigade headquarters to individual villages and hamlets. The cadres visited each household to see that all villagers slept in the shelter. In the evening of August 23, a broadcast alerted the villagers that an earthquake and a subsequent tsunami were predicted to happen that night, and nobody was allowed to stay in the house or the shelter. However, nothing happened that night. In the following few months, the villagers were still on high alert of a possible earthquake and were afraid of entering their houses. They remained on the alert and slept in the shelters until mid-1977, when the alarm was removed (QD1 2000).

Regulating Team Cadres

Fighting Economic Corruption

Unlike many brigade leaders who bore the brunt of Red Guards' attacks and lost their jobs or power during the first three years of the Cultural Revolution, most production team cadres in Qin village, and in the rest of the country, kept their positions. Nevertheless, the team cadres found themselves in a situation more difficult than before when a new campaign, called "Struggle, Criticism, and Correction" (*dou pi gai*) swept both the cities and the countryside, whereby Mao intended to terminate the three-year nationwide political turmoil and to "consolidate the achievements" of the Cultural Revolution (WG3 1969). In the spring of 1970, that campaign further evolved into the so-called "One Attack and Three Antis" (*yida sanfan*), namely, attacking "sabotage activities by counter-revolutionaries," and opposing "graft and theft," "speculation and profiteering," and "extravagance and waste" (GNW 1981b: 882–885).

In both campaigns, all team cadres, including team leaders, accountants, and storehouse-keepers, had to attend the endless "study sessions" (*xuexi ban*) held at the brigade office and the recurrent meetings at the commune seat. During the study sessions, which lasted about half a month each time and repeated three or four times a winter, the cadres normally first studied the latest documents and policies issued by the Party, and then conducted a self-examination, in which each of them confessed his political and economic problems, such as whether he had mistreated poor and lower-middle peasants, whether he had shown favor to friends and relatives in workpoint recording and income distribution, whether he had been derelict in supervising "class enemies" and "bad elements," or whether he had embezzled the team's funds and grain or recorded excessive workpoints for himself or his family members. Finally, all attendants of the study session had to participate in "mutual criticism," to accuse each other of any problems that they knew by posting a "big-character poster" (*dazibao*) on the wall of the brigade's buildings. The more *dazibao* one wrote, the more active and sincere he was thought to be in reforming himself and helping his comrades. Everyone came under strong pressure to reveal the problems of his colleagues in the same team or brigade. Obviously, the methods that the state used in curbing the abuses of grassroots cadres in the early 1970s were a combination of the methods that had been used in the Socialist Education movement in the early 1960s and those that had been widely adopted during the height of the Cultural Revolution.

These methods turned out to be quite effective. By April 1972, when the campaign came to an end, 895 cadres in the commune were found to have economic problems; they had embezzled a total of 98,920 yuan in cash, 55,865 catties of grain, and 4,665 feet of cloth coupons, and, as a solution to their problems, repaid their respective teams a total of 74,480 yuan in cash, 41,326 catties of grain, and 1,995 feet of cloth coupons (*Qindong gongshe shezhi* 1981: 38). Many wrongdoings by the cadres in Qin village were thus exposed. One of such misconducts had to do with the brigade cadres' "illegal division" (*sifen*) of collective funds that had occurred as far back as 1958 and 1959. In those years, the cadres frequently sold the brigade's marsh reeds for money to cover their expenses for attending meetings at the commune or county seats or to share among themselves as subsidies. Everyone involved had strictly kept the secret in the next 10 years. However, during the *dou-pi-gai* campaign, the pressure of mutual criticism was so intense that a former brigade cadre eventually confessed it. As a resolution, all cadres involved had to repay the brigade a sum of money varying from about 20 or 30 yuan to as much as about 400 yuan.[2]

Duiweihui

Another device to limit the team cadres' power and curb their possible abuses was the "production-team management committee" (*shengchan-dui guanli weiyuan hui,* or *duiweihui* for short), which was created nationwide in the early 1960s, when production teams became the basic accounting unit, and remained in force during the rest of the collective era (GNW 1981b: 461–463). In Qin village, the *duiweihui* of the No. 11 team consisted of six or seven members, including several team cadres and several representatives of ordinary team members from different descent groups. In the 1970s, for example, the team's three representatives in the *duiweihui* were a Chen, a Zhang, and a Jiang, all in their fifties.

Jiang was also a Party member since the land reform in the early 1950s and therefore was particularly respected by both team cadres and ordinary members. Unlike the *minzhu licai* members who had to be literate, these representatives were all illiterate, but all enjoyed a good reputation among team members for their frank opinions and inclination to complain at team members' meetings.

The team leader convened a *duiweihui* meeting whenever the team encountered an important matter and he alone was unable to made a decision or unwilling to shoulder the responsibility for the decision. The matters they discussed typically included how to revise the methods and criteria for labor remuneration, how much of the team's marshland should be reclaimed, which part of the team's farmland should be used to grow a specific type of crop, what kind of farming tools the team should buy, which households were qualified as "households-in-difficulty" to receive the team's subsidy at the year-end distribution and how much the subsidy should be, and so forth. Therefore, the *duiweihui* members met irregularly, depending on the occurrence of such matters. They could meet as frequently as twice a week or as rarely as once a month.

When discussing those matters, all *duiweihui* members appeared to be just and concerned primarily with the interests of the collective. Although the team cadres and representatives came from different descent groups and might have ill feelings toward each other, they normally did not support or oppose a proposal simply because of their personal relationship. Therefore, it was not difficult for them to reach a consensus and make a decision quickly over the matter being discussed. However, there were also prolonged discussions over issues when they disagreed with each other. A good example is about the team's sale of oxen in 1974. To have enough money to buy a tractor for plowing and raking, at a *duiweihui* meeting in the early spring, the team leader proposed selling the team's two oxen. However, both Zhang and Jiang openly opposed that idea at the meeting, saying that oxen had been indispensable for farming since the ancient time while using a tractor would cost the team a lot of money for diesel oil and maintenance. In fact, they disagreed with the leader also because it had been rumored among team members that the leader wanted to sell the team's two oxen in order to share the commission in secret with ox brokers who had frequently visited the team to lure the cadres into a deal with potential buyers from outside; for each transaction, the broker would draw a commission of 20 yuan. The team thus gave up the idea until the following year when many other teams in the brigade had already bought a tractor, which turned out to be much more efficient than using an ox. The *duiweihui* thus played an important role in a production team's decision-making process and effectively checked the team leader's potential abuse of power; this was especially likely where the *duiweihui* members, including both team cadres and team member representatives, came from different descent groups and did not readily concur with the team leader over the issues they discussed.

Curbing Cadre Privileges

The grassroots cadres had a hard time during the Cultural Revolution not only because they had to deal with possible accusations of economic problems but also because they had fewer privileges than before. Since the early days of collectivization, the rural cadres had enjoyed two major privileges: partial exemption from doing manual work and receiving workpoint subsidies. In the early 1960s, the state allowed brigade and team cadres to receive annual subsidies in workpoints up to 2 percent of the brigade's total workpoints in a given year, and allowed team cadres to receive annual subsidies up to 1 percent of the team's total workpoints (GNW 1981a: 465, 488, 551). Realizing that most rural cadres rarely joined the labor force, the state required commune and brigade cadres to attend collective manual work for at least 60 and 120 days a year, respectively. Team cadres were expected to routinely participate in production, and their workpoints should be assessed and recorded the same way as other team members (GNW 1981a: 646). This participation, according to the state's explanation, would not only lessen the peasants' burden in supporting the cadres, but also allow the cadres to establish "the most wide-ranging, most frequent, and closest contact with the laboring people" and prevent them from degenerating into "old-style masters riding roughshod over the people" (GNW 1981a: 712, 873).

The actual performance of the grassroots cadres, however, was disappointing in general. Deng Zihui, head of the CCP central committee's Department of Rural Work, found in several localities he had investigated in 1962 that the subsidies in those places often accounted for as much as 14 percent of the brigades' total workpoints. Some brigade leaders subsidized themselves with as many as 600 workdays. Villagers treated such cadres as the *baozhang* before Liberation, complaining that nowadays they had to provide for many *baozhang* while in the old days they had supported only one (GNW 1981a: 579, 584).

The team cadres in Qin village seemed to conform to state regulations on workpoint subsidies. In 1960, for example, the Suqin Brigade allowed a total of 11,829 points as subsidies to the cadres of its five production teams, or 0.82 percent of the brigade's total workpoints in that year (QD4 1960: 30). In 1963 and 1964, the cadres of the No. 8 team were subsidized a total of 2,800 and 2,200 points, respectively, which accounted for 0.81 and 0.84 percent of the team's total points, well within the 1 percent limit allowed by the state (DT28 1964). Nevertheless, the team cadres had other ways to record unearned points to themselves or those whom they favored. A survey compiled in 1961 by the brigade's general accountant classified the team cadres' misdeeds in workpoint recording into several types, such as "embezzling workpoints" or increasing their own points by tampering the accounts; adding workpoints "by mistake" to their own accounts when recording; showing favoritism to certain team members by awarding them excessive points; and increasing the rate when giving workpoints to themselves (QD4 1961).

During the first three years of the Cultural Revolution (1966–1969), when the Dazhai workpoint system prevailed and "workpoint in command" (*gongfen guashuai*) was condemned, the brigade and team cadres in Qin village totally lost the privilege of receiving workpoint subsidies. At the same time, they came under unprecedented pressure to participate in farm work during the campaign of "Learning from Dazhai in Agriculture" when the government warned against rural cadres' "three divorces" (*san tuoli*): divorcing oneself from the masses, the reality, and manual work.[3] As a result, the team cadres, including the leader and the accountant, had to join the team members from time to time, doing some light tasks, such as drying the grain or straw in the sun or weeding the field with a hoe. However, they rarely did strenuous jobs, such as transporting household manure, removing crop bundles, or digging drains.

The cadres refused to do manual work for their own reasons. The team leader normally spent his days traveling between different worksites to supervise the team members. He was also responsible for assigning tasks to different groups of laborers early in the morning and again after lunch, and recording workpoints in the evening. The accountant took care of the team's many accounts, traveling to different fields to lay lines for digging drains and measuring the size of a mud mound to determine the workpoints for those who had dredged up or removed the mud. Quite often the team cadres had to attend various meetings at the brigade, commune, or county level and visited a model production team or brigade. In other words, the team cadres failed to do farm work frequently because they had no time to do so. However, because supervising team members and managing team accounts were much less strenuous than doing manual work, the leader and accountant could not give themselves workpoints higher than those for top-grade farmers; whereas the latter normally earned 10 or more points a day, they could only receive 7, 8, or 9 points a day. Because they had no workpoint subsidies during the first three years under the Dazhai system, the grassroots cadres earned only about 3,000 points or less a year, while a strong male normally could earn more than 3,500 points. It was no wonder that many cadres openly complained at brigade or commune meetings that "being a cadre is meant to lose" (*dang ganbu chikui*) (WG3 1969).

In the early 1970s, when the Dazhai system was abolished, the team cadres once again were allowed workpoint subsidies from their own team, to augment the total amount of their annual workpoints to a level equal to that of first-rate male laborers, but the total number of their subsidies could not exceed the traditional 1 percent limit. To push the team leaders' interest in improving team production, the brigade linked the amount of subsidies with the team's overall performance. The brigade would cancel or lower the subsidies for team cadres if they failed to increase the team's output, such as the case of the No. 11 team in 1976 and 1977, when its total output and per capita income plunged to their lowest levels in the 1970s. Consequently, not only did the leader lose his job, but the subsidies for the team cadres were also reduced to only 0.45 and 0.48 percent of the team's total workpoints, respectively, in those two years (QD5 1976; QD5 1977). Later in 1979, however, the team beat out all other teams in the commune in cotton sales, thus bringing its members' per capita income to 140 yuan, which more than doubled their income in the previous years. As a result, the team leader received a subsidy of 2,670 points, which increased his total workpoints to a whopping 6,050, a record number in the history of the team. The team accountant also received a subsidy of 2,500 points, augmenting his total points to 5,800 (QD5 1979). Both of them earned far more than any other male laborers in the team did. By that time, to be sure, the Cultural Revolution had been over for three years. Production teams throughout the countryside had greater autonomy in planning their economic activities and controlling their products. The team cadres no longer participated in team production. The gap of workpoints between laborers of different grades and between cadres and ordinary members widened, owing to the wide application of the piece-rate system and the use of workpoints as the only incentive to maximize land yield. What the Cultural Revolution had attempted to achieve was largely undone.

Everyday Power Relations

Cadre-Villager Relations

In the opinion of a former brigade leader in Qin village, the team members in his brigade fell largely into three types in terms of their relationship with the cadres. The first was what the villagers called the "slippery fellows" (*huatou*) or troublemakers, who made up about one-tenth of the male members in a team; they tended to argue with the cadres, bargain for more workpoints, or stage a strike after the bargain failed. They did not hesitate to complain when they felt that the team leader was unfair in assigning tasks or recording workpoints or when they found that the leader had done something to favor certain people at the expense of others. The second were the honest and diligent members, who were respectful and obedient to the cadres. Again, these people were the minority in a team. Most team members were between the two types. They often joined the troublemakers demanding more workpoints but they rarely took the lead in disputing with the cadres. Without the "slippery fellows" to start trouble, they could be as submissive as people of the second type. How to deal with the troublemakers, therefore, was the most difficult task for the grassroots cadres in managing a team.

When asked why these few villagers were contentious with the cadres, the informant offered a couple of reasons. One had to do with their personalities. Some of them were known for their outspokenness; they argued with the cadres to show their ability and toughness, to enhance their standing in the team, and to safeguard themselves against possible discrimination by the cadres. A second reason had to do with their personal resentment against certain cadres; to argue with the cadres was a way to vent their anger. They could be resentful when the cadres deducted their workpoints for their poor job or asked them to repeat their work for the desired points, or when the cadres criticized them for their misdeeds. As a third reason, some villagers had difficulties in supporting their families that had many dependents but few workers. They often felt frustrated at home when their wives complained to them of, say, wasting money on cigarettes. Therefore, they could easily harbor resentment toward the cadres when they failed to obtain financial aid from the team or received a reduced number of workpoints because of poor performance. A member of team No. 11 once secretly moved more than 20 bundles of rice crop from a boat to his private plot when he was shipping the team's crop from a field to the threshing ground. The same night, however, a witness reported it to the team leader. When the leader visited his home and found the crop that he had stolen, the man asked the cadre to forgive his first-time offense. The team leader agreed but insisted that the team member had to send the stolen crop to the threshing ground, but the latter refused. The leader thus had to take away the crop on his own. Since that episode, the member was deeply resentful of the team leader and several times complained to a visiting brigade or commune cadre of the team leader's nonparticipation in manual work, unfamiliarity with farming skills, or incompetence as a team leader.

Depending on their personalities and personal relations with the troublemakers, the team cadres treated them differently. Some cadres were sensitive to the team members' attitudes and avoided arguing with the unhappy villagers; they thus often yielded to the troublemakers' demands, which only encouraged those team members to become even more "troublesome." Some cadres had been treated well by the "slippery fellows," and therefore were unwilling to be too strict with them when recording workpoints or distributing grain. There were also some cadres who tended to be tough on the troublesome individuals when they wanted to build a good reputation or improve the team's overall performance in order to get a promotion. Conflicts were unavoidable between such cadres and the "unruly" team members. In the spring of 1975, for example, a certain member of team No. 11 started a quarrel with a cadre, which evolved into a fist fight, causing the brigade's involvement and organizing a team meeting, in which the man made a formal apology to the cadre.

Unlike the troublemakers, most team members appeared to be cooperative, if not submissive, to their cadres. They routinely accepted the team leader's assignments and workpoints, and they rarely "bothered" (*darao*) the cadres unless they learned that their workpoints were missing from the publicized monthly report. There were also a few among them who wanted to win the cadres' particular favor by pleasing them in every possible way. A case in point here is the two fishermen of the No. 11 team, who wanted to be completely exempt from team production and yet to share in the team's distribution of grain rations. Toward that end, they never failed to give fish to each team cadre at every festival. Whenever a cadre wanted to buy their fish, they would charge him a nominal fee or simply gave him the fish for free. Nevertheless, people like these fishermen were exceptions in the production team. The majority of the team members felt no need to please or to quarrel with the team cadres when the latter assigned them routine tasks and recorded them the expected workpoints.

This is not to say, however, that ordinary villagers had no social interactions with the cadres. Whenever a family had a wedding feast, for example, the host would invariably invite the team cadres to join the guests. For the host, the cadres' attendance made the event more formal and important. The cadres who were present at the banquet also felt obligated to give the bride a "red envelope" (*hongbao*) of one yuan or a bit less, just like the other guests, to show their generosity and goodwill. When parents were "dividing the household" (*fenjia*) with their married son, the cadres were also indispensable; they acted as voluntary mediators and even arbitrators when the parties involved disputed over the division of properties. Although their opinions on such matters were not mandatory, they were well respected by the villagers, especially if the cadres had a good reputation among them. During normal times, the team members frequently turned to the cadres for a letter of introduction to travel somewhere or an application for relief funds or changing a bride's *hukou* (household registration and residence status) after marriage. And the cadres routinely and dutifully helped them without expecting a gift or other kind of reward from the team members.

Thus, although there were some members in a production team who needed the cadres' special favor and therefore maintained special relations with them, and although there were also a few who were hostile to the cadres, neither group made up the majority in a production team. Most team members were neither the cadres' "clients" under their favoritism nor "nonclients" suffering their discriminations. Nor should the few resentful members be equated with victims of the team cadres' possible abuse of power. The reverse could be true under certain circumstances. Instead of being victimized, the "slippery fellows" were the most active in demanding high workpoints and criticizing the cadres; it was difficult, if not at all impossible, for the cadres to covertly or openly discriminate against them. By and large, the relationship between ordinary team members and grassroots cadres under the collective system, as seen in Qin village, was much more equal than the "patron-client" model suggests in explaining power relations in collective-era China (Oi 1989).

Kinship Ties

Qin village comprised many descent groups. Among the 48 households of the No. 11 team in 1974, for example, there were eleven Jiangs, ten Zhangs, seven Chens, five Lis, four Pus, two Huangs, two Mengs, two Waangs, one Fang, one He, one Pan, one Wang, and one Yuan (QD3 2003). This mixture of different surnames in a single community reflected the environmental instability in the history of the Lixiahe region, where the repeated flooding uprooted many dwellers, who had to move in or out of the village for a better chance of survival before the Communist Revolution. It was no wonder that none of the Qins, after which the village was named, still resided in the community in the twentieth century. The same was true of the neighboring Su village, where there were no Su families at all. Most of the descent groups in the community had a recent history. The Huangs and the Chens, for example, moved into the village as late as the 1940s. Understandably, none of the descent groups had an ancestral temple or kept a record of clan genealogy. The weakness of lineage ties in Qin village and much of the rest of the Lixiahe region contrasts sharply with the elaborate and strong clan organizations in some areas in southern and southeastern China, where many villages are large communities of a single descent group comprising dozens or hundreds of households, who were often involved in armed conflicts between different clans (Gao 1999). Qin villagers never saw or heard of such feuds.

This is not to say, however, that lineage ties were unimportant to Qin villagers. Kinship mattered a great deal in their economic and social lives. All of the Jiang families in the No. 11 team, for example, had the tradition of fishing. The heads of two of them were full-time fishermen; all other families worked for the team in the daytime and went fishing in their spare time. In the late 1960s and early 1970s, when most of the Jiangs counted on fishing as the major source of their cash income, they did not work as hard as team members of other descent groups to earn workpoints; they only wanted to earn enough points to

compensate for the grain rations they received from the team. Therefore, the Jiangs rarely disputed with team cadres over workpoint
rates or other matters. In general, they appeared to be honest and
well-behaved in the eyes of the cadres. The Zhangs were another large
descent group in the team. Because the team leader was a Zhang, all
team members from this group tended to cooperate with his leadership, although most of the males were either too old or too young in the
late 1960s to dominate the team's labor force. The Lis were the exceptions. The heads of the five Li households were the team's accountant,
machine operators, an irrigation caretaker, and an old-age widower
who received collective welfare benefits. None of them actually did
farm work for the team. The male full laborers of the team were dominated by adults from the Chen families. Because none of them served
as the team's cadres, the Chens always felt underrepresented in the
team and appeared defensive and resentful in dealing with the cadres. Their indispensability to the team's labor force also made some of
them the toughest "slippery fellows." One of the Chens, who served
as a member of the team's "democratic finance management group,"
turned out to be the most active and contentious in checking accounts. To pacify the Chens and make them less resentful, the team
cadres selected a young man from a Chen family as the team's vice
leader in 1974.

Families of the same descent group always gathered together when
a life event occurred to a group member, such as a betrothal, a wedding, a birth, or a funeral, as local customs required. They also supported each other when any of them had an important family event
that needed help, such as the building of a house or working together
for a joint business. A case in point was the Zhangs' cooperation in
running a ferryboat. There is a major waterway in the north of the village, and each day many people crossed the river from either side. In
the early 1950s, six Zhang families pooled their money to buy a boat,
and every two days they took turns ferrying passengers, charging two
cents per person in the 1950s and three cents in the 1960s and 1970s.
The business was especially profitable during the few days around
April 10 each year when there was an annual fair in a neighboring
town and thousands of villagers crossed the river for the event. In
those days, all of the six families worked together, using two boats to
ferry people. It is interesting to note that the Zhangs treated fellow villagers and outsiders differently. To ask a traveler of the same team or
the same village for a fee of a few cents was embarrassing. As a solu-

tion, they always ferried fellow villagers free of charge and instead received an annual lump-sum payment by the individual production teams of the village. The fees were applied only to travelers outside the village. The business came to an end when a bridge was built on the river in 2002.

All in all, the importance of lineage ties in the village should not be overestimated. Because families of different descent groups resided together, most villagers found their neighbors to be people of different surnames. Their relations with the neighbors were in fact no less important than with their kin in everyday life.[4] A Chinese saying best describes this kind of relationship: "a neighbor close by is no less helpful than a relative far off" (*yuanqin buru jinlin*). On the other hand, families of the same descent group, while often working together for a shared purpose, could also have conflicts of interest with each other. The fiercest quarrels in the village often broke out between two families of the same descent group over their respective duties and rights in a common undertaking.

Conclusion

The state had two goals that often conflicted with each other in governing the rural society throughout the socialist period, especially the 1970s: to reverse the radical policies that had dampened the morale of both team members and team cadres in collective production, and at the same time to fight any economic and ideological deviations that would undermine the collective economy and lead to the revival of capitalism in the countryside. The state had no difficulties in achieving the first goal by ending mass agitation and the worship of Mao while reviving many economic policies that had prevailed before the Cultural Revolution. Doing so, however, often ran counter to the second goal that had concerned Mao more than anything else. The reintroduction of the piece-rate system in labor remuneration, for example, would cultivate the villagers' concern with self-interests and presumably cause an increasing gap in income distribution between strong and weak laborers. The revival of workpoint subsidies for cadres and the reduced pressure for them to participate in farm work would further separate the privileged cadres from the laboring masses. The overall relaxation of the political atmosphere would once again open loopholes for grassroots cadres to engage in malfeasance and lead to the growth of autonomy in local collectives, evidenced in the enlargement of private plots and increasing noncollective economic activities, which would compete with the collective for manpower and other resources and lead to the "spontaneous capitalist tendency."

The state, therefore, worked hard to instill the villagers with socialist ideologies, to cut the "capitalist tails" in the countryside, and to discipline the cadres with study sessions in which they had to repeatedly confess their mistakes and expose each other's wrongdoings. These measures, as seen in Qin village, were not totally ineffective. Throughout the 1970s, the collective system successfully dominated the local economy. Family sidelines and other noncollective elements were largely limited to a scope allowed by the government. Thanks to the many years of political campaigns and propaganda, all cadres and almost all team members had a strong awareness of political correctness; they all knew well what they could say and do in public and what they could not. What the state failed to solve in controlling the rural society, however, was a contradiction inherent to the collective economy: the limited income from the collective that provided only a bare subsistence, the income distribution policy that increasingly linked one's labor input with reward, and the wide existence of noncollective economies, all caused the villagers, including both cadres and ordinary team members, to seek opportunities enriching themselves at the cost of the collective and despite the socialist ideology. Not surprisingly, many measures and policies that the state made in educating the villagers, disciplining the cadres, and curbing nonsocialist elements were only perfunctorily carried out and, therefore, short-lived once the pressure from above lessened or disappeared. The villagers' traditional commitment to family interests and old types of social relations, especially kinship, continued to dictate their everyday social and economic behavior.

This dilemma, it should be noted, was not limited to the years following the height of the Cultural Revolution; it was in fact a problem that constantly challenged the state throughout the collective period. To safeguard the socialist system in the countryside, the state always strived to penetrate the village society as deep as it could by indoctrinating the villagers with its ideology and tightening its control of the collective organization, which time and again led to the introduction of radical policies as seen during the "high tide" of collectivization, the Great Leap Forward, and the Dazhai system in the Cultural Revolution. On the other hand, however, the policy makers of the Party had to provide the villagers with necessary material incentives, in the form of private plots, piece rates in labor remuneration, and a degree of autonomy of the production team in economic planning, to maintain the productivity of the collective economy and the subsistence of the rural population, which would inevitably lead to the "restoration of capitalism" as Mao repeatedly warned. The dilemma did not find a final solution until Deng Xiaoping decided to abolish the collective system and revive the traditional family farming in the early 1980s.

It was in this inextricable dilemma of the socialist economy that the relationship between the socialist state and villagers evolved; we cannot appropriately understand that relationship unless we put it in this historical context. Past studies on state-society relations in contemporary China have either assumed the decisive role of the newly created political structure and economic system after 1949 in shaping the political behaviors of the elites as well as the masses (Schurmann 1968; Harding 1981; Lieberthal and Oksenberg 1988) or emphasized the influence of traditional Chinese culture and preexisting social practices in the formation of new political ecology after the Communist Revolution (Pye 1968, 1988; Solomon 1971; Nathan 1985). Along the two contrasting lines of thinking, researchers of rural China have either proposed the cellularization of the peasant society under the Party-state that purportedly turned the cadres of the agricultural collectives into its agents and peasants into victims vulnerable to state penetration and cadre abuse (Siu 1989; Kelliher 1992; Zhou 1996) or argued for the continuation of the traditional social norms and interpersonal ties in shaping the relationship between the cadres and the masses that functioned for the good of rural elites and those under their protection at the cost of the state (Madsen 1984; Shue 1988; Oi 1989).

Both explanations are partly true but fail to appreciate the full complexity of the changing state-peasant relations from a dynamic perspective. Overall, the collective era witnessed the unprecedented penetration of the state into the rural society, as evidenced in its abilities to shape the everyday economic and social lives of peasant families through the collective organizations and various means of mass mobilization. During the turbulent years of the initial introduction of grain procurement, the transition to advanced cooperatives, the "three winds" of the Great Leap Forward, and the implementation of the egalitarian systems in the Cultural Revolution, the rural cadres did indeed behave as agents of the state, carrying out its unpopular policies at the expense of the interests of fellow villagers and local communities. However, the state found it neither possible nor necessary to incorporate the millions of the grassroots cadres into its formal bureaucracy and thereby extend its administrative arm directly to each household. By devolving the basic accounting unit to the production team of approximately 30 households of the same village or neighborhood, where the traditional kinship ties and the norms of interpersonal relations still predominated, the state not only allowed the team cadres, who were chosen from among the villagers, a degree of autonomy in managing the collective economy but also acknowledged the legitimacy of existing community ties as an integral part of the basis of the collective organization. Therefore, the traditional social norms and networks continued to regulate the interpersonal relations within the team, which at once lubricated the everyday operation of the collective system and opened the loopholes for the cadres' abuse of power for self-aggrandizement and nepotism.

Nevertheless, with the economic system and social structure completely transformed after 1949, and with the tremendous pressure from both above and below during the recurrent campaigns against cadre corruption, the grassroots leaders could never be as powerful and abusive as the former landlords and local bullies in dictating the lives of ordinary villagers, nor were the team members as dependent on the cadres as the landless or land-poor on the landed elites before the Communist Revolution. To liken the cadres to the gentry elites of the imperial times or to assume the universality of patron-client ties as the dominant pattern of cadre-peasant relations, therefore, oversimplifies the social realities in rural China under the collective system.

PART THREE

Individuals, the Family, and the Collective

CHAPTER 8

Everyday Strategies for Team Farming

THE INTRODUCTION of a household-based farming system in place of team production in rural China in the early 1980s has caused scholars to enquire into the reasons behind the "failure" of collective agriculture. Most explanations have focused on the problem of work incentives under the collective. Some authors have attributed that problem to factors extrinsic to the collective system and therefore emphasized the detrimental effects of the state's egalitarian policies, especially its preference for time rates over piece rates in labor payments and its policy that grain should be distributed to villagers mainly according to need rather than effort. Had the state allowed the collectives a degree of autonomy in labor management, it is suggested, the collectives would have been able to achieve greater efficiency by using proper incentives (e.g., Putterman 1987, 1988; Kung 1994). Other scholars have highlighted problems characteristic of collective agriculture per se, especially the difficulty of monitoring each person's labor. Poor work quality and inefficiency, viewed in this light, were more of a problem inherent to collective farming, rather than a result of externally imposed policies (e.g., Nolan 1983; Lin 1988, 1990, 1999). Both interpretations assume that shirking was a common strategy in collective production because of a poor connection between effort and reward; both perceive Chinese peasants as self-interested, rational actors, sensitive to material incentives and able to adjust their labor input under different remuneration systems.

What is obscure in both views, however, is the social and historical context in which the villagers pursued private and collective goals. When involved in everyday farming activities, they considered not only the imposed, formal economic policies but also informal institutions embedded in the village communities, such as customary practices, kinship ties, power relations, gender roles, community norms, and various forms of social sanctions. The collective, in other words, was not merely an economic organization operating under state policies but more importantly a community where a set of implicit rules and social relations informed the villagers' everyday thinking and practice. My central concern in this chapter, therefore, is how the imposed systems interacted with indigenous institutions to create workday norms that shaped the peasants' perceptions and strategies for team farming. The aim is to look into the day-to-day functioning of the norms—the implicit and explicit rules of expected behavior—in order better to comprehend the issue of work incentives and efficiency.

A common practice under the collective system was to classify team members into different labor grades according to their sex, age, physical strength and working skills, and credit their effort according to work hours (hence the so-called time rates) or the quantity they finished (piece rates). In addition, during the radical years of the Cultural Revolution, the Dazhai-style workpoint system (named after a model village in North China) prevailed in much of the countryside instead of both time rates and piece rates. This system based a team member's daily "basic workpoint" on his or her self-evaluation of the work effort, followed by fellow members' public appraisal, which took into account not only the person's actual working abilities but also his or her political attitude. The team then awarded workpoints to each member according to his or her basic workpoint evaluation and the number of days he or she had worked (see Chapter 6).[1]

The following sections will begin with a discussion of the differences between the time-rate and piece-rate systems as they were practiced in Qin village in the mid- and late 1970s, focusing on the reasons for using each, their respective effects on villagers' performance, and the critical role of team leaders in labor management. I will then discuss the villagers' strategies under these two systems. Attention will also be paid to the performance of male and female workers in team farming.[2]

Labor Management Under the Workpoint System

Piece Rates Versus Time Rates

In the summer of 1978, after a long-lasting drought, bollworms ran rampant in the cotton fields of the No. 11 team. The repeated use of pesticides was fruitless: the bolls had grown big enough for the worms to hide inside, protected from poisons. Cotton was the major cash crop in this area. Almost one-third of the team's gross income came from cotton sales, and that portion of income was equivalent to the year-end cash payment to team members. Thus a failure of the cotton crop would drastically reduce the families' cash income from the team; many households would receive no money at all, regardless of their year-round work for the collective.

To save the cotton, the villagers needed to catch the worms by hand. To do so, each person used a chopstick, with one end split and sharpened, to get each of the worms out of the boll and drop it into a bottle of salty water. This job could be done only in the morning because it was too hot in the afternoon to stay for hours in the cotton field. The team leader asked all the women and children of the team, totaling more than 60 people, to join in the task. As compensation, each adult woman received five workpoints, adolescents between the ages of 16 and 18 received four points, and those under age 15 earned three points. In other words, the reward was the same for people of the same labor grade, no matter how many worms they actually caught. The leader did not base their workpoints on the actual number of worms they caught because there were too many for him to count. On the first day, however, the leader found that the number of worms caught varied greatly. Some adults killed fewer than a hundred worms, while some teenage girls skewered as many as 500 worms yet received fewer workpoints than the adults. The pests would be out of control if the work continued at this pace.

He announced a new policy the following morning before the work started: everyone would earn one workpoint for every 100 worms, regardless of his or her labor grade and the daunting task of counting. When the work ended at noon, the leader was surprised by the result: almost everyone came up with a full bottle of worms. To count the worms, he invited all the team cadres, including the deputy head, the accountant, the granary manager, and several group leaders to join him. Most workers had caught between 600 and 700 worms.

The third day, to facilitate his counting, the leader asked all the workers to count the worms themselves by putting every 30 worms into a pile so that he only needed to count the piles. However, he soon found by random checks that only a few people were honest enough to put the full 30 worms into each pile. To prevent this kind of cheating, he asked them to arrange their piles again, warning that if anyone was found to have put less than the required number into a pile, all the other piles of the person would be treated as that pile. This policy turned out to be effective. Piles with fewer worms became rare thereafter, and the task proceeded smoothly. In two weeks, the bollworms were basically eliminated.

As seen above, the villagers' performance varied significantly under different methods of labor remuneration. Under time rates, people had no interest in increasing their catch but only focused on how many hours they stayed in the cotton field. In sharp contrast, the piece-rate system offered them a strong incentive to maximize their catch because this was directly linked to the workpoints they would receive.

However, the piece-rate system could not be applied to all tasks. Normally, using piece rates effectively required three conditions. First, the job must be able to be done individually—catching bollworms met this requirement. Second, the work must be able to be measured accurately. Third, and no less important, it had to be the type of task where labor efficiency would be demonstrably improved. Yet the team leader, as well as many workers, did not always favor piece rates even when all three of these conditions could be met. For the leader, it greatly increased his workload. As shown later in this chapter, sometimes he had to negotiate with the workers over the workpoint piece rate for the assigned task, and after the work was done, he had to evaluate their work individually and even had to argue with those workers who disagreed with his assessment. Many team cadres thus treated piece rates as "troublesome" and avoided using it whenever possible.[3] They preferred time rates, for their simplicity and the light duty on themselves and adopted piece rates only when they felt it absolutely necessary or faced pressure from above to do so. Some team members, especially those who were physically weak, also disliked piece rates because it widened the disparity in workpoint earnings between the weak member and the able-bodied members.

The government had promoted the piece-rate system since the early years of collectivization, and reasserted it in the early 1960s after the Great Leap Forward and again in the 1970s to correct the "ultra-leftist" policies of the Cultural Revolution and to implement the socialist distribution principle of "from each to his best, and to each according to his work" (*ge jing suo neng, an lao fenpei*).[4] The accountant of Team No. 11 observed in his notebook that, at four consecutive commune-wide meetings he attended between May 1973 and February 1974, the commune leaders repeatedly required that the piece-rate system be applied to "all kinds of tasks" (QD4 1973: 26, 27, 30, 39; QD4 1974: 77). After these meetings, the team discussed and announced a set of standard workpoint rates and criteria for different tasks.

Workpoint Rates

Critical to implementing the piece-rate system was setting an appropriate workpoint rate for a given amount of work. If the rate was set too low, team members would have no incentive to do the assigned work; if too high, it would devalue workpoints. By the government's repeated requirements, each production team had to set up its own workpoint rates for different kinds of tasks through "democratic discussion" (*minzhu pingyi*) among team leaders or representatives of the farmers. Team No. 11 worked out its workpoint standards for 20 major tasks during several meetings in 1973 (see Table 2).

A basic factor in determining the workpoint rate was the difficulty of the task. Tasks that demanded greater physical strength earned higher workpoints. For men, the "heavy tasks" included digging water drains, carrying bundled rice or wheat from a field to the threshing ground, delivering dried river sludge as fertilizer, and so on. An able-bodied male could normally earn 15 to 20 points a day for such tasks. The most toilsome task was to participate in water-control projects. Those who joined this task had to work 10 hours a day in the harsh winter weather, digging the earth with a spade and removing it by shoulder pole. The payment for this work was normally 20 to 25 points a day. Heavy tasks for women included transplanting rice seedlings and cutting rice or wheat, for which they also could earn 15 to 20 points a day. Light tasks came with lower workpoints. As a rule of thumb, adult men usually earned about 10 points a day for doing light tasks and women 7 to 8 points a day.

It should be noted that in practice these standard rates only served as a guideline. When assigning tasks and recording workpoints, the team leader had to modify the rates, taking into account several other factors. One was the changing difficulty of the task. For instance, consider

TABLE 2

Workpoint Rates in the No. 11 Production Team, 1973 and 1974

	Tasks	Workpoint standards
Tasks for men	Dredging up river sludge	4.2 points per cubic meter
	Delivering mud	2 points per cubic meter
	Removing manure	0.25 points for two buckets moved to a boat; 0.1 points for two buckets moved from the boat to the field
	Removing bundled rice	7 points per mu
	Digging water drains	8 points per 150 meters
	Soaking rice seeds	100 points per 1,000 catties
	Tilling and steeping green-manure field	2 points per mu for tilling; 1 point per mu for harrowing and leveling
	Piling up bundled rice	1 point per mu
	Running stone roller over rice on the ground	3 points per mu
Tasks for women	Sowing cotton seeds	15 points per mu
	Cutting rice	13 points per mu
	Pulling up cotton stalks	14 points per mu
	Turning over topsoil	10 points per mu
	Reseeding cotton field	6 points per mu
	Selecting cotton seeds	20 points for 100 catties
Tasks for both sexes	Spreading rice straw on the threshing ground	4.5 points per mu
	Turning over rice straw on the ground	1.8 points per mu
	Collecting rice straw on the ground	4 points per mu
	Drying rice and straw in the sun	5 points per mu
	Cleaning up and deepening water drains	2 points per mu

SOURCES: QD4 1973, QD4 1974.

catching bollworms. During the first few days, when the bollworms remained out of control, team members earned one workpoint for every 100 worms caught. Later, as the worms became more difficult to locate, the rate was adjusted to 70 worms, and finally to 30 worms for one point. The distance of the worksite also affected workpoint rates. If a man delivered river sludge to a distant place, for example, the reward would be increased from 7 to 8 points per cubic meter. Likewise, carrying the bundled rice from a distant place was also rewarded with higher points than for carrying the rice from a field close to the threshing ground. In addition, the team leader had to consider the availability of suitable workers for a certain task when determining its workpoints. Sometimes he had to yield to the demand for higher rates when there was a shortage of labor for the job, as described below.

It was not impossible for the team leader to show favoritism when determining workpoint rates. For example, the leader could increase the rate by half a point or a point when his wife, children, or friends were among the workers. Therefore, some team members preferred to work with people whom they believed were in the good graces of the team leader. However, the team leader rarely showed his favoritism in an overt manner. He had to find an excuse for increasing the rate, such as hot weather or unexpected rain. It would be too transparent to change the rate simply because of the presence of people he favored, which would lead to a loss of face in front of his fellow team members. A team leader who regularly acted like this could rarely stay in his position for long.

Task Assignments

Another important factor for the successful implementation of piece rates was to assign tasks to the proper people. Normally team members had no right to choose what to do; it was up to the leader to assign them a task. The assignment was usually based on established practices and the workers' labor grade. It was generally assumed that able-bodied adults ("full laborers") did heavy tasks while adolescents and young adults did light jobs. As Table 2 indicates, most tasks were gender-specific. Adult women were only assigned "womanly tasks" such as cutting rice or picking cotton bolls. These tasks were suitable for women because, the villagers said, women had a softer waist and could tolerate bending over for hours. Men, in contrast, could only perform "manly tasks" such as carrying mud by shoulder pole or digging water drains. These tasks were proper for men because they not only demanded greater physical strength but also allowed them to stay upright. Married men and women thus seldom worked together. To let a woman perform men's work was unthinkable, and to ask a man to do woman's work seemed ridiculous. Young people, though, were often assigned to a task regardless of their gender because they were said to have similar physical strength. Disputes between team leaders and members over job assignments were rare, whereas the workpoint rates often caused conflicts.

It should be noted that, although team members had no freedom to choose a task, they nevertheless had a right to decline an assignment, in which case they would have nothing to do if the leader refused to offer them another task. Some villagers chose to stay home to do family chores when there were no high-point tasks. However, under the collective system, especially during the radical years in the late 1960s and early 1970s, noncollective income sources were very limited and during some periods were even prohibited by the government. Thus, most families had no means to make a living other than working for the team. They asked for absences only when they were sick or had family business, such as working the private plot or visiting a relative.

The team leaders held advantages, as in arranging for appointments to privileged high-workpoint and light-duty positions inside and outside the team. One instance that occurred in Team No. 11 in the mid-1970s had to do with the team accountant's two younger brothers, who were appointed as the brigade's supervisor of machine operators and as the team's machine operator, respectively. Some villagers complained that none of the three brothers, all full laborers, did manual farm work. The brothers had their own justifications: the second brother obtained his position as a supervisor owing to having the highest score on a test taken by applicants from all the teams of the brigade; the third brother obtained his job because he was the most literate among the team members and he had learned a great deal about machine operation and maintenance from his second brother. Nevertheless, resentments about the team accountant's possible favoritism never ceased within the team.

The accountant, when he later became team head, pushed the government's policy to give priority to the so-called "disadvantaged" and "revolutionary" families. For example, he sent two young men to the brigade's factory, one an orphan and the other a son in a family with many dependents. He also allowed the youngest son of a family to be recruited by the brigade's broadcasting station, since his brother was away serving in the army. Whenever possible, the team leader had to appear impartial in making coveted appointments while posing any favoritism in a justifiable light.

The Role of Team Leaders

The team leader played a critical role in the everyday management of team production. When assigning tasks, for example, the most important thing for him was to estimate how many workers were needed for a certain job. An inexperienced leader could use too many or too few people, or sometimes the task was actually unnecessary or was too early or too late in the farming season. The villagers called such arbitrary planning "blind commanding" (*xia zhihui*). In contrast, an experienced leader knew how to assign a certain task at the right time, and how to appoint the right persons to the task and reward them at the right rates. The team leader's skills, more than other factors, determined the efficiency of farm activities and the morale of the members.

Not surprisingly, Team No. 11 fared differently under different leaders. In the late 1960s and early 1970s, the team was under a man whom some informants viewed as "weak and incompetent." He often turned a blind eye to sloppy work and yielded to the few "unruly" adult males who demanded higher workpoints. From time to time he also protected his family members and followers when assigning tasks or giving workpoints. Although he tried to be nice to all team members, he lost their respect when the team's economy stagnated during his tenure and the numbers of "overdrawn households" (*chaozhi hu*) increased. The brigade eventually removed him from office in 1976.

Without appropriate candidates available from within the team, the brigade appointed the deputy head of a neighboring team as the new leader. Arrogant and strong-minded, he turned out to be even more irresponsible than his predecessor. How the team fared did not affect his income, especially since the brigade had promised to guarantee his annual workpoints. He thus rarely stayed around to supervise the workers. Informants complained that every day he herded them to the fields and then returned home to cook breakfast. After breakfast, he reappeared in the fields for a short while and then quickly returned home again to do chores and cook lunch for his family. Sometimes he did not show up until 5:00 or 6:00 p.m. when he had to give out workpoints. His poor performance in 1976 resulted in the lowest level of cash value of workpoints in the team's history: 0.38 yuan per workday, lowest among all 11 teams that year.

The brigade thus quickly dismissed him in early 1977 and appointed the accountant of the team to the position. He had a strong motivation to do a better job. He had three small children and his wife had been sick for an extended period of time, and without other means to support the family he had to run the team well in order to increase his income from the collective. He also wanted to obtain Party membership, and the best way to achieve this was to be successful as team head. So he implemented piece rates as often as possible and insisted on quality. For example, he required that the dried mud be distributed to a field in the right way: a shoulder-pole load of mud had to be placed every two meters, and workpoints would be deducted if the workers failed to meet this standard. His strict discipline displeased some. An anonymous villager was so resentful that he poisoned several of the new team leader's chickens. Nevertheless, work quality and labor efficiency steadily improved during his tenure. The cash value of 10 workpoints increased from 0.38 yuan in 1977 to 0.54 yuan in 1978 and 0.84 yuan in 1979 (QD5 1977–1979). Once his reputation was established among the farmers, they became accustomed to his requirements. Slackers who were required to repeat their tasks also showed much less resentment than before. In recognition of his success, he was selected by the county government to attend a meeting of "model agricultural producers" in Nanjing in 1979 and was subsequently promoted to the position of head of the brigade.

In short, given the central role of labor management, collective production varied significantly under team leaders of different abilities. Because most team leaders were appointed from within the team, they could not be irresponsible when planning and monitoring the team's farming activities. On the other hand, most of them had no ambitions for promotion and saw no immediate personal benefits in strictly disciplining the labor force. They also wanted to keep their position because it came with high workpoint rewards and other privileges. In this circumstance, most team leaders found it neither possible nor necessary to supervise the team members closely and adhere to stringent quality requirements. Instead, what they expected from team members was the customarily defined level of work quality, which was necessary for the smooth operation of the team and at the same time acceptable to most team members.

Everyday Strategies for Workpoints

Strategies Under Piece Rates

Members of Team No. 11 employed two basic strategies to earn workpoints: bargaining over workpoint rates and shirking. Bargaining was possible because there were no official regulations on remuneration standards. Throughout the collective era, the government never formulated and enforced universal workpoint rates for different kinds of tasks, for the obvious reason that the landscape and economic conditions varied markedly from team to team. Normally, the members just accepted the announced rate of the team leader, if it seemed normal and fair to them. However, it was not uncommon for the villagers to challenge the rate and bargain with the team leader if the latter had a poor reputation for increasing the cash value of workpoints, if he had a weak personality and was unwilling to argue with the discontented individuals, or if he showed overt favoritism to certain members.

Bargaining could also be a viable strategy when the labor available for a certain task was limited. In the mid- to late 1960s, for example, there were only a few adult males strong enough to do heavy tasks, and most of them came from among the Chen families. Therefore, the Chens took advantage of the situation and often demanded higher rates for those tasks. For instance, they asked for six points for dredging one cubic meter of river sludge, which was almost two points higher than the standard rate. The team leader had no option but to yield. In the 1970s, however, the youngsters from other families grew up and, with more strong workers available, the team reduced the workpoint rates for those tasks to the original levels.

According to my informants, there were three or four occasions in the 1960s and 1970s when men from the team staged a strike after they had failed to bargain for higher rates. The men sat on the ridge of the field, waiting for the team leader's concession, and kept chatting until they returned home for lunch. When they returned home for lunch, however, they faced complaints from their wives because they had earned nothing the entire morning. In the afternoon, the men had to go back to the worksite and accept the assignment, while the team leader increased the rate a bit as a token of consideration of their face. A more illustrative story happened to team member Chen in November 1973, when the brigade ordered the team to provide 14 laborers for water work. The team leader soon did so and promised each of the laborers 19 points a day. All others accepted this rate except Chen, who insisted that the rate had to be 21 points a day. The team leader refused and shipped all of the other laborers to the worksite while Chen stayed home, doing nothing but listening to his wife's frequent complaints. Three days later, he willingly traveled to the workplace on foot to join his fellow villagers.

The reason that the villagers had to concede when bargaining with the team leader was that they had no opportunities to earn income other than through workpoints from the team, nor could they appeal to authorities at higher levels when disputing with the team leader. In the absence of any official rules on workpoint rates, the government normally expected the cadres and peasants to settle the disputes by themselves.

Another strategy was to increase the quantity of one's work at the cost of its quality; this was especially likely under piece rates. Take digging water drains, for instance. An irresponsible worker would dig only 12 centimeters deep rather than the 20 centimeters as required, and he would not smash the dirt on the two sides of the drain that he had just dug out. The bottom of the drain would be full of extra dirt, and the drain would look crooked. This way, he could dig as many as five 150-meter-long drains a day. At the standard rate of 8 points for each drain, he would earn 40 points a day! However, an honest man normally could only finish two drains that met the leader's requirements, earning 16 points a day.

Another example had to do with dredging sludge from river beds to be used as fertilizer. Good sludge should look black and be mixed with waterweeds. Some team members, however, preferred to do the job in the nearby shallow creeks within the boundary of the team's territory, rather than in a distant place outside the territory, so that they could save the time required to pole the boat and the energy required to dredge up the mud. Over time, they would find less and less fertile mud available from the local creeks. The team leader thus demanded that they should fetch it from the wider, deeper rivers outside the team or the village. Without the team leader's close monitoring, however, the villagers continued to stay in the nearby creeks for infertile mud and would cover the top of the mud with some waterweeds to deceive the team leader.

To carry the dried mud to the field could also be problematic. By the team head's requirement, the mud must be evenly distributed to all areas of the field. However, those who wanted to earn more workpoints put the mud more in the area around the mud heap than in distant areas. Spraying manure on the field was another method of fertilization. It was required that every bucket of manure had to be mixed with the same amount of water before application. However, without the team cadre's supervision, a dishonest peasant would blend the manure with much less water, or no water at all.

To what extent did problems of poor quality prevail under the piece-rate system? When recalling their experiences in team production, the village informants agreed that this did happen from time to time. However, several factors worked against this. The first was the mutual competition and surveillance among the team members. When working together, the villagers always paid close attention to each other so that they knew how much and how well others had done. A person who worked too fast or too seriously could possibly became a target of envy or resentment from others because the team leader would use him or her as a model worker and pacesetter, and determine the workpoint rate and quality requirements for the entire group according to his or her performance. Likewise, it was unacceptable to most members if a team member worked too carelessly yet received the same workpoints as others. Thus, there was always an invisible pressure among the group that forced people to work the same way and, if possible, to proceed at the same pace. This peer pressure was especially strong among those of the same age group or the same labor grade. To be sure, the physical strength and abilities were not identical. Members could tolerate a person who worked far ahead of others if the quality of his or her job was no poorer than the rest of the group, but such people were not necessarily welcome among fellow members. Meanwhile, the few who worked slower than others had to tolerate the ridicule of the group or complaints from their family members.

The second factor was the team leader's supervision. He did not have to keep an eye on all of the workers all the time because a team usually had over a hundred workers (the No. 11 team had 148 full- or half laborers in the mid-1970s). Close monitoring was both impossible and unnecessary in practice. What was critical for the leader was to adhere to quality standards when checking work and calculating workpoints. The leader himself, to be sure, could also be derelict from time to time when performing his supervising duties. However, just like the peasants who could never freely loaf on the job, the leader could never totally shirk his responsibilities because sooner or later he would be removed from office if his poor performance caused persistent stagnation or decline of agricultural output.

The third factor was shared assumptions in team production. When asked about the importance of the team leader's supervision, the villagers usually replied that they did not feel any pressure from the leader because the latter was mostly absent when they were working; they did their work according to their own "consciousness" (*zijue*) about how to do it properly. The team leader, too, often felt no need to explain to the members his specific requirements. When assigning tasks in the early morning, he only told the team members where they should go, what they were going to do, and how the workpoints would be awarded.

Rather than doing a perfect job or making a complete mess, what the team head anticipated, as well as what the team members presumed they would achieve, was usually work that was "so-so on the whole" (*dati shang shuo de guoqu*). This informal "so-so" criterion was the basic guideline for team members and the minimum requirement for the team leader to check their work.

A team member had to pay proper attention to the quality of his or her work not only because it was subject to the surveillance of his or her coworkers and team cadres, but also due to the fact that the production team was the principal source of his or her income; how the team fared directly affected the well-being of all the members. The relationship between the team leader and members, in other words, was not the same as between an employer and employees or between a supervisor and the supervised; they both belonged to the same collective and shared the output of their collaborative effort. Both sides had to be responsible for the common good.

Strategies Under Time Rates

Aside from heavy and urgent tasks that entailed the use of piece rates, there were many routine jobs that were light and easy, such as manually selecting seeds, weeding with a hoe, crushing soil with an iron-toothed rake, clipping cotton branches, or attending a meeting of the team or the brigade. Team members normally had no problem finishing them at the expected pace. A team thus thought it unnecessary to use piece rates for these tasks. Instead, a team head would announce a fixed workpoint for the task, and all participants would receive the same points if they finished the task properly. The team's attendance record on September 23, 1977, shows, for instance, that 11 unmarried women who did gardening all earned 8 points for the entire day, while 26 married women who visited the commune clinic for a physical exam in the morning all received 3.5 points (QD6 1977).

As explained earlier, the team leader would prefer time rates whenever possible. The members, too, preferred this system to piecework when the task was easy and all participants were able to do it. Thus, while cutting rice was a task for able-bodied females only, selecting cotton seeds was open to all women. Because no competition was involved under the time-rate system, the villagers felt relaxed and worked at a pace they felt comfortable with. When weeding, for example, the female workers on different strips normally formed a horizontal line to move forward together. Although there were a few who were a bit ahead or behind the line, they could easily adjust their pace to keep in line with each other. Because of the light duty and fixed reward, the pressure that drove them to move fast was much less than under piecework. Those who were weak welcomed this system because it allowed them to work with the able-bodied and to receive the same workpoints.

My informants agreed that work quality under time rates was in general better than under piece rates because they did not have to hurry to achieve a higher quantity, which meant that they had more time to pay attention to the quality of their job. Close monitoring was unnecessary for these routine tasks; both the team leader and workers took it for granted that the jobs would be done properly. However, the team members were likely to do a sloppy job if the leader totally gave up his duty to monitor, showing up on the farm only in the last few minutes when he had to check the work and record workpoints. When a few undisciplined workers took the lead in slacking, all the others might follow suit in the absence of the team leader, like "ducks set free" (*fang yeya*). Farm work became particularly inefficient when the time-rate system was applied to strenuous tasks for which the piece-rate system was far better suited. Under such a circumstance, if time rates were used, few people were willing to work as hard because everyone received the same points regardless of effort. This phenomenon was known to the villagers as "going to work without putting in effort" (*chu gong bu chu li*).

The effects of different workpoint systems thus were complex. The villagers no doubt had a stronger willingness to increase their input under piece rates, but they were likely to do so at the cost of work quality. The piece-rate system, in other words, did not necessarily improve farming efficiency if the team leader failed to perform his duties in labor management. On the other hand, the time-rate system did not necessarily lead to inefficiency if it was applied to the right task and if the team leader monitored the workers properly. What was critical here was the everyday interaction between the team leader and ordinary members in team production. The team leader's abilities in task assignment, work supervision and workpoint rewards, as well as the team members' mutual competition, surveillance, and sanctions, combined to shape the work norms in collective farming.

This is not to say, however, that state policies were less important than the embedded norms. The state's intervention and enforcement of extremely egalitarian systems in labor remuneration could be disastrous to agricultural collectives. This was obvious in the late 1960s, when the Dazhai-workpoint system was implemented in much of rural China. Under that system, team members who worked a full day received only a preset "basic workpoint" (*jiben gongfen*) based on their overall attitude toward laboring well, whatever the nature and quantity of their labor. The Dazhai system was effective in the beginning. Many informants recalled that, to show their zeal for the collective and receive higher basic workpoints in the public appraisal, they even sneaked to the fields at night to cut rice without letting team cadres know, and thus were praised as selfless "anonymous heroes" (*wuming yingxiong*) the next morning when the team leader discovered what they had done. However, as time went on, the villagers gradually quarreled with each other over their mutual appraisal of basic workpoints.[5] In the absence of immediate material incentives, no one was willing to do arduous tasks such as dredging river sludge. As a result, the team simply asked those who were assigned that task to finish only two boat compartments of sludge a day. In contrast, they had dredged as many as four or five a day under the piece-rate system. Because of the application of the Dazhai system in the radical years, team farming became less efficient, as evidenced in the low annual yields of Team No. 11, which ranged between 352 and 385 catties per mu from 1966 to 1970, much less than the output in the first half of the 1970s, when the reintroduction of the piece-rate system, together with improvements in farming conditions (construction of irrigation projects, use of chemical fertilizers, pesticides, new strains of crops and so on), drove output to about 500 catties per mu. Output rose further in the second half of the 1970s, when the full use of the piece-rate system and a full-scale "green revolution" resulted in a yield of more than 700 catties per mu (QD5 1966–1979).

Gender Discrepancy in Work Norms

When asked whether and how women behaved differently from men in team farming, a former leader of Team No. 11 pointed out that women were obedient (*tinghua*). He added that, during his 30 years as a team and brigade cadre, women seldom argued with him over task assignments or workpoints, and he never witnessed any strikes by women. But when asked whether this obedience to team leaders was rooted in women's traditional subordination to male dominance in the patriarchal family that predominated before the Communist Revolution and persisted thereafter, he only partly agreed and offered his own explanations.

First, he believed that, compared to men, women were more concerned about the subsistence needs of their families (*gujia*). To "support the family and feed the mouths" (*yangjia hukou*), they would seize every opportunity to earn workpoints. Most women would never miss a day of work in the team if they could help it, no matter how few workpoints they received. Second, women were more subject to peer pressure. According to the former team leader, this was especially true for those who were physically strong, or who were activists and therefore had to work hard for the sake of their own reputation. It was thus critical, in the team leader's view, to use these women as model workers and pacesetters, and to offer them various bonuses, such as giving them the opportunity to attend the meetings of activists or representatives of team members, naming them as group leaders, praising them at team meetings, and giving them awards at the end of the year. These activists not only cooperated with the team leader when he assigned tasks but also exerted a pressure on the rest of the group, forcing them to work harder and more responsibly (WG2 1976).

A third reason lay in the fact that the team had sufficient female hands for "women's" tasks, which made it hard for them to bargain for higher points. In 1977, for example, the team had 51 women between the ages of 19 and 47 and 54 men between 20 and 49. All of them were classified as full laborers. Among the males, however, only 17 (31 percent) were available for regular farm work; the remainder (37 men, or 69 percent) had fixed jobs, including three team cadres; three diesel and tractor operators; four ox herders; three workers in brigade factories; three pig raisers; two kiln workers; three persons responsible for the fishing ponds, grain grinders, and pesticide application, respectively; two fishermen; three carpenters; and one smith. These people were not included in the team leader's list for daily task assignments. In contrast, among the 51 adult women, 39 were regular, able-bodied workers. The team leader was always able to find enough hands for almost all of the women's tasks. Thus, while the shortage of able-bodied male workers enabled them to request higher rates, women did not have such leverage.

However, the women's obedience should not be equated with their being simpleminded and merely following instructions; they had their own tactics to earn more workpoints. My informants provided several stories in this regard. One had to do with smashing soil lumps with a rake. After the field was plowed and raked, there were always large lumps that had to be smashed to prepare the field for sowing wheat seeds. The field was usually divided into strips at the standard width of 2.6 meters (3.6 meters for growing cotton), and each woman was assigned one strip for this job. She would be rewarded according to the number of strips she finished, and the workpoints for each strip were the same. However, the widths of the strips were not always identical. Thus, when a group of women was sent to a field for this task, each woman tried to get there early to occupy narrow strips. If they all arrived at the same time, a quick-witted woman who predicted that a wider strip would be assigned to her would quickly walk away for a few minutes on any excuse, and then came back for another chance. Those who lacked this knowledge or arrived later had to accept the wider ones that would cost them more time and energy.

In another instance, when cutting wheat, the women would try to get to the field early to occupy as many strips as they could. To do so, a woman would first cut a small area on each of the strips that she wanted. Latecomers had to avoid the strips that had been "touched." Likewise, when pulling out cotton stalks, those who arrived first tried to seize strips in the same way. Others who arrived very late often found that no strips were left. Obviously, such competition was unfair to young mothers, who were unable to leave home early because they had to take care of their children and do family chores if they had no elderly parents or teenagers to help. Realizing this problem, the team later took measures to limit the number of strips that a woman could occupy to guarantee opportunities for latecomers.

Therefore, there were subtle differences between men and women in their strategies for workpoints. Both the male and female peasants, to be sure, wanted to earn as many points as possible. Women, too, sometimes might do their job as hastily and carelessly as some males. However, the villagers could quickly point out the differences between men and women in their attitudes toward team farming. Whereas the males tended to be contentious over workpoint rates and careless under piece rates, women instead tried to earn more workpoints by seeking more opportunities and maximizing their labor input. Overall, women played a role no less important than men in team production. A former team leader estimated that women "did at least 70 percent" of farm work in his team.[6] In his view, without the full use of women as labor force, the production team could not exist at all.

There was also a noticeable discrepancy between the genders in rewarding workpoints. To be sure, occasionally an able-bodied woman could earn more points than a man, especially when transplanting rice seedlings or cutting crops. Some women were able to earn 15 to 20 points a day at this work; in contrast, male workers on the threshing ground normally earned only 10 to 12 points a day (QD6 1977). Under most circumstances, however, women's points were significantly lower than men's. In harvesting rice, an able-bodied man who carried the bundled rice to the threshing ground typically earned 20 to 25 points a day, much higher than the points for the women cutting rice. When transplanting rice seedlings, a woman normally earned an average of 18 points a day, while a man dispatching bundled rice seedlings earned about 25 points per day on average. A woman doing everyday tasks, such as drying straw in the sun, typically earned 8 points a day, while a man who collected and piled up straw earned 9 or 10 points a day. On average, women's daily workpoints were one-third less than men's.

An obvious reason behind the gender disparity in labor remuneration was the changing physical strength and work opportunities of men and women during different phases of the life course (see Chapter 9 and Li 2005b). However, underlying this preferential treatment of men was also the villagers' assumption that men's labor *ought* to be more valuable than women's. A woman stated this notion directly: "Men are masters of the family (*yijia zhi zhu*). They of course deserve higher workpoints. If a man earned the same as a woman or even less, how could he have face in his family and the neighborhood?" According to a 1977 report from the "Joint Investigation Group of the County- and Commune-Level Women's Federations," some adult males in Qin village earned 30 to 40 percent more than females, although they went to work later and returned home earlier than women. The report quoted two sayings by the men to illustrate their mindset: "With the status of a full laborer, a man is never worried about earning enough workpoints"; "In the moment of smoking a cigarette, what a man does equals what a woman does for half a day" (DT29 1977).

However, in the 1970s, especially during the "criticizing Lin and Confucius" campaign, the government promoted "equal pay for equal work" (*tonggong tongchou*), touting this policy as the key to improving women's economic status and freeing them from the yoke of traditional practices. In response to this policy, in 1972, a team in Qin village organized a number of unmarried young women into a "shock squad" (*tuji ban*) to do heavy tasks traditionally reserved for men. According to the aforementioned report, which picked the village as a model brigade in promoting the equal-pay policy, one day when three "iron girls" (*tie guniang*) from the group were digging water drains together with adult males, they finished 200 meters in good quality. Meanwhile, a man named Liu finished the same length, but his drain was "shallow, narrow, and crooked," so he had to repeat his job. The report did not mention how other males did their work and how long they had taken to finish. Nevertheless, that example was used as evidence of the iron girls' competitiveness. In another instance included in the report, the team appointed 38 women to thresh rice from evening to midnight and the same number of men for the same job from midnight to morning for the same number of hours. It turned out that the women finished 520 bundles, while the men finished only 490 bundles. Men's superiority was greatly challenged in this instance. In the winter of 1976, more than 20 of the young women were sent to join a water-control project, which had been a task exclusively for men. The report asserted that the earth removed by the women was "no less than" what the men achieved, and therefore the best of the women earned more workpoints than some of the men did. One day, for instance, the team assigned more than 20 women to dig water drains in the morning, and everyone finished 100 meters. In the afternoon, each of them picked 50 catties of cotton. And in the evening, every woman cut 500 catties of yam vine as forage. Thus, according to the fixed workpoint rates for those tasks, each of them earned 18 points. On the same day, however, some adult males dug only 200 meters of water drain and received 14 points. Again, the report omitted the workpoints of other adult males. As evidence to support its conclusion that this shock brigade had "basically achieved" the goal of "equal pay for equal work," the county report picked two of the women, who earned 3,542 and 3,600 points in 1976, to compare with a man who earned 3,648 points (DT29 1977).

As some villagers pointed out, however, the two "iron girls" were the ablest among all female team members, while the man was one of the weakest among the men. In actuality, most able-bodied males earned at least 4,500 workpoints a year. As a former team head pointed out, to put men and women together on the same task and to use the same rates for both was only a temporary response to the political demands from above. Such practices, in his opinion, could not last for long. "It was fine for the young women to do men's work for one or two days," he noted. "However, you cannot use them just like men. After all, they were girls and young mothers. They were not as strong as men. How could you expect them to do men's work all the time?" Therefore, even during the heyday of the campaign of "equal pay for equal work," he routinely assigned male and female workers to different tasks at dif-

ferent rates. The biological differences between male and female laborers, together with traditional notions about gender roles in the rural
community, prevailed over the imposed policies in shaping the everyday farming practices under the collective.

Conclusion

This discussion of the behavior of team members and cadres in Qin
village underscores the importance of workaday norms in team farming. Where the team leadership was stable, established practices would
develop over time to govern members' performance of routine tasks.
Disputes between team members and the leader over task assignments
and over workpoints, though occurring from time to time, were unlikely to become habitual when both sides had the same or similar
expectations of work quality and remuneration. Covert and minor
slacking occurred, but flagrant shirking was unlikely to prevail where
the villagers were subject to informal and formal constraints, including the surveillance and competition of fellow workers, the shared
sense of collective survival that underpinned various forms of group
pressures, and the team leader's supervision. Such constraints, needless to say, were not limited to the village under investigation; with
varying effectiveness in localities of different landscapes and team
leadership, they existed across rural China, as villagers worked under
similar collective organizations and earned workpoints or derived most
of their income from the same sources under similar arrangements of
labor remuneration.

Women performed differently from men in team production, owing
in large part to their greater sensitivity to peer pressure, their greater
concern with the everyday needs of family subsistence, their disadvantage in labor supply, and their traditional subservience to male dominance. Such cultural and social conditions again were not confined to
the locality examined. In general, female workers were less argumen-
tative than adult males. They were more concerned with maneuvering
for better work opportunities rather than for workpoint rates, and were
paid much less than the adult males. Nevertheless, the women under-
took most of the routine farm tasks. Their participation and hard work
were critical to the normal operations of the collectives.

Obviously, state policies alone did not determine the morale and
motives of the team members. What shaped their attitudes toward
team farming were a multiplicity of formal and informal institutions

operating in the local communities, which motivated as well as constrained the members in their pursuit of private gain and participation in team production. The villagers expected, and were expected, to perform their duties for the collective in a manner in keeping with the team's norms, which meant that under most circumstances they had to strike a subtle balance between the quantity and quality of their tasks and between their personal desire to work less as against their commitment to the collective well-being.

The central role of work norms in everyday team farming suggests that we should rethink the problem of work morale under the collective from a new point of view. We cannot attribute the problem of inefficiency in China's collective agriculture merely to the state's egalitarian policies or to difficulties in monitoring farming activities that discouraged the use of piece rates under the collective. Customarily, both the team leader and members knew well the requirements and the range of remuneration for different kind of tasks. Therefore, the team leader routinely applied piece rates to a variety of tasks for men and women whenever he deemed it necessary. Nor did the team leader feel it problematic to "supervise" the workers because there were established practices to guide both the team leader's expectations and team members' performance of the assigned jobs. For routine tasks, the team leader did not feel the need for close supervision at all; strict monitoring was necessary only when the team encountered an unusual task, or when a routine task occurred in exceptional circumstances, or when a few "slippery fellows" challenged the routines. Once solutions were developed to deal with them, both the team leader's requirement and workers' performance of these tasks became quite predictable.

The problem of work incentives in team production, then, is not so much about the externally imposed policies or the team leader's monitoring and supervision as about the norms or established practices that shaped the expectations of both the team leader and ordinary workers about task performance and labor remuneration. Needless to say, as state polices shifted and as local social and political settings varied, the work norms changed over time. Among the many factors, the most critical was no doubt the team leader's personality and style of management. By the state's expectations, the team leader was supposed to assign different tasks skillfully to workers of different abilities to utilize their labor fully and hence maximize farm output. Before the Cultural Revolution and during much of the 1970s, he was also supposed to use piece rates as often as possible, closely supervise the workers, and reward them according to the quantity and quality of their performance. These requirements, in other words, were essentially no different from the "rational" and "impersonal" principles for running a modern enterprise.

In reality, however, except for the few team leaders who were motivated by a desire for promotion, the vast majority found themselves unwilling or unable to manage their collective in this manner. Unlike a private business owner committed to profit maximization, the team leader did not see any immediate benefit in setting strict standards when he used piece rates. His relationship with the workers was far different from that of a private business owner/manager and wage workers. The team leader himself was a member of the community and his standing within the team was no less important than the marginal increases of output that could have been produced by the strict use of piece rates. A "defect" of the collective, in other words, was the impracticability of its requirement for an impersonal mode of labor management despite the environment in which it operated; namely, the production team as a cooperative community that involved interpersonal ties embedded in local society. The collective organization no doubt could and did work to stimulate production, provided that there was an identity of interest between the leaders and the led. If the two were at odds, it was least efficient. When congruent, a great deal could be done.

CHAPTER 9

The Family Cycle and Income Disparity

MUCH HAS BEEN written about income disparity in rural China under the collective system. It is estimated that in 1979, the eve of decollectivization, the richest 10 percent of rural households shared 28 percent of total household income from all sources, whereas the poorest 40 percent received only 16 percent as a whole (Selden 1988: 146–147). Studies of the lowest-level agricultural collectives (or production teams) in different parts of the country also show that the per capita income of the richest quarter of households in the collectives tended to be two to three times that of the poorest quarter (Blecher 1976; Nolan and White 1981; Vermeer 1982; Selden 1988: 134–135; Hsiung and Putterman 1989: 406–445). An important reason behind this inequality, as noted in past studies, was the changing laborer-to-dependent ratio in the rural families, which in turn reflected the different positions of the households in the family cycle (Nolan and White 1979, 1981; Selden 1988: 132; P. Huang 1990: 238). In general, households with many able-bodied workers and few dependents earned higher per capita income than those in the reverse situation in the late 1970s (Parish and Whyte 1978: 62; Griffin and Saith 1982; Zweig 1989: 177; Judd 1994: 6–7). Rather than a social differentiation based on unequal landholding, what prevailed in the Chinese collectives thus may be called "demographic differentiation," a process that A. V. Chayanov outlined in the 1920s for rural communities in prerevolutionary Russia.[1]

Exactly how a rural household went through different phases of the family cycle, how the changing laborer-to-consumer ratio affected its income from the collective, and how government policies in birth

control and labor remuneration in the 1970s influenced the family cycle and income distribution among the peasant households, however,
have never been systematically proved with solid evidence in the past
studies on rural China, due largely to the unavailability of detailed
and reliable demographic and economic data of the collectives. Drawing on the data from the No. 11 team of the Zhigang Brigade in Qin
Village, this chapter examines those issues.

Under the collective system, peasants earned income from the production team through two sources, working for the team and turning
in the household's manure to the collective, both of which were credited in "workpoints" or "workdays" (1 workday = 10 workpoints). In
the No. 11 team, labor credits constituted 83 percent to 95 percent of
the total workpoints of peasant households, while manure credits accounted for 5 percent to 17 percent. In addition, the peasants also
earned extra income from private "family sidelines" such as raising
pigs, chickens, ducks, rabbits, goats, and sheep, or engaging in fishing,
construction, the kiln industry, and other kinds of off-farm occupation.
In general, such noncollective sources constituted 20 to 30 percent of
the total income of peasant families (Griffin 1982: 706–713; Griffin and
Saith 1982: 172–206). At any rate, workpoints earned by working for the
collective constituted the basic source of income for most peasant families during the collective era.

The cash value of workpoints was determined at the end of a year
when the collective did a final accounting to determine its net income
by deducting all productive and nonproductive costs, as well as agricultural taxes and funds for welfare and production, from its gross income and then determine the value of each workpoint by dividing the
net income with the total workpoints of all households in the production team. How much income a member obtained from the team thus
depended on two factors: the number of his or her annual workpoints
and the cash value of the workpoint. Needless to say, the collective income of peasant families varied from year to year, since the cash value
and the total workpoints they had earned changed every year.

The amount of cash a family would receive from the team at the
year-end final accounting was determined by deducting the cost of all
collective distributions in kind, such as grain, vegetables, and straw,
during the year from its total annual workpoint income. The distribution of grain and straw, however, was in most part based on the number of mouths in a family rather than its workpoints. The mouth-based
grain (or the "basic rations") usually accounted for 85 to 90 percent of

the total amount of grain from the team. Therefore, families with more mouths and few laborers, unable to earn enough workpoints to cover the cost of grains they had received, often ran into debt to the collective, thus being labeled as "overdrawn households" (*chaozhi hu*). Meanwhile, families with more laborers and fewer dependents received more cash payment from the team at the year-end final accounting. The per capita amount of cash a family received from the team, therefore, was largely a function of its labor-to-mouth ratio.

The Family Cycle in Rural China

The use of the family-cycle concept since the 1930s and 1940s in sociological, anthropological, and economic literatures has resulted in a variety of models to distinguish the stages through which all families in a given society and time undergo changes and transitions in their size, composition, and socioeconomic circumstances. The stages are usually defined in terms of the presence and ages of children in the families, and the number of the phases varies from four to nine, depending on the criterion used to demarcate the phases and the objects of research (Glick 1947: 164–174; Glick 1955: 3–9; Duvall 1957; Glick 1977: 5–13; Waite 1980; Duvall and Miller 1985). In general, the transition points that divided the stages involved critical family events such as marriage, birth of children, child rearing, and departure of children from the family (Hogan 1985; Glick 1989). Despite significant changes in marriage and family patterns in the West in recent decades that have caused increased criticism on the "rigid, arbitrary criteria" for determining the stages and their failure to capture differences in individual families (Hanson 1983; see also Nock 1979; Norton 1983), the family cycle is still accepted as a "useful theoretical as well an empirical tool" in the studies of family-related issues (Kapinus and Johnson 2003).

The concept of the family cycle is particular useful in understanding the economic conditions of rural households in China during the collective era for two obvious reasons. First, unlike the families in contemporary United States and other Western societies that have become increasingly diverse because of the mounting rates of divorce, premarital birth, step-parenthood, and bachelorship, Chinese families in the rural collectives remained very stable and traditional owing to the rarity of divorce and the virtual absence of premarital birth among them. It is thus probable to describe transitions in their size and structure in terms of distinct "stages" that were applicable to most of them. Second, after collectivization in the 1950s, all families derived most of their income from the collective through participation in the collective labor force. The workpoints a laborer received from the production team depended on the pieces or hours of work that he or she had done for the team, as well as his or her labor grade that was based on the laborer's age and physical strength. Therefore, the number and age of the members in a family became the major determinants of its income from the collective. It is thus plausible to examine changes in the collective income of peasant households in the context of the family cycle in which the number and age of family members, or more exactly the worker-to-consumer ratio, varied in different phases. The life events that shaped this ratio in a household included marriage, childbearing, transition to adulthood, and family division. Taking these factors into account and using the number and age of children in the families as the major criterion, all households in the collective are placed into four groups, each representing a distinct phase of the family cycle.

The first phase ("beginning families") starts with a family division whereby a couple, with or without children, separated themselves from their parents (in-law) and set up their own household, and ended with their bearing of up to three children when the couple were still in their late twenties or early thirties, and the children were mostly under age 10. The size of the families in this group varied from two to five members, mostly having three or four. Villagers customarily called such families as "small households" (*xiaohu*). What characterized these households were their relatively small size, the strong working abilities of the young parents, and therefore a balanced or slightly favorable worker-to-dependent ratio.

The second phase ("maturing families") started when the family had four or more children, and ended when the eldest child reached age 17 or 18, ready to fully enter the collective labor force. The problem with these families was known to every villager; that is, *kouduo laoshao* ("numerous mouths but few laborers"). With the parents as the only full laborers and all children remaining dependents or partial workers, these families faced the most unfavorable labor-to-mouth ratio and therefore were often the poorest in the collective.

The third phase ("mature families") commenced when the eldest child entered adulthood and became a full laborer, and ended when most children had married and established a separate family. These families were distinctive in the eyes of villagers for their *"renduo liqiang"* ("numerous people and strong labor force"). They often had the largest size (normally seven members in each family; some had as many as nine or ten). As most children had grown up, the biggest advantage of the mature families was their strong labor force, when the children had joined their parents to earn workpoints as full or partial laborers, while the parents themselves remained full laborers in their forties or early fifties. Therefore, they also had the highest worker-to-dependent ratio among all family groups.

The final phase ("aging families") of the family cycle began when the parents entered their mid-fifties and became partial laborers or retirees, while their married children had left the household to start their own family. As a result, the size of the family quickly shrank to a few members, usually including one or two parents and, if any, a grown-up son who failed to find a wife, or the married youngest son who, together with his wife, stayed with the remaining or both parents and his unmarried brother or sister. Such aging families continued to enjoy a favorable laborer-to-consumer ratio because the children and daughter-in-law earned workpoints as full laborers, while the parent, mostly the father, still worked as a partial laborer until his late fifties or early sixties and, after that, received workpoint subsidies from married children who had left the household.

It must be emphasized that, despite the stability and homogeneity of the families in rural China that permit the use of the family-cycle approach, the phases of the cycle underwent significant changes during the 1970s in terms of their timing and duration because of the birth-control policy and survival pressure. The most remarkable changes, as to be shown later, occurred to the first two phases. The delayed marriage and lowered fertility in the mid and especially the late 1970s postponed the inception of the first phase and prolonged its duration, and at the same time slowed and shortened the second phase of the family cycle. Concurring with these changes was the shift in the government's economic policies from the egalitarian orientation in labor remuneration in the late 1960s and early 1970s to the new one in the mid- and late 1970s that increasingly emphasized work incentives. As shown later, both changes had immediate effects on the family cycle and income disparities among peasant households.

To illustrate the characteristics of each of the four phases of the family cycle and their implications for economic differentiation of the rural households, my examination will first focus on the team's situation in 1974, when a transition was underway from early marriage and high fertility to late marriage and low fertility in family practices, and from egalitarianism to work incentives in economic policies. I will then high-light the contrasts and comparisons of the households' situations be-tween the two ends of the 1970s (1970 and 1979), in order to illustrate the impacts of the government's demographic and economic policies on the family cycle and income disparities in the rural collective.

The Family Cycle and Income Distribution

Figure 1 shows the population size and per capita annual workpoints of all households in the No. 11 team of Qin village in 1974. The data in the figure (as well as the three tables in this chapter) are arranged ac-cording to the age of the wives in the households because it was pri-marily the age of the wife (or mother), rather than any other family members, that affected the couple's marriage, childbearing, and their children's transition to adulthood, marriage, and separation from the family; all of these family events in turn shaped the presence and num-ber of children in the family and hence difference phases of the family cycle (Hogan 1985). As shown in the figure, the size of the households in the production team varied according to their positions in the cycle: it was relatively small during Phase 1, expanded in Phase 2, reached the height in Phase 3, and shrank to the lowest level in Phase 4. The per capita annual workpoints of the households showed a different trend line. It began at a relatively high level during Phase 1, fell to the lowest in Phase 2, resurged in Phase 3, and fluctuated in Phase 4.

Phase 1: Beginning Families

After marriage, a young couple did not immediately have their own household; they usually lived with the husband's parents as members of the stem family. The workpoints that they earned therefore belonged to that family. However, in the second or third year of their marriage, especially when they had their first child, the couple normally sepa-rated themselves from the stem family and established their own, hence entering the first phase of the family life cycle, and remaining in this phase until they had more than three children.

Nine families in the production team were in this phase, and the age of the wives in these families ranged from 22 to 31 years. On average, each of them had 4.11 members (see Table 3). The labor force in these families was strong in relation to the number of mouths. The husbands, all in their twenties or early thirties, were able-bodied, each earning

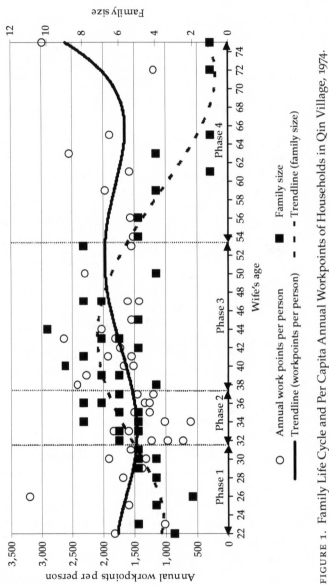

FIGURE 1. Family Life Cycle and Per Capita Annual Workpoints of Households in Qin Village, 1974.
Source: QD5 1974; QD14 1973.

TABLE 3

Family Life Cycle and the Collective Income of Households
in Qin Village, 1974

Phases	Beginning families	Maturing families	Mature families	Aging families
Wife's age	22–31	32–37	38–53	54–75
Number of households	9	15	16	8
Family size	4.11	6.00	6.94	2.75
Per capita workdays	157	125	190	196
Per capita cash payment (yuan)	9.22	–15.00	24.27	30.00

SOURCES: QD5 1974; QD13 1964; QD14 1973.

about 4,000 workpoints a year on average. The wives' working ability was greatly impaired by childbearing, which lasted from six months to more than a year each time. However, still in the prime of life, they could quickly recover from childbearing to become full laborers. Meanwhile, the young couple had only one or two (at most three) children to support. Therefore, there was a relatively balanced worker-to-dependent ratio in these families. Each family member shared an average of 157 workdays among the nine households, which was close to the average level of the entire production team (163 workdays per person); most households in this group, therefore, received a year-end cash payment of 9.22 yuan per person from the team after deducting in-kind distributions from the total value of their workdays.

Of course, the actual situation of the individual families in this group varied. The most advantageous ones were those in which both of the couple were full laborers, who had only one child or no children at all, such as the family of Zhang Changgui. With only one child, the couple, at ages 23 (husband, or H) and 22 (wife, or W), earned a total of 539 workdays, averaging 180 workdays per capita, and received a total of 103 yuan in cash from the team at the end of the year. The poorest families in this group were those with five members, such as the family of Zhang Baocai. The couple, at ages 25 (H) and 23 (W), together earned 547 workdays, which was even more than Zhang Changgui's total but significantly lower when divided by the family's five members: only 109 workdays per person. With three children at ages one, three, and five to support, the couple owed the collective 137 yuan in

1974. This family was the only one among the nine families who ran into debt. On the whole, the beginning families of the first phase fared reasonably well (QD 5 1974).

Phase 2: Maturing Families

Fifteen households, whose wives were 32 to 37 years old, were in this phase. In the absence of birth-control policies in the late 1960s and early 1970s, women continued to give birth to children in their late twenties and thirties. Thus, most families during this phase had six members or more, and a few of them had as many as seven or eight. Families of four, common in the first phase, disappeared when the wives turned 30 or older.

Although the family size expanded, the labor force in these families did not grow proportionally. For most maturing families, the major laborers remained the couple. The husbands, usually in their thirties, remained strong laborers, whose annual workpoints ranged between 3,500 and 5,000 per person. The wives, mostly having finished childbearing after their mid-thirties, became regular laborers, whose annual workpoints ranged between 2,500 and 3,500 per person. Meanwhile, the parents also felt a bit relaxed in child rearing as their children grew up. The eldest child, usually around 10 or older, became a helper in family chores and an occasional "extra laborer" for four or five workpoints a day. Teenagers after 15 further became regular "half laborers," who earned six to seven workpoints a day. However, in families with older children, the number of the children also increased to five or more. The burden to support them outweighed the income the eldest children brought in. What characterized the maturing families thus was the limited labor force in relation to many mouths. On average, the families in this group earned only 125 workdays per person, the lowest among all of the four family groups.

Because of the low per capita workdays and hence low income from the team, this family group had the highest percentage of overdrawn households. Of the 15 families in this group, seven (47 percent) were in debt to the collective, each owing an average of 271 yuan. One such household was that of Jiang Deyuan. Although the couple, at ages 34 (H) and 32 (W), worked extremely hard to earn a total of 8,154 workpoints, they had five children at one, two, four, six, and nine years of age to support. As a result, each member in the family shared only 116 workdays, much lower than the average level in the group. Not surprisingly, this family owed the team 180 yuan at the end of the year (QD5 1974).

Phase 3: Mature Families

There were 16 "mature families" in the production team. At ages 38 to 53, the wives in these families married at age 18 or 19 in the 1940s and early 1950s. Most families in this phase were larger than the maturing families of the preceding phase. The largest three families had nine or ten members. Another nine families had six to eight. On the whole, the families in this group each had an average size of 6.94 members, the largest among all family groups. This enlarged size reflected two facts. One was the high fertility rate of women in the late 1950s and the 1960s, when no birth-control policies were enforced. The other was the continuation of the custom that required newly married couples to live with the husbands' parents before family division.

What characterized the mature families was their high laborer-to-dependent ratio. Most women before the age of 45 and men before 50 remained full laborers, while their children, from age 12 to 22, became extra, half, or full laborers. The families' ability to earn workpoints thus reached the peak over the entire family cycle. After age 45, women earned fewer and fewer workpoints as their physical condition deteriorated. The same was true for men after 50. However, most of their children remained unmarried. The daughters, mostly in their late teens and early twenties, hit the height of their ability to earn workpoints. The newly married sons also lived with their parents and worked as full laborers, while the arrival of the daughters-in-law provided the family with additional labor force, who greatly offset the aging parents-in-law's loss of working abilities.

Together, the 16 mature families earned an average of 190 workdays per person, much higher than both the beginning and maturing families. Overdrawn households completely disappeared during this phase. Most families received more than 100 yuan in cash from the production team in the year-end distribution. On average, each of the 15 families received 168 yuan in cash, or 24.27 yuan per person, which was well above the average level of 9.02 yuan per person in the entire production team.

The most well-to-do families in this phase were those whose members were all able workpoint earners. One example was the family of Chen Changrong. The couple, both at age 43, were full laborers and earned a total of 6,443 workpoints. They had four children at the ages of 22 (son, or S), 20 (S), 18 (S), and 15 (daughter, or D), respectively. The first two were full laborers, and the other two half laborers. Thus, all of the six members in the family were able workers. Together, they earned 15,919 workpoints in the year, bringing their year-end cash income to a whopping 311 yuan, the highest in the entire production team!

On the other side, the least favorable families were those who had many mouths yet insufficient labor force. Take the family of Chen Changhe, for example. It had nine members, including two parents aged 41 (H) and 40 (W), and seven children aged 22 (D), 20 (D), 18 (D), 15 (S), 15 (S), 11 (D), and 10 (S). The wife rarely worked in collective farming and only earned 510 workpoints in the entire year. Thus, there were only three full laborers and one half laborer in the family. The mother and the two male twins were insignificant extra laborers. To-gether, the family earned 13,753 workpoints in the year, which were large enough to cover all in-kind distributions from the team. How-ever, with nine members to support, the family received a year-end cash payment of only 55 yuan, which was the lowest among all of the 15 families in this group. Nevertheless, the family avoided running into debt owing to the hard work of the grown-up children. On the whole, the families in this phase were much better off than their counterparts in other phases (QD5 1974).

Phase 4: Aging Families

When women turned 54 and older, their families usually entered the final phase of the family cycle. In most cases, their children had mar-ried and established their own families, who had to contribute to the parents a varying amount of workpoints depending on the parents' actual needs and their mutual agreement. The younger children, mostly between the ages of 15 and 25, remained unmarried and still lived with their parents. The size of the families in this phase thus decreased sig-nificantly, mostly having only a few or up to five members. Women in their mid-fifties or older usually ceased to work for the collective, and the husbands in their late fifties or older only worked as half laborers, or stopped earning workpoints at all. However, most of their unmar-ried children had become half or full laborers, whose workpoints, to-gether with the workpoints earned by the parents and those contrib-uted by the married brothers, were sufficient to cover the distributions in kind and to ensure a decent amount of year-end cash payment, usually above 100 yuan per household. Older parents in their sixties often found that all of their children had married. They had to either join the family of the youngest son and receive workpoint contributions from other married sons, or stay alone and live on workpoint contributions from the married sons.

A typical family was that of Zhang Yonggen. The couple, both at the age of 56, had eight children. The four eldest daughters and the eldest son had married and had their own families. They still had two daughters, at the ages of 14 and 19, and one son at age 18 staying with them. The family thus had five members. Together, the three unmarried children and their father earned 7,818 workpoints. With a contribution of 502 workpoints from the married son, this family gained a total of 8,320 workpoints, which produced a year-end cash payment of 121 yuan. In another instance, Li Weiji, a 61-year-old widower, lived by himself and received 2,160 workpoints as contribution from his only son and subsidy from the team, which allowed him to get a year-end cash payment of 41 yuan.

By and large, the families in this phase fared quite well, owing to the able labor force of the unmarried children and/or workpoints contributed by married sons. Each member in these families shared an average of 176 workdays, which was about the same level of the mature families at the preceding phase, and 30 yuan in the year-end distribution, which was actually better than the level of the mature families, owing to the fewer mouths in the aging families (QD5 1974).

The Impact of Changing State Policies

Birth Control and the Family Cycle

The Chinese government's birth-control policy in the 1970s brought about remarkable changes to the life cycle of rural families. On the whole, the average age of marriage for women in rural China was delayed from 20.32 in 1971 to 22.25 in 1978. The total birth rate also declined rapidly, from 6.01 in 1971 to 2.97 in 1978 (Yi 1991: 38–39; Chang 1992: 22). Qin village underwent similar changes. In 1970, the average age of the five youngest wives was 21.6 years. The youngest of them was 18 years old. Another four women, at the ages of 19, 22, 24, and 25, respectively, had married between 18 and 21. In contrast, in 1979, the five youngest wives' average age was 24.4 years, and their children were one or two years old, indicating that they had married at 23 or 24. In general, women in the collective delayed their marriage by three to five years

during the 1970s. At the same time, their birth rate declined significantly. For wives between the ages of 20 and 40, the family size was 6.19
on the average in 1970, and by 1979, it had decreased to 4.5 (see Figure
2). The immediate reason behind the delayed marriage and lowered
birth rate was the government's late-marriage policy that regulated 23
as the legal age for women to marry and imposed on them a three-year
interval between births. Meanwhile, many families also voluntarily
delayed marrying out their daughters, whose workpoint earnings were
critical to the family's well-being.

The impact of the changing marriage ages and birth rates in the
1970s on laborer-to-dependent ratio and family income was most evident among the beginning and maturing families. To illustrate this, a
comparison of such families in 1970 and 1979 is in order. In 1970, early
marriage and high fertility remained typical. After marrying at the age
of 20 or earlier, women typically gave birth to their first child at age 22,
the second at 25, and the third at 27, thus quickly bringing the first
phase of the family cycle to an end. Still in their early or mid-twenties,
however, the women could quickly recover from childbearing and re-
enter the labor force. Therefore, the per capita workdays of the eight
beginning families (128 workdays on average) were much more than
that of the maturing families and close to that of the mature families
(see Table 4). In contrast, late marriage and low birth rate in the late
1970s resulted in a longer span of the first phase. Wives during this
phase typically had one child at 24 and 25, two between 27 and 33, and
three between 34 and 36. The first phase thus lasted for fully 12 years,
or 9 years longer than in 1970. When giving birth to the second and
third children, the women were already in their late twenties and early
thirties. It thus took them longer to recover from childbearing as they
had passed their prime years, and their abilities to earn workpoints
also deteriorated. It was understandable, then, that the families of the
first phase in 1979 found themselves in the least favorable situation
among all family groups. Their per capita workdays were 134 days on
average, lower than any other group (see Table 5).

The maturing families underwent a reverse course in the 1970s.
Early marriage enabled young wives in 1970 to enter the second phase
as early as 28 years old when they typically had four children. However, the eldest child did not fully join the labor force until the mother
reached the age of 35. Therefore, throughout this phase, the children
remained basically dependents, while the parents, especially the
mother, had passed their best years to earn workpoints. Mothers

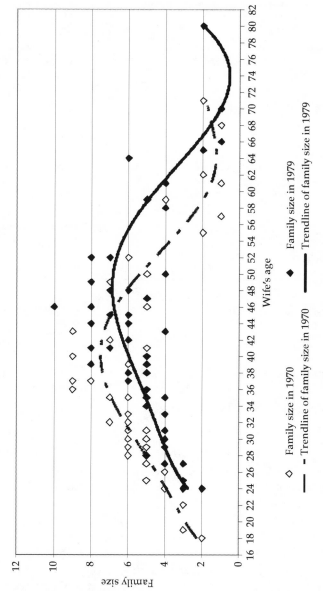

FIGURE 2. Family Size in Qin Village, 1970 and 1979. *Sources:* QD5 1970, 1979; QD13 1964; QD14 1973.

TABLE 4

*Family Life Cycle and the Collective Income of Households
in Qin Village, 1970*

Phases	Beginning families	Maturing families	Mature families	Aging families
Wife's age	18–27	28–35	36–52	53–71
Number of households	8	20	13	7
Family size	3.75	6.05	6.92	1.86
Per capita workdays	128	99	130	165
Per capita cash payment (yuan)	–1.70	–22.66	–11.43	17.69

SOURCES: QD5 1970; QD6 1970; QD13 1964; QD14 1973.

TABLE 5

*Family Life Cycle and the Collective Income of Households
in Qin Village, 1979*

Phases	Beginning families	Maturing families	Mature families	Aging families
Wife's age	24–36	37–40	41–55	56–80
Number of households	18	10	18	8
Family size	3.83	5.7	6.72	3.12
Per capita workdays	134	148	185	153
Per capita cash payment (yuan)	49.80	56.51	85.79	63.16

SOURCES: QD5 1979; QD6 1979; QD13 1964; QD14 1973.

between 28 and 35 thus found their families in the most difficult situation when they had to support a growing family and their aging grandparents with limited workpoints. On average, each family in this phase only earned 99 workdays per person, the lowest level among all family groups (see Table 4). By contrast, the maturing families in 1979 were relatively well-off. When entering the second phase at age 37, the mothers had basically finished childbearing, and fully reentered the labor force, although their earnings were less than girls in the late teens and early twenties. Because of their late marriage and the long span of the first phase, their eldest children had also reached the age of 15 to 18 during this phase, thus becoming half laborers, and their youngest children were also 8 to 13 years old, whose growing abilities to help themselves greatly reduced the parents' burden of child care, allowing them more time and energy to work for the collective. It was no accident, therefore, that these families earned more workdays (148 per person) than those in the first phase of the family cycle (134 workdays per person) (see Table 5). Obviously, the government's efforts of population control in the 1970s had profound effects on the family cycle, causing dramatic changes in the laborer-to-dependent ratio and economic differentiation of the rural families in the first two phases of the family cycle.

The Family Cycle Under Egalitarianism

Another factor that affected the collective income of the villagers was the government's economic policies, especially changes in the workpoint system. During the radical years of the Cultural Revolution (1966–1976), for example, the Chinese government promoted the egalitarian Dazhai system in the countryside as a means to advance equality among the laborers, and at the same time criticized the piece-rate system as "workpoint in command" (*gongfen guashuai*) for its employment of material incentives. When radicalism was over, however, the government encouraged the use of the piece-rate system to implement the socialist principle of "from each according to his ability, to each according to his work" (see Chapter 8). The impact of these two systems on peasant income and its implications for income disparities of families at the different phases of the family cycle is best seen when the two years 1970 and 1979 are compared.

The Dazhai system was fully practiced in Qin village in 1970. An immediate result was the low level of annual workpoints of all workers. The 48 households of the team earned a total of 29,711 workdays, or 117 workdays per person, in that year. In contrast, in 1979, when the task-rate system was widely used, the 54 households in the team earned a total of 43,894 workdays, or 161 workdays per person (QD5 1970). In other words, team members in 1970 earned 27 percent less than they did in 1979.

The limited labor input and poor quality of farm work under the egalitarian system in 1970 further resulted in low agricultural output, which in turn caused the low value of workpoints (0.451 yuan per workday). The low workpoints and low workpoint values combined to produce a very low income from the collective, averaging at 61.91 yuan per person (QD5 1970). By comparison, in 1979, the high workpoints under the task-rate system and the high workpoint value (0.844 yuan per workday) generated a per capita collective income as high as 147.7 yuan on the average, or 2.4 times the 1970 level (QD5 1979).

These changes in the workpoint system and hence the changing standards of labor remuneration had different implications for peasant households at different positions of the family cycle. Under the piece-rate system, households in the third phase of the family cycle found themselves in the best situation among all families in the collective. With more laborers than other family groups, they earned more work-days (185 per person). Although these families had the largest size (6.72 persons per family on average) and therefore paid the most to the team for in-kind distributions that were largely based on the number of mouths, the high cash value of workpoints and high level of work-points enabled them to receive the highest level of cash payment (85.79 yuan per person) at the year-end distribution after deducting in-kind distributions from their total workpoint income (see Table 5).

This advantageous situation of the mature families in 1979 under the piece-rate system contrasted sharply with the unusual hardship that the same family group endured in the radical years, especially 1969, when the workpoint value was so low that every family failed to use its workpoints to cover in-kind distributions from the team. As a result, all of them fell in debt to the team—and the more mouths a fam-ily had, the greater the debt they owed the team, no matter the worker-to-consumer ratio in the family. Families of eight or nine mouths gen-erally owed the team 200 to 300 yuan per household. Thus, although the 13 mature families in the team each earned an average of 130 work-days per person in 1970, which was higher than the earnings of both the beginning and maturing families, most of them had owed the team over 100 yuan and even as high as almost 300 yuan to the team in the previous year (1969), averaging at 22.45 yuan per person. Consequently, they found that the workpoints they earned in 1970 were insufficient to pay off their old debts and cover the in-kind distributions of the cur-rent year. Among the 13 mature families, only 4 received cash at the end of the year. All other 9 families owed the team amounts varying from 43 to 360 yuan. On average, each family in this group shared a debt of 11.43 yuan per person to the collective (see Table 4).

The impoverishment of the mature families under the Dazhai sys-tem was most striking when compared with the situation of the begin-ning families in the same year (1970). With a slightly lower laborer-to-dependent ratio, the beginning families earned an average of 128 workdays per person in 1970, which, as mentioned earlier, was a bit less than the mature families (130 workdays per person). However, the beginning families had fewer mouths (3.75 per family) than the latter (6.92 per family), and the accumulative debt that they had owed to the team prior to 1970 were only 10.66 yuan per person, much less than the latter's. Therefore, among the eight families in this group, five of them were able to pay off their old debt and to cover the in-kind distributions in the current year, thereby receiving a cash payment of 10 to 40 yuan at the end of the year. Altogether, the eight families only owed the collective an average of 1.70 yuan per person, which was much less than the new debt of the mature families in 1970 (11.43 yuan per capita), although the latter actually earned more workdays (see Table 5).

The Changing Income Inequality in the 1970s

To fully understand the economic differentiations caused by the changing laborer-to-dependent ratios over the family cycle and government policies, it is necessary to compare the workdays and workpoint-based cash income of different family groups between 1970 and 1979. Table 4 shows that in 1970 when the Dazhai system prevailed, the biggest gap of workdays occurred between the maturing and aging families. The former earned an average of 99 workdays per person, which was 40 percent less than the latter's. The cash value of workpoints in that year was 0.451 per workday. After deducting the value of in-kind distributions and debt from the previous year, each of the maturing families owed the team an average of 22.66 yuan, whereas the aging families received a net cash payment of 17.69 yuan per person at the end of the year.

In 1979, when the piece-rate system was regularly used, the gap between these two family groups were greatly narrowed; the maturing families earned only 3.3 percent less than the aging families' workdays, and their per capita cash payment (56.51 yuan per person) was only 10.5 percent less than the latter's (63.16 yuan per person). The biggest gap of workpoint earnings took place between the beginning families (134 workdays per person) and the mature families (185 workdays); the former earned 27.6 percent less than the latter (QD5 1979). It was obviously narrower than the biggest gap in 1974 that occurred between the maturing and aging families.

These facts suggest the narrowing gap of collective income between different families groups in the late 1970s. It is worth recapitulation of the two factors behind the reduced inequality: changes in the family structure and increases of the workpoint value. At the beginning of the 1970s, the collective witnessed a sharp contrast between the maturing and aging families. The former had a large size yet low laborer-to-dependent ratio, whereas the reverse was true for the latter. The result was the striking disparity between them in their per capita workdays. At the same time, the low value of workpoints at the beginning of the 1970s under the Dazhai system caused the ever-increasing accumulative debt of the maturing families to the collective because of their inability to use the low-value workpoints to cover the in-kind distributions that were based on their numerous mouths, whereas the small size of the aging families explains their limited debt or even cash payment from the team. Therefore, theoretically, the gap between the two family groups would be ever increasing if there were no changes in the family structure and workpoint values. Ironically, the Dazhai system, intended by radical leaders to promote equality in the rural collectives, in effect produced the widest gap between different family groups when it was compounded with the traditional patterns of marriage and childbearing. At the end of the 1970s, however, the size of the maturing families became smaller while their laborer-to-dependent ratio increased, thus resulting in higher per capita workdays. In general, the gap of per capita workdays among different family groups was greatly narrowed because of the changed structures of the households. Meanwhile, the improved labor productivity and increased cash value of workpoints enabled all maturing families to not only pay off their debt to the team but also receive a net cash payment from it. Although income disparities between different family groups remained significant, the inequality was greatly reduced when virtually all households got rid of the accumulative debt to the team.

Conclusion

The economic fortune of village households was closely related to their size and laborer-to-dependent ratio, which varied constantly over the family cycle. Families during the initial phase of the cycle generally enjoyed the strong labor force of the young couples and the small size of their family. Their situation, however, turned unfavorable as the parents gave birth to more and more children while the labor force remained largely unchanged during the second phase. Mature families of the third phase were often the largest among all families, and they also had the largest number of laborers when the children grew up and entered the labor force. Finally, as the children married and left their parents during the last phase, the families became smaller again, but the parents had the advantages of having yet-to-marry children with them and/or receiving workpoint subsidies from the married sons or the collective.

However, the timing of life events such as marriage and birth that demarcated different phases of the family cycle changed significantly in the 1970s, owing to the enforcement of birth-control policies in the rural collective. These changes in the family cycle coincided with changes in the ideologically charged economic policies, as reflected in the use of different workpoint systems. Therefore, the laborer-to-dependent ratio and the well-being of the rural families during a given phase of the family cycle were not always the same throughout the 1970s. It is necessary to summarize here the changes experienced by each of the four family groups that represented the four phases of the family cycle.

Beginning families. At the beginning of the 1970s, when the low workpoint value under the egalitarian Dazhai system caused widespread indebtedness of rural households to the collective, the beginning families owed much less debt than those in the second and third phases of the family cycle because of their small family size and the able labor force of the young parents. In other words, they were relatively better off in the collective. However, in the late 1970s, as the first phase was prolonged by three or more years owing to the birth-control policy, the wives' working ability deteriorated in their late twenties and early thirties during childbearing while their families' burden to support aging grandparents increased. Thus, although the families earned more workpoints and the workpoints were more valuable in 1979 than a decade earlier, their situation turned out to be the most difficult among the four family groups in that year.

Maturing families. These families were often the poorest in the early and mid-1970s, when the parents were the only major laborers and their many children remained basically dependents. Because their workpoints were insufficient to cover the in-kind distribution from the team that was based on the number of mouths, the maturing families usually owed the highest debts to the collective in 1970. By the end of the decade, however, the prolonged first phase caused the families to enter the second phase when the wives were already in their late thirties, thus fully recovered from childbearing, while their children had become helpers in home chores or partial workpoint earners. As workpoints became more valuable under the task-rate system, they earned more cash per person from the team than the beginning families in 1979.

Mature families. The biggest advantage of these families was their many workers, as their children had grown up and earned workpoints while the parents remained full or partial laborers. In 1970, however, when the cash value of workpoints was very low, the many mouths in these families became a burden, whose in-kind distribution from the team far surpassed the value of workpoints they earned. Therefore, their per capita debt to the team was only lower than the maturing families. In the mid- and late 1970s when workpoints were valuable, the mature families not only earned the highest per capita workpoints but also received the largest amount of cash payment per person among all family groups in the collective in 1979.

Aging families. These families usually had the smallest size, and the aging parents also became partial laborers or retirees in their late fifties or older. However, with married or unmarried children who still stayed with the parents and earned "big workpoints" for them, or with workpoint subsidies from married children who had left the family, these families were well-to-do throughout the 1970s. They were the only ones to receive a year-end cash payment from the production team in 1970 when most households in all other family groups ran into debt. Their per capita workdays and cash payment were second only to the mature families in 1979.

Obviously, because of the government's changing policies on birth control and labor remuneration, the family cycle changed significantly in the 1970s, which in turn had immediate influences on the economic situation of village households at different stages of the family cycle. Contrary to the purported goal to promote equality in rural collectives, the "egalitarian" workpoint system, when coupled with the traditional pattern of the family cycle, actually resulted in the greatest inequalities between different family groups during the radical late 1960s and early 1970s. By contrast, the piece-rate system that prevailed in the later years of the collective era not only permitted remarkable income increase for all families but also significantly narrowed the income gap between different family groups. Finally, it should be noted that the production team under investigation, on which these findings are based, should not be seen as an isolated case. Given the fact that the same workpoint systems, demographic dynamics, and economic trends prevailed simultaneously in many other areas, we may take the changes in family cycle and income disparities in the collective of Qin village as a microcosm of demographic and economic trends in rural China during the collective years.

CHAPTER 10

Agricultural Growth and Social Change

THROUGHOUT THE COLLECTIVE ERA, the state strived to prove the superiority of socialism by accentuating the successes of the collective system in the countryside, such as the mobilization of manpower in changing natural environments, the increased agricultural output in the entire nation, the substantial improvement in the living conditions of rural population, and so forth. In contrast, government officials of the reform era tended to downplay the collective system by underscoring the inefficiency in team production and widespread poverty of the rural people, a way for them to justify the necessity of agricultural reforms that substituted collective system with family farming. Outside China, scholarly interpretations of the collective agriculture in Maoist China are equally divided. Some researchers praise the commune system for its achievements in introducing modern inputs in agricultural production, reducing inequality in income distribution, and bringing modern education and health care to the rural residents. Others acknowledge the significant growth of total output in agriculture enabled by the introduction of modern technologies and the full mobilization of manpower but stress the stagnation of labor productivity and living conditions in the rural area under population pressure during the collective years.[1]

In fact, these contrasting opinions, as contradictory as they seem, can be valid at the same time and be applicable to even the same locality during different years, given the vast regional variations in local ecological conditions and economic performances throughout the country during the collective era. Thus, instead of proving the "success" or "failure" of the collective economy in Qin village, this chapter focuses on how the economic and social institutions under the collective system enabled as well as constrained economic changes and how those changes affected the villagers' daily lives. It scrutinizes the major economic events and trends in the community and the larger Qindong township, including the construction of water-control and irrigation systems, the green revolution in agriculture, the intensification of labor input, and the state's extraction of agricultural surpluses. A close examination of the villagers' living conditions under the collective is also indispensable for a comprehensive understanding of economic and social changes in the community.

"Overturning Heaven and Earth"

Reshaping the Landscape

Qin village, as well as the neighboring communities, is located in one of the lowest parts of the Lixiahe area, north of the Yangzi river. Until the 1960s, most of the area around the village was reed-growing marshes crisscrossed with rivers, rivulets, and ponds (see Map 2). Since the early eleventh century, dwellers in the area had reclaimed the marshland when Fan Zhongyan (989–1052), the famous administrator and scholar of the Song dynasty, served as an superintendent of salt producers within the territory of today's Dongtai county and sponsored the construction of the famous Duke Fan's Dike (*Fan gong di*) to reduce the inflow of salty seawater into the area. But the reclamation was slow and limited because of the lack of water-control projects to protect the farmland from recurrent flooding and waterlogging during the summer. From 1522 to 1948, for example, 95 major floods struck the Lixiahe region, averaging once every four years. Local, small-scale flooding took place almost every year in July and August. In addition, farmland suffered the repeated inflow of seawater owing to the break of Duke Fan's Dike, which occurred eight times during the Republic years from 1912 to 1949 (*Qindong gongshe shezhi* 1981: 64–73).

An effective method of flood control was building dikes around the low-lying fields. In the autumn of 1952, Qindong district built the first dike, three meters high and one meter wide, in Xialong xiang, which effectively protected its fields from a medium flood in 1953. In July 1954, an unprecedented flood swamped the entire Lixiahe region; by July 25, the water level in the district had reached 3.29 meters, or 1 to 1.5

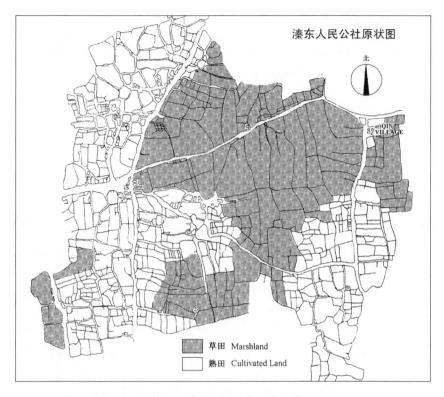

MAP 2. The original condition of Qindong People's Commune.
(Source: *Qindong gongshe shezhi*, 1981)

meters above the ground in most of the district. To save the crops, villagers in the seven xiang of the district built 64 dikes surrounding a
total of 8,965.8 mu or 17.6 percent of the rice fields in the district, and
pumped water day and night from within the dikes using waterwheels
or windmills. Two of the dikes were within the Suqin xiang, which included Qin village. However, by the time the dikes were built and the
water was drained, most rice crops had died and decomposed. The
entire district harvested only 3.21 million catties of rice in the autumn,
or 24.3 percent of its normal yield (*Qindong gongshe shezhi* 1981: 76–80).

After the 1954 flood, the district government was determined to
build a complete network of dikes to encircle all fields in the district, a
decision that became feasible after most households had joined the cooperatives and turned in their farms to the collectives. In the winter of
1955, all of the existing 64 dikes were widened and heightened. In the

following four winters, the 64 dikes, together with other newly built ones, were merged into 49 longer dikes, totaling 86.17 kilometers. But the government soon realized that these dikes remained too fragmented to efficiently drain the flood from encircled fields, and the dikes themselves still had to be further widened and heightened to prevent leaking at the time of flooding. To solve these problems, the district government decided to construct wider and higher "grand dikes" (*dawei*) to surround even larger areas. From November 1959 to May 1960, the first grand dike was finished; it was four meters high, two to three meters wide at the top, and 16.1 kilometers in circumference, covering an area of 10,343 mu. The grand dike worked effectively during the flooding in August 1960, shortly after it was finished, when the villagers closed all eight openings of the dike and kept the water level within the dike 0.55 meters lower than the level outside the dike. Later, the government promoted grand dikes for the rest of the district. By 1965, 18 such dikes were eventually finished that covered all fields in the district (*Qindong gongshe shezhi* 1981: 81–86; see Map 3).

The next task was constructing sluicegates for the dikes. Without sluicegates, the villagers had to fill the 203 openings of the 18 dikes with earth every time a flood was coming and remove the earth when the flood was over. Sometimes an opening had to be dug and filled several times a year because of the repeated floods. In November 1960, the first sluicegate was built on the first grand dike in the district. Made of bricks and concrete, it was 5 meters wide and 5.5 meters high, and could be shut or opened by installing or removing wood beams along the slots on the two sides of the gate. Later the sluicegate was upgraded by installing two permanent concrete doors that could be conveniently closed or opened. Throughout the 1960s and 1970s, the construction of sluicegates continued, peaking in 1973 when 19 gates were finished, which consumed 625 tons of concrete and 24 tons of steel. By 1980, there were 169 gates in the commune (*Qindong gongshe shezhi* 1981: 92).

An even more daunting task was building electric pumping stations. In the 1950s, the villagers mainly relied on windmills to pump water from within the dikes. In 1957, the first water-pumping diesel was installed on a dike in the district. By 1965, the Qindong commune had 18 such water pumps, and 213 by 1980. As a result, windmills, a typical landmark of this area, disappeared in the early 1970s. The water pump, however, had its own drawbacks. Usually installed on a

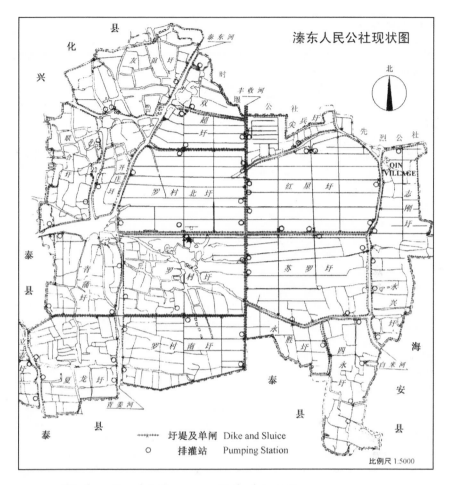

MAP 3. Qindong People's Commune in the late 1970s.
(Source: *Qindong gongshe shezhi*, 1981)

boat, it could not be freely moved in and out of a dike during a flood
when the sluicegates were closed. Despite the increased number of water
pumps, they were not powerful enough to rapidly drain the flood from
within a dike. To construct electric pumping stations thus became im-
perative. In March 1966, the commune built its first pumping station for
about 150,000 yuan. The construction continued in the following
years. In 1973 alone, for example, 29 pumping stations (including two
in Qin village) were built, costing a total of 650,000 yuan, half of
which was funded by the state and half by the commune itself. The

construction of grand dikes, sluicegates, and pumping stations completely solved the problem of flooding and waterlogging that had plagued the area for thousands of years. In July 1974, a torrential rainstorm increased the water level by 1.27 meters overnight. With all pumping stations at work, however, the level of water within the 18 grand dikes dropped quickly, and 21,081 mu of rice and 15,505 mu of cotton survived (*Qindong gongshe shezhi* 1981: 95–97).

The commune also made tremendous efforts to reclaim the marshland and to rework the waterways within each dike. By 1978, a total of 27,650 mu was reclaimed; once a dominant landscape in the area, the marshes completely disappeared. Because most rivers and creeks in the area were narrow, shallow, and crooked, which made the drainage of floodwaters difficult, an ambitious plan of reworking the water system and farmland began in the winter of 1970. More than 4,000 villagers removed 843,000 cubic meters of earth in six months and dug a 6,412-meter-long horizontal canal that runs through the entire commune. In the following autumn, about 2,000 villagers dug three additional canals, totaling 9,680 meters in length. During the remainder of the 1970s, they filled many irregular creeks and ponds within each dike and in their place dug numerous vertical or horizontal canals, drainage ditches, irrigation channels, and rectangular ponds. By the early 1980s when the collective era came to an end, the landscape of the commune had been completely reshaped. A complete irrigation and flood-resisting system covered the entire commune and provided a stable and secure environment for agricultural production (*Qindong gongshe shezhi* 1981: 97–100). In the absence of any modern construction machines, the thousands of male villagers worked extremely hard in the harsh winters during those years, when they manually dug the canals and removed earth with their shoulder poles.

Recalling the persistent efforts to transform the local environment during the collective era, Mr. Zhou, a former commune leader described the changes that took place in the area as "overturning heaven and earth" (*fantian fudi*). But he admitted that the commune cadres had disputed among themselves over various plans of dike construction and other projects; they sometimes "took a roundabout course" (*zou wanlu*) when they had to remove some small dikes and in their places build larger ones or divide the larger ones into small ones to accommodate the local natural river system. To save money, they built some sluicegates in the late 1960s that proved to be too small or too simple and had to be rebuilt in the 1970s. After the complete reclamation of the marshes, households had a shortage of cooking straw. *Lanze,* a popular herb that had widely grown in the marshland, completely disappeared.

The Green Revolution

The collective era also witnessed fundamental changes in agricultural production, such as the introduction of high-yield crop strains and new techniques of farming, and the increased use of pesticides, chemical fertilizers, electricity, and machines; all of them amounted to a true "green revolution" that, coupled with the improved natural environment, dramatically boosted agricultural output in Qin village and the rest of the Qindong commune.

Two major varieties, *yangxian* and *huangjiaoxian,* dominated the rice cultivation before 1949, but they tended to fall down during a rainstorm or a gale and yielded only 300 to 400 catties per mu under normal conditions. In the 1950s and early 1960s, seven or eight new varieties of rice were introduced in succession but none of them were satisfactory, including *nante,* which had more productive spikes but easily fell off. Another strain that failed in the area was the so-called "world rice" (*shijie dao*), which supposedly could yield as high as 600 to 700 catties per mu but required ample fertilization. Without enough chemical fertilizers at that time, farmers could only harvest 200 to 300 catties per mu. In the second half of the 1960s, the villagers gradually switched from round-grained, high-stem strains to long-grained, low-stem ones, which increased the average output to above 400 catties per mu. In the early 1970s, six or seven new varieties were introduced one after another, which generally yielded more than 500 catties per mu. A dramatic change took place in the late 1970s, when a hybrid rice, called *nanyou* (literally, "excellent in the south"), was introduced in the commune. First experimented with on two small farms in 1977 and 1978, the *nanyou* was widely grown in 1978 and fully cultivated over the entire commune the following year, pushing the commune's average output up to 830 catties per mu in 1979. Some farms reached as high as 1,000 catties per mu (QD1 2000).

Coupled with the introduction of new crops were changes in the cropping system. Before 1949, two different cropping systems prevailed in Qin village and neighboring areas. "Double cropping" dominated well-cultivated farms (*shutian*), where the farmers grew wheat in the winter and rice or cotton in the summer. The newly reclaimed, low-lying farms could support only one cropping a year; farmers grew rice in the summer and soaked the farm in the winter for fertilization. In the 1950s and 1960s, the one-cropping farms still accounted for about 50 percent of all arable land in the area. In the early 1970s, however, as all marshes were reclaimed and a drainage system was developed, single cropping finally yielded to double cropping throughout the commune.

To maximize farm output, the commune vigorously promoted the triple-cropping system in the 1970s. Under that system, farmers grew barley in the winter and harvested the crop before May 15, which averaged 300 catties per mu. Then they grew rice twice in the summer. The first cropping began with the soaking of the rice seeds on April 5, which was followed by transplanting the rice seedlings on May 16 and 17 and harvesting on July 31; this practice normally yielded 400 to 500 catties per mu at most. The second cropping of rice started on July 12 with the soaking of the seeds. Rice seedlings had to be transplanted before August 8 to guarantee a normal harvest of 300 catties per mu or 400 catties in a good year. This new system increased a production team's labor and capital input by one-third, and farmers worked extremely hard to ensure that the transplantation and harvesting were done in a timely manner. Some women who transplanted the seedlings for an extended period of time suffered back pain and inflamed fingers. Nevertheless, the annual output of a farm from the three croppings totaled only about 1,000 catties per mu, just a bit higher than its annual output (about 900 catties) under the double-cropping system. After deducting the additional labor and capital input for the third cropping, the actual return of the triple-cropping system was basically the same or even less than that of the double-cropping system (QD1 2000). Thus, despite the commune government's requirement to widely use the triple-cropping system, the leader of the No. 11 team in Qin village limited it to only 20 percent of its rice fields. In the entire commune, it was limited to only about 13 percent in the late 1970s (*Qindong gongshe shezhi* 1981: 142). By the late 1970s, when the pressure lessened, the team completely gave up that system and returned to the traditional double-cropping system. With the introduction of the high-yielding *nanyou*, this system easily generated an annual output of more than 1,200 catties per mu (QD1 2000).

The government also made great efforts to promote new farming techniques. Each production team had an "agricultural technician" (*nongjiyuan*), who received frequent training on new techniques at the commune's agricultural technology promotion station. His basic duty was supervising the team's use of pesticides. Traditionally, farmers used fermented grass liquid or ox urine to kill pests. In the 1960s, chemical pesticides became increasingly available. By the 1970s, the No. 11 team used about 300 one-liter bottles of pesticides a year (the entire commune used 147 tons in 1980, or about 2.45 liters per mu). The team had a special pest-control group, consisting of 14 male and female youngsters, each equipped with an atomizer to spray poison. Sometimes adult men and women joined them when the pests ran rampant. Using the right type and dose of poison at the right time for a specific pest was key to a bumper harvest. The farmers strictly followed the commune station's forecasting and instructions when using the poison (*Qindong gongshe shezhi* 1981: 145).

New methods were also used in preparing seeds, growing seedlings, and planting the different kinds of crops. Some of them were effective and widely accepted; others proved to be impractical and quickly abandoned. In 1976, for example, the government introduced the method of intensive planting for cotton cultivation. By that method, a 3.4 meter-wide strip had to be planted with six lines of cotton plants, and the distance between individual plants on a line had to be 13 centimeters. This intensive planting, in fact, reduced not only the nutrition of the soil available to each crop but also the sunshine and air received by the plant. Therefore, during the first two years of its application in the No. 11 team, its cotton output stagnated and even decreased. Later in 1978, the newly appointed team leader ignored the commune's requirement and decided to extend the distance from 13 to 33 centimeters. He also reduced the use of fertilizers at the time of planting seeds as the commune required, and instead delayed the heavy use of fertilizers to the time when the crop blossomed, to stimulate the growth of bolls. The result was stunning. The team beat all other 191 teams in the entire commune and harvested 254 catties of ginned cotton per mu, a record high in the commune's history. To celebrate this unusual achievement, more than 300 commune, brigade, and team cadres from all over the commune were gathered at the team's threshing ground for a meeting, where the commune leader highly praised the team leader and subsequently promoted him to the position of brigade head. None of the outsiders, however, knew the secret behind the team's miracle (QD1 2000).

The increased investments, especially the use of chemical fertilizers and agricultural machines, also contributed to the agricultural growth of Qin village and the commune during the 1960s and 1970s. Chemical fertilizers were first introduced in 1954, when each village received about 300 catties from the district government. Each household in Qin village obtained a few catties but most villagers doubted its effectiveness. Instead of spraying the fertilizer on the crops, many villagers simply put the entire amount they had received at the root of a tree or a plant, causing the "burning" and death of the tree or the plant. Other villagers who sprayed the fertilizers on their vegetable garden saw the magic; the vegetables grew rapidly. The villagers thus gradually accepted chemical fertilizers in the late 1950s and early 1960s, and learned to use different fertilizers for different purposes. They used ammonium bicarbonate, for example, to prepare the paddy field before transplanting rice seedlings and applied urea after the transplantation to accelerate the growth of seedlings (QD1 2000). By 1980, the entire commune consumed 3,055 tons of chemical fertilizer a year, or about 100 catties per mu (*Qindong gongshe shezhi* 1981: 145). The problem with the use of chemical fertilizers in most collective years was their limited availability. In the early 1970s, for example, Qin villagers used only about 30 catties per mu annually on average, which were too little to be effective, accounting for only one-fourth of the amount the farmers used in the 1980s and 1990s (100 catties and 20 catties per mu before and after the transplantation) (QD1 2000).

Qin village also saw the increased use of machines in the 1970s. In irrigation, for instance, the villagers had long relied on windmills or man-powered waterwheels to pump water into the paddies. Since the purchase of a diesel-powered water pump in 1969, the windmills and waterwheels became less and less useful and were finally abandoned in the early 1970s. After the construction of an electric pumping station in the village in 1973, the powerful electric pump and an irrigation network that reached most fields made irrigation very convenient; the use of a diesel pump was only limited to farms that the network did not cover. In 1975, the No. 11 team purchased a Dongfeng-12 tractor, which partially replaced the farm oxen to plow and rake the fields. Traditionally, the farmers threshed crops mainly by running a stone roller drawn by the oxen. Later, they used a windmill-powered wooden thresher made by a local carpenter. In 1976, the team bought a diesel-powered thresher. In 1980, it built an electric mill to husk and grind the crops. However, all other farm tasks still had to be done manually, including transplanting and harvesting rice crops, and all tasks in cotton cultivation.

To summarize, tremendous efforts were made during the three decades of the collective era in transforming local environment and farming conditions. The biggest achievement was no doubt the completion of an efficient, modern flood-control and irrigation system, the most important precondition for a productive agriculture and sustainable rural development. Also impressive was the revolutionary changes in farming techniques, including the incessant introduction of ever-improving new crop strains and the increased use of chemical fertilizers and pesticides, which resulted in a switch from what the villagers called "farming by old experiences" (*ping laojingyan zhongtian*) to "scientific farming" (*kexue zhongtian*). Although the state's excessive extraction and therefore the team's limited capital accumulation (to be discussed later) only allowed a moderate progress in agricultural mechanization in the 1970s, all these changes laid a solid foundation for rapid agricultural growth and rural development in the next two decades.

Agricultural Growth

Labor Intensification

What shaped the agricultural performance in Qin village during the collective era, especially the 1970s, was not only a remarkable increase in modern inputs as just outlined, but also an increased labor input. Table 6 shows the annual records of labor input in the No. 8 team in 1963 and 1964 (the team was divided into two new teams, No. 8 and No. 11 in 1966), and in the No. 11 team from 1969 to 1981. Each laborer in the No. 8 team earned an average of 163 and 171 "workdays" (*laodongri*, 1 workday = 10 workpoints) in 1963 and 1964, respectively. The average annual workdays increased to more than 200 per laborer at the beginning of the 1970s, and more than 300 per laborer in the late 1970s. The intensified labor input is best seen in the increased annual workdays per mu of farmland. The farmers spent about 34 and 38 workdays per mu in 1963 and 1964, respectively; 62 to 70 workdays in the early 1970s; and more than 100 workdays after 1974. In general, it is safe to say that the farmers' annual workdays almost doubled during the two decades from the early 1960s to the early 1980s, and the labor input per unit of farmland more than tripled during the same period of time.

Several factors explained the intensification of labor input during the collective years. The first is the increased supply of labor force in relation to the limited farmland. In 1963 and 1964, the No. 8 team had 143 and 153 laborers, respectively, to cultivate its 690 mu of farmland; each laborer thus shared an average of 4.8 and 4.5 mu in those two

TABLE 6

Labor Input and Productivity in Qin Village, 1956–1981

Year	Population	Laborers	Farmland Total (mu)	Farmland Per laborer	Workdays Total	Workdays Per laborer	Per mu	Gross income per workday	Cash value per workday
1956	613	310	1,215	3.9	17,429	56	14	2.88	1.912
1957	637	342	1,290	3.8	27,898	82	22	2.48	0.82
1963	374	143	690	4.8	23,253	163	34	2.11	0.93
1964	398	153	690	4.5	26,235	171	38	1.84	0.85
1965	420	142	667	4.7					
1966	225	97	350	3.6					
1967	232	96	350	3.6					
1969	254	134	344	2.6	24,096	180	70	1.14	0.41
1970	257	135	443	3.3	30,004	222	68	1.14	0.45
1971	258	135	447	3.3	27,639	205	62	1.68	0.72
1973	260	141	400	2.8	38,774	275	97	1.2	0.56
1974	265	148	400	2.7	42,518	287	106	1.02	0.46
1975	266	148	400	2.7	45,236	3,306	113	0.96	0.45
1976	269	148	400	2.7	43,599	295	109	1.09	0.49
1977	270	148	400	2.7	45,900	310	115	0.87	0.38
1978	272	148	400	2.7	45,900	310	115	1.19	0.55
1979	272	148	400	2.7	45,118	305	113	1.71	0.84
1980	273	140	400	2.9	45,254	323	113	1.49	0.75
1981	276	140	400	2.9	37,352	266	93	1.93	1.03

SOURCES: DT21 1957; DT23 1957; DT27 1960; DT28 1964; DT 30 1963–1968; DT31 1969–1978; QD5 1966–1981; QD6 1970–1979.

NOTE: Data for 1956–1957 refer to the entire Qindian Advanced Agricultural Cooperative; data for 1963–1965 refer to the No. 8 production team of the Suqin Brigade; data for 1966–1981 refer to the No. 11 production team of the Zhigang Brigade.

years (DT30 1963). The average size of farmland per laborer shrank to about 3.3 mu in the early 1970s and 2.7 mu after 1974 in the No. 11 team, owing to the increased number of laborers on the one hand and the limited size of the farmland in the 1960s and the 1970s (DT31 1970–1978). The second is the wide application of the piece-rate system in the 1970s (see Chapter 8), which greatly stimulated team members' incentive in maximizing their labor input and therefore contributed to the rapid increase of total annual workdays in the No. 11 team. The third is the increased use of laborers in the construction of water-control projects in the late 1960s and the 1970s. As a mandatory task without any compensation from the superior governments, each winter a production team had to supply a number of male laborers to join a project in or outside the commune. Because the task was exceptionally hard, the team had to offer its members high workpoint rates to recruit enough laborers for the project. In 1974, for example, the No. 11 team promised to pay each of the 14 male adults who would join the project 15 points a day. In actuality, the 14 laborers worked only 23 days (or 40 days, including the raining days and traveling days when they did not work) and earned a total of 9,712 workpoints, averaging 694 points per person or about 24 percent of an average laborer's annual workpoints in the team (QD4 1974). The fourth factor behind the increased labor input was the introduction of new cropping patterns and farming methods in the 1970s. The introduction of the double-cropping system in rice cultivation, as mentioned earlier, doubled the team members' labor input. The introduction of many new techniques also increased labor input. Consider, for instance, the digging of subterranean ditches, which was widely practiced in the early 1970s. This task required three steps. A farmer had to first dig an open ditch 30 centimeters deep, and then on the bottom of the ditch he needed to dig a narrow ditch of the same depth. Finally he had to cover the narrower ditch with earth and fill the open ditch above. This way, an adult male could only finish about 100 meters a day, whereas he would otherwise finish 450 meters a day when digging a traditional open ditch. His labor input for digging the subterranean ditch, in other words, increased by 4.5 times.

Agricultural Output and Labor Productivity

As a result of the increased modern agricultural inputs and labor intensification, grain yield in Qin village increased from 270 catties per mu in 1957 to 353 catties in 1964, 500 catties in 1974, and 886 catties in 1979 (see Table 7). Similar growth was also observable in the commune and nationwide. The grain production in the entire Qindong commune increased from 253 catties per mu in 1957 to 329 catties in 1964, 895 catties in 1974, and 1,166 catties in 1979 (*Qindong gongshe shezhi* 1981: 152–153). The national average of grain output in those three years was 195, 205, and 371 catties per mu, respectively (Guojia tongjiju 2000: 40). In general, the grain yield per unit of area in Qin village, the commune, and the entire country more or less doubled from the late 1950s to the late 1970s.

The growth of agricultural output during the collective decades further resulted in steady increases in both the per capita gross income of the production team and the per capita net income distributed to individual team members. The population of the No. 11 team, for example, increased by 8.66 percent, from 254 in 1969 to 276 in 1981, while its gross income increased by 161.71 percent, from 27,490 yuan in 1969 to 71,945 yuan in 1981, much faster than the team's population growth. The result was a steady growth in per capita gross income (see Table 7).[2] The team members' per capita income from the team (i.e., the team's gross income after deducting its production costs, taxes, and collective accumulations and being divided by its population) also increased at 5.63

TABLE 7

Grain Output and Distribution in Qin Village and
Qindong Commune, 1956–1981

	Total output				Grain procured		Grain distributed	
	Qin village							
Year	(catties)	(catties per mu)	(catties per capita)	Qindong commune (catties per mu)	No. 11 team (catties)	Percent of total output	Qin village (catties per capita)	Qindong commune (catties per capita)
1956	39,3026	324	641	351	31,917	8	480	
1957	34,7807	270	546	253	9,415	3	411	449
1958				391				467
1959				331				364
1960				339				328
1961				279				297
1962				237				309
1963	213,756	284	563	316	24,353	11	421	410
1964	225,331	353	523	329	21,000	9	430	399
1965	196,500	367	468	369				394
1966	118,940	352	529					440
1967	139,000	416	599	384				425
1968				458				444
1969	132,300	417	521		9,000	7	395	424
1970	202,000	385	786	1,008	18,000	9	450	454
1971	243,600	522	944	918	32,000	13	510	456
1973	226,560	461	871	947	37,000	16	520	477
1974	242,000	500	913	895	42,000	17	525	480
1975	218,526	437	822	932	29,000	13	512	487
1976	240,000	800	892	947	37,000	15	515	485
1977	238,000	793	881	861	31,000	13	515	487
1978	246,900	823	908	1,097	29,500	12	520	501
1979	265,800	886	977	1,166	36,900	14	560	531
1980	239,100	797	876	1,118	33,000	14	530	512
1981	245,000	490	888		39,191	16	535	

SOURCES: *Qindong gongshe shezhi*: 152–153; DT21 1957; DT23 1957; DT27 1960; DT30 1963–1968; DT31 1969–1978; QD5 1966–1981.

NOTE: Data for Qin village in 1956–1957 refer to the entire Qindian Advanced Agricultural Cooperative; data for Qin village in 1963–1965 refer to the No. 8 production team of the Suqin Brigade; data for Qin village in 1966–1981 refer to the No. 11 production team of the Zhigang Brigade.

percent a year during the same period, from 37.78 yuan per capita in 1957 to 73 yuan in 1964, 88.23 yuan in 1976, and 141.05 yuan in 1981 (see Table 7).[3]

However, the increases in grain output per unit of area and in the villagers' per capita income from the team were achieved in part by intensifying the team members' labor input. Thus, during the decade from 1969 to 1979, while the team's grain production increased by 7.23 percent a year, its gross income by 10.9 percent a year, and its total income for distribution to team members by 11.7 percent a year, the team's total workdays also increased by 6.47 percent a year. The result was a slow growth in labor productivity, or the team's gross income per workday, which was 1.14 yuan in 1969 and 1.71 yuan in 1979, increasing at only 4.14 percent a year. If we compare the late 1960s and the 1970s to the earlier period, however, then there was actually a decline in the team's gross income per workday: from 2.48 yuan per workday in 1957, to 1.84 yuan in 1964 and 1.20 yuan or below in most of the 1970s. Another way to gauge the change in the team's labor productivity is looking at the cash price of a workday (10 workpoints), or the team's total payment to team members divided by their total workdays in a year. The value of a workday declined from 0.85 yuan in 1964 to 0.41 yuan in 1969 and then fluctuated between 0.38 and 0.72 until 1979 when it reached 0.84 yuan. Thus, although labor productivity grew moderately in the 1970s, it saw no breakthrough during the entire collective period, owing to the limited increase in farmland and hence labor intensification (growing at 7.52 percent a year in terms of the team's annual workdays per mu) that surpassed the gross output per unit of farm area (only 2.77 percent a year from 1964 to 1979). The same trend in fact also prevailed in the entire commune (see Table 7) and other parts of the country during the same period.[4]

The stagnation of labor productivity, however, cannot be attributed merely to the increasingly unfavorable land-to-worker ratio and the consequent labor intensification, a trend widely seen in different parts of rural China before agricultural collectivization. Equally responsible for the stagnation and decline of labor productivity was the state's agricultural policies during the collective years, especially its excessive extraction of agricultural "surplus" (i.e., a collective's total output after deducting the minimal amount for maintaining its production and team members' subsistence). This policy severely limited the rural collectives' abilities to accumulate capital and increase modern agricultural inputs and hence hindered their improvement in labor productivity. This is clear when we look at how the agricultural output in Qin village was divided among the different parties.

Dividing the Harvest

A production team's annual gross income was divided into four parts: production cost, tax, collective accumulation, and payment to team members. Table 8 shows the structure of the annual gross income in the No. 11 team (including the former No. 8 team) of Qin village during the collective years. Production cost includes expenses on seeds, fertilizers, pesticides, irrigation, repair of tools and machines, collective sidelines (such as raising pigs and silkworms), and management fees for the team and the brigade. The production cost in the No. 11 team increased from 12,853 yuan in 1969 to 23,278 yuan in 1981, or 5.07 percent a year, while the team's gross income increased 8.35 percent annually during the same period. As a result, the proportion of the production cost in the team's gross income steadily declined during those years, from 47 percent in 1969 to 32 percent in 1981, signifying improved farming efficiency in the collective.

The proportion of the tax in the team's gross income also decreased during the same period, from 6.7 percent in 1969 to 3.2 percent in 1981, although the actual amount of the tax paid to the state increased by 26.7 percent over the 12 years, or 1.99 percent a year, which was much slower than the growth of the team's gross income. In rural China as a whole, the rate of agricultural taxes decreased from 11.6 percent in 1957 to 7.7 percent in 1964, 6.7 percent in 1969, 5.1 percent in 1974, and 3.2 percent in 1981 (Caizhengbu 1994: 411). The decreasing rates of agricultural taxes did not necessarily mean, however, that the state lessened its extraction of the collective's economic surplus. This will be clear when we analyze the state's price policy in grain procurement shortly.

Collective accumulation was deducted from the team's gross income to replenish or increase the collective's funds for investment in public facilities, welfare, grain reserves, and other collective purposes. Its percentage in the team's gross income fluctuated remarkably in different years. In general, the team increased its accumulation when its gross income increased and reduced it when the team suffered a poor harvest in order to increase the proportion of payment to team members. In 1969 and 1977, for example, the collective accumulation accounted for only 1 percent and 2 percent, respectively, when the team's per capita gross income was 110.84 yuan and 146.51 yuan, respectively, significantly lower

TABLE 8
Income Distribution in Qin Village, 1956–1981

Year	Gross income				Production cost		Tax		Collective accumulation		Distribution to team members		
	Total (yuan)	Per capita (yuan)	Farming income (yuan)	Percent of gross income	Yuan	Percent of gross income	Yuan	Percent of gross income	Yuan	Percent of gross income	Total (yuan)	Per capita (yuan)	Percent of gross income
1956	50,254	82			11,859	24	3,192	6.4			34,995	57	70
1957	43,240	68			11,038	26	4,639	10.7	3,025	7	24,072	38	56
1963	36,370	97	35,191	97	14,860	41	2,606	7.2	4,245	12	21,511	58	59
1964	48,196	122	46,499	96	20,664	43	2,857	5.9	6,718	14	27,532	69	57
1969	27,490	111	25,647	93	12,853	47	1,837	6.7	258	1	12,542	51	46
1970	34,330	128	32,991	96	14,177	41	1,907	5.6	3,646	11	14,600	57	43
1971	46,573	180	41,855	90	16,197	35	2,373	5.1	6,769	15	21,200	82	46
1973	46,569	179	43,509	93	19,626	41	1,854	4	3,740	8	21,714	91	47
1974	43,418	164	37,996	87	19,536	45	1,854	4.3	2,388	6	19,641	74	45
1975	43,507	164	37,451	86	17,111	39	1,998	4.6	3,898	9	20,500	77	47
1976	47,661	177	41,662	87	19,553	41	1,970	4.1	4,738	10	21,400	80	45
1977	39,830	147	33,976	85	13,960	35	1,970	4.9	942	2	17,624	73	44
1978	54,620	201	44,859	82	17,394	32	1,970	3.6	6,202	11	25,200	93	46
1979	77,087	283	68,627	89	27,207	35	2,328	3	9,472	12	38,080	140	49
1980	67,704	248	55,248	82	2,5125	37	2,328	3.4	5,854	9	34,398	126	51
1981	71,945	261	63,427	88	23,278	32	2,328	3.2	7,410	10	38,929	141	54

SOURCES: DT21 1957; DT23 1957; DT27 1960; DT28 1964; DT30 1963–1968; DT31 1969–1978; QD5 1966–1981.

NOTE: Data for 1956–1957 refer to the entire Qindian Advanced Agricultural Cooperative; data for 1963–1964 refer to the No. 8 production team of the Suqin Brigade; data for 1969–1981 refer to the No. 11 production team of the Zhigang Brigade.

than in other years. When the team's per capita gross income increased drastically in 1971 and peaked in 1979, its accumulation also reached the highest levels, accounting for 15 percent and 12 percent of the team's gross income, respectively.

After deducting the portions of production cost, the tax, and collective accumulations, the remainder of the team's gross income was for distribution to team members. Likewise, the percentage of this distribution varied remarkably from year to year, mostly between 43 and 47 percent of the team's gross income, and there was no significant growth until the last three years of the collective era. Nevertheless, the team's actual amount of income distribution to its members more than tripled between 1969 and 1981, growing at 9.9 percent a year, much faster than the team's gross income—and the per capita income distributed to the team members also grew from 50.57 yuan in 1969 to 141.05 yuan in 1981, or 8.92 percent annually.

What needs to be further clarified is the actual amount of the state's extraction of agricultural surpluses through taxation and grain procurement. A production team always fulfilled its tax obligation by paying a certain amount of grain and cotton at a price determined by the government. To extract additional grain from the rural collectives, the state deliberately set the price at a very low level, usually one-fourth or one-third of the prevailing price of the grain in private trading. In the 1950s, for example, the official price of rice and wheat crops in Dongtai county was only 0.07 or 0.08 yuan a catty, whereas their actual price in private trading was about 0.2 to 0.25 yuan a catty. In the Great Leap Forward years, the official price remained unchanged while a nationwide famine pushed the price of rice to as high as 1.4 yuan a catty and husked rice 2.00 yuan a catty in the black market. In the rest of the 1960s, the official price of rice and wheat crops was 0.09 to 0.1 yuan a catty, while the market price was 0.4 yuan a catty. From 1969 to 1977, the official price of both crops was about 0.10 yuan a catty, while the market price was about 0.30 yuan. The official and market prices of the crops reversed directions in the following years. In the early 1980s, the government increased its grain price to 0.14 or 0.15 yuan a catty, to offer greater incentives for farmers to increase agricultural output, while the market price of rice and wheat crops dropped to 0.20 yuan a catty, as a result of the increased supply of grain in relation to market demand.[5]

The cash value of the grain that the team paid as taxes or sold to the government to fulfill its procurement obligation thus was much greater than what the official price reflected. The actual tax burden of a production team in the 1960s and most of the 1970s should be three to four times the official figures shown in Table 8. By paying the production team only one-fourth or one-third of the market price for the grain it procured, the state deprived the rural collectives of an additional amount of grain that was often more than the tax burden in the 1960s and 1970s. Take, for example, the No. 11 team's tax and grain procurement obligations in 1974. To fulfill its tax liability of 1,854 yuan, the team paid 18,540 catties of grain to the government at 0.1 yuan per catty. The market price of the grain in the local area, however, was 0.30 yuan. Therefore, the actual value of the grain paid as tax to the state was 5,562 yuan, or three times the official tax burden. In the same year, the team also sold 42,000 catties of grain to fulfill its duty in state procurement, which were worth 12,600 yuan, but the government only paid the team 4,200 yuan and took away the remaining 8,400 yuan as an "indirect tax," which was more than its real tax burden and 4.5 times its nominal tax burden. Altogether, the state extracted a total of 13,962 yuan from the No. 11 team in 1974, while the team's collective accumulation was only 2,388 yuan, or 17 percent of what the state extracted. The actual value of the grain the state extracted from the team through taxation and procurement amounted to about 118,000 yuan during the decade from 1970 to 1979, averaging 11,800 yuan (about 43 to 45 yuan per person) a year, while the team's collective accumulations during the same period totaled about 45,000 yuan, averaging 4,500 yuan a year, only 38 percent of what the state actually extracted.

The state's excessive extraction greatly impaired the team's ability of collective accumulation and impeded its investment in modern agricultural equipment. The average amount of 11,800 yuan that the state annually extracted from the team would have allowed the team to buy, for example, 7 walking tractors, or 15 water pumps, or 25 threshers, or 42,000 kilograms of chemical fertilizers. In actuality, however, with the limited amount of public accumulations, the team had only one tractor, one water pump, and one thresher, and consumed only about 1,500 kilograms of chemical fertilizers a year in most of the 1970s. In other words, because of the overextraction by the state, the production team could only make minimal investments in modern inputs and maintain a "simple reproduction" of the collective economy.

The stagnation of labor productivity in the collective, obviously, cannot be simply attributed to the deteriorating land-to-worker ratio and hence labor intensification. Equally responsible was the state's excessive extraction of the collective's economic surplus that prevented it from increasing modern inputs and improving the farmers' living standards. To safeguard the collective economy and concentrate its limited resources on industrializing the urban sector of the national economy, the state also implemented strict policies to limit the farmers' private sidelines and off-farm economic activities, and prohibited their free migration to towns and cities. All these measures, as we will see in the next chapter, further prevented the farmers from seeking additional income sources and employment opportunities. Once the state reduced its extraction from the rural economy and freed the farmers from the collective organization, agricultural modernization quickly advanced while the labor on farming decreased. The result was the steady improvement of labor productivity in agriculture during the last two decades.

Living Conditions in Qin Village

Despite the low labor productivity and the state's excessive extraction, the living conditions of Qin villagers improved significantly during the collective era, owing to the improved ecological environment and the green revolution in agricultural production that greatly increased land productivity and hence the income distributed to team members, which averaged roughly 40 to 60 yuan per person in the 1950s, 60 to 70 yuan in the 1960s, 70 to 90 yuan in the 1970s, and more than 100 yuan by the end of the collective period (see Table 8). Therefore, significant progress took place in the community in housing, diet, clothing, medical treatment, education, and social welfare.

Housing

Before the 1950s, most houses in Qin village were thatched cottages without bricks and tiles. With adobe walls and straw roof, a cottage typically had three rooms: a living room in the middle and two bedrooms on the sides. Some families had a separate kitchen next to the house; others simply constructed a stove in a bedroom. In the 1950s and 1960s, these cottages continued to dominate the community, and a family usually had to spend about 300 yuan to build such a house. Beginning in 1963 and 1964, about five or six families in the village built new houses with walls of adobe coated by bricks and a thatched roof edged with two lines of tiles. In the 1970s, more and more households built new houses with walls of the same materials and an all-tile roof, which accounted for about 40 percent of the houses in the village by the mid-1970s. To build such an all-tile and partial-brick house usually cost about 1,000 yuan. A family usually needed to spend years to accumulate enough money for the materials and other expenses of a new house. As their income from the team increased after 1978, the number of such houses increased rapidly. By the end of the collective period, the all-tile and partial-brick house had basically replaced the traditional thatched cottages in the community. The best of them had walls all made of bricks and ceilings of thin bricks.[6]

Diet

During the 1950s and earlier, Qin villagers normally ate three meals a day: porridge that was made of rice, oatmeal, or ground barley, or a mix of these, as breakfast and supper, and steamed rice or oats, or a mix of both, as lunch. When there was a poor harvest they ate only two meals a day of porridge, which was usually made of oats or rice blended with a number of carrots, yams, or other vegetables; they added a lunch only during the busy season. Their meals improved in 1956 and 1957, when the state reduced its procurement of the grain from the co-ops while the grain distributed to co-op members increased to more than 400 catties per capita. The villagers suffered food shortage during the Great Leap Forward. In 1961, for instance, the grain ration dropped to less then 300 catties per capita (see Chapter 4 for details). Their per capita grain distribution recovered to the level prior to the Great Leap Forward in 1963 and further increased to more than 500 catties after 1970 (see Table 8). As a result, the villagers regularly ate three meals a day in the second half of the 1960s, often having rice mixed with oats. Ground barley became rare in their diet. In the 1970s, oats also gradually disappeared from their diet; rice became the staple food of their three daily meals. Pancakes and dough drops (*geda*, or dumplings without stuffing) were often part of their breakfast. The villagers normally had enough vegetables to eat for most of the year. Each household had a garden next to the house where bok choy, eggplants, peppers, chives, onions, green beans, pumpkins, and other kinds of melons and vegetables were planted.

However, the availability of cooking oil was limited. During most of the collective years, a team member received only about two catties of oil a year from the collective. Some families therefore had to grow sesame or rape on the private plot and sold their seeds to the state-owned store for extra cooking oil. During the Great Leap Forward, everyone had a ration of only 0.3 or 0.4 catty of oil a year or none at all. It was not until 1978 and 1979 when the team members consumed more than five catties of oil a year because of the increased output of cotton and hence the increased supply of cottonseed oil.

Meat was rare in the villagers' daily diet. There were only a few occasions a year when most families included meat in their lunch: the Duanwu Festival on the fifth day of the fifth lunar month, the Mid-Autumn Festival on the fifteenth day of the eighth lunar month, and of course the lunar New Year, when they ate pork braised in brown sauce or meatballs daily for a week or more. The team usually slaughtered a few pigs before the New Year and distributed several catties of pork to each household. Occasionally, the villagers bought pork to entertain their relatives or guests. Sometimes they also bought pork for self-consumption when a neighbor or a fellow villager butchered a pig, especially during the summer when the price of pork dropped to 0.52 yuan a catty (normally 0.74 yuan in the 1960s and 1970s). In general, they ate pork as rarely as once every few weeks or months.

Many families who had the skill, tools, and spare time for fishing often supplemented their diet with various kinds of fish, crabs, and shrimp. Other families rarely bought these items for self-consumption. However, most villagers were able to get spiral shells, clams, and mussels from the rivers and creeks during the summer to enrich their meals and increase their intake of animal proteins. The villagers rarely consumed eggs, though each family raised a number of chickens. Instead, they sold the eggs for cash (at 0.70 yuan a catty) to buy salt, kerosene, soy sauce, matches, cigarettes, and other daily items that they could not produce by themselves. The villagers did eat hard-boiled, fried, or steamed eggs more often than pork, but in general, the eggs were for sale rather than self-consumption. Tofu or bean curd was another source of protein in the villagers' diet. At 0.02 yuan a piece (about half a catty), it was more affordable and therefore frequently became part of their lunch. In general, however, the villagers' intake of fat and protein was far from sufficient. It is no wonder that when buying pork, most villagers preferred fat to the lean meats in those days, while the reverse has been true since the 1980s.

Clothing

The villagers' clothing changed remarkably between 1950 and 1980. Because of the frequent flooding and hence the limited yield and poor quality of cotton, cotton spinning and weaving had never become a family industry in Qin village and the surrounding areas before the 1950s. For centuries, dwellers in this area relied on hand-woven "native cloth" (*tubu*) bought from a market town or a peddler. Each piece of the native cloth was one *chi* (1.094 feet) wide and three chi long, dyed in dark blue or black, and worth 2.25 catties of rice. In the early 1950s, however, machine-made, large-size cotton cloth (*yangbu*) in various colors gradually replaced the *tubu*. This change occurred when the state-owned marketing co-ops replaced the traditional marketing networks and sold only the cloth made by state-owned factories or imported from the Soviet Union. The machine-made cloth was usually 0.20 to 0.30 yuan per chi; the poor-quality cloth manufactured by local commune-owned factories sold at only 0.18 yuan per chi. Beginning in the late 1960s, polyester fabrics such as Dacron became more and more available and popular among the villagers, but it was more expensive than the cotton fabric. Therefore, only well-do-to families, young adults, and village cadres wore such clothes in the 1970s.

The villagers customarily made new clothes before the lunar New Year, so that on the New Year's day everyone had a set of new clothes to wear. Not every family, to be sure, was able to provide each of its members a set of new clothes during the collective years. When they had a tight budget, the parents made only one piece of clothing, normally the upper outer garment, for themselves, but they would make every effort to ensure that their children each had a complete set of new clothes. Another time to make new clothes was before and during the summer, when they had to wear short pants and short sleeves, which were more affordable than the winter clothes made for the lunar New Year. Too, a bride-to-be had to prepare several sets of new clothes for her wedding, which usually cost 40 yuan in the 1950s and more than 100 yuan in the 1970s.

After buying a piece of cloth, a woman usually made the clothes by herself. She would ask a skilled woman in the village to help her cut out the cloth according to the desired style and size.[7] The villagers never bought ready-made clothes from a store. In fact, there were no such clothes available from the market at all. The style of the villagers' clothes changed a great deal over the years. All homemade clothes were traditional, with knotted cloth ropes as buttons down the front for men and on the right side for women. Almost all villagers wore such clothes in the 1950s. The few exceptions were the village cadres, who asked tailors in the market towns to make machine-sewn Western-style shirts, short sleeves, and most importantly the Mao-style tunic with two up-per small pockets and two lower pockets, known to the villagers as "the cadres' garment" (*ganbufu*). Thus, a cadre could be instantly dis-tinguished from ordinary villagers by his jacket, the fountain pen clipped to the upper left pocket of his *ganbufu*, and the cigarettes that he smoked; ordinary villagers smoked only cut tobacco in the bowl of a long-stemmed pipe (it was not until the early 1980s that the pipe to-bacco was finally replaced by cigarettes among the villagers). During the Cultural Revolution (1966–1976), most villagers, especially young and middle-age men, gave up the traditional jacket and turned to the mili-tary uniform–styled garments or the Mao-style tunic. By the end of the collective era, traditional-style clothes had become rare among both male and female villagers.

The villagers' shoes also changed. Traditionally, it was the duty of the mother or wife to make shoes for her family members, so that each family member would have at least a pair of new shoes for the lunar New Year. When doing heavy tasks, adult men usually wore their handmade straw sandals, rather than the cloth shoes. Such straw san-dals were gradually replaced by rubber-soled shoes bought from the market in the second half of the 1970s. Also since the mid-1970s, plastic sandals became increasingly popular among the villagers, especially students, in the summer. The villagers never wore leather shoes that were expensive and rare in the market. It was not until the mid-1980s that some young villagers began to wear leather shoes during the lunar New Year or other occasions when they did not do farm work. During raining days, the villagers traditionally wore what they called "nailed shoes" (*dingxie*) because they were made of layers of cloth coated with tung-tree oil and fastened with many nails. Hard and uncomfortable, such shoes gradually yielded to rubber boots in the 1960s and early 1970s.

The raincoat also changed from that made of the alpine rush by the villagers themselves to plastic coats bought from the market; these became popular in the early 1970s. By and large, it can be said that the villagers underwent a clothing "revolution" during the collective period, not only in the style and materials of their clothes but also in the way the clothes were made.

It is worth noting that, in addition to the significant improvements in housing, diet, and clothing, the villagers began to buy "luxurious" goods in the second half of the 1970s. Portable or desktop radios became a popular item among the few well-to-do families. A few villagers also had a wristwatch and even a bicycle. However, such goods did not enter most households in the village until the early 1980s, when their disposable income increased greatly under the household responsibility system.

Education

With the district government's assistance, Qin village established a primary school in 1958. Housed in the teacher's own home, the school had two classes for first and second graders, respectively (students of the third grade and above had to go to the primary school in the neighboring Su village about one mile away). Mr. Zhao, the only teacher, taught the two classes alternately, usually teaching one class while leaving the other doing classwork. He offered four courses: reading, arithmetic, music, and art, and taught the two classes together only when it was time for music. In the early 1960s, most families in the village sent their children to the school, and about 70 percent of the students were boys. In 1972, the Zhigang Brigade rebuilt the school at a different site, which had two separate brick buildings, each having two rooms. With four glass windows, the classroom was bright and comfortable. The school also expanded to include the third and fourth grades, and each grade had its own room and teacher. Almost all school-age children of both sexes in the village, totaling about 130 to 140, attended the primary school at that time. The school charged each student 1.50 to 2.50 yuan as tuition and textbook fees per semester, which were affordable to all families.

The brigade had a separate, more formal and complete primary school in the neighboring Su village, which started in 1950 and had six classes from the first to the sixth grades. During the Cultural Revolution, the school was expanded to have two middle-school classes for sixth and seventh graders (the primary school was shortened to five years).[8] The courses offered there included Chinese, mathematics, English, physics, chemistry, physical education, art, music, history, and geography. About 80 to 90 percent of boys and 50 percent of girls in Qin village attended the middle school.

After graduating from the junior middle school, some students continued their education in the high school located at the seat of the Qindong Commune, about five miles from Qin village. During the 10 years of the Cultural Revolution, only three male students from Qin village attended the high school; they were recommended by brigade cadres and representatives of poor and lower-middle peasants from individual production teams based on their academic records as well as their family backgrounds. When the Cultural Revolution was over, students had to take an entrance examination to enter high school.[9] By 1980, when the collective system almost came to an end, the villagers' literacy rate had significantly improved. About 30 percent of middle-aged and older males, who had received a few years of education in the village's school in the 1950s or earlier, were basically literate; they could read newspapers and understand production team accounts. Among the villagers between the ages of 20 and 35, about 90 percent of males and 30 percent of females were basically literate, for they had attended school for several years in the 1960s. All teenage boys and about 60 percent of teenage girls in the village received at least four or five years of education in the primary school, and all school-age children under the age of 12 went to school. Altogether, about 60 to 65 percent of the village's population was literate by the end of the 1970s, whereas in the early 1950s, the literacy rate was less than 10 percent in the community.

Health Care

The collective era also witnessed a fundamental change in the villagers' health condition. Before the 1950s, the biggest threat to the health of the rural population was epidemics, especially cholera, which hit the locality in 1932 after a flood and again in 1938 during a long-lasting drought, causing at least one death for every three households in the local area (*Qindong gongshe shezhi* 1981: 224). When they fell ill during other times, the villagers usually turned to a traditional doctor for herbal medicine or, if that did not work, visited a local temple or a simple shrine to say prayers. In 1958, the Suqin Brigade (including Su and Qin villages) created a clinic, officially called the "health station" (*baojianzhan*), with two doctors who dispensed herbal and Western medicines to villagers and referred patients in serious condition to the commune's hospital. The local government made tremendous efforts in preventing epidemics and curbing infectious diseases. In 1963 it launched a campaign to search and eliminate *oncomelania* (a type of snail that was the intermediate host of blood flukes and thrived in the marshes) and to cure the patients who suffered from snail fever. Beginning in 1965, all children in the commune under 15 years of age had to receive vaccines against tuberculosis, smallpox, measles, meningitis, and diphtheria. Since the late 1960s, adult women were paid workpoints for a visit to the local clinic or the commune's hospital to receive an examination for women's diseases. In 1969, for example, 3,643 women were found to have various diseases and 1,742 were cured. Beginning in 1977, all women in the commune under age 60 received an annual screening for cervical cancer. Each year, two to four women were found to have the cancer. As malaria became rampant in the commune in the early 1970s (the patients increased from less than 1,000 in 1960 to 7,453 in 1974, or 21.1 percent of its population), the government distributed free preventive medicine to all residents, and each brigade assigned a number of individuals to distribute the tablets and supervise the villagers' regular use of the medicine.[10] As a result of the effective prevention, malaria patients in the commune decreased drastically to 453 in 1975 and 78 in 1977 (*Qindong gongshe shezhi* 1981: 230).

The biggest achievement in public health during the collective years was the establishment of the "cooperative medical service" (*hezuo yiliao*) system in 1969. Under the system, each team member in the commune contributed 0.50 yuan to the commune's funds for maintaining the service. In addition, each production team contributed an additional 1.5 yuan for each team member to the funds. Whenever a villager fell sick and visited the brigade's clinic, he or she needed to pay just 0.05 yuan as the registration fee to see a doctor and receive free medicine. If the patient had a serious medical condition that the local clinic could not handle, he or she would be transferred to the commune's hospital or, if necessary, to the more advanced hospital at the county seat. When hospitalized, the patient was responsible for 20 percent of the cost of the medicine; all other costs involved would be covered by public funds (QD1 2000).

An integral part of the system was the training of "barefoot doctors," who were recruited from educated young villagers. After taking the necessary courses and finishing their internship in a hospital, they were assigned to the clinic of their home brigade. By 1980, the commune had trained 52 of these doctors, averaging two for each brigade-level clinic (*Qindong gongshe shezhi* 1981: 229). They were called "barefoot doctors" not only because they came from among, and served, the villagers, but also because they were rewarded only with workpoints, just like ordinary farmers, rather than with salaries from the state. The annual workpoints that the brigade paid to its doctors were normally 500 points higher than the average level of strong adult male laborers (QD1 2000). Because of the government's persistent efforts in improving public health, epidemics had disappeared by the end of the collective era, and all patients were able to receive necessary treatments under the cooperative medical service system.

Social Welfare

From the start of the collective period, the rural collectives offered different kinds of benefits to qualified members. One was the "five guarantees" (*wubao*) for orphans and elderly villagers who were unable to work and who had no children to provide old-age support. This program "guaranteed" their food supply, clothing, housing, education (for orphans), and burial (for the aged). Qin village had three such old-age villagers covered by the program in the late 1950s, each receiving 45 yuan from the cooperative in 1957 (DT23 1957). The No. 11 team had no *wubao* households until 1979 when a childless man turned 66 and received 65 yuan to buy grain and other daily necessities and an additional 140 yuan as his subsidies (QD5 1979).

Another program was workpoint or cash subsidies for "households in difficulties" (*kunnanhu*). Three basic factors caused difficulties or poverty to such households: many dependents but few workers; sickness and especially hospitalization of a team member that caused his or her loss of working abilities for a certain period of time; and the loss of property because of fire or theft. The production team identified its *kunnanhu* at the end of a year before finalizing its distribution plan; a number of team members' representatives (usually one member from each descent group) were gathered to deliberate the actual condition of individual households. In general, they determined a family's eligibility according to the amount of its debt to the team. Different amounts of workpoints were granted to reduce the debt or to prevent it from becoming an "overdrawn household." The Qindian advanced co-op had seven such households out of its 125 member households, each receiving 120 to 1,420 workpoints in 1957 (DT23 1957). The No. 8 team of the Suqin Brigade had seven *kunnanhu* among its 81 households in 1964, and each received 100 to 300 points as subsidy (DT28 1964). In the 1970s, the No. 11 team (part of the former No. 8 team) supported two to six households each year, each receiving 10 to 70 yuan in cash in the mid-1970s and up to 95 yuan in the late 1970s, so that they could buy the necessary goods for the lunar New Year (QD5 1970–1979).

The rural collectives also offered "preferential treatment" (*youdai*) to veterans' or soldier's families. In 1957, for example, each of the five veterans' families in the Qindian co-op was granted 100 to 150 workpoints

(DT23 1957). In the 1960s and 1970s, this benefit was limited to soldiers' families only. Each of the five such families in the No. 8 team, for example, received 100 to 500 points in 1964 (DT28 1964). The No. 11 team had only one serviceman's family in the 1970s, who received 1,500 to 2,200 points in the mid-1970s.

Conclusion

We can draw three conclusions from the foregoing discussion. First, the construction of a modern flood-control and irrigation system, increased modernization in agriculture, and the wide application of new crop varieties produced a long-term growth in both land productivity and per capita agricultural income from the 1950s to the 1970s. It is important to note that these changes were not limited to Qin village and the surrounding areas; rather, they reflected an unprecedented nationwide effort to improve agriculture and maximize land output during the collective years. To illustrate this point, let us look at some basic indicators at the national level in 1957, 1970, and 1979. The total area of farms irrigated by mechanical and electrical equipment, for example, increased from 4.4 percent to 41.6 and 56.3 percent of total irrigated areas in those three years, respectively (Nongyebu jihuasi 1989: 318). The machine-plowed farms accounted for 1.7, 12.7, and 28.4 percent of all farming areas in the country (Nongyebu jihuasi 1989: 318, 130–131). The use of chemical fertilizers averaged 1.5, 12.8, and 47.6 catties per mu (Nongyebu jihuasi 1989: 340–341). Increased modernization in agriculture explained a steady growth in agricultural output in the country. The national average of grain yield was 196, 268, and 372 catties per mu, respectively, in those three years (Nongyebu jihuasi 1989: 146–148). More importantly, the per capita agricultural income of the rural population increased significantly: from 79 yuan in 1957 to 113 yuan in 1970 and 151 yuan in 1979 (Nongyebu jihuasi 1989: 76–77, 84–87).

Second, despite the remarkable growth in land productivity and per capita income of the rural population, labor productivity in agriculture remained basically unchanged in Qin village as well as the rest of the country. Labor intensification under the increasing population pressure and diminishing marginal return were an important reason behind the stagnation in per workday output but were not the entire story. This chapter has emphasized the state's excessive extraction of rural surpluses through the compulsory procurement of grain, the collection of agriculture taxes, and the requisition of agricultural labor

force for public projects; all of these measures hindered the agricultural collectives' capital accumulation and technological investments
and hence halted their improvement in labor productivity. The slow
progress of labor productivity during the collective era, in other words,
was a new phenomenon under the socialist state; it should be distinguished from what had happened before for centuries in the country
when population pressure solely propelled labor intensification.

Finally, although labor productivity remained low, the substantial
increases in agricultural output per unit area and in per capita agricultural income during the collective years permitted a remarkable improvement in the villagers' living conditions. Qin villagers experienced
significant changes in their housing, diet, clothing, education, public
health, and social welfare, which bespoke a breakthrough in social
progress and development in the truest sense. It is worth emphasizing
that all those changes took place before the collective system came to
an end, rather than thereafter, and they were not unique to Qin village
but observable at the national level, as well indicated in the increase of
the average life expectancy of the rural population in the entire country from about 35 years in 1950 to 69 years in 1980 (Zhongguo tongjishi
shiwusuo 1997: 32).

Top: Located in the lowest area of the Lixiahe region, farmland in Qin village was only about two feet above water level after a heavy thunderstorm in the summer of 2005. *Bottom:* One of the three sluicegates on the dikes surrounding the farmlands in Qin village. Next to it is a pumping station that is pumping water from the inside of the dike to the outside.

Top: New techniques of rice transplantation were introduced to the village in the 1990s. Rice seedlings on the left and right sides of the paddy field here were planted by manually "throwing the seedlings" (*paoyang*) and using a transplanting machine, respectively. *Bottom:* One of the kilns around Qin village. Next to it are freight boats that shipped tiles and bricks to neighboring markets.

Top: One of the six chicken ranches in the village in the early 2000s. *Bottom:* A factory in the village that produces steel pipes.

Top: The author (far left), the author's brother (far right), and the three cadres of Qin village, including Mr. Zhang, the director of the village council (second from left); Mr. Zhang, the accountant (middle); and Mrs. Zhu, the director of the village's Women's Federation (second from right). *Bottom:* A traditional ritual at a funeral in 2006.

Top: Newly built two-story houses at the "central village." Next to them are a paved roadway with street lamps and a textile factory. *Bottom:* A new house under construction at the "central village." The owner, Mr. Wang, is a carpenter.

PART FOUR

The Reform Era

CHAPTER 11

Decollectivization

THE EXISTING LITERATURE of decollectivization in rural China generally traces the origin of the household responsibility system and its replacement of the collective system to the audacious action of peasants in Xiaogang village, Fengyang county of Anhui province. It is widely believed that the 18 households of a production team in that village, driven by the hunger and despair that they had suffered for an extended time under the collective system and the difficulties they faced in breaking the team into subteam groups for more efficient farming, surreptitiously allotted the collective farmland to themselves for independent, family-based farming on a winter night in 1978. The 18 families were allowed to keep whatever they produced after fulfilling the team's collective duties in agricultural taxes and grain procurement. The next year, the villagers saw a miracle: their crop output reached a total of 132,000 kilograms, four times the previous year's level. Encouraged by local authorities and finally endorsed by the central government, more and more teams in Fengyang county and the rest of China followed Xiaogang's example of *dabaogan* (literally, the complete allocation of responsibilities [to individual households]) in the following years (see, e.g., Huang Yiping 1998; Li Jin 2000; Yin and Yang 2004; Fishman 2005). Whether the story of Xiaogang villagers was true and whether the figures of agricultural output before and after *dabaogan* in that village were deliberately exaggerated and even fabricated have been subject to the controversy among Chinese scholars and journalists (Chen and Zeng 2006). Nevertheless, the story has been frequently cited by government officials and pro-reform scholars in

China to illuminate the initiatives of Chinese peasants in decollectivization, to underscore the spontaneity and the grassroots nature of the
process, and to prove the necessity and legitimacy of the reform policies in the countryside. It comes as no surprise that, in celebration of
the thirtieth anniversary of the inception of economic reform in China,
Hu Jintao, the general secretary of the CCP, visited Xiaogang village on
September 30, 2008, praising the villagers for initiating the household
responsibility system in the countryside (*Renmin ribao*, October 1, 2008).

The actual process of decollectivization in Qin village does not jibe
with what the official media tried to make people believe. The previous
chapter has shown that the last few years of the 1970s (i.e., the eve of
decollectivization) were the best years in the history of the collective
economy in the village. As a result of the state's promotion of the use of
material incentives in team farming, the late 1970s witnessed a steady
increase in both the output of rural collectives and the per capita income of their members. The grain yield in Qindong commune, for
example, increased from 861 catties per mu in 1977 to 1,097, 1,166, and
1,118 catties in 1978, 1979, and 1980 (*Qindong gongshe shezhi* 1981: 152). In
Dongtai county, grain yield increased from 786 catties per mu in 1977
to 947, 1032, and 1014 catties in the following three years (Dongtai xian
nongye ju 1987b: 116). The same was true in the entire country, where
the grain yield increased from 314 catties per mu in 1977 to 338, 372,
366, and 378 catties in the following four years (Nongyebu jihuasi 1989:
148). The net income of rural population in the country also increased
from 134 yuan per capita to 160 yuan in 1979 and 191 yuan in 1980
(Nongyebu jihuasi 1989: 128). Instead of terminating the collective system, local governments in many provinces were interested in elevating
the basic accounting unit of the collective organizations from the production team to the brigade; that is, to make the collective system more
collective and socialistic in nature in 1978 and 1979 (GNW 1981b: 956,
992). Therefore, there was no sign that the collective agriculture was
bound to collapse.

This chapter shows that decollectivization in Qin village, as in the
rest of rural China, was primarily a top-down process planned and
imposed by the state, rather than a result of local initiatives. However,
the introduction of the household responsibility system nevertheless
spurred the farmers' unprecedented enthusiasm for production and
ushered in a new era of rural development. To show how the transition
to family farming changed the economic life in Qin village, this chapter focuses on the villagers' new strategies for farming and increasing

family income in the 1980s and beyond. It also sheds light on a new dynamic of economic growth, in which off-farm employment, modern inputs in agriculture, and improvement in labor productivity combined to propel the modern transformation of the rural economy at a pace unseen during the collective era. However, unlike the popular media and the existing literature on rural China that highlights the contrasts before and after the reform, this chapter emphasizes both changes and continuities in the countryside during the reform era.

The Reform

Dividing the Field

The transition from team production to family farming in rural China officially began in September 1979, when the Party allowed *baochan daohu*, or "contracting fixed output quotas to households," for families with "special needs in sideline production" and therefore unable to join team production and to those that were located "in remote mountain areas and inconvenient in transportation" (GNW 1981b: 992). Given the long history of the collective system and the established ideology that equated the collective system with socialism in the rural area, the Party was particularly cautious in introducing family farming. Therefore, the Party officially forbade dividing the field for independent farming when announcing the aforementioned *baochan daohu* policy. Endorsed by the Party's famous Third Plenary Session of the Eleventh Congress in December 1978, the latest version of the "Sixty Articles" as government regulations guiding rural economic organizations acknowledged the people's commune as the fundamental system in the countryside; virtually all of its prescriptions about labor management and income distribution in the commune remained the same as they had been before the Cultural Revolution. In March 1979 the Party even denounced the pre–Cultural Revolution practice of "contracting fixed output quotas to households" (*baochan daohu*) as a "retrogression" (GNW 1981b: 1010), and prohibited the attempt of "dividing the field for independent farming" (*fentian dangan*) in September 1979 (GNW 1981b: 992).

However, Deng Xiaoping and the pro-reform leaders were determined to push the rural reforms through when they consolidated their control of the Party. In September 1980 the Party allowed *baochan daohu* in not only poor areas but also "ordinary areas" where "*baochan daohu* has already been implemented and the masses do not want to change it" (GNW 1981b: 1051). Finally, in December 1981, the Party accepted *baochan daohu* as a permanent system in all areas regardless of their economic conditions. In fact, by that time, more than 90 percent of the production teams in the country had divided their fields and distributed them to individual households for contracted output quotas and other obligations (Du Runsheng 2003: 266–283).

Grassroots cadres' reactions to the Party's reform policies varied from place to place. The production team and brigade leaders in poverty-stricken areas who had already divided their collective fields for independent farming when *baochan daohu* remained illegal embraced the new policies enthusiastically. However, cadres and team members in the relatively well-to-do places, such as Qin village, felt no urgent need to abandon the collective system in the early 1980s, when they witnessed steady increases in their teams' output and a continuous improvement in their living standard. In 1979 and 1980, the leaders of the Zhigang Brigade (including Qin and Su village), for example, refused to delegate the power of production management from the production team to subteam groups by contracting fixed workpoints for fixed output. The commune and brigade leaders also refused to divide the collective fields and distribute them to individual families for *baochan daohu*, believing that this practice should be limited to the poor mountain areas and was inapplicable to areas on the plains (such as the commune) as the superior authorities ordered. In early 1981, the higher authorities suggested that the production teams should be allowed to distribute part of their farmland as "grain-ration fields" (0.5 or 0.6 mu per person) to member households so that they could grow crops on the plots as their grain rations and the team would no longer be responsible for distributing the rations to them. For the No. 11 team in Qin village, it meant that 164 mu, or more than 40 percent of its farmland, had to be allotted as grain-ration fields to its 273 members. The brigade and team cadres resisted this policy for the obvious reason that once the grain-ration fields were distributed to the team members, the latter would concentrate their energy on their individual grain-ration fields and engage in other private businesses, and no one would be interested in working the remaining 60 percent of the team's farmland. However, by mid-1981, the drive for *dabaogan* (that is, to divide a team's entire farmland among its member households for contracted output, taxes, and other obligations) had swept the entire nation and the pressure from above to dismantle the collective system mounted.

Without other options, the brigade decided to start *dabaogan* in all production teams (QD1 2000).[1]

The No. 5 team of the Qindian Brigade (formerly the No. 11 team of the Zhigang Brigade and after 1984 the No. 5 group of Qin village) divided its fields in August 1981 before harvesting the rice crop, and the team members actually received their land in November so that they could sow wheat seeds on their own fields.[2] The size of the land that a household received from the team depended on the number of its mouths to feed and its laborers. By the rule of the team, each team member would receive 0.6 mu as his or her "grain-ration field," and each laborer would receive an additional 1.7 mu as a "laborer's field." Thus, if a family had four mouths and two of them were laborers, it would receive 5.8 mu of land in total, including 2.4 mu as the grain-ration field for its four members and 3.4 mu as the laborers' field for its two working adults. In addition, the family also kept its preexisting private plot and garden land (QD1 2000).

It should be noted that the households did not own the land they received from the team; the ownership of all land in the country legally belonged to the state, a fact remaining true in the following decades. The villagers only had the right to cultivate the land, for which they had to assume and share all of the obligations that the former production team had held to the state, including the payment of agricultural taxes and fulfillment of grain procurement quotas, a topic to be discussed later. Because the land was allotted according to a household's number of mouths and laborers, the team made minor adjustments every few years and two major reallocations in 1990 and 1996, when birth, death, and marriage had caused significant changes in the number and size of the team's households.

Strategies for Family Farming

The cadres in Qin village were ambivalent toward the *dabaogan* reform. On the one hand, they were relieved when the fields were allotted to the villagers; they no longer had the daily tasks of planning farm work and recording workpoints for each team member, and they were no longer responsible for the team's output. Still, they held certain privileges, such as their continual control of public funds and subsidies for their positions. On the other hand, however, each cadre had to cultivate his own field, no matter he was a leader of the "villagers' group" (*cunmin xiaozu*, formerly the production team), or the administrative village (formerly the brigade), or a cadre of the township (formerly the people's commune). Whereas during the collective years, the commune leaders often complained of the grassroots cadres' spending too much time in office and nonparticipation in farm work, now they complained of the reverse: they often found no cadre staying in the village's office, especially during the harvesting season, when the village leaders were preoccupied with their own plots.[3] Indeed, the reform greatly narrowed the gap between the grassroots cadres and the villagers in terms of their participation in agricultural production, a result unexpected by both the government and the cadres themselves.

Ordinary farmers reacted to the reform differently. Some young villagers were worried about their lack of knowledge of certain techniques, such as soaking rice seeds, preparing the seedling bed, or using pesticides. To reduce their anxiety, the No. 5 team hired some experienced villagers to soak rice seeds for all the households in the spring of the first year of independent farming (1982). Some families who had few laborers and many dependents were anxious about their inability to work the many mu of land allotted to them. From time to time, the villagers talked about how a couple in a certain village, unable to finish their work in a timely manner, quarreled badly at the time of rice transplantation or harvesting, causing the wife to commit suicide by drinking poison. Therefore, some of them expressed their unwillingness to divide the field, saying to the cadres, for example: "we prefer that you yell to us on a megaphone every morning and tell us what to do; that makes us feel at ease" (QD1 2000). Indeed, over the 30 years of collective agriculture, the villagers had developed a mentality of being dependent on the cadres. It was hard for them to alter their established lifestyle. The villagers who were most unwilling to accept *dabaogan* were those who had an off-farm sideline or job as their major source of income, such as the fishermen, the carpenters, the smiths, the bricklayers, the lacquerers, the teachers, and the barefoot doctors. They earned more money from their own trades than the farmers and received low-cost grain rations from the production team by paying the team a small sum of money for the necessary workpoints to cover the rations. They had been happy with the existing arrangements under the collective system.

The villagers who were most supportive of *dabaogan* were the families with able laborers but no off-farm income sources. They complained that under the collective system it had been "for the dark-skinned to support the light-skinned" (*heipi de yang baipi de*). The "dark-skinned" meant themselves, or those who always toiled in the sun. The "light-skinned" were those who did no farm work but received rationed grain from the team. Thus, when asked how they responded to *dabaogan*, the villagers' answer was that the dark-skinned welcomed it and the light-skinned disliked it. In general, the dark-skinned accounted for more than 70 percent of all households and the light-skinned less than 30 percent.

No matter which group they belonged to, all villagers had to work as diligently as possible to increase the output from their own fields. Farming efficiency increased remarkably after decollectivization. Take transplanting rice seedlings, for example. During the collective years, the No. 11 team had only about 20-odd adult women for that job, and it usually took about 40 days for them to finish the task. After dividing the field, however, all available laborers in a family had to join that task. In the No. 5 group (the former No. 11 team), more than 100 laborers were involved in the task, and it took them only 7 to 10 days to finish transplanting the rice seedlings on all paddies. Likewise, whereas under the production team the farmers normally spent 15 days to harvest wheat and 7 days to harvest barley, it now just took them about 5 days for each task.

Even more dramatic was the change in gender roles in farming. Under the collective, women did all of the routine, strenuous farm tasks that required them to bend over, such as picking cotton bolls, pulling out cotton stalks, removing and transplanting the rice seedlings, and cutting the rice and wheat crops, supposedly because women had a "soft waist" and could bend over for hours (see Chapter 8 for details). Males, on the other hand, avoided those tasks on the pretext that they had a stiff body and therefore could only do tasks that kept them standing. The female laborers thus ridiculed the men, saying they had a body as stiff as a rolling pin (for flattening the dough to make noodles). The 20-odd strong female laborers thus drudged all year round, and many of them were exhausted. The most laborious task for them was no doubt transplanting rice shoots. For about six weeks in May and early June, each day the female laborers woke as early as 3:00 or 4:00 a.m. They put their bare feet in cold water to remove the seedlings from the seedling bed while suffering from the mosquitoes in the air and leeches in the water. After breakfast, the women transplanted the seedlings into the paddy fields for the remainder of the day, taking a break only for lunch time. After the fields were allotted to individual families, however, the situation was reversed. Almost all adult males joined the women in those tasks, and they had no problems bending over all day in their field. In the words of the female villagers, the men had removed the rolling pin from their waists! Many men took over the hard tasks from their wives and let them do the lighter home chores. A saying went: "male laborers become tigers and female laborers leave hardship behind" (*nan laoli ru hu, nü laoli tuo ku*) (QD1 2000).

Cooperation Under Family Farming

Before decollectivization, many villagers, as well as critics of the reform policy, had doubted whether the individual families could finish certain tasks that required group effort in a timely manner, and whether they would be able to maintain the irrigation network and other public projects that required coordination among different households. After dividing the fields, however, the farmers quickly showed their ability to cooperate in those activities. Take, once again, the transplantation of rice seedlings. Usually a typical family of four or five had a rice paddy of five or six mu. Obviously, the two or three laborers of the family alone were unable to finish the task in their field in a single day. However, that job could not be done over several days because seedlings transplanted on different days would grow differently, which would be a problem when draining water from the field or harvesting the crop. Therefore, it was necessary to invite five or six helpers to finish the task in a single day. Normally the villagers had no problem finding enough helpers; they could be their neighbors, relatives, friends, or simply any laborer in the community. There was no conflict between different families over the sequence of their cooperation in transplanting the rice seedlings for each of them. The sequence was determined by the location of their plots: the No. 5 group had five or six walking tractors, each responsible for plowing and raking a large area that comprised a number of plots for different families. The helpers would transplant rice seedlings together for a certain family when the tractor moved to its plot. Instead of paying its helpers a wage, the family treated them with good meals and worked for each of them for one day in return. The helpers were typically provided with a breakfast of *zongzi* (glutinous rice wrapped in reed leaves) seasoned with white or brown sugar. The lunch for them included pork, fish, tofu, and other dishes, as well as beer for men and soft drinks for women. When they finished the task around 4:00 or 5:00 p.m., the helpers again were treated with a supper of noodles and several dishes—here again the women found how their situation had dramatically improved. After finishing the task for their own families and their helpers, many women hired themselves out to transplant rice seedlings for wages. In the 1980s and early 1990s, the wage was 10 yuan a day, which increased to 15 yuan in the mid-1990s, 20 yuan in the late 1990s, and 30 yuan around 2005.

Another area where the villagers voluntarily cooperated was irriga- tion and plowing. During the first few years after decollectivization, most families in Qin village relied on the water supplied by the electric pumping station to irrigate their fields through a network of ditches that channeled water from the pumping station. But this irrigation sys- tem had an obvious drawback: the flow of water was too strong in the fields around the station and too weak and slow in distant areas. There were also areas out of the reach of the network that had to be irrigated with a diesel pump on a boat. Even more inconvenient was that each family had to send a person to its field twice a day, first to make an opening on the ridge around the field to let the water in, and then to fill the opening to keep the water. Later, the villagers all turned to the die- sel pump for irrigation. After 1982, three families in the No. 5 group purchased five electric or diesel pumps to provide irrigation service, and each of them was responsible for a large area of plots in the village. When irrigating, the pump operator was also responsible for making and filling the openings for each paddy field being irrigated. The op- erator charged 12 yuan per mu for a year-round service in the 1980s and collected the money from the individual families they had served at the end of the year. Because the supply of diesel oil was limited and rationed to individual families at that time (at 8 to 10 catties per mu), each family had to provide the pump operator with its own fuel for that service. Since the 1990s, the supply of diesel oil was no longer ra- tioned, and the pump operators used their own oil and therefore charged their clients at a higher rate, which increased to 25 yuan per mu a year in 2005. The same operators also plowed fields for all fami- lies in the group, using their walking tractors. For this service, they charged each family 12 yuan per mu each time (not each year) in the 1980s when the family had to provide diesel oil to the operator and 30 yuan per mu each time in 2005 when the operator used his own oil. These facts suggest that the return to family farming did not end the cooperation among the farmers. Unlike the collective production that was relatively inefficient under poor management, the cooperation dur- ing the reform era was voluntary, reciprocal, increasingly commercial- ized, and critical to improving labor productivity.

Economic Breakthroughs

The economy in Qin village, like the rest of rural China, has witnessed two major breakthroughs since the early 1980s: the increased modern inputs that quickly improved labor productivity in crop cultivation, and the diversification of the villagers' economic activities, which contributed to the rapid increase in their income and the improvement of their living conditions more than any other factors.

Farming Productivity

Qin villagers could quickly point out where agricultural production in the early 2000s was different from 20 years earlier: in the 1970s and before, they spent almost all of their time working the farm "in order to have rice to eat" (*gao fan chi*). In the 1990s, farming became increasingly "time-saving and labor-saving" (*shengshi shenggong*), and what they were preoccupied with was not growing crops but making money from other sources. What made these changes possible was the increased use of chemical fertilizers, pesticides and weed killers, new crop strains, new farming techniques, and, most importantly, agricultural machines.

During the collective years, there was an increased use of chemical fertilizers, but they were expensive and their availability was limited. Thus, villagers relied mainly on organic sources, such as household manure, green plants, and riverbed mud, for fertilization. By and large, a production team had to spend one-third of its total workpoints on preparing and applying organic fertilizers. After decollectivization, no families devoted their precious field to growing green plants for fertilization, and few families had the laborers or boats to dredge river mud. By the mid-1980s, the custom of using river mud as fertilizer had completely disappeared in Qin village and other places in the area. Instead, the villagers increasingly turned to chemical fertilizers. Normally they used about 100 catties of fertilizer per mu before sowing seeds or planting crops and added about 20 catties of per mu as the crops grew. A family thus had to use more than 1,000 catties a year in the 1990s, which was about four times the amount used two decades earlier. The increased application of chemical fertilizers and the sharp decrease in organic fertilizers saved the farmers a lot of time, but it also caused the deterioration of soil conditions. The villagers had to alternate between rice and cotton every year to maintain the fertility of their fields; the yield of rice would significantly decrease if it was grown on the same field for two years in a row, a situation that rarely occurred during the collective years.

The introduction of new farming techniques also reduced the farmers' labor input. One example involved rice transplantation. In the 1990s, the villagers gradually adopted a new method of trans- plantation, "throwing the seedlings" (*paoyang*). Instead of inserting every plant of the seedling into the paddy field by hand, a tradition that had prevailed in rural China for thousands of years, the new method allowed the farmer to stand on a side of the field and throw a bunch of seedlings on the area in front of him. This way, a household typically needed just two or three laborers, usually its own members, to finish the task in a single day; it no longer needed to hire five or six additional helpers. In other words, the new method cut the labor on rice transplantation by at least two-thirds, but the yield of rice by this method was no less than that by the traditional one. To be sure, to evenly throw the seedlings required some training, but the villagers had no problem mastering the skill. By the mid-1990s, all families in Qin village had adopted this method.

A more recent innovation in rice cultivation, which was first intro- duced to the village in 2007, was the "direct sowing" (*zhibo*) method. By that method, the farmers first soaked and sterilized rice seeds for two to three days and then sowed the seeds directly onto the field at the amount of 8 to 10 catties per mu in early June. The field was then lightly plowed (at the depth of two or three centimeters), irrigated, and treated with chemical weed killers. This method was revolutionary because it did away with four time-consuming tasks required by traditional methods: preparing and maintaining the seedling bed, removing the seedlings from the bed, transporting the seedlings to the paddy field, and transplanting or throwing the seedlings on the field. Also, this new method was efficient because it only required shallow plowing and a small amount of irrigation and thus saved much of the farmers' ex- penses on fuel and water. But the risks involved in the new method were much greater than the traditional methods. Because the direct sowing was 25 to 30 days later than the germination of rice seeds by the traditional methods, the rice shoots that grew under the new method were more vulnerable to the storms and flooding that were more likely to happen in June and July. The light irrigation of the paddy field also encouraged the growth of weeds and hence made weeding a more challenging task. Nevertheless, because of the greater efficiency of the new method, the shortened growth period of the rice crop (about 30 days less than the growth period by the traditional methods), and higher crop yields (about 5 percent more), almost all of the households in Qin village accepted it in 2008, the second year after its introduction to the village.

Another example involved weeding, a task that consumed a lot of time for the villagers before the 1990s. After transplanting the rice seedlings, the farmers used to spend hours a day for several days in the paddy field, finding and removing weeds by hand. They also needed to hoe the weeds in the cotton field up to 10 times, each time for two or three days, when the cotton plants were growing. In the 1990s, however, a chemical became available to kill the weeds. Each household now only needed to spend about 10 yuan on the poison and a few hours on each application to wipe out the weeds.

Even more drastic in reducing the villagers' time on farming was the use of combines in harvesting. In 2000, three young men in the No. 5 group pooled 120,000 yuan to buy a combine, each contributing 40,000 yuan. There were other two combines in the village, owned by the farmers in the No. 1 and No. 4 groups. For every mu of rice or wheat field harvested, they charged 30 yuan. It usually took an hour or two to harvest a typical plot of five mu. The family that used the service only needed to bag the grain threshed by the machine. The time it saved by this service was huge. Traditionally, a family had to cut and bundle the crop for several days. Then it needed to spend half a day moving the bundled crops to a threshing ground. After threshing the crops for hours, the family needed to further dry the straw in the sun by turning it over several times a day for two or three days before shipping the straw home and piling it in a heap. With the combine, however, all those jobs were done in a matter of a few hours! When the harvesting was done, most families simply set fire to the straw left by the machine and burned it into ashes for fertilizer.

While labor input steadily decreased in the 1990s and early 2000s, farm output greatly increased, owing to both the increased use of chemical fertilizers and the adoption of high-yielding varieties of crops. The ever-improving hybrid rice strains, for example, pushed the output from about 800 catties per mu in the late 1970s to about 900–1,000 catties in the 1980s, and about 1,200 catties in the 1990s. The most productive farms yielded as high as 1,400–1,600 catties per mu in 2005.

As a result, labor productivity in agriculture remarkably improved after 1980. Table 9 is an approximate estimate of the workdays for different tasks of rice cultivation on a standard field of five mu in the late 1970s and the early 2000s.

TABLE 9
Labor Input in Rice Cultivation in Qin Village

	Labor input (estimated workdays)	
Tasks	The late 1970s	The early 2000s
Preparing and applying organic fertilizers	7	0
Applying chemical fertilizers	2	3
Irrigation	6	6
Plowing and raking the field	3	2
Soaking rice seeds and seeding	2	2
Transplanting	10	3
Weeding	15	2
Pesticide application	6	6
Cutting the crop	8	1
Threshing the crop	4	0
Drying, bundling, and piling the straw	8	0
Total workdays	71 workdays	25 workdays
Rice yield	4,000 catties	6,500 catties

SOURCE: Qin villagers' oral estimates of labor input in rice cultivation on an average-size (five mu) farm.

As the table shows, Qin villagers spent only 25 workdays growing rice on the five-mu farm in the early 2000s, or 35 percent of the time they spent on the same job 20 years ago, while the rice yield from the farm increased to 6,500 catties or about 38 percent more than two decades ago. The rice yield per workday thus increased from about 56 catties in the 1970s to about 260 catties in the early 2000s. In other words, labor productivity in rice cultivation increased by more than four times in the past 20 years. To be sure, not all activities in agriculture witnessed the same progress. Cotton cultivation, for example, remained basically a manual task in the early 2000s that required almost the same labor input as it did 20 years ago, except for weeding and fertilizing. Growing cotton on a farm of the same size (five mu), for example, required about 110 workdays for various tasks such as seeding, weeding, picking cotton bolls, and pulling out and removing the cotton stalks. The gross income from this crop was about 12,000 yuan (109 yuan per workday), or one-third of the per-workday income from growing rice. It is no wonder, therefore, that few families were willing to grow cotton; they did so every other year or every third year in alternation with rice cropping only to maintain the fertility of the soil. Overall, farmers in the early 2000s spent on farming only about one-third of the time they used 20 years earlier, while their income from this source increased by 30 percent. Taking all factors into consideration, it is safe to say that labor productivity in agriculture increased by at least three times in Qin village during the decades after 1980.

Off-Farm Employments

Improvements in labor productivity in farming after decollectivization allowed villagers to engage in off-farm activities that contributed increasingly to their income. One of the off-farm options was the so-called "household business" (*jiating jingying*). For example, in the early 2000s, 10 households in Qin village raised fish in man-made or natural ponds that varied from 9 or 10 mu to more than 40 mu each. The family who rented the pond from the village government paid an annual rent of about 4,000 yuan to the village and earned a net income of 8,000 to 20,000 yuan a year. Four families raised ducks, each making about 8,000 to 10,000 yuan a year from its 400 to 500 ducks. Six families owned chicken farms, and each raised about 3,000 up to 10,000 chickens, earning from 6,000 to more than 60,000 yuan a year. One family raised more than 130 goats and made about 13,000 yuan a year. Another family had a cattle farm and raised four to six cattle each year, yielding a net income of 9,200 to 13,700 yuan. There was also a family who grew various vegetables in a greenhouse and sold them at local markets and in the neighboring towns, earning about 12,000 yuan annually.

It is important to note that these household businesses were different from the traditional "household sidelines" (*jiating fuye*) during the collective era. Before the 1980s, each household raised a limited number of chickens, pigs, or goats only to augment its primary income from the production team. The team members, who spent most of their time on collective farms, took care of the domestic animals only during their spare time in the early morning or evening, or let their children or the elderly do so. Therefore, they did not care much about the cost and profit of such sidelines. After 1980, especially from the 1990s onward, raising a large number of such animals became a family business that generated most of the family's income. Therefore, the family had to carefully calculate its labor and capital input to make a profit. Villager Wang Weidong, for example, invested 26,000 yuan in his goat ranch and bought 46 hybrid female "Suining" goats in 1999, to breed the fast-growing animals at opportune seasons. He particularly cared about the composition of the fodder during different seasons to ensure that the goats had a balanced nutrition, kept their weight during the winter, and grew as fast as possible in the remainder of the year.

In another instance, in 1997 villager Fang Lixin spent about 170,000 yuan to build his chicken farm, which was 385 square meters and housed up to 10,000 chickens. Choosing the best breed of chicken was critical to increasing the rate of egg laying and hence the profit of his business. When he learned that the Shenbao breed of chicken had the highest rate of egg laying and a low rate of illness, Fang traveled to a company in the suburb of Shanghai to buy 4,800 such baby chicks. It turned out that the egg-laying rate reached as high as 95 percent during the peak season, and Fang earned 66,000 yuan in that year. Fang's success inspired five other families, who started their own chicken farms in the following years. These farms became part of the huge network of egg marketing and fodder supply in the lower Yangzi region. Each day, a truck stopped by each of the farms to buy eggs and then transported them to Shanghai, Nanjing, or other cities and towns in the area; the price of eggs changed daily, depending on the demand and supply of the product in the regional market. Every few days, another truck delivered to each farm the prepared fodder that was formulated with balanced nutrition. The ranch owners paid the fodder suppliers every three months.

Kilns prospered in Qin village in the 1980s and 1990s, when a wave of new home construction inside and outside the community created a huge demand for bricks and tiles. At the peak of this business in the early 1990s, nine households contracted with the local government to use the 10 kilns in the village, and another eight households operated kilns in other villages. Each of them earned a net income of about 10,000 to 15,000 yuan a year, depending on the size of the kiln. The nine kilns in the village hired about 90 workers. About half of them were men, who burned, uploaded, unloaded, and watered the bricks and tiles, and each was paid 30 to 40 yuan a day. The other half were women, who did light tasks for about 15 yuan a day. There were also about 50 male villagers who dug and shipped the earth for making the bricks and tiles to the kilns, and each earned about 20 to 30 yuan daily. In the late 1990s, however, this business declined. The reason was that the quality of the bricks and tiles burned in such traditional, small kilns was inconsistent and inferior compared to the products by the two large, modern factories next to Qin village. Although those poor-quality bricks and tiles were acceptable to families building the traditional one-story houses in the 1980s and early 1990s, in the late 1990s more and more villagers turned to the expensive but good-quality materials from the factories to build the two-story houses that became popular in the community. As a result, only four traditional kilns in the village survived into the early 2000s, producing mainly the thin bricks used as ceiling materials that the large factories did not make. By 2007, all of them had disappeared because of the government's strict measures against pollution caused by such kilns.

The boom of the kiln industry in the village and surrounding communities during the 1980s and 1990s caused water transportation in the area to thrive. In the early 1990s, 51 households in Qin village owned concrete boats, each with one or two diesel-powered propellers and a capacity of 15 to 50 tons, to ship bricks and tiles from local kilns to areas where people did not produce them locally. The boat owners usually bought bricks at 0.20 yuan apiece from the kilns and sold them at their destinations for 0.21 or 0.22 yuan, thus making about 500 to 1,500 yuan each shipment or about 6,000 to 20,000 yuan a year, depending on the size of the boat and market conditions. In the late 1990s, as the traditional kiln industry declined, the households who engaged in water transportation decreased to only 10. Two of them, however, not only survived but grew to have several iron-coated freighters with the capacity of up to 200 tons. They no longer shipped bricks and tiles in local areas but instead moved their business to Shanghai and other coastal cities, where they transported different kinds of goods for local companies, making about 200,000 yuan a year.

About 45 villagers worked in the local factories. One of the factories in Qin village was a chemical smeltery. Established in 1990 by a 35-year-old villager named Ma, the factory hired four or five workers and made a gross annual income of about 100,000 yuan in the first few years. In the early 2000s, the factory expanded quickly and built a row of new buildings in 2000. In 2005, it hired 32 workers, paying each of them about 400 to 1,000 yuan a month and generating a gross income of more than a million annually. The annual fee the factory paid to the village government for using its land also increased from only about 3,000 yuan a year in the early 1990s to more than 20,000 yuan a year in the early 2000s.

Villagers who worked in the cities as carpenters, lacquerers, or construction workers increased from about 40 to 50 in the 1980s and early 1990s to about 250 villagers in the early 2000s. They usually went to a city and worked there in group of two or three brothers, cousins, or friends. When they became familiar with the locality and established

their business there, the villagers would introduce other fellow villagers to that place. It is no wonder, therefore, that for most of the 1980s and
the early 1990s, almost all carpenters and other craftsmen in the village
flocked to the few cities in Northeast China, which are thousands of
miles away from Qin village. Each of them earned 2,000 to 3,000 yuan
on average in the 1980s, and 4,000 to 5,000 yuan in the early 1990s. After
the mid-1990s, however, fewer urban families hired the carpenters or
lacquerers to make and paint furniture. Instead, they increasingly
turned to furniture stores for up-to-date, stylish furniture that the carpenters could not make. Therefore, those villagers gradually entered
two new businesses in the cities. Some of them became specialized in
finishing the interior of new apartments. This business boomed in almost every city in the 1990s and early 2000s, when the state terminated
the free allocation of housing units to urban residents and promoted
the privatization of housing. The interior of a new apartment that a family purchased was always unfinished, so the owner had to hire carpenters, lacquerers, and other craftsmen to finish the walls, ceilings, floors,
toilets, the kitchen, and the like. The villagers worked as a group for the
task, usually including two or three carpenters and at least one lac-
querer. Normally, it took about two weeks for them to finish an apartment, and everyone in the group could earn about 700 up to 1,500 yuan
each time. In the early 2000s, the approximately 70 carpenters in the village each earned about 15,000 to 20,000 yuan a year, and the 20-odd lacquerers made 20,000 to 30,000 yuan per person annually.

Other villagers worked for construction companies. A contractor
from such companies often hired his fellow villagers and paid each of
them about 40 yuan a day for working in his company, while providing
them with free meals and lodging. The villagers normally went to the
destination city after the lunar New Year and returned home several
days before the New Year; they were among the tens of millions of migrant workers that emerged in China since the 1980s. The rest of the
villagers had their own alternatives. Nine households in the village
owned a grocery store selling cigarettes, alcohol, processed foods, and
other household necessities, each making an annual profit of about 4,000
to 6,000 yuan. There were also two barbershops, three tailor shops, and
an electric welding shop, each earning an income of about 5,000 to
8,000 yuan a year.

The growing importance of off-farm occupations to Qin villagers
was indicative of the same trend that became increasingly prevalent in
the country during the reform era. By and large, three major patterns

of nonagricultural economic development have emerged in different parts of rural China. One is the Sunan model, which prevailed in southern Jiangsu province. The village or township governments in that area took advantage of the close social and economic ties of local communities with neighboring industrial cities, such as Shanghai, Suzhou, and Wuxi, to develop collectively owned factories and absorb the surplus labor force in the villages into the factories (Fei 1986; P. Huang 1990: 252–265; Ho 1994; Zhu and Sun 1994). The second is the Wenzhou model, which predominated in the coastal Zhejiang and Fujian provinces, where individual villagers created tens of thousands of small-scale private enterprises and built a nationwide network to market their goods (Zhang Renshou and Li Hong 1990; Oi 1999: 67–70; Shi Jinchuan et al. 2002). The third is the hinterland model, found in provinces such as Anhui, Hubei, Hunan, Jiangxi, and Sichuan, where tens of millions of young villagers left home to find employment opportunities in coastal cities, usually earning 300 to 500 yuan a month as housemaids or wage workers in the cities (Xie 2005).

What happened in Qin village and the larger Qindong township, however, did not fit into any of these models. In the mid-1970s, the former Zhigang Brigade (Qin and Su villages) was already known as a model collective in the county for its booming industry. Its largest factory hired more than 50 workers to cast metal parts in molds of paraffin wax, generating a profit of more than 80,000 yuan a year. After the mid-1980s, however, its business declined as competitors in the market increased. In the early 2000s, the factory hired fewer than 20 workers. Meanwhile, small private enterprises boomed in the area. Stainless steel manufacturing was especially developed in Qindong township. In 2005, for example, the 196 private factories and 1,275 "industrial households" (*gongye hu*) in this industry in the township produced a total output of 2,065 million yuan, yielding a pretax profit of 444 million yuan. The township itself was known as the "little Wenzhou" in the region for its private enterprises and economic connections with the city of Wenzhou in Zhejiang province, which has been known in China for its highly developed private economy since the 1980s. From time to time, the township government organized village cadres to visit different companies in Wenzhou to learn from their experiences of industrial development. One of the more recent visits was in April 2005, when they traveled to Zhengtai Group in Wenzhou, the largest enterprise in China specialized in manufacturing low-voltage household appliances. As a result of such visits, the numerous private enterprises in Qindong developed close ties with their partners in Wenzhou. Mr. Chen, director of the township's economic and marketing center, estimated in March 2005 that every day at least 100,000 yuan of stainless-steel components were shipped from the dozens of local factories to Wenzhou. But the wages offered by the private businesses in Qindong were far from attractive to local villagers. In April 2005, the township government had to contact its counterpart in Hanzhang township of Nanle county, Henan province, to hire more than 400 workers from that locality to satisfy the demand of local enterprises for cheap labor. The villagers in Qindong, as we have seen in Qin village, preferred to have their own household business or to work as skilled craftsmen for higher earnings. What took place in Qin village and Qindong township as a whole, therefore, was a mixture, and to some degree a microcosm, of different patterns of rural nonagricultural development in the rest of the country.

Achievements and Problems

Improved Living Conditions

The increase in labor productivity in farming and the development of off-farm occupations accounted for the rapid increase in the villagers' income and significant improvement of their living conditions. The per capita annual net income (i.e., annual gross income after deducting production costs) of Qin villagers increased from 210 yuan in 1980 to 850 yuan in 1989 and 3,752 yuan in 1999. Taking price inflation into account, the real net income of the villagers increased annually by 9 percent in the 1980s and by 9.55 percent in the 1990s. Between 2000 and 2007, Qin villagers' annual net income increased further, from 4,060 yuan to 7,900 yuan per capita, or about 10 percent a year.[4] At 10,710 yuan per capita, the annual net income of rural residents in Qindong township in 2007 was still higher than in Qin village and 2.58 times the national level (4,140 yuan per capita), owing to the boom of stainless steel manufacturing and other enterprises in the localities around the township seat.[5]

The most visible sign of the improved living conditions of Qin villagers was their houses. As mentioned in the preceding chapter, brick-and-tile houses basically replaced traditional thatched cottages in the early 1980s. These houses, however, soon became "outdated" in the late 1980s, when most families demolished them (though those houses could last 20 or 30 years) to build the all-brick "seven-beam houses," which were more spacious than the traditional houses that had five beams to support the ceiling, and updated with a layer of thin bricks, instead of reed stems, as the ceiling materials. The cost of building such a house, therefore, increased to about 12,000 yuan in the late 1980s, more than 10 times the cost of a five-beam house 10 years earlier. However, such seven-beam houses became out of date in the 1990s. What became fashionable in Qin village was the two-story house that had three rooms on each floor, totaling 180 square meters. The use of lots of concrete, reinforcing bars, wires, pipes, and lumber also drove the cost of a standard two-story house to about 60,000 yuan in the mid-1990s and about 80,000 to 100,000 yuan in 2005. Thirty-four families, or nearly one-third of all families in Qin village, had built such houses by 2005. These families were relatively well-to-do. Most of them had a son as their single child; having a two-story building was important for them to attract a desirable daughter-in-law when the son reached a marriageable age. Families who had a daughter as their only child were much less willing to build a two-story house. The seven-beam house was already spacious and comfortable enough for the parents to live before and after they married off the daughter.

The villagers' daily lives became more convenient than before because of the increased use of modern facilities. In the 1980s, almost every family had at least one bicycle. The construction of a highway that connects Qin village with the local highway network in 1996 and 1997 caused the increased use of motorcycles, which replaced the bicycle as the primary vehicle for young villagers. Between 1993 and 1996, all families in Qin village installed water pipes and used tap water instead of the polluted water from a pond or creek for cooking and other daily uses. Most families had a gas stove, which increasingly replaced the traditional stove that burned straw. The new two-story homes normally had a flush toilet and a ceramic bathtub. Small black-and-white TVs, limited to a few families in the early 1980s, became a popular item in the late 1980s and early 1990s. In the mid- to late 1990s, most families switched to a color TV of 18 or 20 inches or larger. Refrigerators and washing machines were indispensable items for newlyweds in the early 2000s, although those machines were rarely used; the villagers turned to their gardens for fresh vegetables each day rather than eating refrigerated ones, and they preferred to wash clothes by hand to save power and to avoid the trouble of operating the machine. Telephones were rare in the village in the mid-1990s, when installing a telephone cost about 2,800 yuan. By 2005, however, almost every family in the community had a telephone as the installation fee decreased to only 300 yuan and the monthly fee to 12 yuan. Almost every young man in the village had a cell phone, which helped explain the fact that one in every three people in China had a cell phone in 2006.

Changes were also visible in the villagers' diet and food. The biggest change, as some informants remarked, was that they "ate less rice and more meat" than before. In the 1970s and earlier, an adult normally ate two or three bowls of steamed rice as lunch, using at least one catty of uncooked rice. In the early 2000s, however, they usually ate only one bowl, or one-third to a half of what they had eaten 20 years earlier. The villagers gave two reasons. One was that they used much less energy to do farm work because of the increased use of machines and chemicals and therefore they did not feel so hungry. The other was the increased intake of fat and greasy food. Some estimated that the amount of cooking oil they used in the early 2000s was more than three times what they did in the 1970s when the oil was expensive and rationed. Most families ate pork every few days or at least once a week, rather than every few weeks or months as before. Whereas during the collective years almost all families had to sell their chicken eggs for pocket cash, now they raised a limited number of chickens and ducks only for the self-consumption of eggs and meat. In fact, because of their overeating of fat, some middle-aged men and women in the village became overweight and had high blood pressure and heart disease.

The Cost of Development

Despite these improvements, Qin villagers could quickly point out the costs they paid for them. One problem that they complained about most often was the polluted water. Before the 1990s, the villagers generally felt safe to wash their rice, vegetables, dishes, and clothes by the pond or creek next to their houses or to store water from the pond or creek in a vat in their kitchen for cooking and drinking. The water, however, became increasingly polluted in the next decade as more and more pesticides were used in the fields and eventually flowed into the ponds and creeks. Two other developments made the water even dirtier. In the 1990s, the villagers no longer dredged up the mud and waterweeds from the bottom of the pond or rivers as fertilizer. After threshing the rice or wheat crop, they no longer kept the husks as burning materials for their stoves but pushed them into a nearby river or pond. All these explained in part why all households in the village had to use tap water instead. The villagers also complained that more and more people died of cancer, which they attributed to the excessive use of pesticides and chemical fertilizers that polluted their food and water sources.

Another problem resulted from the excessive development of kilns in the village in the 1980s and the early to mid-1990s. The huge demand for earth to make bricks and tiles caused many villagers to dig the dirt from their farms or anywhere inside and outside the village and ship it to the kilns for about 3 yuan a cubic meter, or 20 to 30 yuan per day per person. The village government attempted to prohibit this activity because it damaged the farms, but it rarely succeeded. Later, even the government itself was involved in selling earth to large kilns under the official pretext of making artificial ponds for fishing. As a result, more than 300 mu of farms, or one-fifth of the farmland in the village, became ponds, which generated a substantial amount of income for the government through the selling of the earth and the annual leasing of the ponds to fishing households.

One more problem had to do with the increasing disparity in household income among the villagers. As demonstrated in Chapter 9, during the collective years, when earning workpoints was the major source of family income, the economic status of a household was basically determined by its worker-dependent ratio that in turn reflected its position in the family cycle. Families with working parents and grown-up children were normally the richest in the community, while those with many dependents and few workpoint earners were less well-off. These dynamics, however, gradually changed after 1980, as the increased use of machines and other modern inputs reduced the labor demands in agriculture and, more importantly, as agriculture itself was no longer the major source of family income. What determined a family's economic status was not the number of its farming laborers but rather the abilities of its members to seek off-farm income opportunities. The richest in the village in the early 2000s, therefore, were those that had members "earning big money" (*zhuan daqian*) as contractors for construction companies. Mr. Wang, one of such successful contractors, earned about 150,000 to 200,000 yuan annually. His villa-like house was also the most expensive in the village. On the other hand, the poorest in the village were those who still relied on farming as their major source of income. Although food and clothing were no longer their everyday concerns, these families earned only 7,000 or 8,000 yuan a year on average, or 5 to 10 percent of the annual income of the richest families.

Conclusion

Economic development in Qin village after 1980 is best seen as both a cumulative result of agricultural progress during the collective era and the immediate consequence of the break with the collective system. Without the solid basis laid by the rural collectives between the 1950s and the 1970s, the rapid increase in agricultural output in recent decades would have been unimaginable. The land that the villagers received from the former collectives, for example, was the farms that had been furnished with a well-developed irrigation and flood-control system. By the time the collective organizations were dissolved, the farmers had been acquainted with the use of modern inputs, such as chemical fertilizers, pesticides, new crop varieties, and some types of agricultural machines. An effective network that connected each household through wired broadcasting guided the villagers in pest control and using new farming techniques. All these provided the necessary conditions for further agricultural growth during the reform era.

The switch from collective production to family farming no doubt offered the villagers a strong incentive to maximize the output of their private farms, which was evident during the first few years after the breakdown of the collective system, when grain yield per land unit increased dramatically in both Qin village and rural China as a whole. However, the return to independent family farming, or the institutional change, was not the whole story behind the miracle. What made possible the rapid increase in labor productivity in crop cultivation, as this chapter has shown, was the increased use of chemical fertilizers, pesticides, chemical weed killers, and, most importantly, agricultural machines, which boosted farm yield while saving the farmers' labor, a development that gained a momentum in the 1990s and early 2000s.

But the most important development in rural China after 1980 was the villagers' increased engagement in off-farm income-earning opportunities rather than the increase in farm output and improvement in labor productivity in agriculture—after all, the villagers' income from farming around 2005 accounted for only about one-third of their total income. A new, self-sustained dynamic thus emerged in the rural economy to propel its modern transformation: the increased income from off-farm sources allowed the villagers to increase their investment in modern inputs and hence labor productivity; the increased labor productivity, in turn, generated more surplus laborers in agriculture and greater demand for off-farm employment opportunities; and the villagers' increased involvement in nonagricultural activities led to greater needs to invest in modern inputs and thereby to reduce the demand for labor in farming. This process is in sharp contrast with the old dynamic of the collective economy: the state's preoccupation with urban industrialization and hence its restriction of the villagers' freedom in migration and off-farm employment caused the intensification of labor input in farming and low-labor productivity. The low-labor productivity in agriculture, coupled with the state's over extraction of rural economic surplus, resulted in the villagers' low income and the collective's limited capital accumulation, and hence its limited investment in modern inputs, which in turn contributed to low-labor productivity in agriculture. The most significant achievement of the rural reform after 1980, in a nutshell, was not the remarkable increase in agricultural production, as the reform designers originally intended, but the unexpected emancipation of the rural labor force and the consequent diversification of income sources of the rural population, which paved the way for economic and social modernization in rural China.

CHAPTER 12

The Retreat of the State: Village Politics and Community Life

IT IS TRUE that economic liberalization inevitably leads to greater political participation and personal freedom. Observers of Chinese politics, therefore, tend to deem it an anomaly that, despite the drastic transition to a market economy and the rapid economic growth for three decades after 1978, China's political system remained largely unchanged. Compared to the economic reforms that resulted in the predominance of capitalism in the late 1990s and early 2000s, the political reform definitely lagged behind (Chi 1986; McCormick 1990; Goldman 1995; Zhao 2000; Oksenberg 2001; Pei 2006). This observation, to be sure, holds true when one looks at the government structure at the township level and above and the political culture in which it operated, but it fails to characterize the changes in local politics in rural China, especially the relationship between villagers and government authorities. This chapter examines the social and political consequences of decollectivization in Qin village. It underscores three forces that shaped the villagers' experiences in the community and the family after 1980, namely the Maoist legacy, especially the state's continuous but increasingly ineffective control of rural society through the Party's network; local customs and practices that governed the villagers' daily social and economic activities; and the introduction of new institutions and values that affected the villagers' standing in the community and self-perceptions. Overall, the reform era has seen the state's weakened presence in the countryside and the villagers' growing autonomy and equality in local politics, social interactions, and family life. Decollectivization, in other words, not only paved the way for the villagers to change themselves from peasants living on subsistence to managerial farmers, business owners, and factory workers, but also made them increasingly aware of their rights and abilities to reorient and achieve their life goals.[1]

Village Leadership

"Grassroots Democracy"

After decollectivization, the three-tier administrative system of the people's commune, the brigade, and the production team was replaced by a new system of *xiang/zhen* (township), *xingzhengcun* (administrative village), and *cunmin xiaozu* (subvillage group). In Qin village, the former six production teams of the Qindian Brigade became the six villagers' groups of Qin village in 1984, and above it was Qindong township, the former Qindong commune.[2] Dongtai county also became a municipality in 1987, although more than 80 percent of its population were villagers at that time.

What changed, however, was not merely the name of the administrative units but also the relationship between villagers and local cadres. Whereas in the collective years the villagers depended on the production team for their livelihood and followed the team cadres' instructions in team production, now they made decisions on their own about what to do on and off the farm. Having lost much of their influence on the villagers' economic activities and household income, the cadres' standing and power in the community dwindled. Ordinary villagers no longer treated the cadres with as much respect and awe as before. It was difficult for the cadres to implement government policies and fulfill their administrative duties without the villagers' consent. Therefore, how to reshape the village leadership and redefine its relationship with the villagers became a challenge to the government.

Foreseeing the inevitability of a new form of village government after decollectivization, reform-minded leaders of the central government proposed the idea of village-level self-government in the early 1980s. Article 111 of the 1982 Constitution, therefore, designed the "village council" (*cunmin weiyuanhui*) as a "self-governing organization of farmers at the lowest level." In the following two years, 948,628 such village councils were established throughout the country.[3] The council of Qin village came into being in 1984 when the Qindian Brigade was renamed Qindian village, and all former brigade cadres became members of the village council, who filled these five positions: director of the council, the financial councilor or the accountant, the councilor for public security, the councilor for women's work, and the agro-technician. As will be discussed shortly, however, the secretary of the village's Party branch remained the most powerful person in the village, though he was not a member of the council. Like their counterparts in the rest of rural China, these cadres were supposedly the most capable members of the community, individuals who had received more education than others or served in the military. Mr. Wang, the secretary of the Party branch, was a veteran of the army. Mr. Zhang, the director of the council, was a veteran of the navy. And the accountant, also surnamed Zhang, was a high school graduate.

According to the 1987 law, the council members should be selected through a "direct election" by all villagers age 18 and above. The first election took place in Qin village in 1986. Afterward, the village council was regularly reelected every three years in accordance with the 1987 law, and one of the more recent elections was conducted on September 7, 2004. Like the earlier elections, the election in 2004 involved what the village cadres called "three ups-and-downs" (*sanshang sanxia*), or three rounds of interactions between the township government and the villagers. The village first set up an election committee of seven members, including Secretary Wang and the heads of the six villagers' groups. Its major task was to nominate the candidates. It was up to Secretary Wang to prepare a preliminary list of candidates through his consultation with other village cadres and a representative of the township government, and to submit the list to the township government for approval before he could convene the villagers to finalize the candidates. This was the first round of "up-and-down."

Then he gathered about 50 to 60 representatives of the villagers (about 10 from each group)—mostly Party members, former production team or brigade cadres, or members of the village's "group for democratic financial management" (*minzhu licai xiaozu*)—to deliberate the qualifications of each candidate on the preliminary list and to select by a vote six members from the nominees as the final candidates. As a second "up-and-down," the secretary submitted the list of the six finalists together with a description of their qualifications to the township government for verification before their names were announced to the public. The villagers were allowed three days to think about their choice of the candidates before the election. Although their choices were very limited, the fact that one of the six candidates would be eliminated in the election and that the candidates had to win at least half of the votes in order to be elected nevertheless produced pressure on the candidates and gave the voters some leverage in the process.

These three days were critical for the candidates to influence the villagers' decision. Most candidates made phone calls to, or directly visited, their relatives, friends, and acquaintances to make sure that the latter would vote for them. One villager thus described how the candidates contacted him through their family members. The wife of a candidate, for example, spoke to him on the evening before the election day: "Uncle, we count on you this time. He [her husband] cannot lose the election. What we worry about is not the loss of his position, but the loss of his face. How could he face the public if he loses the election?" The same evening, the father of another candidate visited his home, saying: "Elder brother, please do take care of him [the candidate]. As you know, his wife is disabled, and his son is still too young to support the family. How could they survive if he loses his job?" The villager's answers to such visitors were almost the same: he always praised the candidates and assured the visitors that he would certainly vote for them. No matter what he actually thought about the candidates, the villager would never say no to any visitors to avoid hurting their feelings. What the candidate or his family members appealed to, as this example indicates, was not the candidate's administrative abilities or his opinions on the future of the community, but the traditional notions about personal reputation and subsistence, which made sense to the villagers.

Likewise, when making his or her choices, a villager would think first about the candidates who were his friends or relatives. This does not mean, to be sure, that a candidate's personal abilities and reputation were unimportant. In fact, quite the contrary; the villagers showed almost unanimous respect to those who were just and upright. Mr. Zhang, for example, won the villagers' wide support for his honesty and integrity in serving as the director of the village council for more than two decades after the mid-1980s. Therefore, he invariably won more than 95 percent of the votes during each of the seven elections between 1986 and 2004. He was also the only candidate who never "campaigned" for himself.

A typical election of the village council members, as seen in Qin village in 2004, proceeded as follows. In the early morning of the election day, more than 800 voters were admitted to the compound of the village office. As an incentive for the villagers to attend the election, each received a free towel or some other gift on admission. The township government sent a representative and a notary to supervise and witness the event; Secretary Wang presided over the entire process. He first named the staff for the election, including the persons for distributing the ballots, reading the selected names on each ballot, recording the results, and supervising the reading and recording process. After the voters showed their consent to the named staff by raising their hands, the ballots were distributed. The villagers then checked the names of the candidates they favored on the ballot and dropped it into a box. They were allowed to add a different name to the ballot that was not included as a candidate. The counting process began when the ballots were gathered from the boxes. The winners would be the five who won the most votes. The secretary then submitted the result to the township government for verification and endorsement before announcing it to the villagers; this was the third "up and down."

Qin villagers' attitudes toward the election varied. According to Mr. Chen, a member of the village council, about a third of the villagers had various kinds of connections with the candidates (such as being the candidates' family members, friends, relatives, or business partners) and wanted those candidates to keep their current positions or get the desired ones. Another third of the villagers, who did not have such relations with the cadres, also showed an interest in the election because they wanted to use their votes to express their support to, or dissatisfaction with, the existing village cadres. The remaining third of the villagers had no interest in any candidates or the election itself at all for the following reasons. First, unlike the production team leaders before the 1980s, whose abilities directly affected the well-being of team members, the council played an insignificant role in the villagers' household economy. Therefore, who would be the village cadres did not matter to them. Second, as mentioned earlier, there were few opportunities for the villagers to nominate their own candidates; they elected the candidates prepared by the Party secretary and township government, and there were only six candidates, from whom five would be elected. Third, and most important, none of the members of the village council that they elected, including the head of the council, were as powerful as the secretary of the village's Party branch in managing the public affairs of the community; the latter was selected by the township's Party committee rather than by the villagers. Therefore, it made no sense for them to be too serious about the election. No wonder that the only reason for many of them to attend the election was to receive a free gift!

The excessive interference by the township government and the Party secretary, and the low interest of many villagers in the election, led to increased concern on the part of the provincial government. Therefore, in its 2005 directive on the eighth province-wide election of village councils scheduled for 2007, the provincial authorities promoted the method of "direct election" (*zhixuan*). By that method, there would be no more nomination of candidates by the Party secretary and township leader or by the representatives of the villagers. Instead, the villagers wrote directly on the ballot the names of those they supported. The election would be valid as long as more than half of the qualified voters attended the election and those who were elected won more than half of the votes.

This direct election, which took place in Qin village in December 2007, involved two steps: a direct nomination by all eligible villagers and voting on the finalists. During the nomination held in late November, each villagers' group was assigned a person to visit every household in his group with a traveling ballot box; there was no longer a village-wide election meeting because of the difficulty of getting all eligible voters (about 900) together. The voter was asked to write up to five names of his or her own choice on a blank ballot. The finalists were the top three who won the most nominations. As the second step, the three candidates' names were printed on the ballots for the villagers to vote, which was conducted on December 5. A villager would vote by simply making a check mark next to a candidate's name or by adding another name to a blank space on the ballot. The top three who won at least half of the votes would become the new members of the village council. As a result of this election, Mr. Wang, a former member of the village council in charge of public security and a newly appointed Party secretary of the village, became the new director of the council; Mr. Meng, whose number of votes were second to Wang's, became the deputy director; and Mr. Zhang, who had been the village's accountant for more than 20 years, continued his position in the new council.[4]

The biggest difference between the 2007 and earlier elections, as just seen, was the way in which the candidates were selected. Whereas in the earlier elections it was up to the Party secretary to determine the candidates, now the villagers' votes were decisive. Many Qin villagers thus were more enthusiastic in nominating their favorite candidates and, as a result, about 60 individuals were named in the 2007 election. Mr. Meng, who had never held any position in the village council, won second place in the nomination and became one of the three finalists, while two former members of the village council lost the election and hence failed to keep their positions. On the other hand, however, there were also many villagers who were as indifferent (*wusuowei*) as before in dealing with the election. This was true especially during the formal election. They simply checked the names of the finalists printed on the ballot without bothering to make any change, assuming that doing so would not alter the result of the election and that the result of the election, whatever it would be, did not matter to them.

The Party Secretary Versus the Village Council

Policy makers in China who designed the village self-government program in the early 1980s intended villagers to have full autonomy in managing their community affairs. In the words of Peng Zhen (1902–1997), chairman of the standing committee of the National People's Congress, the villagers should have the full right to decide "what should be done and what should not; what should be done first and what should be done later" (Bai Yihua 2004). Owing to his steering efforts, the 1987 law on the village council defined it as "a mass self-government organization for the villagers' self-management, self-education, and self-service" (Bai Yihua 1998). To safeguard the villagers' right in self-government, the law avoided mentioning any role of grassroots Party organizations in the village council's activities. But it also failed to specify the concrete duties and rights of the village council in local administration. Therefore, despite the regular reelection of the village council in the 1980s and the 1990s, the secretary of the Party branch in most places, including Qin village, remained as powerful in managing community affairs as before. It was usually the Party secretary who had the final say in making important decisions, such as the amount and kinds of fees to be collected from the villagers; the collection and allocation of the fees; the establishment of a factory or other kinds of collective enterprises; the construction of a bridge, a road, or other public projects and welfare programs; and the negotiation and signing of contracts with external partners over the lease of the collective land of the village or sales of its public resources. Because the secretary was above the village council and not subject to its supervision, his abuse of power was inevitable under certain circumstances (Zhou Xiaohong 2000).

Realizing the negative effects of the unbridled power of the Party secretary in the village, the "Law on the Organization of the Village Council," revised by the central government in 1998, made significant changes. Although it ambiguously acknowledged the "core leadership" of the grassroots Party organizations in rural communities, the law emphasized the "democratic election, democratic decision-making, democratic management, and democratic supervision" of the village council. It urged the Party to "support and safeguard the villagers in implementing self-government programs and directly exercising their democratic rights" (Xu Jing 2006). More important, the new law granted the village council the following rights: the collecting and using of miscellaneous fees, raising funds for public welfare programs, deciding the subsidies for village cadres, using the income from the village's collective enterprises, starting a collective enterprise or a public welfare program, making contracts for the construction or management of collective projects, making contracts with the villagers over their use of land and other collective resources, and regulating of use of land as housing lots. Thus, almost all of the economic power previously controlled by the Party secretary had to be turned over to the village council.

The actual effect of the 1998 law varied from village to village. In some localities, the Party secretary refused to share his power with the newly elected village council, and the latter was as weak as before in making decisions on the village's public business. In other places, the "enlightened" local Party leaders handed over the village's financial accounts and seals to the newly elected village council. This often occurred in places where the collective economy was weak and the burden of managing the village's various affairs outweighed the possible benefits from their current position. Where the collective economy was prosperous and controlling the village's finance mattered a great deal to village cadres' personal interests, however, the introduction of the new law only incurred bitter conflicts between the Party branch and the village council. Once elected, members of the village council would set up their own office, separate from the secretary's, and demand that the Party leader hand over the account books. Unwilling to lose his influence and material benefits, the Party secretary would refuse to do so using whatever excuses he had. In retaliation, the village council would stop paying the subsidies from the funds it controlled to the secretary or any personnel he had appointed. After giving up their financial power, Party secretaries found that their influence in the community became nominal, often complaining that what they were left with was only "a hammer and a sickle," symbols on the Party's flag (Guo Zhenglin 2001).

The Dongtai municipal government attempted to eliminate the conflict between the Party secretary and the village council director by promulgating a regulation in 2002 that introduced two measures. First, it allowed the Party secretary to act as the director of the village council, a measure that presumably would reduce the conflicts among the village cadres, cut down the salaries on the personnel, and improve the efficiency of village government.[5] To prevent the Party secretary from being too powerful and potentially abusive, however, the regulation prescribed another measure: to select this person through the method of "four transparencies, three nominations, and two elections." The selection should have "transparent" goals, requirements, procedures, and results; the candidates should be produced through nominations by the Party organization, by the masses, and by the individuals themselves; finally, the successful candidate should win both the election by the Party members and the "trust votes" from ordinary villagers (Dongtai shiwei 2002).

The actual selection of the Party secretary in a given locality, to be sure, rarely conformed to the announced method. Nevertheless, as a result of the regulation, the two offices did merge into one through the 2004 election of the village council in many localities, including Qin village; this was possible because a Party secretary usually had no problem winning the election by manipulating the nomination of the candidates. The introduction of direct election in 2007, however, changed the situation. As seen in the case of Qin village, a Party secretary could still win the election and become the director of the village council by taking advantage of his influence in the community. Nevertheless, because he could no longer control the nomination as easily as before, his success in the election could not be guaranteed. The awkward relationship between the Party secretary and the village council continued in localities where the former lost the election. No matter whether the Party secretary could become the village council director or not, one thing is certain in either circumstance; that is, the introduction of direct election in 2007 produced an unprecedented pressure for both the Party secretary and incumbent village council members to improve their performance and relationship with the villagers.

Restructuring Villager-Cadre Relations

Cadres and Villagers

The relationship between the grassroots cadres and ordinary villagers changed remarkably during the reform era. Mr. Pu, a 68-year-old Qin villager, thus described the cadres in 2005: "During the collective time, they rarely smiled when running into us in the street and always waited for us to say greetings to them first. They always had a stern face when inspecting in the field and could easily get angry and scold us if we failed to do a good job. Nowadays, the reverse was true. Upon seeing an old villager like me, the cadres would say greetings first and appear nice." The reason behind the changed attitude, as he pointed out, was that "in the past we counted on them but now they count on us." Pu's words were true. Before the introduction of village elections in 1986, what determined a village cadre's career was his relationship with higher authorities and his ability to carry out the instructions from above, rather than the villagers' opinions of him. After 1986, the introduction of the multi-candidate election pressured the cadres to maintain good relationships with the majority of the villagers.

Pleasing the villagers, however, was far from enough to win their respect and trust. A respectable cadre, in the eyes of some villagers, should have an ability to properly manage the village's domestic affairs and, more importantly, to build connections with people outside the community, and to use those external sources to open factories, make loans, obtain raw materials, and market the goods of the local factories. In addition, the cadre should be able to manage the village-owned enterprises so that they could provide adequate employment opportunities for the villagers and generate enough profit to improve the community's public welfare. When talking about such cadres, several mentioned Mr. Meng of the neighboring Meng village, who established five factories that hired more than a hundred villagers in total.

Equally important was the cadre's integrity. Mr. Zhang, director of the village council, stood out in this regard. Unlike other cadres, Zhang rarely accepted a villager's invitation to dinner or joined them in gambling. He was also a competent mediator. Whenever the villagers quarreled with each other, they would turn to him for a resolution. Zhang would carefully consider the appeals of each side and avoid favoritism when making a judgment. Therefore, he was always able to work out a settlement acceptable to both sides or at least reasonable to the public. However, Zhang was such an honest person that he failed to establish close connections with his superiors and build extensive networks with external sources. Experienced villagers agreed that it was difficult for people to "have both ability and integrity" (*de cai jian bei*).

When talking about their public service, the village cadres admitted that they faced pressure from different directions. The pressure first came from themselves and their families. To be a Party secretary or village council head in Qin village came with a subsidy of about 8,000 to 10,000 yuan a year in the early 2000s. Other members of the village council received 5,000 to 6,000 yuan annually. This was only about half of the income of an ordinary adult male or less than one-tenth of the earning of the most successful villagers. Of course, all cadres sought extra income from other sources, which made their standard of living higher than the average in the community. Nevertheless, in the opinion of the cadres, the time and energy they spent on official duties were much more than what they were compensated. The cadres also faced pressures "from above and below" because not only did fellow villagers treat them with high expectations but the township government also was demanding in evaluating their performance. In Qindong township, every Party secretary of a village was subject to a 300-score evaluation system, which measured the secretary's performance in three areas (economic growth, social harmony, and disciplining Party members); each area contained further specific requirements. The secretary had to work hard to keep his score at 200 or above and to avoid a warning from the township government or dismissal from office.

"Government Transparency"

To improve the local cadres' creditability and reduce their misconduct in managing village finances, a nationwide policy, called "government transparency" (*zhengwu gongkai*), was instituted in the 1990s. The policy promoted the villagers' participation in the "democratic management of financial affairs" (*minzhu licai*), a practice that had existed in every production team during the collective years. In Qin village, a *minzhu licai* group of six members, chosen from each of the six subvillage groups, met each quarter to examine the village government's accounts. The members checked every receipt and, if they found that the expense was excessive or unnecessary, would refuse to stamp the receipt. The cadre responsible for that transaction then had to take the receipt and refund the village. However, as one member pointed out, the receipts and all account books for them to review had been screened by the cadres to ensure that no "big holes" would be found. When the group members did find some expenses excessive and argued with the cadres, the latter would justify the receipts with "a thousand reasons." Thus, when performing their duties, the *minzhu licai* members were rarely serious. After all, the financial condition of the village government did not directly affect their own living. Therefore, more often than not, the group members treated their quarterly meetings as a casual occasion to simply chat with each other for hours and to receive their stipend of 10 yuan—after having a free lunch provided by the village government.

Another part of the government transparency policy, introduced in the late 1990s, was publicizing the village government accounts. Fifteen different forms thus were posted in a glass-fronted board, called "the board of government transparency" (*zhengwu gongkai lan*), on the wall of Qin village office in the summer of 2005 when I visited there. These forms covered the village government's revenues, expenditures, annual budgets, the amount of taxes and fees owed by individual households, rent payments by certain villagers for using the village's property for business, the names and the dates of birth and marriage of couples qualified for childbirth, and the like. The purpose of the board was to put the village government's financial activities under the villagers' supervision and forestall possible misconduct. Villagers welcomed the installation of the board because having something publicized was better than having nothing at all. Before creating the board, the villagers knew little about the village government's revenues and expenditures. However, some villagers also complained that the numbers shown in the forms were too general and that they had no idea how the cadres arrived at those numbers. For example, one of the forms showed that the village government's expenditures on magazines and newspapers in 2004 was 2,000 yuan. "Why did the village cadres spend so much on newspapers and magazines? Why was the amount exactly 2,000 yuan?" a villager expressed his doubt when looking at the board. Whether the numbers as publicized on the board were accurate was hard to judge, without knowing the details of the actual expenses and transactions involved, but it was obvious that much work remained for the village government to win the villagers' trust and to make the government truly transparent.

Community Life

Depoliticization

An obvious change in the daily lives of Qin villagers after 1980 was that there were no more political campaigns or frequent mass meetings. The Party's top leadership, to be sure, continued to emphasize the importance of ideological work in justifying its new policies and advocating its ever-changing guidelines, such as the "Deng Xiaoping theory" and the "Three Represents" in the 1990s, and the "Harmonious Society" in the 2000s. However, grassroots cadres lacked the interest in propagating them to the villagers. It was no longer easy for them to convene a village-wide gathering or to organize the villagers into study groups, since the village government lost its effective means of persuading the independent farmers to do so after the transition to family farming, nor did the cadres themselves believe it necessary to spend their time and energy on propaganda. What was important to them was their economic and administrative records; increasing the village government's revenue and fulfilling the tasks imposed from above were above anything else in the township government's evaluation of their performance.

Ordinary villagers had no interest in the state's ideology, either. The village cadres admitted that none of the more than 400 households in Qin village subscribed to any newspaper published by the government or Party organizations. Readers of the few newspapers and magazines kept by the village government were limited to the cadres themselves. Not surprisingly, when I asked several villagers what the "Three Represents" were, none could answer correctly. Indicative of the abating influence of the state's ideology in the village, all signs of official propaganda that had existed during the collective era disappeared in the 1980s and 1990s. There were no more political slogans on the wall of the villagers' houses. The picture of Chairman Mao above the family-god chest in the living room of every house yielded to the portrait of the God of Longevity, the God of Fortune, or other deities.

All these do not mean, however, that the villagers were ignorant of the government's policies and political events going on inside and outside of China. In fact, some of them, especially the young and middle-age males who had received middle or high school education, as well as some older Party members and former cadres, said that they were interested in watching TV news in the evening. Their conversations with

me about the life stories of President Hu Jintao, the Taiwan Party leaders' visits to the mainland, or the U.S. war in Iraq, for example, showed
their curiosity about things beyond their community. They also knew
well the government's policies on issues such as birth control, the village council election, and the reduction of fees and taxes. Although
they counted for only a small fraction (probably no more than
one-tenth) of the village population, these villagers played an active
role in village politics. However, unlike the "activists" of the collective
era, who were cultivated by the government to promote its policies,
the informed villagers of the reform era actively participated in local
politics out of a real concern with the well-being of the community as
well as of themselves. Therefore, they thought independently and were
often critical of village cadres and the government.

The indoctrination of the Party's ideology was limited to a small
number of Party members in the village, 17 all told in the early 2000s.
On the fifth of every month, the Party members regularly met at the
village office to listen to Secretary Wang's reading of new documents
and discuss various matters that concerned the village. At the end of a
year, each member made a self-evaluation, which summarized one's
achievements as well as problems in performing the assigned duties,
and scored oneself accordingly. The self-evaluation and scoring were
subject to other members' discussion and approval. The Party branch
then determined if the person under evaluation was qualified to continue his or her Party membership or was subject to the Party's disciplinary measures, such as receiving an inner-Party warning, being
placed on probation within the Party, or having membership terminated. Although the self-evaluation was perfunctory and no one received any kind of punishment, it was routinely done every year. When
asked about the benefits of being a Party member, the villagers often
explained that having Party membership was like having a "trademark
of high standing" (*paizi ying*); it was an indication of one's reputation
and status in the community.

But few villagers showed interest in obtaining Party membership in
the 1990s and the early 2000s. For years, Secretary Wang had to contact
individual villagers to ascertain their willingness to join the Party. The
primary criterion in choosing candidates for Party membership, as the
Party instructed, was their abilities to "take the lead in getting rich"
(*daitou zhifu*) and to "lead the villagers in getting rich" (*dailing cunmin
zhifu*). As Wang explained, these requirements actually meant finding
candidates from those who owned the largest and most profitable

businesses and hired the most employees in the village. The traditional criteria in recruiting new Party members—that is, the candidate's family background (poor and lower-middle peasants), allegiance to the Party's guidelines, and sincerity in joining the Party—were abandoned. It is no wonder that the few members newly admitted to the village's Party branch were all the "rich persons" (*furen*) and "able persons" (*nengren*). Subsequently, the 17 members of the Party branch normally split into two groups at the monthly meeting during the discussion session. One group consisted of veteran members who had joined the Party during the collective era or earlier; they spent most of their time complaining about the unjust happenings in the village and beyond. The other group consisted of the rich and able persons, whose chatting focused on exchanging information about their businesses. As an old Party member remarked, the Party branch soon or later would become "the club of the rich and the able" in the village when the veteran members passed away.

The Revival of Traditional Customs

Traditional social ties and customs, which withered during the collective years, revived in Qin villagers' everyday lives after 1980. Before the reform, interactions between kinsmen were limited to the exchange of visits and gifts on the occasions of marriages, funerals, sickness, and important festivals. Whenever they encountered particular financial difficulties, the villagers turned to the production team, rather than their relatives, for help. After the reform, however, kinship ties became particularly important in family farming. Reciprocal help in transplanting rice seedlings or harvesting crops occurred primarily between relatives. Villagers with affinal or agnate ties also tended to help each other in running the family business and sidelines. When a villager, named Wang, succeeded in shipping goods with his own freighter in Shanghai and neighboring cities in the 1980s, for example, his three brothers, two cousins, and two brothers-in-law all joined him one after another in the following years. Another Wang was among the first in the village to start a chicken farm, raising more than 5,000 chickens, and earned more than 25,000 yuan a year in the mid-1990s. Later, his cousins and a brother-in-law each opened their own chicken farms with Wang's help. Young villagers who formed a small group as construction workers or contractors in the cities were often brothers, cousins, or brothers-in-law, who informed each other of the new opportunities of business and helped each other in case of sickness or financial difficulties while working in the cities.

Traditional customs in celebrating festivals as well as weddings and funeral rituals were revived and became extravagant. The lunar New Year remained the most important festival. Villagers who worked in the cities, no matter how far they were away from home, all came back for family reunions. Enjoying good food, visiting relatives, watching TV, and playing poker or mahjong were the villagers' main activities during the lunar New Year. There were no more constraints imposed by the government on celebration. Nevertheless, many villagers complained that the festival was not as fun and exciting as before because there was no longer a crowd of kids flocking from one house to the next, calling out greetings and asking for gifts such as candy, a handful of peanuts, or a *hongbao* (a red envelope filled with a small sum of money). The children preferred to stay home playing games; they went out only to accompany the parents visiting their relatives.

Without the government's interference, villagers openly performed sacrificial service to ancestors and deceased family members four times a year.[6] On the Qingming Festival, each family visited the tombs of their ancestors, where the family members replaced the top of the grave with new earth, cleaned the weeds around it, burned fake paper money, and performed kowtow. In addition, the family also offered sacrifices to one's own deceased parents on the anniversaries of their deaths.

In the absence of government intervention, old customs also resurfaced after 1980 for betrothal and wedding ceremonies. Using a matchmaker remained important for a formal betrothal, even if the two individuals involved had already known each other and started courtship on their own initiative. After the matchmaker's proposal, the parents of both sides as well as the two young villagers would visit each other's homes. The parents would pay attention primarily to the economic condition of the other family, while the young man and woman were concerned more with each other's personal qualities. If both sides agreed on the proposal, the host family would treat the visitors with a feast, and the two young individuals would take a betrothal picture. Before marriage, the boy had to send specific gifts to his fiancée's family on important festivals according to the custom. On the Duanwu Festival (the fifth of the fifth lunar month), for example, the gift was 66 *zongzi* or cooked glutinous rice wrapped in reed leaves. On the Mid-Autumn Festival, the list included 20 catties of lotus roots, 36 moon cakes, two carps, 66 duck eggs, and four catties of pork. To prepare for the wedding, the groom's family had to provide the bride with enough cloth to make 8 sets of winter clothes, 12 sets of spring and autumn clothes, and 16 set of summer clothes. On the wedding day, when the groom visited the bride's family to bring her to his own family, he had to provide a certain amount of money to have the door of the bride's home opened to him. He also needed to provide the bride's family as well as her maternal and paternal uncles and aunts with a specific kind and number of gifts. The most important part of the wedding for the groom's family was entertaining the guests with feasts for three days. The guests had to give the young couple a specific kind of gift, according to their relationship with the couple. For example, the gift from the groom's eldest maternal uncle, the most important guest, was a red silk flower accompanied with a pair of red-paper couplets written with blessing words, a pair of red cradles with the golden characters of "fortune" and "longevity," six large firecrackers, and two strings of small firecrackers. A month after the wedding, the newlyweds would pay a visit to the bride's family and stay there for several days (QD1 2000).

While the villagers abided by the old customs in marriage, the material requirements anticipated for a successful marriage changed a great deal in the 1980s and 1990s. For example, when visiting the potential son-in-law's home, the girl's parents usually expected that the boy's family would have a two-story house filled with modern furniture or at least a well-built ranch house. The bride's dowry in the late 1990s and early 2000s typically included a color TV, a washing machine, a refrigerator, and desirably a motorcycle, in addition to traditional items. The groom's attire had changed from the Maoist or military-style tunic to a Western-style suit, while the bride wore the traditional red silk wedding dress or, in an increasing number of cases, a modern-style white dress. The "red envelope" (*hongbao*) or cash gift from each guest to the bride on the wedding day increased from only 10 or 20 yuan in the early 1980s to normally 100 or 200 yuan in the late 1990s.

When asked why the government took no measures to regulate the villagers' expenses on weddings and gift-giving, a former village leader replied with only two words: *duo shi*, or "meddlesome." He explained that marriage was the "major event in life" (*rensheng dashi*) for everyone and therefore it deserved one's expenses to the maximum of his affordability. And gift-giving showed one's responsibility as a relative; kinship made sense only when the relatives exchanged gifts and visited

each other on such events. He added that the government took measures to limit gift-giving and expenses on weddings during the collective years because people at that a time were poor and many were unable to provide the gifts as the custom specified. However, it was
"meddlesome" for the government to do so when the gifts were affordable to all villagers and when exchanging gifts remained the most important way for them to show kinship ties.

The Family

The "Small Family" Prevailed

Despite the survival and revival of traditional practices in Qin village
after 1980, economic reform and the birth-control policy brought many
changes to the villagers' daily lives in the family and the community.
The most significant was the shrinking size of the family and the simplified family relations. Because of the enforcement of the one-child
policy (see the next chapter), "small families" (*xiao jiating*) of four members or less, which accounted for only 24 percent of all families in the
community in 1974, increased to 63 percent in 1984 and to 88 percent in
2005. Families of five or six, which were typical during the collective
era, decreased from 48 percent in 1974 to 31 percent in 1984 and to 12
percent in 2005. Large families of seven or more decreased from 28 percent in 1974 to 6 percent in 1984 and to zero in 2005. Overall, the average
size of the families in Qin village reduced from 5.6 people in 1974 to 4.22
in 1984 and to 3.12 in 2005. The three-member family of one couple plus
a single child became the norm in the 1990s and the early 2000s, increasing from 9 households (16 percent) in 1980 to 17 households (27 percent)
in 1984 and to 49 households (56 percent) in 2005 in the No. 5 group of
Qin village.[7]

An immediate result of the decreased size of the family was the increased privacy of individuals in family life. During the collective
years and earlier, when a family typically had five or six members and
sometimes as many as eight or nine people, the children lived with
their parents in the same bedroom, and it was not unusual for three or
more people to sleep together on the same bed. After 1980, however, as
small families increased and their living conditions improved, the single child or at most two children in a family usually had their own bed
in their own bedroom after they were five or six years old (in most families, young children still lived with their parents in the same bed-

room for better caring). In the early 2000s, most families had only one child while their house had two or three bedrooms. Therefore, almost all school-age children had their own bed in a separate room. The parents also had greater privacy in their own bedroom. However, the disadvantages of these changes were equally obvious. Although the son or daughter, who was usually the only child in the family, received much more personalized love and care from his or her parents than children 20 years ago, the child spent most of his or her time at home alone, without siblings, cousins, or friends to play with him or her. This was especially true in the 2000s for the children whose parents themselves were products of the one-child policy and had no sisters or brothers of their own. In general, social interactions of both children and adults in the village greatly lessened after 1980, as kinship ties attenuated.

Family Relations

The reduced size of the family accounted for significant changes in family relations. In his seminal study of contemporary village life in Northeast China, Yunxiang Yan (2003) demonstrated how changes in the family structure and residential patterns resulted in greater equality between family members of different generations and sexes and greater privacy and intimacy in family life. Similar tendencies were also visible in Qin village. With only one child, parents in the village were willing to spend as much as they could afford on the education of their son or daughter. Growing up as the "little emperor" at home and spoiled by the parents and grandparents, the child did few or no family chores. He or she was also much less obedient to the parents than the children had been in the 1970s and before. This was especially evident in the parents' arrangement of a marriage for him or her when the child reached his or her late teens or early twenties. Although a matchmaker was still involved, as mentioned earlier, the parents usually listened to their child when making a decision. It was up to the son or daughter to decide if he or she would accept the matchmaker's proposal. Forced marital arrangements disappeared.

After marriage, the young couple generally had a better relationship than in the collective years, not only because they had more privacy in their family life but also because family chores, which had been the major source of conjugal conflicts, greatly lessened. Before the 1990s, the villagers were burdened with many farming and domestic tasks.

They had to cut the rice and wheat crops manually during the harvest seasons and raise pigs, goats, sheep, and chickens throughout the year. The wife had to cook three meals a day for the family that often had four or five mouths or more, and hand wash their clothes in the early morning. Quarrels often broke out between the wife and her husband or between the mother-in-law and the daughter-in-law over the division of duties in the family. After the mid-1990s, however, mechanization in crop harvesting greatly reduced the farmers' labor. The increased use of chemical fertilizers also reduced their dependence on animal manure. As a result, few families in the village raised pigs, goats, or sheep in the early 2000s. Cooking and washing were no longer a burden to a wife. In many families, the only person who still ate and lived at home was the wife herself; her husband was working and came back only once a week and even once a year, and her child lived in the boarding school and came home only for the weekend. Therefore, the wife needed to cook only once or twice a day for herself. Except for the busy season, many wives had little farm work or home chores to do. When staying at home together, the couple had more time and privacy to develop their relationship.

There were, however, new causes of disputes between the husband and wife in a small family. Some male villagers worked in the cities for months or year-round, leaving their wives at home. They often would not return home until the lunar New Year or when there was an important family event. The long separation had a negative effect on the marital relationship. Although newly married young males generally kept in touch with their wives through frequent phone calls, some husbands called their wives only about once a month, asking primarily about their child's education or their parents' health. Other husbands never called, unless there was something urgent to discuss. Extramarital affairs occurred for a few husbands and wives. One case that stirred up the entire community in 1997 dealt with Mr. Jiang, a calm, handsome 33-year-old carpenter. While making furniture for a family in Shenyang, Liaoning province, he fell in love with the daughter of the family in the summer of that year. After returning home for the lunar New Year, Jiang revealed the affair to his wife and stated that he wanted a divorce. His wife and parents strongly opposed. Villagers also showed sympathy to the wife. In their eyes, she was a good wife and mother who took good care of her child and the parents-in-law while Jiang was away. After the New Year, a hearing was held in the branch court at a neighboring market town. About 40 Qin villagers, who showed unequivocal support to the wife, attended the hearing. Jiang temporarily gave up the idea of a divorce after the court denied his request but continued his relationship with the woman in Shenyang for the next few years until he finally married her.

In their conversations with me, some young couples shared their concerns about supporting their aging parents in the future. In the collective years, older parents often had support from two or more married sons. These married sons were responsible for their parents' support in their old age, each contributing a certain amount of workpoints to his parents to receive grain rations and other goods from the production team. The reverse was true in the early 2000s. In most new families, both the husband and the wife were the only child of their respective parents; therefore, a young couple had to take care of two old couples. Most of the young couple's parents or parents-in-law, to be sure, were still in their fifties and therefore able to make a living on their own. Parents whose daughters had left them after marriage worked particularly hard to accumulate enough savings for their old age. Therefore, what the young couple worried about was not their ability to provide food and clothing or other goods to their parents or parents-in-law in the future, but the chores of taking care of the two old couples when they were sick or too old to take care of themselves 10 or 20 years from now. Sharing the chores and being fair in treating their respective parents would possibly be a new source of conflict for the young couple.

Lifestyle

Changes were also visible in the villagers' lifestyle. In the 2000s, villagers in their old age as well as some middle-aged women had more leisure than before. Unlike young men, who were busy with their off-farm business in or out of the village, and young women, who worked in factories or joined their husbands in family business, these villagers usually stayed home. As agriculture became increasingly mechanized and family chores lessened, many mothers and the elderly in the village had plenty of time, especially during the slack season. They spent their time chatting with neighbors or gathering together to play cards or mahjong. After supper, villagers usually spent the evening watching TV or VCD movies. Many villagers enjoyed singing karaoke songs, believing it to be a "civilized" form of entertainment, unlike playing cards or mahjong, which involved gambling of money and often caused bitter feelings between players.[8]

Young villagers were quick to accept new ideas and new ways of life. Television was the primary source from which the villagers learned about the world beyond the community, especially the different ways of thought, expression, and life in the cities. The improved transportation conditions also made it convenient for the villagers to visit the neighboring towns and cities shopping for clothes and other goods that they liked. Those who worked as carpenters or contractors in the cities made the same style of furniture and renovated the living rooms or bedrooms for themselves or fellow villagers the same way as they did for urban families. A "generation gap" thus occurred between the young and old villagers. Villagers in their late fifties and older distinguished themselves from the young not only in their clothing but also in their values. They lived a frugal life and showed a strong dislike of those who wasted food. Having suffered the hardship of the Great Leap Forward, grandparents in a family frequently reminded their children or grandchildren of "the time when people ate at the collective canteen," although the latter had no idea what the canteen was like. They also expected their children and grandchildren to be obedient and, therefore, were frustrated frequently when the young disobeyed. When talking about their experiences in the collective era or recent changes, the older villagers still showed a special feeling about Mao Zedong and a degree of fear of mentioning anything negative about the cadres or the government that would cause trouble for them.

Villagers from their teens up to their forties, in contrast, not only showed a strong interest in new things from the outside and a willingness to accept or imitate them, but also had different life goals. Better educated and informed, the young villagers played a more important role than their parents in making decisions for the family. They judged fellow villagers, including the cadres, by looking at how successful they had been in doing business rather than anything else. They acknowledged the gaps between themselves and "townsmen" (*chengliren*) and between country and city, but they worked hard to narrow the gaps. When talking about the future of their family, almost all middle-aged parents placed their hopes on their school-age children; although they had failed to change their own status as villagers, the parents wanted their son or daughter to receive a good education, to leave the village, and to enter a world that they had yearned for but never experienced in their own lives. Indeed, after finishing their high school, almost all teenagers in the village successfully entered a college. The few who failed the college entrance examination either planned to take the exam again or found a job in a local factory or in a city. None of them wanted to be a farmer or to stay in the village for life.

Conclusion

Qin villagers' everyday experiences in the community and the family after 1980 were subject to the influences of three factors. The first is the Maoist legacies, especially the state's control through the Party's organizations and propaganda. The abolition of the collective system, to be sure, weakened the administrative basis of the state's presence in the countryside, causing the government to increasingly turn to economic leverages, rather than compulsory measures, to enforce its policies. But the post-Mao state's retreat from the rural society was sluggish and reluctant, as seen in the township government's attempts to put village election under its control and in the Party branch secretary's dominance of village government. Another heritage of the Maoist era was mass participation in local politics through various devices that sought to put the grassroots cadres under the villagers' supervision. The election of village cadres, the regular auditing of the village government's accounts, and the implementation of the "government transparency" policy should best be seen as the continuation of the Maoist tradition of popular politics. By and large, however, the reform era witnessed the waning influence of the state in the village society, both administratively and ideologically. Both the state's top-down control and the villagers' bottom-up supervision of the village cadres deteriorated.

The second is the continuity and change in village traditions, especially the indigenous values and practices that regulated interpersonal relations in the community before the Maoist era. The customs in family events, ranging from childbirth to burial, revived and became even more extravagant. But they lost their traditional meanings that had been embedded in popular values; instead the villagers used the ceremonies and events primarily to affirm and maintain their standing in the community. Kinship ties were particularly important for the villagers seeking money-making opportunities in the booming private economy, although their personal wealth and abilities, rather than the blood or fictive ties, played a more decisive role in their quest for economic success. Changes were also noticeable in family relations. The enforcement of the one-child policy, coupled with the steady improvement in living conditions, led to not only the downsized family and simplified family relations but also to the further decline of the traditional hierarchy and the inherent notion of subordination in the family.

The third is the emergence of a series of new economic, political, and cultural dynamics, which can be put together under the rubric of "modernity"; they made possible the significant changes that led to the villagers' greater independence and equality in the family, the community, and society. We have seen in this and the preceding chapters how decollectivization led to the thriving of family farming and private businesses, the subsequent economic autonomy of individual households, and the enhanced standing of the villagers in their relationship with the cadres. The introduction of self-government programs in the countryside, especially the election of village councils, is best seen as the state's recognition of the new economic and social realities in the reform era. Unlike the farmers of the Mao era, who were economically dependent on the collective and therefore subject to the exploitation of the state and the possible abuse of local cadres regardless of their imagined superiority in political discourse, villagers of the reform era not only achieved economic independence but also developed an awareness of equality in social and political relations. For the younger generation of villagers growing up in the reform era, the traditional gap between the city and the countryside was no longer unbridgeable; they strived to change their status from the stigmatized *peasants* to *citizens*, who would be on equal footing with the rest of the nation and whose individual rights and choices would not be compromised.

CHAPTER 13

From Government to Governance

RECALLING THEIR experiences in the reform era, the cadres in Qin village agreed that their work was exceptionally hard in the 1980s and early 1990s, when they were preoccupied with "three major tasks" (*san da renwu*) that they had never encountered before: enforcing the one-child-per-couple policy, promoting cremation and forbidding earth burial, and collecting taxes and fees from individual households. These tasks challenged the villagers' traditional notions and customs about birth and death and affected their livelihood. Therefore, the cadres had a difficult time dealing with the noncompliant villagers who condemned their jobs as "demanding money and lives" (*yaoqian yaoming*). Since the mid-1990s, however, the relationship between the cadres and villagers ameliorated as the latter became accustomed to the new family practices and as the state shifted its focus from extracting agricultural surplus to accommodating the needs of the rural population. The cadres also paid more attention to the community's own projects, such as rebuilding and upgrading water-control projects, promoting cooperation in medical care, and improving community infrastructures. This chapter describes how the village government changed its role from merely carrying out the mandatory orders from the township government, often at the cost of the villagers and involving the use of coercion, to showing greater concern with the issues of the local community. It ends with a discussion on the problems associated with the transition from *government* or the state's one-way penetration of rural society to *governance* that entailed the villagers' cooperation and voluntary participation.[1]

In the Name of the State

Birth Control

The most challenging task for village leaders in the 1980s and early 1990s was to enforce the one-child-per-couple policy, which was the No. 1 criterion used by the township government to judge their performance in local administrative activities and determine their annual subsidies. If there was one couple in the village who gave birth to a second child, the village cadres would receive the lowest rating and the lowest subsidy at the end of the year, no matter how well they had performed the remainder of their duties. This was what they called "negation by one case" (*yi piao foujue*). To effectively carry out the policy, each village created a new organization called "the birth control group," headed by the secretary of the village's Party branch. The head of the village's Women's Federation (*fulian*) branch, also a member of the group, was responsible for its routine tasks. One of the tasks was to see that all married women in the village used an IUD after the birth of their first (and only) child and that all women who had two children were sterilized. An even more important task was tracking the whereabouts of all women of child-bearing age and checking them every two months, mainly through a urine test performed by the village clinic's nurse, to ensure that none of them had conceived a second child. Once an unplanned pregnancy was detected, the woman had to be sent to the hospital at the township seat to have a surgical abortion.

The township government also imposed a fine on couples who violated the one-child policy in 1980. The fine increased by 200 yuan every year in the following five years, to 1,200 yuan in 1985. It was no doubt a burden for violators who earned income mainly from farming, but those who had become rich through household sidelines or off-farm businesses in the early 1980s could easily pay off the fine and thereby give birth to a second child. To deter potential violators, the township government dramatically increased the fine to 6,000 yuan in 1986, 10,000 yuan in 1987, 15,000 yuan in 1991, and 20,000 yuan in 1993. The fine in fact became so exorbitant that it went far beyond the affordability of many families. To make the penalty more practical, the government changed the flat rate of the fine to a flexible one after 1993, which in general was three times the violating couple's annual income.

Villagers reacted differently to the one-child policy and the concomitant measures. Those who had given birth to a son had no problem in accepting it, and all young mothers in such families voluntarily used an IUD after giving birth to the child. Resistance came only from the couples whose first child was a girl. These couples had several practical concerns. First, marriage in the rural area remained basically patrilo-cal. Upon marriage, the daughter moved out to live with her husband at the husband's home. In the eyes of the villagers, therefore, a daugh-ter who was married off was just like a basin of water that was thrown away; she no longer belonged to her birth family. Having no son thus was tantamount to terminating the family line, which was unfilial to one's ancestors. Second and more important, without children to live with them or at least to live in the same village, the parents had to take care of themselves during their old age. This could be a problem when they were sick or too old to cook and to do other home chores. Third, the couple had worked hard and saved for years to build a new house or a two-story building; they wanted to have a son to inherit the prop-erty. Without a son to continue the family line and to live with them, the parents also faced the problem of property inheritance. For these reasons, almost all couples who already had a daughter wanted to have a second child, but few of them had the ability or the opportunity to do so because of the government's ever-increasing fine and the village cadres' close surveillance.

Nevertheless, a few couples in Qin village successfully produced a second child by taking advantage of their occupation as freight-boat owners in long-distance transportation and escaping the village cad-res' control. Among such examples were villager Meng and his wife, who had a transport business in Jiangnan (southern Jiangsu). Upon hearing that the wife conceived a second child, the village government sent three men to search for them in the summer of 1988. The search ended in vain a month later after more than 2,400 yuan had been spent on the trip. The village government soon received a letter from Meng, who informed the cadres that his wife had given birth to a lovely boy with "tender skin, shining hair, and bright eyes," as a village cadre later recollected. Irritated, the village cadres threatened to dismantle Meng's house as a way to punish him and deter other potential viola-tors. But no one took the lead in doing so, unwilling to offend Meng and his relatives. At the end of the year, Meng and his wife came back to the village with their two children. The village government imposed a fine of 8,400 yuan, which included the fine and travel expenses. They paid only 4,800 yuan before returning to Jiangnan after the lunar New Year. In the next few years they eventually paid off the remainder of the fine. In 1989, another couple in the village gave birth to a second child and was fined 6,000 yuan. The son thus got the nickname Liu Qian Kuai, or "six thousand yuan," for the fine his parents had paid for him. In 1993, a third couple in the village paid a fine of 15,000 yuan for breaching the rule.

Although the hefty fine might have been a deterrent to many villagers of average income, it did not discourage the few who were determined to have an additional child. The village government, therefore, had to count on other means that they deemed necessary to thwart the attempts of such couples. One case in point concerned a villager named Zhang. In 1995 Zhang and his wife, who already had a daughter, left the village with their freight boat when the wife was pregnant again. Five months later, it was finally reported to the township government, when the couple was far away from the village and no one knew their whereabouts. So the township cadres could only summon Zhang's father to the government office. Rumors had it that during the six or seven days in the hot summer when Zhang's father was "detained," the old man was fed only porridge each day. Without a tented bed on which to sleep, he suffered mosquito bites at night. Zhang's cousin, a cadre in the village, found himself in an embarrassing situation because his uncle's prolonged detainment hurt both his conscience and his reputation. He finally learned where the couple was and went there in person to bring them back. By the time Zhang's wife returned to the village, she had been pregnant for six months. She had no choice but to have an abortion.

As Mr. Xiao, the director of the township government's Planned-Birth Office, explained, to prevent unplanned pregnancy and to force the women involved to have an abortion, the government had to use compulsory measures under certain circumstances that no official regulations allowed. Putting one's parent under custody, he explained, was the only method available to the government when a pregnant woman and her husband were missing. If the woman was available but refused to abort the fetus, they had to threaten with the use of the compulsory "three ones" method: one piece of door plank to carry the woman, one rope to tie the woman to the door, and one group of people to perform this task. In actuality, he quickly pointed out, they rarely resorted to coercion. Whenever a woman had an extra pregnancy, the *fulian* director and other village cadres would spend a lot of time with the couple, persuading them to voluntarily terminate the pregnancy. Most of the couples gave up in the end and went to a clinic for an abortion. To facilitate the task, the village government always provided a diesel-powered boat to send the woman to the clinic and then bring her back. The *fulian* director also accompanied her the entire day and gave the woman some nutritious foods as gifts from the village government after she returned.

After the mid-1990s, birth control became much easier than before in Qin village and the rest of the township. Unplanned pregnancies basically disappeared during the first five years of the 2000s, whereas in the 1980s there were at least five or six such cases each year in the village. In fact, as Mr. Xiao explained, although there were more than 500 couples in the township who were qualified to have a second child, only about 40, or less than one-tenth of them, were willing to do so; all others voluntarily gave up the opportunity.[2] For several reasons, the young couples were unwilling to have a second child. The first had to do with the villagers' changed opinion about childbearing. After enforcing the one-child policy for more than 10 years, families with only one child had become increasingly predominant in the community in the 1990s and early 2000s. It became acceptable for most young couples to have a daughter as their only child after marriage; having a son to continue the family name was no longer a serious concern for them. Second, as their income increased steadily, most couples no longer worried too much about their old age; unlike villagers of earlier generations, who generally counted on their children for old-age support, the young couples in the early 2000s were confident about saving enough to support themselves. Third, and no less important, the cost of raising a child dramatically increased over the years, and much of the cost had to do with the child's education. The tuition, miscellaneous fees, and other costs, for example, increased from about 20 or 30 yuan in the early 1980s to more than 2,000 yuan a year in the early 2000s for an elementary-school student, from about 30 to 40 yuan to more than 4,000 yuan for a middle-school student, and from about 100 yuan to more than 7,000 yuan for a high-school student. To have two children would double these figures, which would become a real burden for parents of average income. If the student was fortunate enough to enter an outstanding school, the cost involved could be more than twice that of a regular school. Most parents thus had to give up the idea of having two children and focus their energy and savings on the only child. To have only one child thus became a voluntary choice. Birth control, which had been the most difficult task for the village cadres before, was no longer a major concern in their quotidian duties in the early 2000s.

Funeral Reform

Funeral reform began nationwide in the late 1950s and early 1960s, when its primary goal was to eliminate superstitious and wasteful customs in funeral service, such as making and burning paper decorations, inviting Buddhist or Taoist monks to perform rituals, hosting a lavish feast for guests, and keeping the coffin at home for three years before burial. During the Cultural Revolution, such "superstitious" activities completely disappeared, although the villagers secretly continued some old customs for the dead, such as observing the anniversaries of the death of the deceased. In the 1970s, promoting cremation in place of the traditional burial in the ground became a new task for the cadres, as the population pressure mounted and the shortage of farmland became severe. Cremation and the use of a cinerary casket, according to the government, would reduce the use of land for tombs as well as the lumber needed for coffins. This reform, however, encountered strong opposition from the villagers, not only because the incineration of the dead sounded dreadful to the elderly but also because that many people still believed in the notion that "only a burial brings peace to the dead" (*ru tu wei an*). Moreover, most old villagers had already had a coffin for themselves before the new reform was introduced; to destroy the coffins would be equally wasteful and deeply hurt the feelings of their owners. The only measures that the government took in the 1970s were encouraging villagers to accept cremation by providing a boat free of charge to ship the dead to a crematory and by prohibiting carpenters from making new coffins. The government punished the carpenters who violated the rule by charging them a fine of 30 yuan and confiscating their tools. These measures, however, were much less successful than the government expected because those who already had a coffin could be buried in the ground after death without punishment, and others could easily make a coffin in secret or buy it from neighboring counties where no punishment was enforced on coffin makers. As a result, only 481, or about 30 percent of the dead in the entire township, were cremated in the 1970s (*Qindong gongshe shezhi* 1981: 211).

In response to the state's new regulation on funeral reform, a vigorous campaign took place in Dongtai county in 1985 to enforce cremation in the county. By that regulation, all residents had to be cremated (except for individuals of ethnic minorities and overseas Chinese who died in China); the ashes of the dead could be deeply buried in the ground but no tombs could be built; and the making and selling of coffins and other burial supplies were strictly prohibited. In Dongtai county, the government set a specific date of its enforcement: those who died before September 1, 1985, were still allowed to be buried with a coffin in a tomb; the new regulation would be applied thereafter.

This regulation caused panic among many elderly villagers who feared the burning of their bodies after death. Some of them moved out of the village to live with their daughters' families in other counties where no deadline was enforced. Granny Jiang, for example, was already 92 in 1993. Whenever she was sick, she would quickly move to her daughter's home in the neighboring Haian county. Those who wanted to bypass the new regulation after the deadline had a dreadful experience. Villager Zhang Yongwang, for example, died on September 2, 1985, right after the regulation took effect. Normally, whenever a villager died, his or her children would immediately announce the passing of their parent to neighbors and relatives, and the latter would pay a visit to show their condolence. Mourning the dead was in fact a public event of the entire community. This time, however, Zhang's son, Baofu, as well as his family members, kept the death of his father a secret, knowing well the effective date of the new regulation. He shipped the coffined remains to the river bank north of the village one night and buried his father there. Nevertheless, the village government discovered the unreported death and the illegal burial four days later. Jin Renkuan, the village's Party branch secretary, immediately phoned the township government for help. After a township cadre arrived in the village, Jin led all village cadres and Party members, each carrying a spade, to the site where Zhang was buried to unearth the coffin. Upon learning about what was happening, Baofu rushed to the site and cried helplessly while the crowd was digging up the tomb. Eventually, the corpse was taken out of the coffin and burned at a crematory about 20 miles from the village.

This event was shocking to the villagers. Traditionally, digging up a tomb and taking the corpse from a coffin for smashing or burning was believed to be the most severe punishment of the dead; only those who committed a capital crime were treated that way. Baofu later complained, therefore, that he was not as sad at the moment his father died as when his father's coffin was excavated and smashed. The villagers believed that Secretary Jin was able to do so because he was from the neighboring Gao village. As an "outsider" to the village, he did not have to worry about offending anybody in the community. Jin, however, knew well the possible resentment against him from the Zhang family, so he invited the township cadre as well as all other village cadres and Party members to do the digging together, to show that the excavation was a decision made by the government rather than by himself.

Although to many villagers Jin's action was seen as cruel, it intimidated those who would have attempted to do the same as Baofu. No villagers violated the regulation thereafter. However, a new problem soon surfaced after the enforcement of cremation, namely, where to place the cinerary casket that contained the ashes of the dead. According to the new regulation, the casket should be preserved in the "memorial hall of the laboring people," to be built and maintained by the village or township government; alternatively, it should be buried in the ground without a tomb above it. In the late 1980s and early 1990s, however, no village in the township had such a hall. The villagers thus turned to another option. Without the village cadres' close supervision, most of them put the casket in a coffin and buried the coffin the same way as they had in the past. Some villagers even built concrete tombs aboveground. Moreover, traditional funeral rituals were revived. Before cremation, the family of the dead would invite a group of lay monks to perform the traditional service at home. The family would also hire a band to play both traditional and popular music when the dead was sent to the crematory and when the cinerary casket was brought back home after cremation. The family made a number of paper houses, pavilions, and various kinds of furniture and home appliances, and burned all of them when burying the casket. Thus, all of the traditional rituals that had been attacked in the 1960s and 1970s as superstitious and wasteful were revived and became even more extravagant. Except for the universal enforcement of cremation, the funeral reform failed to achieve its original goals: to save land, to reduce the villagers' financial burden, and to fight superstitions.

Taxes, Fees, and Grain Procurement

During the collective era, individual households of a production team paid no taxes and miscellaneous fees to the government, nor did they have the duty to sell grain to the government at a price preset by the state. Instead, it was the team that paid the agricultural tax and fulfilled its duty in grain procurement (see Chapter 10). After the reform, however, all those obligations were shifted to the households. To collect the taxes and fees and to see that all the households finished their duties in a timely fashion for the mandatory grain sales thus became a new task of village cadres.

The burden of the agricultural tax and other duties, as a percentage of a household's total net income, was heavy in the 1980s and early 1990s. In 1982, the first year after decollectivization, all households in Qin village fulfilled their duties to the state through the production team. The total burden of all 65 households in the No. 5 team, including the agricultural tax, fees, and the water-work contribution, was 8,012.51 yuan (123.27 yuan per household, or 29.78 yuan per person), or about 9 to 10 percent of the team's average per capita net annual income in 1982 (QD7 1982). In 1983, as the collectives were dismantled in the county, all households paid the agricultural tax and sold the required amount of grain directly to the government on their own. The tax on a household was based on the number of its members. The tax rate was 8.526 yuan per person. The total amount of the tax in the No. 5 team of Qin village was 2,327.67 yuan. The quota of grain procurement on the team in that year was 40,000 catties, which was allocated to its 65 households at the rate of 146.5 catties per person. By selling the grain quotas to the government, every villager thus actually lost 6.154 yuan (a hidden form of agricultural tax) in comparison to selling the same amount of grain in the free market.[3] In addition, each villager had to pay the team 36 catties of grain (worth 7.20 yuan) as a contribution to the team's grain reserve, 45.04 yuan as contribution to its public funds, and 11 yuan as contribution to water-control projects. The total burden that a team member shouldered thus amounted to 77.92 yuan, or 19 to 20 percent of the average level of a team member's annual net income (QD8 1983; QD9 1983).

The burden was significantly lessened in 1984 when the cash contribution to the team was reduced to 21.132 yuan per person, the grain reserve contribution was reduced to 21.25 catties, and the grain procurement quota was reduced to 141.4 catties per person, while other obligations remained the same as the previous year. Each team member thus shouldered a burden of 49.46 yuan (QD10 1984; QD11 1984). For the remainder of the 1980s, the burden of agricultural taxes and fees, including the loss of income in grain sales to the government, increased moderately, reaching 86.6 yuan per capita in 1990, 110 yuan per capita in 1995, and 123 yuan per capita in 2000. Although the absolute amount of the burden increased over the years, its share in the villagers' annual net income steadily decreased, from 12 percent in 1984 to 8.6 percent in 1990, 5.5 percent in 1995, and 3 percent in 2000 (QD12 1990–2000).

Compared to duties paid to the government in imperial times and in the late 1990s, which ranged between 3 and 4 percent of their income, the villagers' burden in the 1980s and the early 1990s was heavy. It was also unfair to the extent that the burden was based only on a household's number of members, rather than its actual income. However, unlike the collective years, when the income of a household was largely determined by its size, especially the number of its laborers (see Chapter 9), the reform years saw a more complicated pattern of income differentiation among the rural households. As shown in the preceding chapter, the villagers' personal ability, rather than the number of workers in the family, became a more decisive factor in determining its income. In the early 1990s, a few households in the village, who had an adult working as a contractor or business owner, were able to earn up to 30,000 yuan or more a year, yet their burden of taxes and fees remained the same as those who had the same number of members but earned only a few thousand yuan a year. Although the burden was a small fraction of the annual income of the wealthy families, it accounted for as high as 20 to 30 percent of that of the poor.

The village cadres, therefore, had a difficult time collecting taxes and fees from low-income families in the 1980s and early 1990s. The collection normally started in early April, when the village government announced the details about the kinds and rates of the taxes and fees for the current year and the actual amount owed by each household. Most households in Qin village paid their dues within the first two or three weeks. The village government awarded each of them a washbasin or a thermos as an incentive, and included the photo of the household head in the village's "honor board." There were, however, always about 10 to 20 households that delayed their payment by several months and even to the end of the year or the following year. To deal with them, the village government typically assigned several Party members and village council members to visit each of them. After explaining government policies on payment of taxes and fees, the visitors invariably used a number of precedents to explain how futile it was to delay the payment. Under their pressure, most delinquent households paid off their dues right on the spot or soon after the visit. If a household did indeed have financial difficulties in making its payments, the village cadres and Party members would visit it again to determine a solution. Usually the village government would agree to exempt the household 20 to 30 percent of its dues and offset that part with the village government's own funds. Meanwhile, the household and its relatives had to pool enough money to pay off the reminder of what was due.

Every year, however, there were a few households who paid only the agricultural tax they owed to the state but refused to pay the fees to be kept by the village or township government, for reasons other than financial difficulties. They insisted, for instance, that they would not pay the fee to the village until the latter paid off its own debt to them for hiring them to repair a dike, for the damage caused to their crops when constructing the highway, for using their lumber or bricks to build the village office, or for other reasons. The village cadres had to take care of such requests and clear the debt if they found the requests justified. If the claim was unwarranted and the villager failed to fulfill his duties by the end of the year, the village government would impose a fine on the delinquent household, which was usually 7.5 percent of the original amount of the tax and fees. Sometimes the village cadres turned to the village's primary school for help in dealing with the delinquents, since many of the fees had to do with local education. The school would announce to students the names of the parents who had delayed the payment, and issued a ticket to the children of delinquent villagers; the ticket detailed the amount of fees that were overdue and the deadline for payment. Those students who failed to persuade their parents to pay off the fee before the deadline would be subject to the teacher's open criticism. Predictably, the student, normally the only child in his or her family and spoiled by the parents and grandparents, would make a fuss at home and even refuse to go to school until the parents agreed to pay the fee.

The villagers' burden of taxes and fees was greatly reduced in the early 2000s. In the autumn of 2001, the state finally terminated the contractual procurement of grain from rural households in the entire country; farmers no longer had to sell a required amount of crops to the government at a low price. In 2005, the Jiangsu provincial government announced the permanent abolition of the agricultural tax and surtaxes. Consequently, in Qin village and the rest of the county, farmers only needed to pay three kinds of fees that were determined by the size of their farmland or number of mouths or laborers in their family: a water-control construction fee of 8 yuan per mu, a contribution to local projects of 20 yuan per person, and a "labor substitution" fee of 64 yuan per laborer. Together, these fees amounted to 70.84 yuan per person, or only about 1.5 percent of the village's average per capital annual income. To pay the fees was no longer a burden to all households in the village.

Serving the Community

The role of village cadres in the community changed significantly over the years. Whereas in the 1980s and most of the 1990s they were obsessed with the burdensome and thankless "three major tasks" (discussed earlier), the local leaders paid more attention to the well-being of their community from the late 1990s onward as the state terminated the compulsory procurement of grain and the collection of the agricultural tax and at the same time emphasized solving the problem of rural poverty and the widening gap between the cities and the countryside in economic and social development. Three new tasks thus emerged as the village government's priorities: rebuilding water-control networks, cooperation in medical service, and community infrastructure projects.

Rebuilding Water-Control Networks

As shown in Chapter 10, the construction of a systematic water-control network was one of the major achievements in the local area during the collective era. In the 1980s, however, no major effort was made to expand and upgrade the water-control projects because of the village and township governments' limited budget and preoccupation with other tasks. By the early 1990s, the condition of the dikes, sluices, and pumping stations in Qin village and the rest of Qindong township had deteriorated to varying degrees. Thus, in late June and early July 1991, when an unprecedented flood struck the lower Yangzi region, several dikes in the township broke and caused flooding within the area encircled by the dikes. Qin village and all of its farmland survived the flood, thanks to the dikes surrounding the village and the pumping stations that worked day and night draining the water out of the dikes. At the height of the flood, the water level outside the dikes was more than a meter higher than that inside. Any breach in the dike thus would result in the complete drowning out of crops, cause major damage to household properties, and threaten lives. Danger indeed occurred from time to time during the flood, when water seeped in through some sections of the dike or flowed over the top of certain parts of the dike. The village government, therefore, mobilized more than 200 male volunteers to patrol the dike 24 hours a day, checking for breaches or seepage, raising the sections that were too low, and fortifying the parts where water seeped in. In the county, however, more than 60 percent of farmland suffered from the flood, and the grain yield decreased by about 30 percent that year.

The government learned a lesson from the 1991 flood. Afterward, serious efforts on water-control projects revived. Using the relevant fees collected from the villagers, the township government recruited thousands of laborers to widen and heighten all dikes in the local area in the following winters. Beginning in 1998, the county government spent 4 million yuan each year as extra funding on flood-control projects. After another damaging flood in 2003, the county government allocated an additional 10 million yuan as a special budget to strengthen the dikes and to upgrade the pumping stations and sluices. In the next two years, 229 pumping stations were rebuilt and upgraded with a more powerful electric pump, including the one in Qin village (Chen Weiguo 2004).

In 2005, the abolition of the agricultural tax allowed the government to increase the collection of fees by almost three times, which in turn provided a generous budget for water-control projects. A new effort was under way to dredge the 2,200-odd waterways in the county. This task was necessary because many rivers, canals, and creeks had become choked with waterweeds and silt after being used for more than 20 years without a systematic dredging. Before the 1980s, the waterweeds and silt had been used as organic fertilizers, and each production team had a couple of laborers to dredge them. After the mid-1980s, especially in the 1990s, however, all farmers switched to chemical fertilizers, leaving the silt to build up and waterweeds to grow freely, which not only polluted the water but also caused problems in water transportation, flood draining, and irrigation. The county government thus organized more than 4,000 boats to form about 700 teams for that task. From March 20 to April 5, 2005, the season when waterweeds germinated, they cleaned about 40,000 mu of waterways, dredging up more than 800,000 tons of waterweeds and 3.7 million cubic meters of silt.[4] Qin village provided six boats and 12 villagers to form a team. Two teams on the diesel-powered boats cut the weeds; those on the other boats removed them.

Reviving the Cooperative Medical Service

Rebuilding a cooperative medical service program was another major endeavor of the government in the early 2000s. As described in Chapter 10, Qin villagers benefited from a collective health program in the

1970s, which provided them basic treatments at a minimal cost. This program, however, collapsed in the early 1980s when the collective economy that had sustained it gave way to family farming. Although the village clinic survived, the cost of the medicine it dispensed steadily increased. By the early 2000s, for example, a villager had to spend 20 to 30 yuan for the simple treatment of a fever or cold. Having surgery or being hospitalized in a neighboring town or city was much more costly, ranging from a few thousand yuan for a simply surgery to tens of thousands for complicated conditions. Therefore, many villagers were hesitant to see the doctor at the start of the illness, when the symptoms were minor, but went later, often when it was too late to get an effective treatment; several males thus died in their late fifties or sixties. Those who received an expensive surgery lost their savings of several years and even ran into debt. The breakdown of an effective, low-cost health system in the rural area was one of the major failures of the government's public policies in the reform era.

It was not until October 2002 that the central government decided to create a "new-type rural cooperative medical system." Aimed at providing partial compensation to villagers for treatment of severe medical conditions, this program required participants to pay an annual premium of 10 yuan per person; the local governments subsidized the program to augment the premium to 30 yuan per person. The program took effect in Dongtai county in 2003. By the beginning of 2005, about 758,000 villagers or 93 percent of its rural population, including all Qin villagers, had participated in the program. In 2004, 24,349 patients benefited from it, receiving a compensation of 12.56 million yuan in total or 515.71 yuan per person.[5]

Qin villagers showed little interest in the program when it was first introduced in the spring of 2003. Because participation was completely voluntary, many refused to pay the 10-yuan premium. The villagers' major complaint was that the program did not cover patients' registration for seeing a doctor and only paid them 20 percent for the cost of an outpatient service and 25 percent of the expense on hospitalization that was less than 1,000 yuan (the program further paid 35 percent of the cost of hospitalization between 1,001 and 3,000 yuan, 45 percent of the cost between 3,001 and 8,000 yuan, 55 percent of the cost between 8,001 yuan and 20,000 yuan, and 65 percent of the cost over 20,000 yuan, up to 30,000 yuan per person per year). This coverage was indeed limited, compared to the cooperative health service during the collective years that covered 80 percent of the cost of hospitalization. Although the village cadres visited every household to solicit its participation, only about 55 percent of the households in the village paid their premiums in full in 2003, which was far less than the target of 95 percent set by the township government. To ensure that all households joined the program in 2004, the village government simply deducted the full amount of the premium from the government's grain subsidy for each of them before the subsidy was issued to the households. Participation in the program, in other words, became compulsory.

The villagers' attitude to the program changed a great deal in the next year when they witnessed its benefits. One woman, named Qian, received a compensation of 7,181 yuan in 2004 for surgery for her lung cancer. Four other villagers each were compensated more than 1,000 yuan for hospitalization. Another 23 villagers each received more than 500 yuan from the program. To participate in the cooperative medical service made sense to the villagers. Therefore, in 2005, all households in Qin village voluntarily paid their share of the premium, which was increased to 30 yuan per person, while the government also increased the maximum of reimbursement to 50,000 yuan per person.

Building a "Civilized Village"

Even more burdensome to the village cadres were the various tasks associated with the project of building a "civilized village" (*wenming cun*). One of the tasks was "changing the water and altering the toilet" (*gai-shui gaice*)—installing tap-water facilities and new-style toilets for all households. According to a directive from the provincial government, 95 percent of rural households had to have tap water installed by 2005, and at least 70 percent of households had to use various kinds of the new-style "innocuous and sanitary" toilet, preferably the ceramic flushing toilet, by 2008. Qindong township, including Qin village, in fact was far ahead of the rest of rural Jiangsu in "changing the water." In the early 1990s, most households in Qin village as well as the remainder of the township had switched to tap water because the water from natural sources such as ponds and creeks had become severely polluted. The waterworks at the township seat was responsible for all costs involved in installing the pipes to individual homes, and the latter were responsible for buying the faucets and pipes in their own houses. The monthly fee for using tap water ranged from 7 up to 20 yuan, which was easily affordable for the villagers. By 2005, the tap-water system had covered all households in the village as well as in the entire county; the county itself also became a model in the province in the "changing the water" project.

"Altering the toilet" was necessary because the old-style privy could easily pollute the waters when the waste overflowed into the neighboring pond or stream after a heavy rain or in a flood; it also polluted the air in the hot summer and disturbed local residents. To promote this project, the health department of the central government formulated concrete technical requirements for various types of new-style toilets that fit the ecological and residential conditions in different parts of rural China. It also provided financial support to train specialists in "altering the toilets" and offered a subsidy of 150 yuan per household for installing the underground part of the sanitary toilets that met the official standards.[6]

Qin villagers' reaction to this program varied. Many of them who had built a two-story house in the late 1990s and the early 2000s included a flushing toilet in their new homes, but most households still used the traditional privy. In general, young couples preferred to have a flushing toilet in their house, which not only allowed them to get the subsidy from the government but also made their lives "civilized." About 20 households thus indeed "altered the toilet." Opposition came primarily from elderly villagers, who adhered to their old way of life and believed the new-style toilet to be unnecessary. The village cadres failed to meet the township leaders' requirement that at least 30 percent of the households in the community had to have a sanitary toilet in 2005; they lacked any leverage to force the villagers to do so. The only measure that they took was requiring that villagers who were building a new house include a flushing toilet before the construction plans were approved and the new house passed the government's final examination. By mid-2008, only about 45 percent of the households in Qin village had updated their toilets, far below the goal of 70 percent set by the provincial government.

Another part of the "civilized village" program was improving transportation in the rural area, including linking all villages to the highway network with concrete-paved roadways, widening and paving all intra-village dirt paths with concrete or gravel and building reinforced concrete bridges on all major ferry crossings. All these tasks, according to a directive of the provincial government in 2003, had to be finished within three years. The provincial and county governments were responsible for 70 percent of the cost involved in constructing the concrete roadways and all cost in building the bridges, while local communities shouldered the remainder of the costs. Qin villagers enthusiastically supported those projects. Traditionally, without paved roadways connecting local communities, the villagers had to travel several miles on foot, by bicycle, or by boat to visit a market town. The dirt paths in the community also created an inconvenience for the villagers on rainy days when the paths turned muddy and slippery. The ferry crossing on the river north of the village was a big hassle for travelers when there was no ferry service at night. Therefore, when they were asked to participate in widening and paving the dirt paths and to contribute labor to the construction of an assigned section of the concrete roadway, the villagers cooperated with or without compensation. After working off and on for about half a year, the villagers finally finished the assigned tasks. A construction company hired by the government also finished building an 80-meter-long bridge in the northwest of the village in the summer of 2003. Bus service became locally available thereafter. Young villagers especially enjoyed the wide and smooth roads in and out of the village that allowed them to ride their motorcycles freely.

What challenged the cadres, as well as the villagers, however, was the construction of a "central village" (*zhongxin cun*), the key component of the "civilized village" project. In response to the ordinance of the central government, the Dongtai municipal government mandated in 1999 that every administrative village had to designate a residential area, called the central village, for villagers to build new houses. Those houses had to meet the government's quality and design requirements, such as including necessary pipes, wires, electrical outlets, and of course flushing toilets. The central village would provide its residents with necessary infrastructure facilities, including power, water, telephone and TV cables, paved walkways, street lamps, an underground drainage system, a market area, and a public toilet. The advantages of the central village were purportedly numerous. Traditionally, without the government's strict planning, villagers randomly built their houses wherever they preferred so that the homes occupied a lot of farmland. Laying water pipes and cables to the outlying houses was difficult and costly. Going to school was also an inconvenience for students from the distant areas. To relocate their houses to the central village, therefore, would eliminate all those problems.

Qin village planned its own central village, about 50 mu in size, in 2000. Many villagers, however, opposed this project. In their opinion, the size of the lot for each house in the central village was too limited;

it did not allow the space for a vegetable garden, a henhouse, and a pigpen, which were indispensable for farmers who lived the traditional lifestyle. Moreover, some villagers complained that the central village was too far away from their farms; it would be inconvenient for them to do farm work after moving to the central village. But not all villagers took issue with the project. Several owners of two-story houses in the central village said that they liked its location (it was next to the highway) and that they had no problem with the size of their lots. In fact, as they pointed out, many of the households in the village had given up the custom of raising chickens and pigs years ago, so they no longer needed such things as a henhouse or a pigpen.[7]

The biggest problem in promoting the central village project, as the village cadres explained, lay in the fact that most villagers had built their houses at a location other than the central village in the late 1980s and the 1990s. It was impossible for them to dismantle their houses, which were still in good condition, and move to the central village. Realizing the difficulties involved in the project, the township government only expected that 1.5 percent of the total households in the township would move into the central villages each year. But the cadres in Qin village were optimistic that in 15 or 20 years, most households in the community would move to the central village and the villagers would be able to live a life not too different from that of the townspeople thereafter.

Conclusion

The state's termination of compulsory grain procurement in 2001 and abolition of agricultural taxes in 2005, and its increased subsidization of farming, medical service, public education, and the construction of infrastructures suggested a reorientation of the government's rural policies from extracting agricultural surpluses for industrialization and urban development, which characterized the history of the People's Republic in its first five decades, to accelerating rural development with the state's growing input derived from nonagricultural sectors. This change enabled a corresponding switch in the role of grassroots cadres from primarily enforcing the state's exploitative policies at the expense of local communities to concentrating on a series of programs aimed at improving the living conditions of villagers.

This transition, however, did not come with a reversal of the state's role in rural society. Quite the contrary, in all those recent programs, including the reconstruction of local water-control projects, the cooperative medical service, and various efforts associated with the promotion of "civilized villages," the government's planning, regulation, and input remained decisive. Two factors explained the state's continued intervention after 2000 despite its reversal of the extraction policy. One had to do with the traditional top-down approach of government in the Maoist and reform eras, when the state was used to imposing its will on the society regardless of the needs and wants of the latter. It was difficult, therefore, for government leaders as well as local cadres to give up that mindset when the state no longer needed to penetrate the countryside in the traditional way. The villagers, on the other hand, were also accustomed to accepting whatever the government imposed; they showed no institutionalized efforts to manage community affairs and promote public goods on their own initiatives. Therefore, it remained a challenge for them to cultivate the spirit and abilities of self-government after having lived under an all-powerful state for half a century.

The other had to do with the nature and purposes of the developmental state in rural China. The government's active role in planning and regulating economic development has been central to the success of East Asian countries in "catching up" with Western industrial societies in the postwar years (Johnson 1982, 1995; Woo-Cumings 1999). In many ways, China's economic growth in the reform era resembled the experiences of its Asian neighbors; the transition from a planned economy to a market economy and the replacement of the collective system with family farming did not reduce the role of the state in shaping the priorities of economic development and pursuing a sustainable growth strategy. The policy makers adopted the same approach in the countryside; they believed that the government's extensive involvement through planning, regulation, and subsidization would accelerate the modern transformation of rural society. To accomplish the overall goals of various programs that purportedly benefitted the entire community, the rights and interests of individuals had to be compromised. Instead of encouraging the initiatives of individuals, the critical role of local government in achieving economic prosperity was emphasized. To be sure, the planning and leadership of the government were indeed vital to the development of rural industries in its early stage, as seen in the rise of the collectively owned "township and village enterprises"

(TVEs) throughout the countryside in the 1980s (Oi 1999). But the local government's excessive involvement in economic activities also increased the likelihood of mistakes in decision making and misconduct for self-aggrandizement by the grassroots cadres in the absence of effective means of supervision by higher authorities from above or by the villagers from below. The increased privatization of the TVEs in the 1990s and early 2000s suggested the problems inherent to such enterprises (Oi and Walder 1999). Thus, although the government's initiation and sponsorship were indispensable for the economic and social projects aimed at promoting public good, it was difficult for them survive and prosper without the villagers' initiatives. For both the policy makers and the villagers, it remained a daunting task to transform their relationship from that of top-down *government*, or the one-way flow of power from the political center to local communities, to a true form of self-government—or *governance*—in which the self-motivated villagers interacted fruitfully with the state to advance their collective as well as individual interests.

CHAPTER 14

Conclusion

Chinese Villagers: From Righteous to Rightful

Villagers in post-1949 China played a key role in shaping the state's agrarian policies. It was their everyday resistance and open defiance, rather than the will of the Party or the enthusiasm of grassroots cadres, that accounted for the final form of those policies and the way they functioned in the countryside. This is most evident in the "unified purchase and sale of grain" and agricultural collectivization in the 1950s, the two most critical measures that shaped the basic economic and social institutions in rural China for the next three decades.[1] As demonstrated in this study and in a separate article (H. Li 2006), it was precisely under the pressure of the villagers' persistent and widespread resistance that the state finally gave up or drastically adjusted its unrealistic plans in order to make them workable in the rural area. Chinese peasants, as it turned out, were not as powerless and subservient under the socialist state as conventional wisdom would suggest.

The villagers' reactions to the state's relentless policies fell largely into two categories. One can be called *righteous resistance*, which prevailed in the early years of peasant protests when the Party and the new state were yet to establish its organizational and ideological control in the villages. To defend their economic interests, the villagers turned to traditional tactics of noncompliance that were based on their everyday social practices and shared values, especially the widely accepted assumption of the right to subsistence. To reduce their loss in selling grain to the state under the compulsory procurement program in the early 1950s, for example, the villagers underreported their harvest, hid their grain, reduced landholdings by dividing the household or giving away farmland, made complaints, threatened to commit suicide, quit farm work, or slaughtered farm animals when farming no longer made sense to the villagers under the government's policy of "bottomless" procurement. Meanwhile, to increase their quota of grain purchase from the government, the peasants sought protection from local cadres by giving gifts, offering a good meal or sex, or creating fictive kinship; all those activities were essentially no different from what had been done with the community leaders, yamen runners, or any other kinds of power holders in the prerevolutionary period for the same purposes. Later in the course of agricultural collectivization, the villagers who were most unwilling to join the co-ops clandestinely sold their oxen, dismantled their boats or windmills to make furniture, or simply took back their farming tools and animals that had been collectivized. Those who had joined the co-ops under the government's pressure secretly harvested and divided the collective's crops, lowered their attendance in collective production, or withdrew from their cooperatives when they found that collective farming could not secure their livelihood (see Chapter 3).

But the villagers did not limit their actions to such individual, everyday forms of resistance. When their frustration reached a climax, they did not hesitate to act collectively and violently. Thus, the protesters surrounded local government offices to air their resentment, staged a traditional ceremony to show off their collective strength, or beat up the cadres who failed to satisfy their demands, as seen in the heyday of rural unrest against collectivization. The cadres who forced the individual households to sell grain in the winter but failed to sell grain back to the latter in the spring and the cadres who took away their properties and forced them to join the co-op thus became the direct targets of popular grievances. They beat and cursed the cadres and threatened to smash their offices in a method no different from what they had used to deal with the abusive landlords, rent collectors, or rice shop owners before the Communist Revolution. No matter whether their actions were individual or collective, passive or aggressive, the villagers believed that they were *righteous*, not only because the languages, symbols, and methods that they used in defending their interests had been familiar and available to them for ages, but also because they felt that they had a good reason behind their actions, that is, to secure their livelihood. In a peasant community where subsistence remained the villagers' primary concern, the right to survival was above anything else in justifying one's claims and actions.[2]

However, as the socialist state established its dominance in the villages through economic reorganization, social restructuring, and ideological indoctrination, the villagers gradually changed their strategies for dealing with the state. They gave up the old methods, which were now condemned as backward, superstitious, and even reactionary; instead the villagers turned to the new notions and channels promoted by the socialist state to articulate their interests. Those who were most active in such *rightful* activities were usually the literate and informed in a community, such as teachers, retired soldiers, family members of soldiers in active service, former village leaders, doctors, or Party members. With access to newspapers, broadcasting, or other forms of public media, the village "elites" were familiar with government policies and events outside their community. They were able to use the language that they had learned from official media and take advantage of the means allowed by the government to make their actions appear justifiable. Therefore, the elite villagers never openly challenged the policies or systems imposed by the state; instead they focused their attacks on local cadres who had abused their power in carrying out government policies or running the collectives, especially their favoritism in issuing grain-purchase certificates, misconduct in managing co-op finances, and inability to increase production and distribute enough food to co-op members. Even when petitioning for quitting agricultural cooperatives, which was officially allowed, the villagers would promise to fulfill their tax duties and abide by state laws while excluding landlords, rich peasants, and other "bad elements" from their ranks. Their activities, therefore, fell into the new category of *rightful resistance*. Reflecting the growing influence of the state in the countryside, this type of action first prevailed in the heyday of peasant protests during cooperativization in the late 1950s (see Chapter 3 and H. Li 2006) and revived in the post-collective years, when the increased burden of taxes and fees and rampant cadre abuse again drove the villagers to act collectively in defense of their interests (O'Brien 1996, 2002).

The Socialist State: From Antagonistic to Conciliatory

The socialist state, too, changed its strategies in dealing with the villagers. In its initial attempts to curb unrest in grain procurement and cooperativization, the government as well as local cadres invariably turned to the methods they had used during the previous campaigns of Land Reform and Suppressing Counterrevolutionaries to treat all those involved in the disturbances. They presumed any resistance to the campaigns to be a sign of "antagonistic contradiction" between the socialist state and its traditional opponents in the countryside (including landlords, rich peasants, and counterrevolutionaries), and tended to respond to the resistance with violent repression, such as arrests, imprisonment, and the execution of the leading activists in mass riots. However, as the grassroots cadres and the government soon realized in the early-to-mid 1950s, those who opposed the state policies were rarely the conventional enemies; instead, the protest came primarily from ordinary villagers, including poor and middle peasants, who had allied with the state during the earlier years of the Communist Revolution and Land Reform.

The increasing inapplicability of its old construct of rural conflicts to the new realities caused the state to adjust both its representation of the new issues and its strategies to cope with them. Instead of perceiving rural unrest as hostility from conventional enemies, the practical Party leaders came to recognize the resistance as a form of "contradictions among the people," which was in itself a result of the contradiction between the "advanced social relations of productions and the lagging forces of production" in the newly created socialist society (Mao Zedong 1957). The state first admitted this new reality in 1955 during the heyday of peasant protest against the grain-procurement program and fully used the concept of "contradictions among the people" to deal with peasant disgruntlement during the cooperativization in the following years. Instead of suppressing the discontented villagers with violence, the state emphasized the use of persuasion and education to handle the unrest. To pacify the villagers, local government leaders and work team members openly censured the grassroots cadres for their mistakes, removed the most unpopular of them from office, or asked them to make self-criticisms at mass gatherings. The state itself also made significant adjustments of its policies. Following the nationwide protests against the grain procurement program, the central government announced the "three fixed" policies to limit the amount of grain purchased by the state (H. Li 2006). The protests during the cooperativization caused the state to implement a series of policies regarding financial management in the co-ops, the distribution of collective income to co-op members, local cadres' participation in labor work, and the relationship between grassroots cadres and ordinary villagers. All of those measures remained largely effective in the following decades and constituted the basis of the collective system in the countryside.

These facts indicate the central role of the villagers in shaping the final form of the state's rural policies. They also suggest that the state itself was pragmatic in addressing rural problems and willing to concede when its policies threatened the livelihood of peasants and incurred disgruntlement. As seen in Chapter 4, its concession reached the climax after the disastrous Great Leap Forward, when the state accepted the production team, a subvillage neighborhood of 20 to 30 households, as the basic accounting unit and even allowed independent family farming under the "contracted output" arrangement. The state's pragmatism was unchanged even during the radical years of the Cultural Revolution, when the production team remained the basic collective unit and when individual households were still allowed to keep their private plots and other "capitalistic tails." Except for the very few years in the late 1960s when the state attempted to experiment with the short-lived egalitarian Dazhai system in labor remuneration, all economic policies that had been introduced in response to peasant protests in the 1950s and early 1960s remained in existence throughout the collective era.

It is worth noting in this context that the state did revive the political discourse of class struggle in the 1960s and the 1970s (until the death of Mao) and emphasized the use of "dictatorship" or violence to deal with the old categories of "class enemies" (former landlords, rich peasants, and counterrevolutionaries) as well as the newly emerged "capitalist roaders" (*zouzipai*) within the Party. The state did so for two reasons: one had to do with the intra-Party "line struggle" between the radical Maoist ideologists and the capitalist roaders; reintroducing the discourse of "class struggle" was the most legitimate means for the radicals to secure and enhance their position within the Party and to continue their policies. There was, however, also a practical reason: to safeguard the collective economy against the erosion of capitalist elements and thereby to ensure the state's complete control of agricultural surpluses for its needs of massive investments in modern economic sectors. Thus, once the line struggle receded after Mao's death and once industrialization in China finished its initial stage of capital formation, tight ideological and economic control became obsolete and unnecessary; the state was ready to make further policy adjustments that allowed local collectives and individual households greater autonomy in the late 1970s and culminated in the introduction of the household responsibility system. Decollectivization in the early 1980s, therefore, is best seen as both a departure from the preexisting agricultural policies and a continuity of the state's time-honored pragmatism that accounted for its repeated adjustments of rural policies throughout the collective period.

Grassroots Cadres: To Supervise and to Be Supervised

Local politics in rural China centered on the relationship between the masses and the grassroots cadres, primarily production team leaders; it was with the team cadres, rather than brigade or commune leaders, that the ordinary villagers interacted on an everyday basis. As seen in this study, the team members employed a variety of tactics to deal with the cadres in collective production and played a critical role in restraining the possible abuse of power by the latter. The "patron-client" model that has prevailed in interpreting power relations in post-1949 China cannot fully explain the complexity of village politics in the Maoist era and thereafter.

The key to understanding the activism of ordinary villagers in local politics has to do with the state's two basic yet conflicting strategies for regulating the cadres. One was stabilizing the ranks of grassroots cadres and, unless necessary, not removing them from office, for the obvious reason that able and literate individuals qualified for local leadership were rare among the villagers. But the grassroots cadres were so numerous (more than 6 million in the country in the 1960s and 1970s) that it was impossible for the government to put them under its direct control—the state's formal bureaucracy stopped at the commune level, and hundreds of production teams were under the commune. Therefore, another indispensable and more important method to discipline the cadres was using the masses to supervise them from below. To this end, the state promoted a new political culture in the village community, which centered on a discourse that assumed the supremacy and political correctness of ordinary villagers or the poor and lower-middle peasants. This imaginary superiority helped cultivate the villagers' political awareness. It also legitimated the various institutions whereby the peasant masses were empowered to supervise the cadres, such as openly criticizing the latter for their mistakes during the recurrent political campaigns, writing "people's letters" and drawing big-character posters to reveal their misconduct, participating in the periodic meetings of the "democratic management of finance" to examine production-team accounts, and making complaints against the team cadres to higher authorities.

Not all team members, to be sure, had access to such means or were able to use them to express their concerns and resentment. From time to time, these means became a tool of different factions of village cadres and their supporters to fight each other. But the successive political campaigns, the mutual accusation among the cadres during repeated study sessions, the periodic account checking by team members, and the horror stories of governmental investigations of cadre abuses following the submission of a "people's letter" imposed a constant and powerful constraint on the grassroots cadres. In addition, the cadres were also subject to the everyday surveillance of team members, who always kept a close eye on the cadre's activities in task assignment, workpoint recording, and income distribution. They would argue with the cadres, make complaints, or even turn to covert revenge activities when they felt that the cadres were unfair. Therefore, under normal circumstances, the room for team leaders to abuse power was limited; when they did so, they had to keep their wrongdoings in a hidden and, whenever possible, officially justifiable manner. Open favoritism to certain team members and discrimination against others did exist among some cadres but rarely prevailed in the rural collectives.

Mutual surveillance and confrontation, however, was only one aspect of the relationship between the villagers and cadres. The other aspect was their shared economic interests and collaboration in dealing with the state. Unlike the salaried commune cadres, who were part of the state bureaucracy, production team and brigade cadres received no salaries from the state and instead lived on workpoints and grain rations from their respective teams just like ordinary members. Therefore, they identified themselves with fellow villagers more than with the state when managing local economic activities. Some village leaders thus underreported the grain yield in their production teams or brigades in order to reduce the procurement burden on fellow villagers in the 1950s. Production team leaders tended to underreport the crop acreage and output in their own collectives in order to keep more grain for team members, distribute private plots much larger than permitted by the government to individual households, and even allow young villagers to leave the team and apprentice with craftsmen regardless of government prohibition.

In addition to their identity with ordinary team members, the grass-roots cadres were also involved in the intricate network of local social ties. The cadres and team members were not merely the supervisors and the supervised within the collective; they were also neighbors, kinsmen, and friends or foes of each other. The cadres and team members formed different attitudes toward each other not only according to their status within the team but also according to their personal position in the social network. Tensions and open conflicts took place not just between the cadres and ordinary villagers but more often than not between people of different descent groups or any other kinds of social ties that comprised both the cadres and team members. A cadre rarely carried out state policies or local regulations without taking into account his personal relationship with team members. This embedded-ness of grassroots cadres in local social webs explained, at least in part, why the state was unable to eliminate the "capitalist tails" and "super-stitious" practices even during the Cultural Revolution, when the state's institutional and ideological control of society was unprecedented.

Therefore, power relations in the rural collectives were complex. Despite the state's penetration into the village through agricultural col-lectivization and political indoctrination, leaders of production teams did not act merely as agents of the state; as members of local communi-ties, they represented the interests of fellow villagers rather than that of the government when managing their collectives or carrying out the tasks imposed from above. At the same time, however, their relations with community members cannot be simply likened to the patron-client ties between the landed elites and the landless or land-poor who depended on the former for a living before the Communist Revolution. The grassroots cadres, in fact, were no different from the rest of team members in terms of their economic and social statuses. This gross equality, coupled with a new political culture that exalted the political role of poor and lower-middle peasants and the introduction of many campaigns and institutions, enabled the team members to counterbal-ance the power of the cadres and limit their possible abuse. A produc-tion team in collective-era China was in essence a semiautonomous body in which both the imposed institutions of political participation and the embedded social ties and practices combined to shape the rela-tionship between the grassroots cadres and ordinary villagers.

Substantial changes took place in village politics after decollectiviza-tion in the early 1980s. Because of the dissolution of production teams, local politics now centered around the relationship between cadres of the newly created "administrative village" (equivalent to the former brigade in most cases) and ordinary villagers, instead of that between production team cadres and team members. However, unlike the brigade and production team cadres who had been responsible for agricultural production in their collectives and received income from the same collectives as other team members, the village cadres' major duties after the reform were collecting taxes and fees from individual households in the name of higher authorities, and much of their income came from the fees that they had collected. Therefore, the relationship between the village leaders and villagers in the 1980s and early 1990s was full of tension and conflicts when the former were concerned primarily with carrying out the state's harsh policies at the expense of the latter and as the deterioration of the disciplinary measures led to possible abuses of power in performing their duties.

The relationship between the cadres and villagers improved in the late 1990s and early 2000s, as the state terminated the compulsory procurement of grain, abolished the agricultural tax, reduced the fees imposed on villagers, increased the subsidies to farmers, and provided the villagers with some social welfare programs. The major duties of village leaders, therefore, have shifted from enforcing the unpopular policies on behalf of the state to serving local communities, primarily improving public welfare and community infrastructures. At the same time, the villagers began to show a genuine interest in the self-government program, as seen in their participation in the election of village cadres and voluntary involvement in public projects that directly benefited them. What characterized the changes in village politics thus was a transition from *government* or the state's top-down control of the village to *governance* that involved the villagers' voluntary participation in the management of community affairs and advancement of public well-being.

The Logic of Collective Agriculture

There is no doubt that labor productivity in rural China greatly increased under the household responsibility system after 1980. But this fact alone should not lead us to conclude that agricultural production under the collective system in the preceding two decades was necessarily inefficient; nor should we attribute the low labor productivity in those decades mainly to the collective organization itself. One of the central propositions in this study is that team farming during the collective years was not as inefficient as conventional wisdom would have it; instead, a multiplicity of factors—social, biological, and managerial—explain why farmers had to increase their labor input and maintain a minimum level of productivity in collective agriculture.

The workpoint system, which directly linked an individual's labor input with his or her income from the collective, played a key role in team production. It is true that throughout the collective era rural households received their income from their production team primarily in the form of grain distribution rather than cash payment, and most of the grain distributed was based on the household's need, or the number of its members (hence called *kouliang* or "rationed grain"), rather than its workpoints or labor contribution to the team (hence *gongfenliang* or "workpoint grain"). But this fact does not mean that the workpoints were unimportant to the team members. Every household in the production team knew that the *kouliang* it received from the team was not free; it had to be purchased with the workpoints the household had earned. Only after paying the workpoints needed to cover the cash value of the rationed grain could the household receive the year-end cash payment for the remainder of its workpoints. The cash payment was small but critical for the household to make ends meet; unable to receive cash payment or unable to pay off the rationed grain with workpoints and hence becoming an "overdrawn household" (*chaozhi hu*) meant not only dishonor but also great hardship to the household. Therefore, team members used every opportunity to increase their workpoints, and they participated in collective production only for workpoints and nothing else.

Contrary to the received assumption that workpoint awarding under the collective system was egalitarian, unable to reflect the quality and quantity of a team member's labor input and therefore causing widespread shirking and farming inefficiency, this study has shown that the egalitarian methods of labor remuneration existed only during the short-lived Great Leap Forward and the peak years of the Cultural Revolution, which did cause the farmers' low morale. What prevailed in the rest of the collective years, however, was a workpoint system based on piece rates or time rates, which linked a team member's workpoints to the quantity or hours of his or her work for the team. Several reasons explain why shirking in collective farming was not as rampant as many observers have surmised. First and foremost, the production team, as a basic accounting unit normally comprising 20 or 30 and even up to 50 or 60 households, allowed its members to develop a strong sense of group identity because the public good produced by the team was more directly linked with the income of individual households than previously under larger collectives, such as the advanced cooperatives in the mid-1950s or the people's commune during the Great Leap Forward. The group identity was also strong among team members because all of them were acquaintances—neighbors, friends, or kinsmen—from the same neighborhood, who tended to identify and vie with each other in social and economic life; the abilities to earn workpoints, to do farm work quickly, and to do a decent job were the necessary means to establish one's standing among his or her peers. It goes without saying that this group solidarity enabled the team members to exercise a necessary degree of mutual competition and surveillance in collective production to ensure the production of the public good, thus safeguarding the livelihood of individual families. This group identity and scrutiny, together with team cadres' monitoring, produced a variety of constraints on the team members against overt shirking and outright dereliction in collective production.

Needless to say, to keep such constraints at work, it was necessary to limit the size of a collective organization to no more than that of a neighborhood of approximately 30 to 50 households, as represented by the primary cooperatives in the mid 1950s and the production teams from the early 1960s to the early 1980s, when farming still relied largely on manual labor. It is no wonder that, after the disastrous Great Leap Forward, Party leaders cautiously followed this *social* logic of collective agriculture under traditional farming conditions and persistently kept the production team as the basic accounting unit even during the most radical years of the Cultural Revolution, a lesson they had learned from the failure of the gigantic people's commune before.

In addition to the social constraints that were at work in the team, other factors also shaped farmers' motivations for team production. It is demonstrated in this study and elsewhere (H. Li 2005b) that families in the second phase of the "family cycle" ("maturing families"), with more dependents and fewer workers, had the strongest need to work for the team. Female workers in general were more concerned with the opportunity to earn workpoints rather than the rate of workpoints and therefore were also more cooperative with, or subservient to, team leaders; unmarried women had a yet stronger motivation for earning workpoints than women of any other age group did when they were in the prime of their lives and had the individual needs of preparing dowries. These factors constituted the *biological* logic of collective agriculture under traditional conditions, where the individual households depended on the collective for their incomes and determined their labor contribution to collective production according to the changing needs of the family during different phases of its life cycle, as well as the changing needs of the individuals during different phases of their own life course.

Even more important in shaping the morale of team members in collective production was the role of team leaders. Two conflicting motivations influenced their strategies for team management. On the one hand, those leaders, like ordinary team members, depended on the team for most of their family incomes. Therefore, they had the same concerns with the well-being of the team as did regular members. In fact, their incentives for improving the collective economy were stronger than any others because their reputation among the team members and their position as team leaders depended on their abilities to run the collective and to increase the income of team members. Those who worked toward promotions wanted to demonstrate their abilities by maximizing the team's output. On the other hand, however, the team leaders were different from owners of private enterprises. Their incentives for maximizing production in the most cost-effective way would not be as strong as the capitalists because the return they produced from the increased production went to the team rather than themselves. More importantly, most team leaders were unable to fire any slacking team members to improve farming efficiency, nor were they willing to be so strict in labor management as to sacrifice their personal relationship with the team members. For most of the cadres, therefore, the goal of team management was to keep the collective running and to ensure the livelihood of all households of the team, rather than maximize its returns. These motivations lay at the core of the *managerial* logic of collective agriculture.

The social, biological, and managerial aspects of the logic of collective farming combine to explain why the efficiency of team production in rural China was not as low as widely believed. There is no doubt that the team members as well as team leaders were less motivated to increase production than the independent farmers after 1980. However, the shared interests of team cadres and ordinary members in the collective economy from which they derived most of their income and the various constraints against overt slacking in team production and dereliction in labor management did allow them to maintain the necessary level of productivity in collective farming, which proved capable of supporting a rapidly expanding rural population and increasing its life expectancy while meeting the state's demands for rural surpluses during the entire collective years.

Development as a Continuum

The steady growth of agricultural output in collective-era China did not bring about a comparable increase in labor productivity. But the slow progress, and even stagnation, of labor productivity in collective agriculture was primarily a result of the state's excessive extraction of rural resources, rather than that of the collective system itself; and this sluggishness did not prevent the significant breakthroughs in agricultural production and the overall improvement of living conditions of rural people.

My analysis of the collective economy in Qin village has emphasized three state policies that impeded the improvement in labor productivity in the locality and much of the rest of rural China. The first is the state's extraction of agricultural products through the systems of compulsory grain procurement and taxation. In Qin village, the team No. 11 alone turned in to the government an average of 11,800 yuan annually during the 1970s, which was more than 40 yuan per capita, or more than half of each team member's total income from the team, more than the year-end cash payment each member received from the team, and about three times the team's annual accumulation of public assets (QD5 1970–1979). The state's excessive extraction greatly impaired the team's ability to invest in agricultural modernization and improve the living conditions of team members.

The second is the state's mandatory requisition of the team's labor force for water-control projects that did not directly benefit the team itself. Each winter during the collective period, for example, a production team had to send its most capable male workers to such projects for about a month or two. The team received no compensation from the state but had to pay its participants in the project at the highest workpoint rate, which was normally more than twice what the workers usually received. In general, the workpoints a team spent on such projects accounted for about one-fifth of its total annual workpoints, which greatly depreciated the cash value of the workpoints and made the labor force much less productive as measured against the team's output.

The third is the state's policy that strictly limited team members' migration and engagement in noncollective economic activities. Under that policy, people who were born into a team member's family automatically obtained lifetime team membership, and the team had to employ them when they reached the working age. As the team's population steadily expanded during the collective years, the number of its surplus laborers also increased. The ample supply of the labor force and the limited accumulation of public funds caused the team to increase its output by intensifying labor input rather than capital input in agricultural production, a strategy that boosted land productivity but failed to increase labor productivity proportionally.

Low labor productivity does not mean no economic or social development. In fact, there were impressive improvements in the ecological and technological conditions of agricultural production and living standards of rural residents during the collective era. Despite the limited funds available to them, local collectives throughout rural China took advantage of their ample labor force and made tremendous efforts in constructing flood-control and irrigation projects, which fundamentally improved the natural environment for agriculture. They also persisted in introducing new varieties of crops, promoting new farming techniques, and using chemical pesticides and fertilizers. By the time the collective system came to an end, substantial progress had been made in the green revolution, which successfully transformed the traditional farming that was based on farmers' old experiences and vulnerable to natural disasters into a new one backed by modern techniques and water-control systems. Farm output in Qin village, therefore, increased from about 300 catties per mu in the 1950s to about 800 catties per mu in the late 1970s. Farmers' income from the collective also increased from about 50 to 60 yuan per capita in the 1950s and early 1960s to more than 120 yuan per capita in the early 1980s in the same locale, which made possible substantial improvements in their living conditions, as evidenced in the obvious changes in their housing, clothing, and diet, and in the implementation of many programs in public health, education, and social welfare (see Chapter 10). It should be noted that Qin village, the focus of this study, was far from a model collective; its output and per capita income were only slightly higher than the national level during the collective era (see Chapter 1). What happened to this community is best seen as a microcosm of the changes that took place in much of the rest of rural China.

The changes during the collective era paved the way for the further development of rural economy and society from the 1980s onward. There is no doubt that under the family farming system, cultivators had stronger incentives than before to increase farm output, a fact that explains the rapid growth of grain yield during the first few years following decollectivization. Between 1981 and 1984, the total grain yield in the country increased at 8.5 percent annually, much faster than the rate of grain yield (4.1 percent) during the 18 years from 1962, when the production team was universally installed as the basic accounting unit in collective agriculture, to 1980, when the collective system came to an end (Guojia tongjiju 2000: 37, 40). But the effects of the new incentives under the family farming system did not last long; in the next five years, the total grain yield in the entire nation stagnated. On the whole, the total grain yield in the country from 1981 to 1999 increased by only 2.5 percent annually and the per-land-unit yield in the country increased by only 2.6 percent annually, significantly *lower* than the records of the prior 18 years under the production team, which were 4.1 percent and 4.4 percent, respectively.[3]

What accounted for the increase in rural households' incomes during the reform era was not the farmers' stronger incentives for agricultural production or the increased output of the family farms, but the state's loosening and removal of the measures that it had enforced to control rural resources. The first and foremost was its reduced extraction of agricultural surpluses, as seen in its repeated increases of the prices of grain it procured during the 1980s, its reduction of the compulsory procurement of grain and introduction of contractual procurement that offered competitive prices in 1985, its termination of the grain procurement system in 1993, and, finally, the nationwide abolition of agricultural taxes in 2005 and 2006. By allowing farmers to keep more and more of their harvests, those policies contributed to the continual growth of the incomes of rural households. Even more important in increasing their income was the state's removal of prohibitions against rural residents' free migration and choice of occupation. The "freed" villagers, as seen in Qin village, increasingly left the farm and earned income from other occupations as craftsmen, contractors, construction workers, business owners, or factory employees. For most rural families, earnings from such nonagricultural sources constituted the major part of their income in the 1990s and 2000s. The family farm, normally worked by women and the elderly with the increased use of machines, became less important to the household economy.

What has emerged in the rural economy in the reform era thus is a dynamic totally different from that of the collectivized agriculture. Whereas under the collective system the state's extraction of agricultural resources and its strict limit on the free flow of the labor force drove the collectives to intensify labor input rather than capital input as the major strategy for improving output, the villagers' increased income since the 1980s enabled them to increase modern inputs in agriculture, as seen in the widespread use of chemicals and machines, which drastically reduced manual labor and allowed more of the labor force to enter nonagricultural occupations. The villagers' increased engagement in nonagricultural activities in turn increased their demand for agricultural mechanization, while their additional income from this new source further enabled them to do so.

Underlying the different dynamics of economic growth, however, was the continuity of the rural economy during the two periods. Despite the state's exorbitant extraction that precluded significant increase in labor productivity, the production team provided necessary incentives for both local cadres and team members to increase farm output at a pace no slower than what occurred during most of the reform period and to substantially improve the ecological and technological conditions of agricultural production under the collective system. Further economic growth during the reform years was possible not only because the preceding collective economy had provided the farming households with a solid technical and ecological basis, but also because the state had loosened and finally removed the means of extraction that had restricted the economic growth during the collective years. Instead of juxtaposing the different agricultural systems during the collective and reform periods, therefore, this study has emphasized rural economic and social development as a continuum throughout the two periods.

Village-State Relations in Perspective

Three political heritages of prerevolutionary China influenced state-village relations after 1949 and will continue to shape the evolving patterns of rural governance in the future. The first is the self-governing tradition before the twentieth century, as manifested in the cooperation in communal welfare, self-defense, criminal control, seasonal farming, tax payment, and so forth, on the basis of lineage ties, community networks, or gentry initiatives. The state's efforts to penetrate village communities after 1900 under the name of "new administrative measures" (*xinzheng*) and "local self-government" (*difang zizhi*) did not necessarily destroy or weaken that tradition. In fact, the villagers' voluntary participation and initiatives, which undergirded the traditional self-governing practices, continued to form the basis on which many of the new policies, such as the installation of village government, the election of a village headman, and the establishment of primary schools, were carried out. In the environmentally stable and agriculturally productive "core" areas of the North China Plain, where village organizations and lineage ties were highly developed, as my study of south-central Hebei (H. Li 2005a) has demonstrated, the survival of such organizations and cooperative practices also helped mitigate the mounting pressure of state penetration, stem the intrusion of abusive outsiders in taxation and local administration, and prevent the collapse of village leadership. What prevailed in such core areas in the early twentieth century thus was the continuation of the self-governing tradition and its incorporation into the newly imposed program of self-government.

The second was the tendency of "state involution" in prerevolutionary China. The enforcement of the *xinzheng* programs, and later the intensified military conflicts among the warlords in the late 1920s and early 1930s, it is suggested, caused an upsurge in the tax burden on the villagers, which in turn accounted for the collapse of traditional community leadership, the rise of local bullies to power, and the multiplication of entrepreneurial personnel who engaged in tax collection and local administration only for self-aggrandizement at the cost of taxpayers and the state (Duara 1988). Prevailing primarily in the ecologically insecure and poverty-stricken areas where the village communities fell short of cooperative traditions for self-protection and thus were vulnerable to intrusive outsiders, state involution became conspicuous during the Japanese occupation in the late 1930s and early 1940s, causing the erosion of preexisting social ties and cultural practices on which the imperial state had built its legitimacy in the rural area. Although the breakdown of the village community and the rampant abuse of power by "native bullies" (*tugun*) and "evil ruffians" (*eba*) were far from a widespread phenomenon in rural China before the late 1930s and definitely not the dominant trend in the core areas, the thesis of state involution nevertheless offered a convenient interpretation for the phenomena of peasant mobilization and the Communist Revolution in the 1940s.

The third legacy of the pre-1949 period, therefore, is the revolution-ization of the peasant society. Beginning with the radical intellectuals' appeal to nationalism in the anti-imperialist agitation in the 1910s and 1920s in urban China, the Communist Revolution successfully accom-modated the needs of the poor in rural areas by conducting land reform and turned them into a revolutionary force. The revolution, however, not only halted the ongoing process of state involution but also weakened the social basis on which the indigenous cooperative arrangements and the imposed self-government programs had existed. The nationwide movement of land reform and collectivization after 1949 further wiped out the educated and landed elites who had played a leading role in the self-government programs; they also under-mined the lineage organizations and community networks that had bolstered the cooperative arrangements in the peasant society.

The agrarian reforms in the 1980s and 1990s can be viewed in this historical context as a process of derevolutionization because they un-did much of what the Communist Revolution and the subsequent col-lectivization had achieved in the countryside and because they accounted for the revival of some of the sociopolitical practices that had prevailed in prerevolutionary China. The dismantling of the people's commune and the consequent weakening of the state's presence in the country-side necessitated the introduction of the self-government program in the villages, especially the election of village council members. At the same time, the retreat of the state also led to the revival of lineage orga-nizations in rural communities. The growing autonomy of the town-ship and village governments and the expansion of their functionaries entailed the multiplication of surcharges and fees imposed on the vil-lagers, hence paving the way for rampant abuse of power by the cadres as well as a new wave of popular protests after decades of general si-lence. All these bore some resemblance to the developments in the ru-ral society under the name of *xinzheng* and *difang zizhi* in the late Qing and Republican periods.

Cognizant of the threat of the mounting discontent among the vil-lagers in the 1980s and 1990s, the state made serious efforts to reorient its agrarian policies from exploiting agriculture for industrialization to "feeding back" agriculture and the rural population when the state no longer relied on agriculture as a major source of revenue after decades of rapid industrialization. New measures thus were introduced to the rural area, including abolishing agricultural taxes and subsidizing the farmers in grain production, the purchase of agricultural machines, participation in the cooperative health program, the construction of local infrastructure projects, and so on. The historical reason behind state involution (i.e., the state's need to extract rural resources and its subsequent penetration of the rural society) no longer existed.

The real challenge to rural China in the twenty-first century came primarily from within the village communities, when the state's termination of its extraction policies, which offered the villagers a better opportunity to prosper, also allowed greater room for the cadres to engage in profiteering activities and abuse of power. Therefore, at the core of that challenge was how to institutionalize the self-governing bodies at the grassroots level on the basis of local initiatives in order to minimize the scope of misconduct by the grassroots cadres. Viewed in this light, the revolutionary legacies that continued into the reform era could be at once conducive and obstructive to the smooth growth of self-government in the countryside. The Party's vertical organizations that reached down to the village, and the supervisory measures based on popular participation that had existed since the Mao era, continued to impose a constraint on the grassroots cadres, despite their limited effectiveness. The Party's leading role in promoting the self-government program also helped overcome the political apathy of many villagers and the obstacle from traditional community networks. At the same time, however, the Party's continuous control of village election and dominance over the village council also impeded the healthy growth of a true form of self-government in rural communities. How to cultivate the villagers' initiatives in local governance and promote their interest in political participation while reducing the state's excessive intervention remained a major challenge to the development of grassroots democracy in rural China.

CHAPTER 1

1. For Chinese-language works that represent this view, see, e.g., Lu Feng, Luo Huanzhen, and Huang Weiping 1987: 31–48; Zhang Yulin 1992: 41–52; Jiang Chongwei 1993: 244–257; Zhang Tiesen, Liu Jinsheng, and Chen Junsheng 1995: 1–55; and Fang Xiangxin 1998: 29–47. In English-language works, this view is most evident in Kelliher 1992: 19–39 and Sachs and Woo 1994.

2. In celebration of the thirtieth anniversary of the inception of agrarian reforms in the late 1970s, the official media in China once again extolled the peasants in different localities for starting the economic and political reforms from the bottom up (*Renmin ribao*, September 29 and October 1, 2008).

3. For discussions on the relationship between grassroots cadres and villagers during the collective era, see, e.g., Oi 1989: 131–154; Siu 1989: 143–169; and Zhou 1996: 30–33.

4. See, e.g., Nolan 1983; Putterman 1987, 1988; Lin 1988, 1990, 1999; Kung 1994; McKinley 1996: 3–23; Zhou Xiaohong 1998: 194–207; and Shi Lei 1999: 59–64.

5. For a criticism of the "new institutionalism" in economics that has emphasized the formal institutional constraints, see Nee 1998.

6. For recent studies on peasant protests in the reform era, see Bernstein and Lü 2003 and O'Brien and Li 2006.

7. Among the many studies on agricultural collectivization and collective economy in rural China under Mao are Shue 1980; Lardy 1983; Perkins and Yusuf 1984; P. Huang 1990; and Friedman, Pickowicz, and Selden 1991. Monographs on social and political life in the rural collectives include Parish and Whyte 1978; Madsen 1984; Burns 1988; Oi 1989; Siu 1989; and Zweig 1989. Village case studies include Potter and Potter 1990; Chan, Madsen, and Unger 1992; and, more recently, Gao 1999.

8. For my examination of peasant resistance to the state's control of grain marketing through the "unified purchase and sales" program in the 1950s, see H. Li 2006.

9. The statistics here are provided by the accountant of Qin village.

10. See Table 8 in this book. In 1976, for example, the net income distributed from the No. 11 team, which contained 51 households and 269 people, was 80 yuan per person, which was lower than 115.3 yuan in the Suzhou region, the richest area of the province, but significantly higher than 49.8 yuan in the Huaiyin region, the poorest in Jiangsu. It was also higher than the average per capita level of 74.1 yuan of the county, 71.5 yuan of the province, and 62.8 yuan for China as a whole. The per capita amount of grain distribution from the team in the same year was 515 catties (see Table 2 in this book), which was likewise higher than the 417 catties average for the county, the 456 catties average for the province, and the 405 catties average in China as a whole. (Data of the per capita income and grain distribution of Dongtai county, Suzhou and Huaiyin regions, and the province in 1976 and 1978 are from JSJW 1976 and 1978, respectively. Data of the country are from Nongyebu zhengce yanjiushi 1979: 105; see also Lardy 1983: 160–161.)

11. The amount of the annual income of Qin villagers in 2005 was provided by the accountant of the village government. The net annual income of rural residents was 5,665 yuan per capita in Dongtai municipality in 2005, according to the municipal government's statistics, 5,276 yuan in Jiangsu province and 3,255 yuan in the entire country in the same year (Guojia tongjiju 2006: tables 10-2 and 10-21).

12. Unless otherwise specified, the information in this and following sections is from QD1 2000.

13. To pay grain as rent to their landlord was an ordeal to all tenants. The grain had to pass two quick checks before it could be accepted. First, when the villager's boat loaded with the grain reached the landlord's house, the housekeeper would drop a handful of grain on water to see if there was floating, and therefore immature, grain. He would allow the villager to unload the grain from the boat to the storage house if the result was satisfactory. Then he would put a handful of the crop on a glossy table to see if the crop had too much dust or other impurities. If unsatisfied, he would have the crop screened by a bellows, to blow off the light, immature crops and other undesired ingredients. If the quality of the grain was too poor, the landlord would refuse the payment and threaten the villagers with terminating the lease of his farmland.

14. In Qindong township, the government confiscated from landlord and rich peasant households a total of 44,772 mu of land, 2,035 rooms of tile-roof houses, 501 rooms of straw-roof houses, 3,906 pieces of furniture, 156 boats, 16 waterwheels, 1,690 *dan* of grain, 7 oxen, and 4 pigs (TG5 1951; *Qindong gongshe shezhi* 1981: 30).

CHAPTER 2

1. By the end of the same year, more than 8 million mutual aid teams, mostly irregular, temporary ones, were created in the county, absorbing 39.9 percent of rural households (Lin and Gu 1995: 81; see also GNW 1981a: 228).

2. Output was 309, 320, 414, and 458 catties per mu in 1952 through 1955, respectively, or 14 percent a year on average (Dongtai xian nongye ju 1987a: 4.5.1).

3. The annual grain output in Songjiang was 513, 535, 531, and 556 catties per mu in 1952 through 1955, respectively (*Songjiang xianzhi* 1991: 9.4.5).

4. Dongtai county had 3,297 primary co-ops with a total of more than 95,400 households in 1955, which were merged into 559 advanced co-ops with 144,596 households in 1956 (Dongtai xian nongye ju 1987a: 3.4.3, 3.4.4).

CHAPTER 3

1. The hungry villagers in southern Jiangsu, for example, felt justified to "eat the great households" (*chi dahu*) in the early 1930s when the price of rice had reached such a level that looting rice shops was no longer an action of bandits. Indeed the rioters made every effort to distinguish themselves from true bandits (Bernhardt 1992; Bianco 2001: 159–161). Likewise, the deprived and dislocated villagers in Qing China joined rebels of various heretic organizations dedicated to their deities or secret societies inspired by legendary heroes because "the officials compel the people to rebel" (*guan bi min fan*); rebellion was the only option for them to escape the government's unscrupulous exaction and outrageous cruelty (see, e.g., Naquin 1976; Perry 1980; Prazniak 1999). In all those cases, the peasants invariably resorted to the "right to survival" to justify their claims and actions.

2. Along with the annual drive for collecting grain tax, the program of "unified purchase and sales" of grain began in Qin village in December 1953 (DT4 1952; DT5 1953). The program incurred peasant protests throughout the country, including Dongtai and Songjiang counties, in the following two years (H. Li 2006). In Songjiang, for instance, the largest protest involved 12 villages and more than 700 villagers (SJ4 1955).

3. This quote and the information in the rest of this section is from QD1 2000.

4. Similar protests also took place in the rest of Qindong district but generally subsided in late 1957 as a result of government persuasion and suppression. The district government reestablished local social and economic orders afterwards (DT24 1958; DT25 1958; DT26 1958).

5. The grain production in the entire country yielded only 188.5 catties per mu in 1956 (Guojia tongjiju 2000: 40); and the average level of grain rations of rural residents in the entire country was 410 catties in 1957 (Nongyebu zhengce yanjiushi 1979: 105).

6. In both the Jiangsu and Henan provinces, according to reports by their respective provincial Party committees, women, the elderly, and children were often among the first to take actions in local disturbances. Strong adult males joined their actions later or did not act at all (GNW 1981a: 677, 688).

7. According to a report by the Party committee of the Jiangsu province, organizers of the disturbances in the province usually only allowed poor and middle peasants to join them, claiming that "what we want is the regular folks, not landlords and rich peasants" (GNW 1981a: 688).

8. No matter whether their actions were righteous or rightful, however, such open challenges to the collective system almost disappeared after 1957, when the state eventually deprived the peasants of their right to exit the collectives, redefined the major contradiction in the country as that between socialism and capitalism, and returned to suppression, rather than "persuasion and education," in dealing with actions that undermined the collective economy.

CHAPTER 4

1. Mao launched the Great Leap Forward for two reasons: to outcompete the Soviet Union in the transition to communism and to materialize his dream of an egalitarian utopia that he had harbored since his youth (Song Haiqing 2000: 199–201, 223–224; Song Liansheng 2002: 170).

2. A nationwide survey shows that 70 percent of the communes had 5,000 households or less; 22.6 percent of them had 5,000 to 10,000 households; 7 percent of them had 10,000 to 20,000 households, and less than 1 percent of them had more than 20,000 households (GNW 1981b: 84).

3. During my childhood, my mother unfailingly reminded me of "the time of mess hall" whenever I wasted some food or left the rice in my bowl unfinished, though I was born several years after the Leap and had no memory of the famine at all.

4. It was reported that by the end of 1959, 72.6 percent of commune members or about 400 million people, had joined the 3,919,000 mess halls in the country. In Henan, Hunan, Sichuan, Yunnan, Guizhou, Shanghai, and Anhui, more than 90 percent of rural population had participated in the mess hall program (GNW 1981b: 292).

5. The per capita monthly ration was scheduled as 20 catties in November and 18 catties in December 1960. During the next five months, the rations were 18, 21, 23, 25, and 26 catties, respectively (QD4 1960). Everyone thus had a total of 113 catties on average during those five months. The ration increased as the busy season approached.

6. In October 1960, for example, the daily rations for the five grades were 0.25, 0.4375, 0.625, 0.8125, and 0.8125 catties, respectively. In the next months, the rations were reduced to 0.1875, 0.3125, 0.4375, 0.625, and 0.8125 catties (QD4 1960).

7. The rural population in the entire country increased at 1.577 percent per year during the six years prior to the Leap (from 503.19 million in 1952 to 552.73 million in 1958). If we suppose that no famine occurred during the three Great Leap Forward years and that the rural population continued to grow at the preexisting rate, then it should have reached 579.29 million in 1961 or 26.56 million more than its actual size in that year. Alternatively, we may use the growth rate after the Leap to gauge the loss of population during those three years. The rural population grew at 2.592 percent a year from 556.36 million in 1962 to 665.54 million in 1969, when there was no major famine and birth

control measures. If we assume that the rural population grew at that same rate from 1959 to 1961, under normal conditions, it should have increased to 596.83 million in 1961, or 65.31 million more than its actual number. I believe that the normal growth rate from 1959 to 1961 should have been certainly higher than 1.577 percent a year but lower than 2.592 percent a year, had there been no widespread famine in the country. If, for example, we accept 2 percent as the likely normal growth rate in those three years, then the population in 1961 should have been 586.56 million, or 55.04 million more than the actual size in 1961 (for the annual number of rural population in those years, see Nongyebu jihuasi 1989: 6–8).

CHAPTER 5

1. In August 1961 there were 55,682 communes, 708,912 brigades, and 4,549,474 production teams nationwide (GNW 1981b: 492). In the mid-1970s, there were 52,615 communes, 677,000 brigades, and 4,820,000 production teams in the entire country (Zweig 1989: 5). In 1982, the end of the collective era, there were 54,352 communes, 719,438 brigades, and 5,977,000 production teams (Peng Xianggang 1995: 15). Each brigade normally had about 10 cadres, and each team had about 3 or 4 cadres.

2. Three key documents guided the movement. The first was the CCP central committee's "Decision on Several Issues Concerning the Current Work in the Countryside" (known as the "Former 10 Articles") issued on May 20, 1963, in which the Party defined the movement's task as to clean up accounts, inventories, properties, and workpoints (the "four minor clean-ups" or *xiao siqing*) (GNW 1981b: 688). Four months later, the revised document (known as the "Latter 10 Articles") further defined the methods and strategies for conducting the movement. Finally, on January 14, 1965, the Party publicized a document, "Some Issues Currently Emerged in the Rural Socialist Education Movement," which clearly defined its task as to "clean up" the politics, economy, organizations, and ideology in local collectives (the "four major clean-ups" or *da siqing*) (GNW 1981b: 821).

3. The "unclean" cadres included 12 of the 13 commune cadres, 100 of the 109 brigade cadres, 465 of the 500 production team cadres, 418 of the 587 subteam cadres, and 5 of the 183 cadres in other government agencies or businesses. Among the "unclean" cadres, 532 "thoroughly confessed" their wrongdoings, 279 "partly confessed," and 128 "incompletely confessed" (SQ7 1965).

4. In the entire Dongtai county, 26,377 cadres, or 80.46 percent of all cadres from the commune level to the subteam level, confessed a total of 2,032,203 yuan of unlawfully obtained grain, cloth coupons, and cotton, or 77.04 yuan per person (SQ6 1964–1965; SQ7 1965).

5. The returned goods included 28,528.72 catties of grain, 1,947.5 feet of cloth coupons, 179.6 catties of cotton, 12 wristwatches, 13.5 housing units, 91 pieces of furniture, 11 woolen sweaters, 18 leather coats, 4 pairs of leather shoes, 3 mosquito tents, and 10 pieces of lumber (SQ7 1965; SQ2 1965: 2, 6–7). In

Dongtai county, the 26,377 "unclean" cadres (80.46 percent of all cadres in the county) had returned by the same date a total of 893,556 yuan of goods (33.88 yuan per cadre), or about 50 percent of what they should have returned, including 748,557 catties of grain, 66,435 feet of cloth coupons, 18,981 catties of cotton, 445 wristwatches, 805 bicycles, 2,442 pieces of furniture, 540 woolen sweaters, 124 leather coats, 233.5 housing units, and 83 gold ornaments (SQ7 1965).

6. During the years of primary and advanced co-ops from 1953 to 1957, the collectives conducted an examination of their financial condition only when the superior authorities asked them to do so, which usually did not involve co-op members. During the Great Leap Forward from 1958 to 1961, a brigade normally reviewed its financial accounts once a quarter to meet the government's requirement, and production teams were not involved in the process because they were not the basic accounting unit and the team cadres, only responsible for labor management and production, were not involved in the management of the collective's financial matters.

7. Unless otherwise specified, the information in this and following sections is based on the author's interviews with Qin villagers.

8. For example, when reviewing the No. 2 team's accounts, the accountant from the No. 11 team made the following comments: "two catties of pork were recorded without a seal" and "stationery was entered as an agricultural expense" (QD4 1973: 4).

CHAPTER 6

1. Unless otherwise specified, the information in this section is based on the author's interviews with Qin villagers and his personal observations.

2. The same was true for the villagers, even when dealing with the so-called bad elements and class enemies in the community. The No. 6 team of the Zhigang Brigade, for example, had several landlord households and rich-peasant households. The 15 male laborers from these households accounted for half of the team's regular male labor force. They were treated the same way as were other team members in task assignment and labor remuneration. The team cadres had no problem in visiting a former landlord's or rich peasant's home for a feast or accepting his gift, though they had to be scrupulous in doing so. The No. 11 team, in another instance, had a "counterrevolutionary" (*fan geming*), named Fang. A former *baozhang* (head of a quasi-official unit comprising hundreds of households for mutual surveillance) at the county seat, Fang was sent to the team to "work under supervision" in 1969 when he was already 60. At the very beginning of his residence in Qin village, some young villagers treated him rudely, often cursing and humiliating him in the public. However, in the following few years, the villagers gradually accepted him, usually calling him Uncle Fang or Lao Fang. The team leader only assigned him some light tasks, such as raising the team's goats or taking care of the team's vegetable garden. Fang had several sons, working as doctors or factory workers at the

county seat, who had been worried about their father's situation in the team but later were satisfied about the team cadres' reasonable treatment of their father. Thus, each time when Fang returned to the village after the lunar New Year, he unfailingly visited each cadre's home in secret at night, bringing with some cookies, cakes, fruits, and medicines.

CHAPTER 7

1. By that time I was already a sixth grader. At the instruction of my father, the team's accountant, I spent a weekend copying several short newspaper essays that criticized Deng onto the posters and drew a cartoon that caricatured Deng as being poked by a pen held in a huge, furious fist. The cartoon and the posters won a visiting brigade cadre's praise. I received no workpoints but was rewarded with a box of watercolors that I desperately wanted.

2. Unless otherwise specified, the information in this and following sections is based on the author's interviews with Qin villagers.

3. In the model Dazhai Brigade of Xiyang county, Shanxi province, the cadres reportedly worked 300 days a year and led in doing "three types of jobs": the strenuous, the dirty, and the important ones (GNW 1981b: 873).

4. During my childhood, for example, the neighbors of my family included the Waangs, the Zhangs, and the Mengs. My family had the closest relations with the Waangs, whose house was next to ours. The two families helped each other; they borrowed things from and exchanged foods with each other frequently.

CHAPTER 8

1. Scholarly discussions have focused mainly on the Dazhai system, which had the alleged purpose of minimizing income disparities between households within the team and of cultivating team members' loyalty to the collective. However, the Dazhai system, as these studies have shown, existed in most localities only for a few years in the late 1960s and early 1970s (Parish and Whyte 1978: 64; Madsen 1984: 141, 237; Unger 1985; Burns 1988: 77; Siu 1989: 231; Chan, Madsen, and Unger 1992: 93, 249). By early 1968, according to an estimate by the Ministry of Agriculture, more than 70 percent of production teams in Shanxi and Shandong provinces, as well as Shanghai and Tianjin municipalities, and more than 50 percent of teams in Guangdong, Guangxi, Hebei, Shaanxi, and Heilongjiang provinces, had adopted the Dazhai system (GNW 1981b: 874). The time-rate and piece-rate systems predominated during the rest of the collective era. To be sure, studies of rural China under the collective have discussed these latter two systems. The best of these studies have discussed the evolution and applicability of these systems in different ecological, socioeconomic, and ideological settings (Parish and Whyte 1978: 59–71; Unger 1985; Oi 1989: 135–137; Potter and Potter 1990: 117–120; Kung 1994). However, due to a dearth of detailed empirical data from the production teams, little research has been

done on the day-to-day realities of the time-rate and piece-rate systems. When discussing work incentives and labor efficiency under the collective, scholars have focused mainly on the defects of imposed distribution policies or problems associated with the collective organization, rather than the actual functioning of different workpoint systems per se. Consequently, many issues remain unanswered, such as how the villagers adjusted their labor input under these systems, how they interacted with team leaders in task assignments and in awarding workpoints, and how the villagers developed everyday strategies for collective production. These questions are critical for understanding the problem of incentives and morale under the collective system.

2. Unless otherwise specified, the information in this chapter is derived from the author's interviews with Qin villagers.

3. The reluctance of rural cadres in adopting piece rates was also observed in other localities (Zweig 1985: 146; Chan, Madsen, and Unger 1992: 249).

4. In response to the 1970 North China Agriculture Conference, which attempted to reverse the radical policies prevailing in the late 1960s, most teams in the country gave up the Dazhai system and returned to time rates and piece rates (GNW 1981a: 892). The piece-rate system was first introduced in the "Exemplary Regulations of Agricultural Production Collectives" in November 1955, and reasserted in the "Revised Exemplary Regulations for the Advanced Agricultural Production Collectives" in 1956. Both documents were enacted by the central government to guide the newly created collectives (GNW 1981a: 493–494, 572). In Qin village, the piece-rate system was first introduced in the winter of 1956 at the instruction of the supra-village district (*qu*) government. According to a former co-op leader, villagers in his unit accepted this system with great enthusiasm when it was introduced. After the transition to the advanced co-ops in 1957, the collective continued to use the piece-rate system and applied it to most tasks. Except for the few years from 1966 to 1969, piece rates and time rates were the two major systems during the 1960s and 70s.

5. For how the peasants reacted to the Dazhai system in the late 1960s and early 1970s, see Unger (1985).

6. Bossen noticed the same phenomenon in Lu village, Yunnan province (2002: 111–112). Many women in Qin village complained that they felt exhausted during the collective years, especially during the 1970s when the double cropping of rice, which almost doubled their effort, was introduced. Some women thus suffered a prolapse of the uterus because of the long-lasting drudgery during the transplanting and cropping seasons. The collectives had to organize married women to visit the local hospital for a check of what they called "the women's disease."

CHAPTER 9

1. Chayanov maintained that peasant household organization was based on demographic factors to the degree that all of its economic activity was de-

termined by the size and age composition of the domestic unit. How hard a peasant household worked was in his view an effect of an internal dynamic, or the ratio of working members to nonworking members. At some stages of the life cycle, therefore, the peasant household contained elements (very young children, aged parents) which, because they were not yet economically productive or were no longer economically productive, had to be provided for by those elements (children, adults) that were. This he labeled the "labor-consumer balance," which in turn gave rise to the "drudgery of labor," or the amount of work it was necessary for economically active members to perform in order to support the economically inactive components of the peasant household. In other words, work is in this context linked closely to the life cycle of the domestic unit (Chayanov 1986: 53–69).

CHAPTER 10

1. Perkins and Yusuf, for example, found that agricultural growth in China from 1949 to the 1970s was "impressive" and "fairly high by international standards." They further found the commune system to be an "effective vehicle" for promoting public health, eradicating illiteracy, reducing inequality, and introducing new technology into the countryside (Perkins and Yusuf 1984: 35, 39, 196–199; see also Bramall 1993 for a similar view). Philip Huang observed that the increased supply of farm labor, together with the introduction of modern inputs and water-control efforts, permitted significant growth of total output in collective agriculture. But the gains in labor productivity from capitalization, he contended, were "almost entirely whittled away by losses from extreme labor intensification." He described this phenomenon as involution or "output growth without an increase in returns per workday." As a result, the majority of rural population continued to live "close to the margins of bare subsistence" throughout the collective era (P. Huang 1990: 16, 240).

2. The per capita gross income grew at 6.1 percent a year between 1957 and 1981 in Qin village, from 62.94 yuan per person in the Qindian co-op in 1957 to 98.30 yuan in the No. 8 team (originating from the Qindian co-op) in 1963, 110.84 yuan in the No. 11 team (part of the former No. 8 team) in 1969, 177.17 yuan in 1976, and 260.67 yuan in 1981 (see Table 7).

3. In the entire Qindong commune, the villagers' net income from the team increased by 6.06 percent annually from 54.9 yuan per person in 1969 to 104.92 yuan in 1980, a bit slower than the No. 11 team's growth rate (8.66 percent a year) during the same period.

4. In a village in Songjiang county in the Yangzi delta, for example, the price of a workday fluctuated between 0.9 and 1.0 yuan during most of the collective years, a phenomenon that Philip Huang ascribed to labor intensification and therefore the diminishing marginal returns to labor (P. Huang 1990: 236–241).

5. The official prices of rice and wheat in the local area were slightly lower than the national averages, which were a bit more than 0.08 yuan a catty in the

1950s, 0.1 to 0.11 yuan in most of the 1960s, and 0.12 yuan from 1967 to 1977, gradually increasing to 0.19 yuan in 1981 and 0.2 yuan in 1985 (Caizhengbu 1994: 412).

6. Unless otherwise specified, information included in this and following sections is based on the author's interviews with Qin villagers and his personal observations.

7. My mother was one of the few amateur tailors in the community. During my childhood in the early 1970s, whenever there was a rainy day and the villagers had no tasks, there were always a number of women visiting my home for that purpose, and the service was free. There was, however, a professional tailor in the village, the schoolteacher's wife, who had a sewing machine and charged 0.20 yuan for a pair of pants and 0.35 yuan for an upper garment. The villagers turned to her only when they bought a relatively expensive piece of cloth and wanted to make a formal garment that they could not make by themselves, especially the upper clothes for adult men. It was not until the late 1970s that the villagers completely gave up the custom of sewing garments at home and turned to professional tailors.

8. I went to that school in 1974 as a fifth grader and finished my middle school there in the summer of 1977.

9. Most of my classmates took that test in the summer of 1977; about one-fifth of them passed and became high school students, including me and two others from Qin village. Three years later I passed the college entrance examination and became the first college student in the village and the entire brigade.

10. As a fifth grader, one of my routines in the school was to swallow the tablets, just like all other students.

CHAPTER 11

1. Unless otherwise specified, the information in this and following sections is based on the author's interviews with Qin villagers.

2. The Zhigang Brigade was split into two brigades in 1981. As a result, the production teams in Qin village formed the Qindian Brigade, while the six teams in Su village formed a separate Suzhuang Brigade.

3. My informants enjoyed talking about how a cadre worked so hard cutting the crop on his own field that he failed to notice that his fountain pen was missing, or how a cadre who had always worn a bright white shirt and kept his hair shiny and neatly combed had to move the household manure to his field by himself.

4. Estimates of Qin villagers' average annual income from the 1980s to 2007 were provided by Mr. Zhang, accountant of the village government. For annual price indexes in China during this period, see http://news.xinhuanet.com/ziliao/2003-01/25/content_707572.htm.

5. Information on the annual net income of villagers in Qindong township is from the official Web site of the Qindong township government at http://www.qindong.net/. Data on the national level is from *Renmin ribao* (January 31, 2008).

CHAPTER 12

1. Unless otherwise specified, the information contained in this chapter is based on the author's interviews with Qin villagers and his own observations.

2. In 1981, the No. 7, 8, 9, 10, and 11 teams of the Zhigang Brigade formed the separate Qindian Brigade.

3. In 1987, the state further promulgated "The Law on the Organization of the Village Council" to regularize the election and operation of the self-government organization in the village. It is interesting to note that the hard-liners in the central government, who briefly prevailed in the decision-making circle following the 1989 Tiananmen Protests, attempted to abolish the village council system, denouncing the "direct democracy" in electing village councilors as unsuitable for China's "national conditions," and instead proposing the creation of a formal village government under the direct control of the township government (see Bai Yihua 1998).

4. The former director of the village council, another Zhang, decided to retire before the 2007 election after serving the community for more than 20 years; by serving as a member of the election committee he automatically lost his candidacy for village council membership.

5. In fact, to merge the two offices has already been a popular practice in many other places, including, for example, 56 percent of the villages in Guangdong province (*Yangcheng wanbao*, May 6, 1999).

6. Every family offered such service at home to its ancestors of the latest three generations (namely, the deceased parents, grandparents, and great grandparents) on the Qingming Festival (April 4, 5, or 6), the fifteenth of the lunar seventh month, the eve of Dongzhi (December 20, 21, or 22), and the day before the eve of the lunar New Year, respectively.

7. The data here are provided by Mr. Zhang, accountant of Qin village government.

8. Similar phenomena are observed in other villages in different parts of China (S. Huang 1998 and Yan 2003).

CHAPTER 13

1. Unless otherwise specified, information in this chapter is based on the author's interviews with Qin villagers and his personal observations.

2. Exceptions to the one-child policy were allowed to qualified couples, if both of the couple were the only child of their respective parents, if the first child was disabled, or if one of the couple was divorced and had one child with him or her before the second marriage and the other had no children.

3. Among the 146.5 catties, 80.6 catties were designated as the basic quota, which was purchased by the government at 0.14 yuan per catty, or 0.06 yuan less than the market price; the remaining 65.9 catties were extra quota, which was purchased by the government at 0.18 yuan per catty.

4. *Nongmin ribao*, May 25, 2005.

5. The data here are provided by the "joint management committee of the new-type rural cooperative medical service" of Dongtai municipal government.

6. For details of this program, see www.moh.gov.cn/uploadfile/200502/2005228141615474.doc.

7. Villager Wang, my childhood friend who had almost finished his house when I was visiting the central village in the summer of 2006, explained that he would not attach a "stinky and ugly" pigpen or henhouse to his beautiful house, even if the government allowed him to do so.

CHAPTER 14

1. For peasant resistance to the unified purchase and sales in Jiangsu province in the 1950s, see H. Li 2006.

2. For studies on the central role of subsistence in the peasant society and the thesis of moral economy in general, see Polanyi 1957; Thompson 1963, 1971; Wolf 1969; Scott 1976; Taylor 1982.

3. The total grain yield in the country was 154,410,000 tons in 1962, 320,560,000 tons in 1980, 325,020,000 tons in 1981, and 508,390,000 tons in 1999. The grain yield per land unit in the country was 1,270 kilograms per hectare in 1962, 2,734 kilograms per hectare in 1980, 2,827 kilograms per hectare in 1981, and 4,493 kilograms per hectare in 1999 (Guojia tongjiju 2000: 37, 40).

References

UNPUBLISHED SOURCES

Note: Documents beginning with DT, LX, SQ, TG, and WG are from Dongtai Municipal Archives (Dongtai shi dang'an guan). Documents beginning with SJ are from Songjiang County Archives (Songjiang xian dang'an guan, renamed Songjiang qu dang'an guan in 1998). The rest of the documents listed in this section are from Qin village.

DT1. 1950. "Qindong qugongsuo shengchan jiuzai gongzuo zongjie baogao" 溱东区公所生产救灾工作总结报告 (Report of Qindong district government on agricultural production and relief work).

DT2. 1952. "Qindong quweihui yijiu wuer nian fengchan wenti yu zuzhi hezuo huzhuzu baogao" 溱东区委会一九五二年丰产问题与组织合作互助组报告 (Report of the CCP Qindong district committee on increasing agricultural output and organizing mutual aid teams in 1952).

DT3. 1952. "Qindong qu weiyuanhui xiaji shengchan gongzuo de chubu zongjie" 溱东区委员会夏季生产工作的初步总结 (The CCP Qindong district committee's preliminary review of agricultural production in the summer).

DT4. 1952. "Dongtai xian Qindong quwei wuer niandu qiuzheng gongzuo zongjie" 东台县溱东区委五二年度秋征工作总结 (The CCP Qindong district committee's review of tax collection in Autumn 1952).

DT5. 1953. "Liangshi tonggou tongxiao baogao" 粮食统购统销报告 (Report on the unified procurement and sales of grain).

DT6. 1954. "Qindongqu nongye shengchan huzhu hezuo qingkuang" 溱东区农业生产互助合作情况 (Mutual aid and cooperativization in agricultural production in Qindong district).

DT7. 1954. "Qindong qu xiaji yilai shengchan gongzuo de jixiang cailiao chubu zongjie" 溱东区夏季以来生产工作的几项材料初步总结 (A preliminary review of several documents on agricultural production in Qindong district since the summer).

DT8. 1954. "Zhonggong Qindong qu weiyuanhui jige cailiao de zonghe hui-bao" 中共溱东区委员会几个材料的综合汇报 (The CCP Qindong district commit-tee's general report based on several documents).

DT9. 1954. "Zhonggong Qindong quwei guanyu zhaokai dangyuan ganbu huiyi qingkuang de baogao" 中共溱东区委关于召开党员干部会议情况的报告 (The CCP Qindong district committee's report on the conferences of Party mem-bers and cadres).

DT10. 1954. "Dongtai xian Qindong qu yijiu wusi niandu gongzuo zongjie baogao" 东台县溱东区一九五四年度工作总结报告 (An annual work report of Qin-dong district, Dongtai county in 1954).

DT11. 1955. "Dongtai xian Qindong qu jin yi shiqi ge jieceng sixiang dongtai ji zhibu gongzuo qingkuang zonghe buchong baogao" 东台县溱东区近一时期各阶层思想动态及支部工作情况综合补充报告 (A supplementary report on the po-litical attitudes of different social groups and the activities of Party branches in recent times in Qindong district, Dongtai county).

DT12. 1955. "Qindong qu xinbanshe de jidian tiyan" 溱东区新办社的几点体验 (Sev-eral lessons from the newly established cooperatives in Qindong district).

DT13. 1955. "Zhonggong Qindong quweihui guanyu Qindong qu gaolidai boxue huodong qingkuang diaocha baogao" 中共溱东区委会关于溱东区高利贷剥削活动情况调查报告 (The CCP Qindong district committee's report of inves-tigation on usury in Qindong district).

DT14. 1955. "Zhonggong Qindong quwei guanyu shiyue shangxun yiqian xu-anchuan gongzuo zongjie" 中共溱东区委关于十月上旬以前宣传工作总结 (The CCP Qindong district committee's review of propaganda work before October).

DT15. 1955. "Zhonggong Qindong quweihui nongshe gugan xunlian dahui guanyu 'ding Mao zhuxi hua zou shehuizhuyi lu' de dongyuan baogao" 中共溱东区委会农社骨干训练大会关于"听毛主席话、走社会主义路"的动员报告 (The CCP Qindong district committee's report on "Follow the words of Chairman Mao and Take the Socialist Road" at the conference for training activists of agricultural cooperatives).

DT16. 1955. "Qindong qu guanyu zhengdun gonggu xinshe tigao laoshe zhengli he fazhan huzhuzu tuanjie dangan nongmin de yijian" 溱东区关于整顿巩固新社、提高旧社、整理和发展互助组、团结单干农民的意见 (Suggestions on consolidat-ing new co-ops, developing old co-ops, consolidating and developing mu-tual aid teams, and uniting with independent farmers in Qindong district).

DT17. 1956. "Qindong qu chuxi diwei shiban gaojishe ganbu huiyi de bucong cailiao" 溱东区出席地委试办高级社干部会议的补充材料 (Supplementary docu-ments for Qindong district cadres to attend the prefectural conference on experimenting with advanced cooperatives).

DT18. 1957. "Zhonggong Dongtai xianwei guanyu dangqian nongcun renmin neibu maodun de fenxi he zhengque chuli renmin neibu maodun wenti de cailiao" 中共东台县委关于当前农村人民内部矛盾的分析和正确处理人民内部矛盾问题的材料 (The CCP Dongtai county committee's analysis of current contradictions among the people in the countryside and materials on correct handling of contradictions among the people).

DT19. 1957. "Zhonggong Dongtai xianwei guanyu Chengdong qu Sitang nongshe chuli sheyuan tuishe wenti de tongbao" 中共东台县委关于城东区四塘农社处理社员退社问题的通报 (The CCP Dongtai county committee's report on handling co-op members' withdrawal from the Sitang Cooperative in Chengdong district).

DT20. 1957. "Chengdong qu Zaoxi nongshe guanyu chuli yufen liangshi zhong fasheng bufen sheyuan naoshi de baogao" 城东区灶西农社关于处理预分粮食中发生部分社员闹事的报告 (Report on handling peasant disturbances during the advance distribution of grain in the Zaoxi Cooperative of Chengdong district).

DT21. 1957. "Dongtai xian Qindong xiang Qindian nongshe banshe qianhou shengchan shuiping de bianhua" 东台县溱东乡秦甸农社办社前后生产水平的变化 (Changes in production output in the Qindian Cooperative of Qindong district, Dongtai county, before and after its establishment).

DT22. 1957. "Qindong xiang Qindian nongshe yijiu wuqi nian qiuzhong guihua he zhunbei gongzuo qingkuang" 溱东乡秦甸农社一九五七年秋种规划和准备工作情况 (The planning and preparation of autumn sowing in the Qindian Cooperative of Qindong district in 1957).

DT23. 1957. "Qindong xiang Qindian nongshe liangshi shouyi fenpei qing-kuang tongjibiao" 溱东乡秦甸农社粮食收益分配统计表 (Statistical table on grain production and income distribution in the Qindian Cooperative of Qin-dong district).

DT24. 1958. "Zhonggong Dongtai xian Qindong xiang weiyuanhui guanyu chunji yilai shengchan, shenghuo, ji sheyuan sixiang dongtai de huibao" 中共东台县溱东乡委员会关于春季以来生产生活及社员思想动态的汇报 (The CCP Qin-dong xiang of Dongtai county committee's report on agricultural produc-tion, living conditions, and political attitudes of co-op members since the spring).

DT25. 1958. "Muqian de zhengshe he caiwu gongzuo huibao" 目前的整社和财务工作汇报 (Report on the current consolidation of cooperatives and financial work).

DT26. 1958. "Qindong xiang Qindian she yijiu wuba nian nongye baochan tongjibiao" 溱东乡秦甸社一九五八年农业包产统计表 (Statistical table on contract-ing out farm output in the Qindian Cooperative of the Qindong xiang in 1958).

DT27. 1960. "Dongtai xian Qindong qu linianlai liangshi zuowu shiji chan-liang tongjibiao" 东台县溱东区历年来粮食作物实绩产量统计表 (Statistical table on the annual output of grain and other crops in Qindong district of Dong-tai county).

DT28. 1964. "Suqin dadui diba shengchandui yijiu liusi nian nianzhong shouyi fenpei shenpi yijianshu" 苏秦大队第八生产队一九六四年年终收益分配审批意见书 (Approved plan for year-end income distribution in No. 8 production team of the Suqin Brigade in 1964).

DT29 (Xian-she Fulian lianhe diaochazu 县、社妇联联合调查组). 1977. "Nannü tonggong tongchou zhengce hao, funü fahui 'banbiantian' zhuoyong da:

Zhigang dadui shixing nannü tonggong tongchou de diaocha" 男女同工同酬政策好，妇女发挥"半边天"作用大——志刚大队实行男女同工同酬的调查 (The equal-pay-to-equal-work-for-both-sexes policy works well, causing women to play a major role as "half-the-sky" : An investigation of the implementation of the equal pay to equal work for both sexes in the Zhigang Brigade).

DT30. 1963–1968. "Dongtai xian renmin gongshe nongye shengchan tongji nianbaobiao: Qindong renmin gongshe Suqin dadui" 东台县人民公社农业生产统计年报表——溱东人民公社苏秦大队 (Annual statistics of agricultural production in the people's communes of Dongtai county: Suqin Brigade, Qindong People's Commune).

DT31. 1969–1978. "Dongtai xian renmin gongshe nongye shengchan tongji nianbaobiao: Qindong renmin gongshe Zhigang dadui" 东台县人民公社农业生产统计年报表——溱东人民公社志刚大队 (Annual statistics of agricultural production in the people's communes of Dongtai county: Zhigang Brigade, Qindong People's Commune).

LC. 1972–1979. "Zhigang dadui di shiyi shengchan dui minzhu licai huiyi jilubu" 志刚大队第十一生产队民主理财记录簿 (Journal of the meetings for democratic management of financial affairs in production team No. 11, Zhigang Brigade).

LX1. 1965. "Zhonggong Dongtai xian weiyuanhui guanyu jinyibu zuohao renmin laixin laifang gongzuo de zhishi" 中共东台县委员会关于进一步做好人民来信来访工作的指示 (The CCP Dongtai committee's instruction on improving the work of handling people's letters and visits).

LX2. 1965. "Zhonggong Dongtai xian Qindong renmingongshe weiyuanhui guanyu renmin laixin laifang gongzuo de chubu zongjie" 中共东台县溱东人民公社委员会关于人民来信来访工作的初步总结 (The CCP Qindong People's Commune of Dongtai county committee's preliminary conclusion on the work of handling people's letters and visits).

LX3–LX5. 1964. "Renmin laixin laifang jie'an juanzong" 人民来信来访结案卷宗 (Complete files of people's letters and visits).

QD1. 2000. "Qincun cunshi huiyi" 秦村村史回忆 (Recollections on the history of Qin village), manuscript by Li Weixiang (1935–2006), who served as the accountant of a mutual aid team, a primary co-op, and then the advanced co-op in Qin village in the 1950s; as the chief accountant of the Suqin Brigade from 1959 to 1961; as the accountant and then the leader of the No. 11 team of the Zhigang Brigade in the 1960s and 1970s; and as the head of the Qindian Brigade in the late 1970s and early 1980s.

QD2. 2003. "Qincun jiefang qian de zhuhu renkou ji jingji qingkuang" 秦村解放前的住户人口及经济情况 (Households, population, and economic conditions in Qin village before Liberation), manuscript by Li Weixiang.

QD3. 2003. "Bencun zubei diaocha" 本村祖辈调查 (A survey of family lines in our village), manuscript by Li Weixiang.

QD4. 1959–1978. "Gongzuo biji" 工作笔记 (work notebooks) by Li Weixiang.

QD5. 1966–1981. "Zhigang dadui di shiyi shengchandui jingji fenpei fang'an" 志刚大队第十一生产队经济分配方案 (Annual economic distribution plan of production team No. 11, Zhigang Brigade).

QD6. 1970–1979. "Zhigang dadui di shiyi shengchandui sheyuan chuqinbiao" 志刚大队第十一生产队社员出勤表 (Attendance record of commune members in production team No. 11, Zhigang Brigade).

QD7. 1982. "Qindian dadui diwu shengchandui 82 nian sheyuan chengbao liangtian gehu jisuan biao" 秦甸大队第五生产队 82 年社员承包粮田各户结算表 (Settlements with individual households on contracted farmland in the No. 5 production team of the Qindian Brigade, 1982).

QD8. 1983. "Qindian dadui diwu shengchandui 83 niandu bagaogan zhenggou ji nongyeshui daohu biao" 秦甸大队第五生产队 83 年度大包干征购及农业税到户表 (Quotas of grain procurement and agricultural taxes for individual households in the No. 5 production team of the Qindian Brigade, 1983).

QD9. 1983. "Qindian dadui diwu shengchandui 83 nian baogan fenpei zherenzhi hetong" 秦甸大队第五生产队 83 年包干分配责任制合同 (Contracts for allocation of responsibilities in the No. 5 production team of the Qindian Brigade, 1983).

QD10. 1984. "84 nian Qindian 5 dui chun ding hetong shengchan ji shangjiao renwu biao" 84 年秦甸 5 队春订合同生产及上交任务表 (Contractual production and grain procurement in the No. 5 team of the Qindian Brigade as planned in the spring of 1984).

QD11. 1984. "Qindong xiang Qindian cun 5 zu yijiu basi nian nongcun liangshi youliao chan liu gou baogan luoshi fenhu qingce" 溱东乡秦甸村 5 组一九八四年农村粮食油料产留购包干落实分户清册 (Contracted tasks of production, reservation, and procurement of grain and food oil for individual households in the No. 5 team of Qindian village, Qindong township, 1984).

QD12. 1990–2002. "Qindong zhen Qindian cun (linian) nongmin fudan gongbu biao" 溱东镇秦甸村（历年）农民负担公布表 (Annual announcement of farmers' obligations in Qindian village of Qindong township, 1990–2002).

QD13. 1964. "Di er ci quanguo renkou pucha dengjibiao: Suqin ba dui" 第二次全国人口普查登记表：苏秦八队 (Registry of the second national census: The No. 8 team of the Suqin Brigade).

QD14. 1973 (updated annually until 1981). "Qindong renmin gongshe Zhigang dadui di shiyi shengchandui hukouce" 溱东人民公社志刚大队第十一生产队户口册 (The household register of the No. 11 production team of the Zhigang Brigade, Qindong People's Commune).

SJ1. 1954. "(Songjiang xian) huzhu hezuo zhong cunzai de jige wenti" (松江县)互助合作中存在的几个问题 (Several problems in mutual aid and cooperation in Songjiang county).

SJ2. 1954. "Chengdong district Xinglong xiang ge jieceng jingjie bianhua qingkuang he dui hezuohua de taidu" 城东区兴隆乡各阶层经济变化和对合作化的态度 (Changes in the economic conditions of different social strata and their attitudes toward the cooperativization in Xinglong xiang of Chengdong district).

SJ3. 1954. "Songjiang xian dangqian nongcun jieji douzheng qingkuang" 松江县 当前农村阶级斗争情况 (The current state of class struggle in the countryside of Songjiang county).

SJ4. 1955. "Guanyu pingxi Songjiang xian Fengjing district Changwu xiang tongxiao zhong qunzhong saodong shijian de baogao" 关于平息松江县枫泾区 菖梧乡统销中群众骚动事件的报告 (Report on suppressing the mass disturbance in Changwu xiang, Fengjing district of Songjiang county during the unified sale of grain).

SJ5. 1956. "Songjiang xian guanyu chujishe sheng gaojishe de jige wenti" 松江县 关于初级社升高级社的几个问题 (Several issues regarding upgrading primary cooperatives to advanced cooperatives in Songjiang county).

SJ6. 1957. "Tiankun qu zi hezuohua gaochao fazhan yilai dui nongyeshe naoshi qingkuan" 天昆区自合作化高潮发展以来对农业社闹事情况 (Report on disturbances against agricultural cooperatives in Tiankun district since the hide tide of cooperativization).

SJ7. 1957. "Zhongguo Sijing quwei guanyu qunzhong naoshi qingkuang de baogao" 中共泗泾区委关于群众闹事情况的报告 (Report of the CCP Sijing district committee on the disturbances of the masses).

SJ8. 1957. "Zhongguo Caojing quwei guanyu nongmin naoshi ji youguan wenti de qingkuang baogao" 中共漕泾区委关于农民闹事及有关问题的情况报告 (Report of the CCP Caojing district on peasant disturbances and other relevant issues).

SJ9. 1957. "Chengdong qu guanyu nongmin naoshi qingkuang baogao" 城东区 农民闹事情况报告 (Report on peasant disturbances in Chengdong district).

SJ10. 1957. "Jiu Chengdongqu nongmin naoshi qingkuang gei Liu zhengwei de xing" 就城东区农民闹事情况给刘政委的信 (Letter to Director Liu on peasant disturbances in Chengdong district).

SJ11. 1957. "Chengxi qu naoshi qingkuang" 城西区闹事情况 (Disturbances in Chengxi district).

SJ12. 1957. "Guanyu chuli xinwu xiang xinwu she naoshi wenti de qingkuang baogao" 关于处理新五区新五乡闹事问题的情况报告 (Report on handling the disturbances in the Xinwu cooperative of Xinwu xiang).

SJ13. 1957. "Sheshan qu guanyu guangming she manma ganbu naoshi qingkuang de baogao" 余山区关于光明社漫骂干部闹事情况的报告 (Report on slandering the cadres and making disturbances in Sheshan district).

SJ14. 1957. "Fengjing qu chuli naoshi wenti de chubu zongjie" 枫泾区处理闹事问题的初步总结 (A preliminary review of handling disturbances in Fengjing district).

SJ15. 1957. "Quan xian nongyeshe naoshi qingkuang" 全县农业社闹事情况 (Disturbances in agricultural cooperatives in the whole county).

SJ16. 1957. "Sheshan qu renmin neibu naoshi qingkuang dengji biao" 余山区人民 内部闹事情况登记表 (Records of disturbances among the people in Sheshan district).

SJ17. 1957. "Tiankun qu renmin neibu naoshi qingkuang dengji biao" 天昆区人民 内部闹事情况登记表 (Records of disturbances among the people in Tiankun district).

SJ18. 1957. "Sijing qu renmin neibu naoshi qingkuang dengji biao" 泗泾区人民内部闹事情况登记表 (Records of disturbances among the people in Sijing district).

SJ19. 1957. "Jin yinian lai quan xian qunzhong 'naoshi' qingkuang jianming biao" 近一年来全县群众"闹事"情况简明表 (A brief survey of the "disturbances" of the masses in the whole county in the past year).

SQ1. 1965. "Zhongguo Dongtai xian Qindong renmin gongshe weiyuanhui guanyu pinnong xiazhongnong daibiao huiyi zongjie" 中共东台县溱东人民公社委员会关于贫农下中农代表会议总结 (The CCP Qindong People's Commune of Dongtai county committee's report on the conference of poor and lower-middle peasant representatives).

SQ2. 1965. "Zhonggong Dongtaixian Qindong renmin gongshe yuanyuanhui guanyu shehuizhuyi jiaoyu dao dui de qingkuang jianbao" 中共东台县溱东人民公社委员会关于社会主义教育到队的情况简报 (The CCP Qindong People's Commune of Dongtai county committee's brief report on the socialist education in production teams).

SQ3. 1965. "Zai mianshang shejiao he liuwu nian shengchan gongzuo zhong congfen fahui le she dangwei ge bumen zuoyong de zongjie" 在面上社教和六五年生产工作中充分发挥了社党委各部门作用的总结 (A concluding report on large-scale socialist education and the full exertion of the functions of different divisions of the commune's Party committee in agricultural production in 1965).

SQ4. 1965. "Zhonggong Dongtai xian Qindong renmin gongshe weiyuanhui guanyu zaokai pinxiazhongnong he sanji ganbu dahui de zongjie baogao" 中共东台县溱东公社委员会关于召开贫下中农和三级干部大会的总结报告 (The CCP Qindong People's Commune of Dongtai county committee's concluding report on the conference of poor and lower-middle peasant representatives and three-level cadres).

SQ5. 1965. "Ziwo gemin jiancha" 自我革命检查 (A revolutionary self-examination).

SQ6. 1964–1965. "Dongtai xian siji ganbu hui daohui renyuan qingkuang paidui biao" 东台县四级干部会到会人员情况排队表 (A survey of the problems of attendees of the conference of four-level cadres in Dongtai county); "ge gongshe mianshang shehuizhuyi jiaoyu diaocha modi qingkuang liaojie biao" 各公社面上社会主义教育调查摸底情况了解表 (An investigation of the socialist education in individual communes); "ge gongshe youguan daji pinxiazhongnong de qingkuang tongji biao" 各公社有关打击贫下中农的情况统计表 (A survey of the situation of retaliation on poor and lower-middle peasants in individual communes); "Qindong gongshe geji ganbu jingji sibuqing qingkuang tongjibiao" 溱东公社各级干部经济四不清情况统计表 (A survey of the four economic uncleannesses of the cadres at all levels in Qindong commune).

SQ7. 1965. "Geji ganbu duochi duozhan, tanwu daoqie, toujidaoba he tuipei qingkuang biao" 各级干部多吃多占、贪污盗窃、投机倒把和退赔情况表 (A survey of excessive eating and taking, embezzlement and theft, speculation and profiteering, and repayment by cadres at all levels); "ge gongshe pinxiazhongnong daibiaohui shang jiejue shedui ganbu sibuqing wenti de tongjibiao" 各公社贫下中农代表会上解决社队干部四不清问题的统计表 (A survey of the handling of the problems of four uncleannesses among cadres at commune, brigade, and production team levels at the conference of poor and lower-middle peasant representatives in individual communes).

SQ8. 1965. "Qindong gongshe pinxiazhongnong daibiao ji sanji ganbu dahui shang dui Suqin dadui ganbu de yijian" 溱东公社贫下中农代表及三级干部大会上对苏秦大队干部的意见 (Criticisms on the cadres of the Suqin Brigade at the conference of poor and lower-middle peasant representatives and three-level cadres in Qindong commune).

TG1. 1949. "Qindong xingzheng quhua renkou ji dang de zhuzhi zonghe tongjibiao" 溱东行政区划人口及党的组织综合统计表 (Statistical table on population and Party membership in different administrative units of Qindong district).

TG2. 1951. "Ganbu dengji biao" 干部登记表 (Register of cadres).

TG3. 1951. "(Qindong qu) zhuzhi qingkuang yu xingzheng gaikuang biao" (溱东区)组织情况与行政概况表 (Table 1: Party membership and administrative conditions in Qindong district); "ge jieceng huafen biao" 各阶层划分表 (Table 2: Determination of different social classes); "tugai qian tudi qingkuang yilan biao" 土改前土地情况一览表 (Table 3: Land ownership before land reform); "tugai zhong moshou dizu yu zhengshou funong miao si xuechan qingkuang biao" 土改中没收地主于征收富农庙寺学产情况表 (Table 4: The confiscation of landlord properties and appropriation of the properties of rich peasants, temples, and schools); "tugai hou ge jieceng suoyou tudi bijiao biao" 土改后各阶层所有土地比较表 (Table 5: A comparison of land ownership between different social classes after land reform); "tugai zhong ge jieceng deyi (wu da caichan) tongji biao" 土改中各阶层得益(五大财产)统计表 (Table 6: The benefits—five basic categories of properties—received by different social classes during the land reform).

TG4. 1951. "Qindong qu tugai zhongzuo jiben zongjie" 溱东区土改工作基本总结 (A general summary of land reform in Qindong district).

TG5. 1951. "Yancheng zhuanqu Dongtai xian ge qu xiang moshou zhengshou tongji biao" 盐城专区东台县各区乡没收征收统计表 (Statistical table on the confiscation and appropriation in different districts and sub-districts in Dongtai county, Yancheng prefecture).

TG6. 1951. "Dongtai xian jige shiqi jieshu tugai jiben zongjie" 东台县几个时期结束土改基本总结 (A general summary on concluding the land reform during different phases in Dongtai county).

WG1. 1969. "Zhigang dadui pinxiazhongnong Mao Zedong sixiang xuanchuandui duiyuan dengjibiao" 志刚大队贫下中农毛泽东思想宣传队队员登记表 (Register of members of the Mao Zedong thought propaganda team in the Zhigang Brigade).

WG2. 1976. "Dongtai xian Qindong renmin gongshe yijiuqiliu nian nongye xue Dazhai jijifenzi dengjibiao" 东台县溱东人民公社一九七六年农业学大寨积极分子登记表 (Register of the activists in the campaign of "In Agriculture,

Learning from Dazhai" in Qindong People's Commune, Dongtai county, 1976).

WG3. 1969. "Zhigang dadui dongji doupigai xuexiban" 志刚大队冬季斗批改学习班 (The winter study session for "Struggle, Criticism, and Correction" in the Zhigang Brigade).

WG4. 1979. "Dongtai xian Qindong renmin gongshe gemin weiyuanhui guanyu Zhang Qianyuan tongzhi youguan wenti de fucha yijian" 东台县溱东人民公社革命委员会关于张乾元同志有关问题的复查意见 (The revolutionary committee of Qindong People's Commune of Dongtai county's comment on the reexamination of the problems of comrade Zhang Qianyuan).

WG5. 1969. "Zhigang dadui jidai jilu" 志刚大队积代记录 (Records of the meeting of peasant activists in the Zhigang Brigade).

WG6. 1969. "Huoxue huoyong Mao Zedong sixiang jiangyong cailiao" 活学活用毛泽东思想讲用材料 (Speeches on the active learning and active application of Mao Zedong thought).

WG7. 1969. "Qindong renmin gongshe huoxue huoyong Mao Zedong sixiang jijifenzi daibiao dengjibiao" 溱东人民公社活学活用毛泽东思想积极分子代表登记表 (Register of representative activists in active learning and active application of Mao Zedong thought in Qindong People's Commune).

WORKS CITED

Bai Yihua 白益华. 1998. "Wo suo jingli de cunmin zizhi zhidu gaige" 我所经历的村民自治制度改革 (The reform of villagers' self-governing institutions as I experienced it). *Zhongguo shehuibao* 中国社会报, December 29.

———. 2004. "Qinli cunmin weiyuanhui zhuzhifa zhiding" 亲历村民委员会组织法制定 (My experience in the making of the Law on the Organization of the Village Council). *Zhongguo renda* 中国人大, 8: 46–49 and 9: 50–52.

Baum, Richard. 1971. "The Cultural Revolution in the Countryside: Anatomy of a Limited Rebellion." In Thomas W. Robinson, ed., *The Cultural Revolution in China*. Berkeley: University of California Press.

Bernhardt, Kathryn. 1992. *Rents, Taxes, and Peasant Resistance: The Lower Yangzi Region, 1840–1950*. Stanford, CA: Stanford University Press.

Bernstein, Thomas P. 1967. "Leadership and Mass Mobilization in the Soviet and Chinese Collectivization Campaigns of 1929–30 and 1955–56: A Comparison." *The China Quarterly*, 31: 1–47.

Bernstein, Thomas P. and Xiaobo Lü. 2003. *Taxation Without Representation in Contemporary Rural China*. Cambridge, MA: Cambridge University Press.

Bianco, Lucien. 2001. *Peasants Without the Party: Grass-roots Movements in Twentieth-Century China*. Armonk, NY: M. E. Sharpe.

Blecher, Marc. 1976. "Income Distribution in Small Rural Chinese Communities." *The China Quarterly*, 68: 797–816.

Bossen, Laurel. 2002. *Chinese Women and Rural Development: Sixty Years of Change in Lu Village, Yunnan*. Lanham, MD: Rowman and Littlefield.

Bramall, Chris. 1993. *In Praise of Maoist Economic Planning: Living Standards and Economic Development in Sichuan Since 1931*. Oxford: Clarendon Press.

Burns, John P. 1988. *Political Participation in Rural China*. Berkeley: University of California Press.

Caizhengbu (Ministry of Finance) 财政部. 1994. *Zhongguo nongmin fudan shi* 中国农民负担史 (A history of the burden of Chinese peasants), vol. 4. Beijing: Zhongguo caizheng jingjie chubanshe.

Chan, Anita, Richard Madsen, and Jonathan Unger. 1992. *Chen Village Under Mao and Deng*. Berkeley: University of California Press.

Chang Chongxuan 常崇煊, ed. 1992. *Dangdai Zhongguo de jihua shengyu shiye* 当代中国的计划生育事业 (Planned birth in contemporary China). Beijing: Dangdai Zhongguo chubanshe.

Chayanov, A. V. 1986 [1925]. *The Theory of Peasant Economy*. Madison: University of Wisconsin Press.

Chen Chuang 陈窗 and Zeng Defang 曾德方. 2006. "Xiaogang cun: Yitiao yue zou yue zai de xiaonong jingji laoluo" 小岗村：一条越走越窄的小农经济"老路" (Xiaogang village: The old way of peasant economy that is increasingly hopeless). *Xueshu Zhongguo* (http://www.xschina.org), June, A.

Chen Donglin 陈东林. 2004. "Cong zaihai jingjixue jiaodu dui sannian ziran zaihai shiqi de kaocha" 从灾害经济学角度对三年自然灾害时期的考察 (An examination of the period of three-year natural disasters from the angle of disaster economics). *Dangdai Zhongguo shi yanjiu* 当代中国史研究, 11(1): 83–93.

Chen Weiguo 陈卫国. 2004. "Minzhu zhishui, duoyuan touruo: Dongtai shi noncun shuili jianshe qingkuang de diaocha" 民主治水，多元投入——东台市农村水利建设情况的调查 (Democracy in water control and diversity in investments: An investigation report of hydraulic projects in Dongtai municipality). *Jiangsu shuili* 江苏水利, August 6. http://www.jswater.gov.cn/.

Chi, Wen-shun. 1986. *Ideological Conflicts in Modern China: Democracy and Authoritarianism*. New Brunswick, NJ: Transaction Books.

Dongtai shiwei 东台市委 (CCP Dongtai municipal committee). 2002. "Dongtai shi cunzhu ganbu guifanhua guanli zhanxing banfa" 东台市村组干部规范化管理暂行办法 (A provisional regulation on the regularized management of village and sub-village cadres in Dongtai municipality). N.p.

Dongtai shizhi 东台市志 (Gazetteer of Dongtai municipality). 1994. Nanjing: Jiangsu kexue jishu chubanshe.

Dongtai xian nongye ju 东台县农业局 (The agricultural bureau of Dongtai county). 1987a. *Nongye zhi* 农业志 (Gazetteer of agriculture). N.p.

———. 1987b. *Nongye zhongzhiye zhi* 农业种植业志 (Gazetteer of agriculture and plantation). N.p.

Du Runsheng 杜润生, ed. 1996. *Zhongguo de tudi gaige* 当代中国的土地改革 (Land reform in contemporary China). Beijing: Dangdai Zhongguo chubanshe.

———. 2003. *Zhongguo nongcun zhidu bianqian* 中国农村制度变迁 (Institutional changes in rural China). Chengdu: Sichuan renmin chubanshe.

Duara, Prasenjit. 1988. *Culture, Power, and the State: Rural North China, 1900–1942*. Stanford, CA: Stanford University Press.

Duvall, E. M. 1957. *Family Development*. Philadelphia: J. B. Lippincott.

Duvall, E. M. and B. C. Miller. 1985. *Marriage and Family Development*. New York: Harper & Row.

Fang Xiangxin 方向新. 1998. *Nongcun bianqian lun: Dangdai Zhongguo nongcun bianqge yu fazhan yanjiu* 农村变迁论——当代中国农村变革与发展研究 (Rural transformations: A study of changes and developments in contemporary rural China). Changsha: Hunan renmin chubanshe.

Fei Xiaotong 费孝通. 1986. *Lun xiao chengzhen ji qita* 论小城镇及其他 (On small towns and other things). Tianjin: Tianjin renmin chubanshe.

Fishman, Ted C. 2005. *China, Inc.: How the Rise of the Next Superpower Challenges America and the World*. New York: Scribner.

Friedman, Edward, Paul G. Pickowicz, and Mark Selden. 1991. *Chinese Village, Socialist State*. New Haven, CT: Yale University Press.

Gao, Mobo. 1999. *Gao Village: Rural Life in Modern China*. Honolulu: University of Hawai'i Press.

Glick, Paul C. 1947. "The Family Cycle." *American Sociological Review*, 12: 164–174.

———. 1955. "The Life Cycle of the Family." *Marriage and Family Living*, 17: 3–9.

———. 1977. "Updating the Life Cycle of the Family." *Journal of Marriage and the Family*, 39: 5–13.

———. 1989. "The Family Life Cycle and Social Change." *Family Relations*, 38(2): 123–129.

GNW (Guojia nongye weiyuanhui 国家农业委员会). 1981a. *Nongye jitihua zhongyao wenjian huibian, 1949–1957* 农业集体化重要文件汇编 (一九四九——一九五七) (A compendium of important documents on agricultural collectivization, 1949–1957). Beijing: Zhongguo zhongyang dangxiao chubanshe.

———. 1981b. *Nongye jitihua zhongyao wenjian huibian, 1958–1981* 农业集体化重要文件汇编 (一九五八——一九八一) (A compendium of important documents on agricultural collectivization, 1958–1981). Beijing: Zhongguo zhongyang dangxiao chubanshe.

Goldman, Merle. 1995. *Sowing the Seeds of Democracy in China: Political Reform in the Deng Xiaoping Era*. Cambridge, MA: Harvard University Press.

Griffin, Keith. 1982. "Income Differentials in Rural China." *The China Quarterly*, 92: 706–713.

Griffin, Keith and Ashwani Saith. 1982. "The Pattern of Income Inequality in Rural China." *Oxford Economic Papers*, 34(1): 172–206.

Guo Zhenglin 郭正林. 2001. "Yige cunzhuang de minzu zhili: Laizi Guangdong Xishan cun de baogao" 一个村庄的民主治理——来自广西西山村的报告 (Democratic governance in a village: A report on Xishan village of Guandong province). In Fan Yu and He Xuefeng 范瑜 贺雪峰, eds., *Cunmin zizhi de cunzhuang jichu: Laizi quanguo shi sheng shi de cunmin zizhi diaocha baogao* 村民自治的村庄基础——来自全国十省市的村民自治调查报告 (Village as the basic for villagers' self-government: A report of investigations on ten provinces and municipalities of the nation). Xi'an: Xibei daxue chubanshe.

Guojia tongjiju 国家统计局. 1980. *Jianguo shanshi nian guomin jingji tongji tiyao* 建国三十年国民经济统计提要 (Brief statistics on national economy in the past thirty years since the founding of the People's Republic). N.p.

———. 2000. *Xin Zhongguo wushi nian nongye tongji ziliao* 新中国五十年农业统计资料 (Statistics of agriculture in the fifty years of New China). Beijing: Zhongguo tongji chubanshe.

———. 2006. *Zhongguo tongji nianjian* 中国统计年鉴 (2006) (The annual statistics of China, 2006). Beijing: Zhongguo tongji chubanshe.

Hanson, Sandra L. 1983. "A Family Life-Cycle Approach to the Socioeconomic Attainment of Working Women." *Journal of Marriage and the Family*, 45(2): 323–338.

Harding, Harry. 1981. *Organizing China: The Problem of Bureaucracy, 1949–1976*. Stanford, CA: Stanford University Press.

Hechter, Michael. 1987. *Principles of Group Solidarity*. Berkeley: University of California Press.

———. 1990. "The Emergence of Cooperative Social Institutions." In Michael Hechter, ed., *Social Institutions: Their Emergence, Maintenance, and Effects*. New York: Aldine de Gruyter.

Ho, Samuel. 1994. *Rural China in Transition: Non-Agricultural Development in Rural Jiangsu, 1978–1990*. Oxford: Clarendon Press.

Hogan, Dennis P. 1985. "The Demography of Life-Span Transitions: Temporal and Gender Comparisons." In Alice S. Rossi, ed., *Gender and the Life Course*. New York: Aldine.

Hsiung, Bingyuang and Louis Putterman. 1989. "Pre- and Post-Reform Income Distribution in a Chinese Commune: The Case of Dahe Township in Hebei Province." *Journal of Comparative Economics*, 13: 406–445.

Huadong junzheng weiyuanhui 华东军政委员会 (East China military and administrative committee). 1952. *Huadong district tudi gaige chengguo tongji* 华东区土地改革成果统计 (A survey of the results of land reform in eastern China). N.p.

Huang, Philip C. C. 1990. *The Peasant Family and Rural Development in the Yangzi Delta, 1350–1988*. Stanford, CA: Stanford University Press.

———. 1995. "Rural Class Struggle in the Chinese Revolution: Representational and Objective Realities from the Land Reform to the Cultural Revolution." *Modern China*, 21(1): 105–143.

Huang, Shu-min. 1998. *The Spiral Road: Change in a Chinese Village Through the Eyes of a Communist Party Leader*. Boulder, CO: Westview Press.

Huang, Yiping. 1998. *Agricultural Reform in China: Getting Institutions Right*. Cambridge, MA: Cambridge University Press.

Jiang Chongwei 蒋崇伟. 1993. *Zhongguo nongcun shehuizhuyi gaizhao yu gaige 40 nian* 中国农村社会主义改造与改革 40 年 (40 years of socialist transformation and reform in rural China). Changsha: Hunan shifan daxue chubanshe.

Johnson, Chalmers A. 1982. *MITI and the Japanese Miracle: The Growth of Industrial Policy, 1925–1975*. Stanford, CA: Stanford University Press.

———. 1995. *Japan: Who Governs? The Rise of the Developmental State*. New York: W. W. Norton.

JSJW (Jiangsu sheng jihua weiyuanhui 江苏省计划委员会). 1976. *Yijiu qiliu nian Jiangsu sheng nongye tongji ziliao* 一九七六年江苏省农业统计资料 (Statistics of agriculture in Jiangsu province, 1976). Nanjing: Jiangsu sheng jihua weiyuanhui.

———. 1978. *Yijiu qiba nian Jiangsu sheng nongye tongji ziliao* 一九七八年江苏省农业统计资料 (Statistics of agriculture in Jiangsu province, 1978). Nanjing: Jiangsu sheng jihua weiyuanhui.

Judd, Ellen R. 1994. *Gender and Power in Rural North China.* Stanford, CA: Stanford University Press.

Kang Jian 康健. 1998. *Huihuang de huanmie: renmingongshe jinshilu* 辉煌的幻灭——人民公社警示录 (The disillusionment of a splendor: Revelations of the People's Commune). Beijing: Zhongguo shehui chubanshe.

Kapinus, Carolyn A. and Michael P. Johnson. 2003. "The Utility of Family Life Cycle as a Theoretical and Empirical Tool: Commitment and Family Life-Cycle Stage." *Journal of Family Issues,* 24(2): 155–184.

Kelliher, Daniel. 1992. *Peasant Power in China: The Era of Rural Reform, 1979–1989.* New Haven, CT: Yale University Press.

Kung, James K. 1994. "Egalitarianism, Subsistence Provision, and Work Incentives in China's Agricultural Collectives." *World Development,* 22(2): 175–187.

Lardy, Nicholas R. 1983. *Agriculture in China's Modern Economic Development.* Cambridge, MA: Cambridge University Press.

———. 1987. "The Chinese Economy Under Stress, 1958–1965." In Roderick MacFarquhar and John K. Fairbank, eds., *The Cambridge History of China,* vol. 14. Cambridge, MA: Cambridge University Press, 144–184.

Lee, Hong Yung. 1978. *The Politics of the Chinese Cultural Revolution: A Case Study.* Berkeley: University of California Press.

Li, Huaiyin. 2005a. *Village Governance in North China, 1875–1936.* Stanford, CA: Stanford University Press.

———. 2005b. "Life Course, Labor Remuneration, and Gender Inequality in a Chinese Agrarian Collective." *The Journal of Peasant Studies,* 32(2): 277–303.

———. 2006. "The First Encounter: Peasant Resistance to State Control of Grain in East China in the Mid-1950s." *The China Quarterly,* 185: 145–162.

Li Jin 李锦. 2000. *Dazhuanzhe de xunjian: Muji Zhongguo nongcun gaige* 大转折的瞬间——目击中国农村改革 (The moment of great transition: Witnessing the reform in rural China). Changsha: Hunan renmin chubanshe.

Lieberthal, Kenneth and Michel Oksenberg. 1988. *Policy Making in China: Leaders, Structures, and Processes.* Princeton, NJ: Princeton University Press.

Lin, Justin Y. 1988. "The Household Responsibility System in China's Agricultural Reform: A Theoretical and Empirical Study." *Economic Development and Cultural Change,* 36(3): S199–S224.

———. 1990. "Collectivization and China's Agricultural Crisis in 1959–1961." *Journal of Political Economy,* 98(6): 1228–1252.

———. 1998. "Tizhi gaige he Zhongguo nongye zengzhang" 体制改革和中国农业增长 (Institutional reforms and agricultural growth in China). Beijing: China Center for Economic Research, Beijing University.

———. 1999. "China: Farming Institutions and Rural Development." In Mieke Meurs, ed., *Many Shades of Red: State Policy and Collective Agriculture.* Lanham, MD: Rowman and Littlefield, 151–183.

Lin Yunhui and Gu Xunzhong 林蕴晖、顾训中. 1995. *Renmingongshe kuangxiangqu* 人民公社狂想曲 (The rhapsody of the people's commune). Kaifeng: Henan renmin chubanshe.

Ling Zhijun 凌志军. 1996. *Lishi buzai paihuai* 历史不再徘徊 (History no longer lingers). Beijing: Renmin chubanshe.

Liu Ruofeng 刘若峰. 1997. *Zhongguo nongye de biange he fazhan* 中国农业的变革和发展 (Changes and development in China's agriculture). Beijing: Zhongguo tongji chubanshe.

Liu Shaoqi 刘少奇. 1958. *Zhongguo gongchandang zhongyang weiyuanhui xiang dibajie quanguo daibiao dahui dierci huiyi de gongzuo baogao* 中国共产党中央委员会向第八届全国代表大会第二次会议的工作报告 (Work report of the CCP Central Committee to the Second Session of the Eighth National Congress). Beijing: Renmin chubanshe.

Lu Feng 卢锋, Luo Huanzhen 罗欢镇, and Huang Weiping 黄卫平. 1987. *Woguo jingji tizhi gaige de huigu he zhanwang* 我国经济体制改革的回顾和展望 (The reform of economic systems: Retrospect and prospect). Beijing: Zhongguo zhengfa daxue chubanshe.

Luo Pinghan 罗平汉. 2000. "Renmin gongshe gongjizhi tanxi" 人民公社供给制探析 (An examination of the free supply system under the people's commune). *Dangdai Zhongguoshi yanjiu* 当代中国史研究, 7(3): 38–46.

Madsen, Richard. 1984. *Morality and Power in a Chinese Village.* Berkeley: University of California Press.

———. 1991. "The Countryside Under Communism." In Roderick MacFarquhar and John K. Fairbank, eds., *The Cambridge History of China,* vol. 15. Cambridge, MA: Cambridge University Press, 619–681.

Mao Zedong 毛泽东. 1955a. "Zhongguo nongcun de shehuizhuyi gaochao xuyan" 《中国农村的社会主义高潮》序言 (Preface to *The High Tide of Socialism in Rural China*). In *Mao Zedong xuanji* 毛泽东选集 (Selected works of Mao Zedong), vol. 5. Beijing: Renmin chubanshe, 218–224.

———. 1955b. "Zhongguo nongcun de shehuizhuyi gaochao de anyu" 《中国农村的社会主义高潮》的按语 (Commentaries on *The High Tide of Socialism in Rural China*). In *Mao Zedong xuanji* 毛泽东选集 (Selected works of Mao Zedong), vol. 5. Beijing: Renmin chubanshe, 225–259.

———. 1955c. "Guanyu nongye hezuohua wenti" 关于农业合作化问题 (On the issue of agricultural cooperativization). In *Mao Zedong xuanji* 毛泽东选集 (Selected works of Mao Zedong), vol. 5. Beijing: Renmin chubanshe, 169–191.

———. 1957. "Guanyu zhengque chuli renmin neibu maodun de wenti" 关于正确处理人民内部矛盾的问题 (On the problem of correct resolution of contradictions among the people). In *Mao Zedong xuanji* 毛泽东选集 (Selected works of Mao Zedong), vol. 5. Beijing: Renmin chubanshe, 363–402.

———. 1977. *Mao Zedong xuanji* 毛泽东选集 (Selected works of Mao Zedong), vol. 5. Beijing: Renmin chubanshe.

Mayhew, Leon. 1971. *Society: Institutions and Activity.* Glenview, IL: Scott, Foresman.

McCormick, Barrett. 1990. *Political Reform in Post-Mao China: Democracy and Bureaucracy in a Leninist State.* Berkeley: University of California Press.

McKinley, Terry. 1996. *The Distribution of Wealth in Rural China.* Armonk, NY: M. E. Sharpe.

Naquin, Susan. 1976. *Millenarian Rebellion in China: The Eight Trigrams Uprising of 1813.* New Haven, CT: Yale University Press.

Nathan, Andrew. 1985. *Chinese Democracy.* Berkeley: University of California Press.

Nee, Victor. 1998. "Sources of the New Institutionalism." In Mary C. Brinton and Victor Nee, eds., *The New Institutionalism in Sociology.* Stanford, CA: Stanford University Press.

Nock, S. L. 1979. "The Family Life Cycle: Empirical or Conceptual Tool?" *Journal of Marriage and the Family*, 41: 15–26.

Nolan, Peter. 1983. "De-collectivization of Agriculture in China, 1979–1982: A Long Term Perspective." *Cambridge Journal of Economics*, 7(3–4): 381–403.

Nolan, Peter and Gordon White. 1979. "Socialist Development and Rural Inequality: The Chinese Countryside in the 1970s." *The Journal of Peasant Studies*, 7(1): 3–48.

———. 1981. "Distribution and Development in China." *Bulletin of Concerned Asian Scholars*, 13(3): 2–18.

———. 1988. *The Political Economy of Collective Farms: An Analysis of China's Post-Mao Rural Reforms.* Cambridge, MA: Polity Press.

Nongyebu jihuasi. 1989. *Zhongguo nongcun jingji tongji daquan* 中国农村经济统计大全, 1949–1986 (Complete statistics of rural economy in China, 1949–1986). Beijing: Nongye chubanshe.

Nongyebu zhengce yanjiushi. 1979. *Zhongguo nongye jiben qingkuang* 中国农业基本情况 (The basic condition of agriculture in China). Beijing: Nongye chubanshe.

Norton, Arthur J. 1983. "Family Life Cycle: 1980." *Journal of Marriage and the Family*, 45(2): 267–275.

O'Brien, Kevin J. 1996. "Rightful Resistance." *World Politics*, 49(1): 31–55.

———. 2002. "Collective Action in the Chinese Countryside." *The China Journal*, 48: 139–154.

O'Brien, Kevin J. and Lianjiang Li. 2006. *Rightful Resistance in Rural China.* Cambridge, MA: Cambridge University Press.

Oi, Jean C. 1989. *State and Peasant in Contemporary China: The Political Economy of Village Government.* Berkeley: University of California Press.

———. 1999. *Rural China Takes Off: Institutional Foundations of Economic Reform.* Berkeley: University of California Press.

Oi, Jean C. and Andrew G. Walder, eds. 1999. *Property Rights and China's Economic Reforms.* Stanford, CA: Stanford University Press.

Oksenberg, Michel. 2001. "China's Political System: Challenges of the Twenty-first Century." *The China Journal*, 45: 21–35.

Parish, William and Martin King Whyte. 1978. *Village and Family in Contemporary China*. Chicago: University of Chicago Press.

Pei, Minxin. 2006. *China's Trapped Transition: The Limits of Developmental Autocracy*. Cambridge, MA: Harvard University Press.

Peng Xianggang 彭向刚. 1995. *Zhongguo nongcun jiceng zhengquan yanjiu* 中国农村基层政权研究 (A study of local government in rural China). Changchun: Jilin daxue chubanshe.

Perkins, Dwight and Shahid Yusuf. 1984. *Rural Development in China*. Baltimore, MD: The Johns Hopkins University Press.

Perry, Elizabeth J. 1980. *Rebels and Revolutionaries in North China, 1845–1945*. Stanford, CA: Stanford University Press.

———. 1984. "Collective Violence in China: 1880–1980." *Theory and Society*, 13: 427–454.

———. 1985. "Rural Violence in Socialist China." *The China Quarterly*, 103: 414–440.

Polanyi, Karl. 1957. *The Great Transformation*. Boston: Beacon Press.

Potter, Sulamith H. and Jack M. Potter. 1990. *China's Peasants: The Anthropology of a Revolution*. Cambridge, MA: Cambridge University Press.

Prazniak, Roxann. 1999. *Of Camel Kings and Other Things: Rural Rebels Against Modernity in Late Imperial China*. Lanham, MD: Rowman and Littlefield.

Putterman, Louis. 1987. "The Incentive Problem and the Demise of Team Farming in China." *Journal of Development Economics*, 26(1): 103–127.

———. 1988. "Ration Subsidies and Incentives in the Pre-reform Chinese Production Team." *Economica*, 55(218): 235–247.

Pye, Lucian. 1968. *The Spirit of Chinese Politics*. Cambridge, MA: MIT Press.

———. 1988. *The Mandarin and the Cadre: China's Political Cultures*. Ann Arbor: Center for Chinese Studies, University of Michigan.

Qindong gongshe shezhi 溱东公社社志 (Gazetteer of Qindong People's Commune). 1981. N.p.

Qindong xiang nongye qingkuang 溱东乡农业情况 (Agricultural conditions in Qindong township). 1987. N.p.

Renmin ribao 人民日报 (People's Daily). 1948–. Beijing: The CCP Central Committee.

Rosen, Stanley. 1982. *Red Guard Factionalism and the Cultural Revolution in Guangzhou*. Boulder, CO: Westview Press.

Sachs, Jeffrey and Wing Thye Woo. 1994. "Structural Factors in the Economic Reforms of China, Eastern Europe, and the Former Soviet Union." *Economic Policy*, 18: 114–115.

Schurmann, Franz. 1968. *Ideology and Organization in Communist China*. Berkeley: University of California Press.

Scott, James C. 1976. *The Moral Economy of the Peasant: Rebellion and Subsistence in Southeast Asia*. New Haven, CT: Yale University Press.

———. 1985. *Weapons of the Weak: Everyday Form of Peasant Resistance*. New Haven, CT: Yale University Press.

Selden, Mark. 1988. *The Political Economy of Chinese Socialism*. Armonk, NY: M. E. Sharpe.

Shi Jinchuan, Jin Xiangrong, Zhao Wei, and Luo Weidong 史晋川 金祥荣 赵伟 罗卫东. 2002. *Zhidu bianqian yu jinji fazhan: Wenzhou moshi yanjiu* 制度变迁与经济发展：温州模式研究 (Institutional change and economic development: A study of the Wenzhou model). Hangzhou: Zhejiang daxue chubanshe.

Shi Lei 石磊. 1999. *Zhongguo nongye zhuzhi de jiegouxing bianqian* 中国农业组织的结构性变迁 (Structural changes in China's agricultural organizations). Taiyuan: Shanxi jingji chubanshe.

Shue, Vivienne. 1980. *Peasant China in Transition: The Dynamics of Development Toward Socialism, 1949–1956*. Berkeley: University of California Press.

———. 1988. *The Reach of the State: Sketches of the Chinese Body Politic*. Stanford, CA: Stanford University Press.

Siu, Helen F. 1989. *Agents and Victims in South China: Accomplices in Rural Revolution*. New Haven, CT: Yale University Press.

Solomon, Richard. 1971. *Mao's Revolution and the Chinese Political Culture*. Berkeley: University of California Press.

Song Haiqing 宋海庆. 2000. *Renmin gongshe xingwang lu* 人民公社兴亡录 (The rise and fall of the people's commune). Urumqi: Xinjiang qingshaonian chubanshe.

Song Liansheng 宋连生. 2002. *Zongluxian, dayuejin, renmingongshe yundong shimo* 总路线、大跃进、人民公社化运动始末 (A chronicle of the campaigns of General Line, the Great Leap Forward, and the people's commune). Kunming: Yunnan renmin chubanshe.

Songjiang xianzhi 松江县志 (Gazetteer of Songjiang county). 1991. Shanghai: Shanghai renmin chubanshe.

Taylor, Michael. 1982. *Community, Anarchy, and Liberty*. Cambridge, MA: Cambridge University Press.

Teiwes, Frederick C. 1987. "Establishment of Consolidation of the New Regime." In Roderick MacFarquhar and John K. Fairbank, eds., *The Cambridge History of China*, vol. 14. Cambridge, MA: Cambridge University Press, 51–143.

Thompson, E. P. 1963. *The Making of the English Working Class*. New York: Vintage.

———. 1971. "The Moral Economy of the English Crowd in the Eighteenth Century." *Past and Present*, 50: 71–136.

Unger, Jonathan. 1985. "Remuneration, Ideology, and Personal Interests in a Chinese Village, 1960–1980." In William L. Parish, ed., *Chinese Rural Development: The Great Transformation*, Armonk, NY: M. E. Sharpe, pp. 117–140.

———. 1998. "Cultural Revolution Conflict in the Villages." *The China Quarterly*, 153: 82–106.

Vermeer, E. B. 1982. "Income Differentials in Rural China." *The China Quarterly*, 89: 1–33.

Waite, Linda. 1980. "Working Wives and the Family Life Cycle." *The American Journal of Sociology*, 86(2): 272–294.

Walder, Andrew G. and Yang Su. 2003. "The Cultural Revolution in the Countryside: Scope, Timing and Human Impact." *The China Quarterly*, 173: 74–99.

Wang Xiao 王道. 2001. "Renmin gongshe gonggong shitang xingshuai zhi lishi yanbian" 人民公社公共食堂兴衰之历史演变 (The rise and fall of the mess hall of the people's commune). *Dangshi yanjiu yu jiaoxue* 党史研究与教学, 157: 13–18.

Wolf, Eric R. 1969. *Peasant Wars of the Twentieth Century*. New York: Harper and Row.

Woo-Cumings, Meredith. 1999. *The Developmental State*. Ithaca, NY: Cornell University Press.

Xie Jianshe 谢建社. 2005. *Xin chanye gongren jieceng: shehui zhuanxing zhong de nongmingong* 新产业工人阶层——社会转型中的"农民工" (The new industrial working class: Migrant workers in the course of social transformation). Beijing: Sheke wenxian chubanshe.

Xu Jing 徐晶. 2006. *Zhonghua Renmin Gongheguo cunmin weiyuanhui zuzhifa zhushiben* 中华人民共和国村民委员会组织法注释本 (The law on the organization of the village council in the People's Republic of China, with annotations). Beijing: Falu chubanshe.

Yan, Yunxiang. 2003. *Private Life Under Socialism: Love, Intimacy, and Family Change in a Chinese Village, 1949–1999*. Stanford, CA: Stanford University Press.

Yang, Dali. 1996. *Calamity and Reform in China: State, Rural Society, and Institutional Change Since the Great Leap Famine*. Stanford, CA: Stanford University Press.

Yi, Zeng. 1991. *Family Dynamics in China: A Life Table Analysis*. Madison: University of Wisconsin Press.

Yin Yongqin 尹永钦 and Yang Zhenghui 杨峥晖. 2004. *Jubian: 1978 nian–2004 nian Zhongguo jingji gaige licheng* 巨变:1978 年–2004 年中国经济改革历程 (The great transformation: The process of China's economic reform, 1978–2004). Beijing: Dangdai shijie chubanshe.

Zhang Renshou 张仁寿 and Li Hong 李红. 1990. *Wenzhou moshi yanjiu* 温州模式研究 (A study of the Wenzhou model). Beijing: Zhongguo shehui kexue chubanshe.

Zhang Shouchun 张寿春. 1996. "Renmin gongshe hua yundong ji renmin gongshe wenti yanjiu zongshu" 人民公社化运动及人民公社问题研究综述 (A review of the studies on the campaign of creating the people's commune and issues pertaining to the people's commune). *Dangdai Zhongguo shi yanjiu* 当代中国史研究, 3: 82–88.

Zhang Tiesen 张铁森, Liu Jinsheng 刘金生, and Chen Junsheng 陈钧生. 1995. *Zhongguo nongcun gaige de zhexue sikao* 中国农村改革的哲学思考 (Philosophical reflections on reforms in rural China). Beijing: Zhongguo nongye chubanshe.

Zhang Yulin 张雨林. 1992. *Cong chuantong nongcun xiang shehuizhuyi xiandai nongcun de zhuanhua* 从传统农村向社会主义现代农村的转化 (Transforming the traditional rural society into the socialist modern rural society). Shanghai: Shanghai shehui kexueyuan chubanshe.

Zhao, Suisheng, ed. 2000. *China and Democracy: Reconsidering the Prospects for a Democratic China*. New York: Routledge.

Zhongguo tongjishi shiwusuo 中国统计师事务所. 1997. *Zhongguo guoqing baogao* 中国国情报告, 1978–1996 (Report on China's national conditions, 1978–1996). Beijing: Zhongguo jihua chubanshe.

Zhou, Kate Xiaohong. 1996. *How the Farmers Changed China: Power of the People*. Boulder, CO: Westview Press.

Zhou Xiaohong 周晓虹. 1998. *Chuantong yu bianqian: Jiangzhe nongmin de shehui xinli jiqi jindai yilai de shanbian* 传统与变迁——江浙农民的社会心理及其近代以来的嬗变 (Tradition and transformation: Social mentalities of peasants in Jiangsu and Zhejiang and their modern changes). Beijing: Sanlian shudian.

———. 2000. "Cong guojia he shehui guanxi kan Zhongguo nongmin de zhengzhi canyu: Mao Zedong he hou Mao Zedong shidai de bijiao" 从国家和社会关系看中国农民的政治参与——毛泽东和后毛泽东时代的比较 (Political participation of Chinese peasants in the perspective of state-society relations: A comparison between the Mao and post-Mao eras). *Xianggang shehui kexue xuebao* 香港社会科学学报, 17 (Autumn).

Zhu Tonghua 朱通华 and Sun Bin 孙彬. 1994. *Sunan moshi fazhan yanjiu* 苏南模式发展研究 (A study on the development of the Sunan model). Nanjing: Nanjing daxue chubanshe.

Zweig, David. 1985. "Peasants, Ideology, and New Incentive Systems: Jiangsu Province, 1978–1981." In William L. Parish, ed., *Chinese Rural Development: The Great Transformation*. Armonk, NY: M. E. Sharpe, 141–163.

———. 1989. *Agrarian Radicalism in China, 1968–1981*. Cambridge, MA: Harvard University Press.

List of Characters

anlao fenpei 按劳分配
anxu fenpei 按需分配
ban laoli 半劳力
bangong 拌工
baoben 包本
baochan 包产
baochan daohu 包产到户
baogong 包工
baojianzhan 保健站
baoshudai 宝书袋
baoshutai 宝书台
baozhang 保长
bei dui bei 背对背
benshi 本事
bi shang Liangshan 逼上梁山
biaobing 标兵
biaoyang xin 表扬信
bing tian 并田
bing xiaojia wei dajia 并小家为大家
bingfang 病房
buchong jiancha 补充检查
buchun fenzi 不纯分子
chai she bing cun 拆舍并村
changnian huzhuzu 常年互助组
chaozhi 超支
chaozhi hu 超支户
chaozhi nuoyong 超支挪用

chen re da tie 趁热打铁
chengliang 乘凉
chengliren 城里人
chi dahu 吃大户
chi fan bu yao qian 吃饭不要钱
chu bu lai de 处不来的
chu de lai de 处得来的
chu gong bu chu li 出工不出力
chujishe 初级社
chun zuzhi, qiu kuatai, kai guo nian lai
    you chong lai 春组织, 秋垮台, 开过年
    来又重来
cu shengchan 促生产
cunmin weiyuanhui 村民委员会
cunmin xiaozu 村民小组
cunmin zizhi 村民自治
da jiazi 搭架子
da laping 大拉平
da siqing 大四清
da xiezuo 大协作
dabaogan 大包干
dagunainai 大姑奶奶
dailing cunmin zhifu 带领村民致富
daitou zhifu 带头致富
dajia 大家
daming dafang 大鸣大放
dan 担

dang ganbu chikui   当干部吃亏

dangan   单干

dangjia   当家

dangquanpai   当权派

darao   打扰

dati shang shuo de guoqu   大体上说
得过去

dawei   大圩

dazibao   大字报

de cai jian bei   德才兼备

deli ganbu   得力干部

dengjia jiaohuan   等价交换

difang zizhi   地方自治

dingxie   钉鞋

diwo maodun   敌我矛盾

dou   斗

dou pi gai   斗批改

douzheng hui   斗争会

duduan zhuanxing   独断专行

duilian   对联

duiweihui   队委会

duo shi   多事

duo zhan   多占

duochi duozhan   多吃多占

duoshi zhi qiu   多事之秋

eba   恶霸

fan geming   反革命

Fan gong di   范公堤

fang yeya   放野鸭

fangren ziliu   放任自流

fantian fudi   翻天覆地

fengchao   风潮

fengjian mixian   封建迷信

fengjian sixiang   封建思想

fenjia   分家

fenkong   分空

fentian dangan   分田单干

fu laoli   副劳力

fudaoyuan   辅导员

fukua feng   浮夸风

fulian   妇联

furen   富人

gaishui gaice   改水改厕

ganbufu   干部服

gao fan chi   搞饭吃

gaochan weixing   高产卫星

gaojishe   高级社

ge jin suo neng, an lao fenpei   各尽所能，
按劳分配

ge jin suo neng, an xu fenpei   各尽所能，
按需分配

geda   疙瘩

gong   公

gongchan feng   共产风

gongfen guashuai   工分挂帅

gongfenliang   工分粮

gongxi facai   恭喜发财

gongye hu   工业户

gongzuo zu   工作组

gongzuo zuofeng   工作作风

guan bi min fan   官逼民反

Guandi   关帝

Guanyin   观音

gugan   骨干

gujia   顾家

guojia ganbu   国家干部

haoren haoshi   好人好事

haozi   号子

hegong   河工

heipi de yang baipi de   黑皮的养白皮的

hezuo yiliao   合作医疗

hongbao   红包

hongbaoshu   红宝书

hongzhuan xiaozu   红专小组

huan sixiang bu huang ren   换思想
不换人

huangjiaoxian   黄脚籼

huatou   滑头

hukou   户口

huli   互利

huo xue huo yong   活学活用

huzhuzu   互助组

*jiajia jiqi xiang, chuchu shi
gongchang*   家家机器响，
处处是工厂

jiang yong hui   讲用会

jiashen 家神

jiating fuye 家庭副业

jiating jingying 家庭经营

jiben fen 基本分

jiben gongfen 基本工分

jiben kesuan danwei 基本核算单位

jide 积德

jieji ganqing 阶级感情

jiji fenzi 积极分子

jinhou haiyao guo rizi 今后还要过日子

jiti naoshi 集体闹事

junshi hua 军事化

kaitian 开田

kaiyou 揩油

kexue zhongtian 科学种田

kouduo laoshao 口多劳少

kouliang 口粮

kunnanhu 困难户

langgong 浪工

lao lianpi 老脸皮

Lao san pian 老三篇

lao youtiao 老油条

laodongri 劳动日

lian 连

liangshi guanli suo 粮食管理所

litou 里头

Lixiahe 里下河

luohou fenzi 落后分子

luohou qunzhong 落后群众

manchan sifen 瞒产私分

mao wan 猫碗

mao xuan 毛选

Mao Zedong xuanji 毛泽东选集

Mao zhuxi yulu 毛主席语录

men qian zhang de yao qian shu, dou da yuan bao gun jia lai
门前长的摇钱树; 斗大元宝滚家来

mian dui mian 面对面

mingong 民工

minzhu banshe 民主办社

minzhu licai 民主理财

minzhu licai xiaozu 民主理财小组

minzhu pingyi 民主评议

nan laoli ru hu, nü laoli tuo ku 男劳力
如虎，女劳力脱苦

nannü tonggong tongchou 男女同
工同酬

nante 南特

nantehao 南特号

nanxia ganbu 南下干部

nanyou 南优

nengren 能人

nongjiyuan 农技员

nongmin xiehui 农民协会

nongye shengchan hezuohe 农业生产
合作社

paizi ying 牌子硬

paoyang 抛秧

pi Deng fanji youqing fan'an feng 批邓
反击右倾翻案风

pi-Lin pi-Kong 批林批孔

ping laojingyan zhongtian 凭老经
验种田

ping liangxing ganhuo 凭良心干活

pinggong jifen 评工记分

pingxiazhongnong 贫下中农

pingxiazhongnong daibiao 贫下中
农代表

po sijiu 破四旧

qiangpo mingling 强迫命令

Qingmiao hui 青苗会

qu 区

qunzhong luxian 群众路线

qunzhong naoshi 群众闹事

ren sui wangfa cao sui feng 人随王
法草随风

renduo liqiang 人多力强

renmin gongshe 人民公社

renmin laixin 人民来信

renmin neibu maodun 人民内部矛盾

rensheng dashi 人生大事

ru tu wei an 入土为安

Rulai 如来

san da renwu 三大任务

san tuoli 三脱离

san ying 三硬

sanbao yijiang 三包一奖

sanshang sanxia 三上三下

saomang zhengshu 扫盲证书

shang ya, zhong ji, xia ding 上压，中挤，
  下顶

shaokou duofen 少扣多分

shehuizhuyi da xiezuo 社会主义
  大协作

shehuizhuyi gaochao 社会主义高潮

shehuizhuyi jiaoyu 社会主义教育

shejiao 社教

shengchandui guanli weiyuan hui 生产
  队管理委员会

shengshi shenggong 省时省工

shezhang 社章

shijie dao 世界稻

shishi jiukong, jiaping ruxi 十室九空，
  家贫如洗

shunkouliu 顺口溜

shutian 熟田

si 私

si ge shouxian 四个首先

si ren 私人

siding huoping 死订活评

si buqing 四不清

sifen 私分

siqing 四清

sishu 私塾

souliangdui 搜粮队

suku 诉苦

tai ping 太平

tanwu daoqie 贪污盗窃

tie guniang 铁姑娘

*ting Mao zhuxi hua ju ju zhen yan; gen
  Gongchandong zhou tiao tiao da
  dao* 听毛主席话句句真言；跟共产党
  走条条大道

tinghua 听话

tonggong tongxiao 统购统销

touji daoba 投机倒把

touzhi 透支

tu huangdi 土皇帝

tuan 团

tubu 土布

tudi fenhong 土地分红

tugun 土棍

tuipei 退赔

tuji ban 突击班

tuo houtui 拖后腿

tuogong 施工

waitou 外头

wangben 忘本

weidong bingtuan 卫东兵团

wen de 文斗

wenming cun 文明村

wogong 窝工

wu de 武斗

wubao 五保

wujiang 五匠

wuming yingxiong 无名英雄

wusuowei 无所谓

wuxian xinren 无限信任

wuzhi ciji 物质刺激

xia zhihui 瞎指挥

xia zhihui feng 瞎指挥风

xiang 乡

xiang/zhen 乡/镇

xiao jiating 小家庭

xiao siqing 小四清

xiao zai jiang fu 消灾降福

xiaohu 小户

xiaomie danganhu 消灭单干户

xiaozu jijian 小组计件

xiguan liang 习惯粮

xinzheng 新政

xingzhengcun 行政村

xue 学

xuexi ban 学习班

ya 压

yangbu 洋布

yangjia hukou 养家糊口

yangxian 洋籼

yaoqian yaoming 要钱要命

yi da er gong 一大二公

yi piao foujue 一票否决

yida sanfan 一打三反

yijia zhi zhu   一家之主
yikufan   忆苦饭
ying   营
youdai   优待
youqing jihuizhuyi   右倾机会主义
yuanbao   元宝
yuanqin buru jinlin   远亲不如近邻
yülu dai   语录袋
zhandou hua   战斗化
zhaofanpai   造反派
zheng laoli   整劳力
zhengwu gongkai   政务公开
zhengwu gongkai lan   政务公开栏
zhengzhi guashuai   政治挂帅
zhengzhi yexiao   政治夜校
zhibo   直播
zhixuan   直选
zhongdui   中队

zhongtian wei gongfen   种田为工分
zhongxin cun   中心村
zhongyang wenjian   中央文件
zhua geming   抓革命
zhuan daqian   赚大钱
zibao gongyi   自报公议
zibenzhuyi weiba   资本主义尾巴
zifa de zibenzhuyi qingxiang   自发的资
    本主义倾向
zijue   自觉
ziliudi   自留地
ziwo jiantao   自我检讨
ziyuan   自愿
zongzi   粽子
zou wanlu   走弯路
zouzipai   走资派
zuixin zhishi   最新指示
zuzhi qilai   组织起来